ISBN: 9781313515214

Published by:
HardPress Publishing
8345 NW 66TH ST #2561
MIAMI FL 33166-2626

Email: info@hardpress.net
Web: http://www.hardpress.net

CHARING CROSS

AND ITS IMMEDIATE NEIGHBOURHOOD

St. Martin's Lane in 1820

THE STORY

OF

CHARING CROSS

AND ITS IMMEDIATE NEIGHBOURHOOD

BY

J. HOLDEN MACMICHAEL

WITH A FRONTISPIECE AND PLAN

LONDON

CHATTO & WINDUS

1906

CONTENTS

CHAPTER I.

INTRODUCTORY.

CHAPTER II.

A CHARING CROSS REGATTA.

CHAPTER III.

THE TAVERNS.

CHAPTER IV.

THE TAVERNS—*continued.*

CHAPTER V.

THE ELEANOR CROSS.

CHAPTER VI.

CRAVEN STREET.

CHAPTER VII.

THE GOLDEN CROSS HOTEL.

CHAPTER VIII.

ROUND COURT.

CHAPTER IX.

SOME OF THE STREETS.

CHAPTER X.

MORE OF THE STREETS.

CHAPTER XI.

THE "LEMON TREE."

CHAPTER XII.

ST. MARTIN'S LANE.

CHAPTER XIII.

ST. MARTIN'S LANE (*continued*).

CHAPTER XIV.

ST. MARTIN'S LANE (*continued*).

CHAPTER XV.

KING STREET.

CHAPTER XVI.

SOME CURIOUS ASSOCIATIONS OF KING STREET.

CHAPTER XVII.

HUNGERFORD MARKET.

CHAPTER XVIII.

NORTHUMBERLAND HOUSE.

CHAPTER XIX.

CHARING HISTORIC AND PRE-HISTORIC.

CHAPTER XX.

THE KING'S MEWS.

CHAPTER XXVI.

THE " ALENTOURS " OF COCKSPUR STREET.

CHAPTER XXVII.

WHITCOMB STREET.

ILLUSTRATIONS.

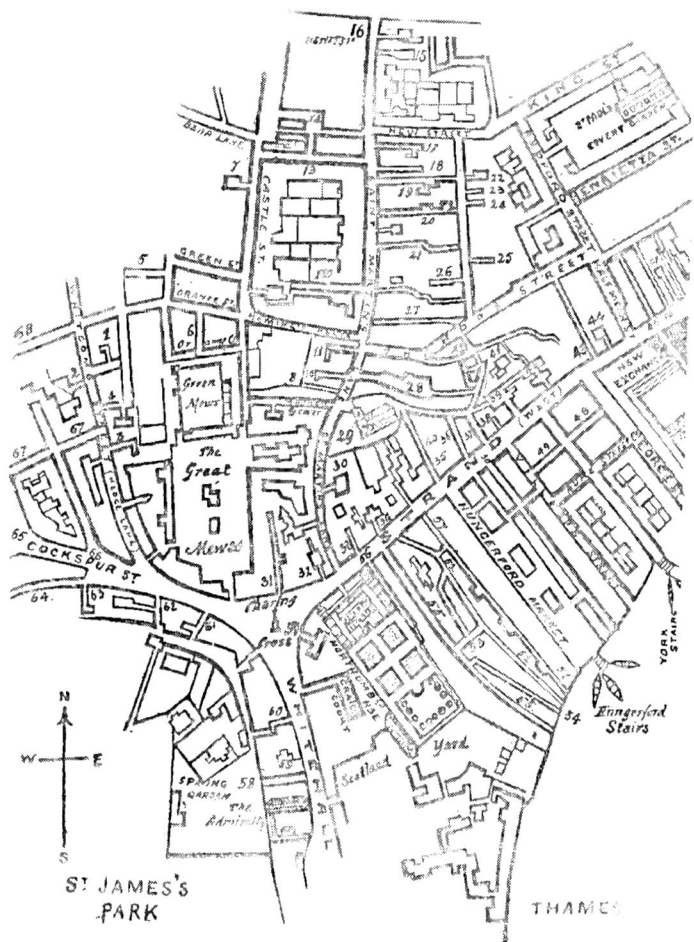

St. JAMES'S PARK

THAMES

1. George Yard.	24. Key Alley.	47. Heathcock Court.
2. Prince's Court.	25. Pipe-makers Alley.	48. George Alley.
3. Monmouth Court.	26. White Hart Yard.	49. Of Alley.
4. The Mews Street.	27. Dawson's Alley.	50. Charles Court.
5. Chapple Court.	28. Moor's Yard.	51. Brewer's Yard.
6. Orange Passage.	29. St. Martin's Church.	52. Spur Alley.
7. Hunt's Court.	30. Hunt's Court.	53. Cross Lane.
8. Red Lion Court.	31. Woodstock Court.	54. Lime Wharf.
9. Duke's Court.	32. Checker Inn.	55. Hartshorn Lane.
10. Grant's Court.	33. Starr Inn.	56. Somerset Court.
11. Ellis Court.	34. King's Head Inn.	57. Angel Court.
12. Peter's Court.	35. St. Martin's Convt.	58. Buckingham Court.
13. Cecil Court.	36. Hewit's Court.	59. Stanhope Court.
14. St. Martin's Court.	37. Church Lane.	60. Pump Court.
15. Castle Court.	38. Robin Hood Court.	61. Mermaid Court.
16. Cross Keys Inn.	39. New Round Court.	62. Red Lion Inn.
17. Goodwin's Court.	40. Round Court.	63. White Horse Court.
18. King's Arms Inn.	41. Back of Round Court.	64. Warwick Street.
19. The Hop Yard.	42. Thackham's Court.	65. Haymarket.
20. Kynaston's Alley.	43. Long's Court.	66. Suffolk Street.
21. Feathers Alley.	44. Harvey's Court.	67. Little Suffolk Street.
22. Bell Yard.	45. Exchange Court.	68. James Street.
23. Goate Alley.	46. Thatched House Court.	

CHARING CROSS

AND ITS

IMMEDIATE NEIGHBOURHOOD

CHAPTER I.

INTRODUCTORY.

CHARING CROSS is the very centre of metropolitan London, situated as it is about midway between Blackwall on the east and Hammersmith on the west. It may, therefore, without entertaining an unduly inflated opinion of its importance, be accurately described as the hub of the terrestrial hemisphere, of which it occupies "nearly the centre," as Sir John Herschel, in his "Natural Philosophy," has pointed out. One cannot but think, therefore, that the Boston man flies his kite rather high when he devotedly claims Boston State-house as the centre of the Solar System, a belief which the "Autocrat of the Breakfast-Table" says you could not pry out of him if you had the tire of all creation straightened out for a crowbar. Paris is justly styled the hub of fashion, and Calcutta, if one may use the word, is a "swagger" city; but London is the centre, not only, as the cabman will tell you, of the four-mile radius, but of the capital of an empire where the sun has actually had to abandon his search for a night's lodging. The Mansion House marks the centre, it is true, of commercial London, but commerce and pleasure—the legitimate pleasures that are "the reflex of unimpeded energy"—go hand-in-hand where human life ebbs and flows past the column that symbolises Britain's dominion of the sea :

> Great God ! I'd rather be
> A pagan suckled in a creed outworn ;
> So might I, standing on this pleasant lea,
> Have glimpses that would make me less forlorn ;
> Have sight of Proteus rising from the sea,
> Or hear old Triton blow his wreathèd horn.

As to the etymology of the place-name of "Charing," the *chère reine* derivation has been described by Professor Skeat as "too funny to be pernicious."[1] And truly its absurdity can best be indicated by the reflection that the village existed long before the death of Queen Eleanor. The cross, in fact, was named after the village from its accidental erection on that spot. A note in Leland's " Collectanea " says, "Anno D. 1292 crux apud Cheringes incepta fuit."[2] But it seems possible, nay probable, that there was a way-side cross standing here before the erection of the more famous work of Richard and Roger de Crundale, who indeed, according to one writer, erected the Eleanor cross "in place of the original wooden cross."[3] The gloss imparted to the *chère reine* interpretation was no doubt acquired from the fact of the first Edward having been so strongly and deservedly attached to the heroic woman, his first wife, Eleanor of Castile. But *nimium ne crede colori*, and the name assuredly had its origin, like so many other place-names, in the geographical situation of the spot, placed as it is at the bend of the river—the only bend between Chelsea Reach and Wapping. This may be seen by referring to the map of London, where the Thames at Charing takes a perfectly rectangular course, with the quondam village at its elbow, *i.e.* at the spot where it turns or bends. Now the Anglo-Saxon word " char " means to turn, whence wood *turned* to coal becomes *char*-coal, a char-woman is one who takes a *turn* at work, and to leave the door a-char is to leave it on the *turn*. One circumstance, in particular, helped to make this bend in the river remarkable, and was probably instrumental in suggesting the name of the village. London was more plainly visible than it is now, and even Loftie, in his " Historical Notes of Whitehall," mentions this " curious bend " in the course of the Thames, on account of which London was nearly as visible from Westminster.[4] The Anglo-Saxon *cerr*, says Skeat, means a *turn* ; Old High German *chér*, a

---

[1] *Notes and Queries*, 7th series, vol. ix. p. 132.

[2] Vol. ii. p. 356.

[3] See also *Manners and Household Expenses of England in the 13th and 15th Centuries*, by Beriah Botfield (Roxburghe Club), 1841, pp. 110, 122. Earlier even than these instances, in a MS. entitled " Liber de Antiquis Legibus," occurs an allusion to the village in the year 1260—thirty-one years before the death of Queen Eleanor, and consequently before the erection of the cross to her memory. See transcript of this MS. among the Archives of the City of London ; also reproduced, I think, by the Camden Society.

[4] " Ing " as a suffix in the names of persons had much the same significance as the prefix " Mac " in Scotland, " O " in Ireland, and " Ap " in Wales.

turning about ; Middle English *cherren, charren*, to turn ; Anglo-Saxon *cerran*, to turn. In Newcastle and some neighbouring towns a *chare* is a local name for a narrow lane, alley, or wynd—in short, for what we should call in less plain Saxon, a *turning*. Reverting to the ancient spelling of the name we shall find reason to conclude that Charing in Kent is exactly identical in its etymology with the Charing now known to us as Charing Cross, for if the map inserted in Furley's "History of the Weald of Kent" [1] may be relied on, Charing in Kent is also situated at a decided deviation of the river's course, and in Domesday and other ancient records is written Cheringes, Cerringes, and Cherring. [2] With regard to "ing" in Charing, Professor Skeat says " we are constantly told that 'ing,' a meadow, is Anglo-Saxon," and he says that " this statement rests on Lye's ' Dictionarium Saxonicum,' where it is calmly assumed that it explains the Northern English, *i e.* the Scandinavian use." " Eng," however, is not even Swedish for " a meadow," which is written äng, the former being the Danish spelling as it is also the Icelandic. [3] The unsoundness, therefore, of the derivation which would make " Char-ing " the turn-meadow, or the " meadow at the bend " (of the river), is evident in the improbability and inconsistency of an " Anglo-Saxon " and a Swedish or Danish combination of syllables.

So far as there can be any certainty about the etymology of such place-names it may, then, fairly be assumed that " Charing " is a substantive with a participial termination like our present word " turning," and that its simple meaning is that of the " turning " or " bending " of the river at this spot, a bend which has been pointed out as a very remarkable one in the course of the Thames, for such geographical peculiarities were commonly taken advantage of in ancient place-nomenclature.

There is an engraving of the village of Charing in Grose's "Antiquarian Repertory," [4] which, if rightly attributed, as it is, to Hollar, goes to prove that even in Charles I.'s time there were only the one or two

---

[1] This map shows the " Ancient and Modern names of the Manors &c., mentioned in the survey of Domesday, compiled A.D. 1086 " (vol ii. part 1). The ancient manor of Charing in the Hundred of Calehill was one of the earliest possessions of the See of Canterbury after the Conquest, and the district of Charing had been taken about the year 839, by Offa, from that See, but restored by Cenulph (Hasted's *Kent*, vol. iii. p. 211).

[2] See also Dugdale's *Monasticon*, vol. ii. pp. 443, 542.

[3] *A Student's Pastime*, by W. W. Skeat, p. 189. See also *Notes and Queries*, 1884 (6th series, vol. x. p. 110).

[4] Ed. 1807, vol. i. p. 371.

dwellings that can at the very least be supposed to constitute a village, the only other symptom of village life, or of any human habitation, being a tavern to the left of the spectator, nestling comfortably beneath a large tree, and next to the cottages alluded to. There was, of course, the alien priory of St. Mary Rouncival, which at the Dissolution came into the hands of the Earl of Northampton, who built upon its site the last of the riverside palaces, Northumberland House, the site and grounds of which are now occupied by Northumberland Avenue. All around Charing, excepting on the east and north-east sides, appears to have been meadow land, as may be seen in Aggas's plan of the village of Charing, 1560, the north being occupied by the Mews, the east by the Strand palaces, and some distance to the west the Hospital of St. James, afterwards St. James's Palace. The lazar- or leper-house of St. James's is described by one chronicler as being as dreary and lonely a spot as could be desired for the isolation of its inmates.[1] What is now St. James's Park was nothing but chaotic marsh land, and so remained until Henry VIII. had it laid out and walled in. Long Ditch, only 720 yards from Charing Cross, so called "for that the same almost insulateth the city of Westminster," was even in Strype's time, at the beginning of the eighteenth century, "a place of no great account for houses or inhabitants." It was situated, I think, between what are now Tothill Street and Great George Street, but the locality is laid down with great exactness in Strype's map of St. Margaret's, Westminster. One of the Westminster prints lately exhibited by Mr. C. E. Jerningham in Westminster Town Hall shows a view from the village of Charing, depicting even Whitehall as wooded meadow-land. Northwards, Long Acre was in 1556 known as the back-side of Charing Cross. An item in Machyn's "Diary" says: "Anodur theyff that dyd long [belong] to one of master comtroller . . . dyd kylle Richerd Eggylston the comtroller['s] tayller, and k[illed him in] the Long Acurs, the bak-syd Charyng-crosse" (p. 121). The village was in fact known principally as the border-land, connected on the one hand, by means of the historic thoroughfare of the Strand, with the City of London, and on the other, by way of the Whitehall and King Street Gates, with Westminster—although of course these gates did not exist before the removal of the royal palace of Westminster to Whitehall. Consequently the spot has been the scene of innumerable because unchronicled events in English history, and those who

---

[1] See Bailey's *Antiquities of London and Westminster*, and J. E. Sheppard's *History of St. James's Palace*.

ventured from either direction so far as Charing no doubt found the inhabitants of the few dwellings which, at a later time, constituted the village—especially the landlord of the rustic tavern that stood there—convenient " middle-gossips " as to what was transpiring either at Westminster or in London. Boniface would recall the exciting time which diversified the normal loneliness of the villagers, when in 1222 a great wrestling match was held near the Lepers' Hospital, now the palace of St. James's, between the men of London and those of Westminster, city and suburban. The Londoners were victorious, but their victory only aroused in the vanquished a desire for revenge such as is unfortunately associated sometimes even nowadays with the noble games of " Socker " and " Rugger." A steward of the Abbot of Westminster—" seneschal " as he was called—was so annoyed at defeat that he resolved on revenge. With the usual live ram as a prize [1] he proposed a second trial of skill a week after the first, i.e. on August 1. The Londoners in great numbers flocked to the rendezvous, where, as bout succeeded bout, it was perceived that the London men were again getting the upper hand, upon which, unarmed as they were, they were attacked by the seneschal's armed followers. The deluded postulants for the ram are described as having been " cruelly maimed and wounded," and forced to fly for refuge within their stout city walls. This was, of course, more than the Londoners could stand. The efforts of the Mayor, Robert Serle, mercer, to restore peace and satisfaction by advising the citizens to complain to the Abbot of Westminster were of no avail. Stronger measures were voiced by one Constantine Fitz Arnulf, who in 1198 had been sheriff under Mayor Fitz Alwin.[2] This firebrand aroused in the general populace such a degree of fury and resentment that they marched at his call on Westminster, with the watchword of the late French invaders on their lips, " God help us and our Lord Lewis," and with the avowed intention of levelling with the ground the houses of the devoted Westmonas-terians. This they accomplished, pillaging them to boot, and

---

[1] Chaucer says of the big and brawny miller, in the Prologue to the *Canterbury Tales* :
> " At wrastlynge he wolde bere away the ram ; "

and again, in the *Rime of Sir Thopas*, it is said of the Knight :
> " Of wrastling was there none his pere,
> There ony ram should stonde."

[2] *Vide* " Calendar of Mayors and Sheriffs " in B. B. Orridge's *Account of the Citizens of London*, 1867, p. 208.

returned in triumph to the city.   But Fitz Arnulf was hanged for his trouble, in spite of large sums offered for his ransom.[1] He was, however, hanged unjustly, as we may well suppose, from all the known circumstances, and the injustice of Hubert de Burgh, the original builder of Whitehall Palace, recoiled on his own head, for on his downfall in 1232 the citizens of London failed not to attribute to him Fitz Arnulf's undeserved death.   It was at the " Admiral Duncan " tavern at Charing Cross that in March 1824 the men of Cumberland and Westmorland in the metropolis met, and resolved to found the annual North Country wrestling matches.[2]   A " scrum " is not dearer to the heart of the festive Milesian than it appears to have been to those who breathed the humid air of Westminster. One Saturday afternoon in July 1722 the " King's Scholars " at Westminster had an *argumentum baculinum* with the lads of several other schools.   The battle was fought with such fury that three lives were lost and others despaired of.   The " King's Scholars " were not satisfied with vanquishing their academical rivals.   Some hackney coachmen chivalrously took upon themselves to aid the weaker side, but paid dearly for their magnanimity, one losing his life and another being placed seriously *hors-de-combat*, while the others were so well beaten that "it is believed they will never for-sake their Coach-Boxes again to meddle on such an Occasion.   We are told several of the Scholars are expelled for this Offence."[3]   In Machyn's " Diary " is an account of " a boy [that] kyld a byge boye that sold papers and prynted bokes [with] horlyng of a stone and yt hym under the ere in Westminster Hall ; the boy was one of the chylderyn that was [at the] sckoll ther in the abbey ; the boy ys a hossear sune a-boyff London-stone."[4]

When in 1397 the Earl of Arundel, as a result of his conspiracy against Richard II., was tried and sentenced at Westminster to be beheaded, the poor—whether or not of the particular neighbourhood does not appear—were seated at Charing Cross to receive alms of the condemned Earl.[5]   In 1542 King Henry VIII. would have no

[1] *Vide* Matthew Paris, and Lyttelton's *History of England*, 1808, vol. i. pp 374–5.

[2] The first record of a code of rules was then made, although the Cumberland and Westmorland Wrestling Society had existed for many years before. *Wrestliana*, by Walter Armstrong, 1870, p. 1.

[3] *London Journal*, July 7, 1722.

[4] 1556, p. 121.

[5] *Annales Ricardi Secundi*, ed. by H. T. Riley, M.A. (Rolls Series), p. 216 : " Egressus primo de Palatio, rogavit ut, laxatis manibus, illa liberfate possct

sword borne before him from Charing Cross whensoever he came to Westminster, *which was never seen before.*[1]

But an event of greater moment than either a wrestling match or an execution was celebrated, in the year 1415, when the neighbourhood of Charing allowed its excitement to reach fever-heat at the news of the hard-fought victory of Agincourt. Monmouth, however—not yet returned from the scene of his sanguinary triumph—was unable to participate in the national thanksgiving in Westminster Abbey, which took place four days after the battle. So that whereas it was the usual custom to go to Westminster on similar occasions in procession on horseback, the Mayor, aldermen, and an immense number of the commonalty, proceeded on this occasion like pilgrims on foot, partly apparently on account of the sorrows and adversities which the campaign had entailed and partly from feelings of humility in the hour of conquest due to a solemn religious service.[2] But a triumphant note was not unvoiced by the people, and a curious ballad-relic has survived in the " Song on the Victory of Agincourt," which, in its original state, says Dr. Rimbault, may justly be considered as the first English *regular* composition of which we have any remains :

> Owre Kynge went forth to Normandy
> With grace and mygt of chivalry ;
> The God for hym wrougt marvellously,
> Wherefore Englonde may calle, and cry,—
>
> Deo gratias.[3]

Our landlord, or his good dame, or perchance his skinker could also tell you how Sir Thomas Wyatt, incensed at Queen Mary's resolve to marry Philip of Spain, marched with an army on London and met with a temporary success at Charing Cross, where he repulsed the attack of Sir John Gage, who was at the head of 1,000 men, and obliged him to seek shelter within the gates of Whitehall Palace, where cries of " Treason " were raised, and there was

perfrui, ut propriis manibus liceret erogare pauperibus, sedentibus ab eo loco usque ad le Charyng Cros, aurum quod in bursa gerebat. Qua libertate sibi concessa, pecunia cum summa devotione distributa, prout ei placuit, brachia sua durissime constringuntur a tergo." See also Stubbs's *Constitutional History of England*, vol. ii. ; Lingard's *History*, 1854, vol. iii. p. 181 ; and *Rot. Parl.* iii. 374–377, 435.

[1] Wriothesley's *Chronicle* (Camden Soc.), vol. ii. p. 135.

[2] Riley's *Memorials of London and London Life*, 1868, pp. 620-1-2.

[3] The melody is " in a modern dresse " as it appears in the first volume of *Old Ballads* in the Pepysian Collection. It was probably modernised in the reign of Charles I. (Rimbault's *Musical Illust. of Anc. Eng. Poetry*, 1850, p. 60).

" running and crying out of ladies and gentlemen, shutting of doores and windowes, and such a shriking and noise as was wonderfull to heare." [1]   And who was the doughty Kentishman who, with his pike, " kept seventeene horsemen off him a great time, but at the last was slaine " ? [2] for by this time Wyatt's army had dispersed, and their leader was riding pillion-wise behind Sir Maurice Berkeley, to whom he had surrendered, and he must, on his way through Charing to the Court at Whitehall, have witnessed his men being appre-hended on all sides by Pembroke's horse.   Later, on February 22, 1554, about 400 of Wyatt's faction were led past Charing Cross to the Tilt Yard opposite Whitehall Palace with halters round their necks, and were there pardoned by the Queen, " who looked forth of her gallery."   They were lucky in thus escaping the fate of another fifty of their leader's adherents, who, a week before, were hanged on " twenty paires of gallowes made for that purpose in divers places about the citie." [3]   Another account says : " The VIIth of Feb. beinge Ash-Weddensday, earlye in the morninge, the Earle of Pembroke, Lieutenant of the Queen's Armie, with the horsemen and footemen of the noblemen, gathered their armies together with the Queen's ordinance, and pitched their field by St. James beyond Charing Crosse to abide the said traytor Wyatt and his rebells.   The Lord Mayor and the Lord Admirall sett the citizens in good arraye at Ludgate, Newgate, and from Creeplegate to Bushopsgate, lest the rebels would drawe to Finnesburie field, they to defend that egde. Then Wyatt with his rebells came to the park pale by St. James about 2 of the clocke in the afternoon, and Knevett, one of his captains with his rebells went by Towtehill, through Westminster, and shott at the Court gates.   But Wyatt perceavinge the great armie of the Queen's campe, and ordinance bent against him sodenlie returned by the wall of the park at St. James, toward Charynge Crosse, with the lightest of his souldiers, when the Earl of Pembroke's men cutt off his trayne, and slue divers of the rebells ; but Wyatt himself with divers other came in at Temple Barre and so thorowe Fleet Street to the Bell Savage, crying ' A Wyatt ! a Wyatt ! God save Queen Marie ! ' " [4]   Another sequel to the general dissatisfaction with which the populace viewed the projected marriage between Philip and Mary was the conflicts which frequently occurred between the Spaniards in London and the Londoners.   These Spaniards were apparently the servants of the ambassadors from the Emperor

---

[1] Stow's *Annales*, p. 1052.   [2] *Ibid.*   [3] *Ibid.* p. 1054.
[4] Wriothesley's *Chronicle*, vol. ii. p. 112 (Camden Society).

Charles, father of Philip, who came over to conclude a treaty for the Queen's marriage. The ambassadors were the Count d'Egmont, Charles Count de Laing, Jehan de Montmorancy sieur de Corriers, Philip Negri, and Simon Renard. "On the iiij day of November" (1554), says Machyn, "be-gane a grett fray at Charyng crosse at viij of the cloke at nyght be-twyn the Spaneardes and Englysmen, the wyche thrugh wysdom ther wher but a fuwe hort, and after the next day thay wher serten taken that be-gane yt; on was a blake-mor, and was brought a-for the hed offesers by the Knyght-marshall['s] servandes."[1] Later, "On the xxvj day of Aprell, 1555, was cared from the Marsalsee in a care thrugh London unto Charying crosse to the galows, and ther hangyd, iij men for robying of serten Spaneardes of tresur of gold out of the abbay of Westminster."[2] "On the xxix day of Aprill was cutte downe of the galows a man that was hangyd the xxvj day of Aprill, a pulter['s] servant that was one of them that dyd robed the Spaneard with-in Westminster Abbay, and he hangyd in a gowne of towny (tawny) fryse and a dobelet of townny taffata, and a payre of fyne hose lynyd with sarsanet, and after bered undur the galaus, raylling a-gainst the pope and the masse, and hangyd iiij days."[3] A Spaniard also was hanged at Charing Cross for killing a servant of Sir George Gefford without Temple Bar.[4]

A tumultuous crowd now appears in the distance—we must, however, give the reins to our imagination of the scene, in the absence of a seventeenth-century cinematograph—the most conspicuous figure in which has left both his ears with the Star Chamber; he is branded, too, on each cheek with S.L. (seditious libeller), but his gait is resolute and his spirit unsubdued. This is the author of "Histriomastix," who had greater reasons perhaps than exist to-day, fortunately, for hurling his anathemas at the theatrical exhibitions then in vogue. Prynne, Burton, and Bastwick came this way on different days to plead their cause in person : the storm of the Great Rebellion was about to burst. Prynne was attended by hundreds of carriages and thousands of horsemen, amidst multitudes on foot, in much the same form, one may well imagine, as the approach of the mob across Westminster Bridge on the occasion, as I remember well, of the meeting in Trafalgar Square, which was projected in the interests

---

[1] *Machyn's Diary*, ed. by J. G. Nichols, 1848, p. 74.   [2] *Ibid.* p. 86.
[3] *Ibid.* p. 86.
[4] *Ibid.* p. 72.   See also Wriothesley's *Chronicle*, vol. ii. pp. 125–128 (Camden Society).

of the release of William O'Brien. The mob that acclaimed the release of Prynne, as they passed the cross at Charing, soon to fall before their unreasoning fury, wore bay and rosemary in their hats as recorded by Lingard, emblems, in these circumstances, of rejoicing and defiance. In "A Perfect Journal &c. of that memorable Parliament begun at Westminster, November 3, 1640," i. 8, is the following passage : "Nov. 28.—That afternoon Master Prin and Master Burton came into London, being met and accompanied with many thousands of horse and foot, and rode with rosemary and bayes in their hands and hats ; which is generally esteemed the greatest affront that ever was given to the courts of justice in England."

In what part of Charing Cross the villas or mansions were situated is not exactly apparent, but soon after Elizabeth had ascended the throne the village appears to have become a fashionable residential suburb, much as Hammersmith, for instance, was in the latter part of the eighteenth century. Sir Nicholas Bacon, the father of the illustrious Francis, had a house here, where he died in 1578,[1] and Sir Thomas Bromley, Lord Chancellor, dates a letter from his house near Charing Cross in 1582.[2] In 1613 Lord Fenton writes to the Lord Mayor for "a quill of water out of the City's great pipe for his house near Charing Cross."[3] And the tenth Earl of Northumberland in another letter also writes complaining that he had lately been deprived of the conduit water which had always served Northumberland House at Charing Cross. He requests permission for a quill of water from the City's pipes, which passed the gates of his residence.[4] This may be said to be the period when London was becoming imperceptibly united, by means of Charing Cross, with Westminster, until its teeming life reached, in Dr. Johnson's time, the "full tide of human existence." London and Westminster were not indeed, at one time, much more than a mile asunder, becoming insensibly incorporated in point of continuity though not of government. The union was greatly accelerated by the influence of a greater Union, that of England and Scotland, "for the Scots multiplying here mightily, neasted themselves about the Court, so that the Strand, from mud Walls

[1] J. T. Smith's *Streets of London*, 1849, p. 91. This was York House, the site of which is now occupied by Buckingham and Villiers Streets, Strand. 1579 is generally given as the year of Sir Nicholas Bacon's death, but Cunningham is wider of the mark still in saying that it was 1594.

[2] The *Remembrancer*, 1878, p. 177.

    Ibid. p. 555.

    1664,—*ibid.* p. 561

and thatched Houses, came to that perfection of Buildings, as now we see." [1]

The majority of the accused in the great State trials at Westminster, although passing close to Charing, probably reached the Courts of Justice by water, as in the case of the Protector Somerset from the Tower. When Somerset was condemned the people supposed that he had been acquitted because they saw "the axe of Tower put downe," and they made such "a shryke and castinge up of caps, that it was hard (heard) into the Longe Acre beyond Charinge Cross." [2] Charles I. went by way of St. James's Park from the Palace of St. James. Dutch William slipped round quietly by water to meet his Parliament, entering his state barge at Whitehall Stairs.[3] Strype speaks of that part of the Strand upon which abutted the stables of Durham House, as "ready to fall and very unsightly in *so public a passage to the Court and Westminster.*" This unsightliness was caused by the ruinous state of the said stables, situated close by the spot afterwards occupied by the New Exchange and Coutts's Bank. When in 1643, soon after the battle of Edgehill, the City was fortified with outworks, of which relics still exist in place-names round what was then suburban London, Charing Cross was one of the ways into the City for which exception was made as to closing it. Other passages that were left open were at St. Giles's-in-the-Fields, St. John Street, Shoreditch, and Whitechapel.[4] But beyond Charing Cross were the musket-proof [5] Chelsea turnpike, a large fort with four bulwarks at Hyde Park Corner mounted with artillery, and a redoubt and battery at Constitution Hill. And again, Charing Cross was the scene of the reception, by the Common Council, of Fairfax at the head of an army that thus became masters both of the City and the Parliament. Then Nemesis !

> O thou, who never yet of human wrong
> Left the unbalanced scale, great Nemesis !
> Thou who didst call the Furies from the abyss,
> And round Orestes bade them howl and hiss,
> For that unnatural retribution.

[1] *Londinopolis,* by James Howell, 1657, p. 346. There are still a Thatched House Tavern in the Strand, and the Thatched House Club in St. James's Street.

[2] Wriothesley's *Chronicle* (Camden Society, 1877), vol. ii. p. 63.

[3] Strickland's *Queens,* 1847, vol. xi. p. 31.

[4] See Maitland's *London,* 1739, p. 237.

[5] An old expression meaning to be in no danger from a musket. Butler, in his *Hudibras,* employs a similar expression in "halter-proof"

> "Both might have evidence enough
> To render neither halter-proof."—(Part III. canto 1.)

There are, of course, two views of this retribution : whether a bloodless revolution might not, in time, have been consummated, without cutting people's heads off, or whether the scaffold was a *sine quâ non*. At all events, the shedding of blood recoiled, as it very often does, like a boomerang, and Charing Cross was made the scene of one of those orgies of blood, a taste for which seems to have been ingrained from the cradle among Royalist and Roundhead, Catholic and Protestant alike. The majority of the regicides were executed at Charing Cross. When, three days after the execution of Harrison, John Cook and Hugh Peters were drawn upon sledges to the place of execution, Harrison's head " was placed on the sledge which carried Cook, with the face uncovered and directed towards him." [1] The atrocities—usual to the times, however—which attended the hanging, drawing, and quartering of Harrison are not desirably repetitional.

On subsequent occasions, two historic personages, Lord Balmerino, and Sir Edward Seymour, Speaker in the time of Charles II., by their British composure in what one would have thought were trying circumstances, strikingly emphasised the imperfection of Goldsmith's saying that " philosophy is a good horse in a stable, but an arrant jade on a journey." The former, on his way to the Tower from his trial at Westminster, stopped the coach at Charing Cross, to buy what he, a Scotchman, called honey-blobs, but which we know as gooseberries. [2] And when Sir Edward Seymour's coach broke down at Charing Cross, he coolly ordered the beadles to stop the next one passing and bring it to him. The gentleman occupying it was much surprised to be turned out of his own coach ; but Sir Edward told him that it was more proper for him to walk the streets than the Speaker of the House of Commons, and left him so to do without any further apology. [3]

Titus Oates's infamous plot had already filled London with a renewed fear and horror of the " Papists," and some of the noblest had been beheaded on his perjured evidence, when a semblance of truth was imparted to his rascally fictions by the murder of Sir Edmondbury Godfrey, the magistrate, whose funeral was with great pomp attended by thousands to St. Martin's Church in the Fields, where he was buried. That Godfrey had always shown himself the

---

[1] *Memoirs of Lieutenant-General Ludlow*, 1690, vol. iii. p. 75.
[2] Walpole to Montague, Aug. 2, 1746.
[3] Lord Dartmouth in *Burnet*, ed. 1823, ii. 70 (quoted by Cunningham).

steadfast friend of the Roman Catholics,[1] however, did nothing to counterbalance the predisposition of the mob to assign to him a "Protestant Martyrdom," and the perjured Oates delivered a fierce oration at Charing Cross, where the bier rested, in which he called upon every citizen to avenge him. A terrible massacre of the Roman Catholics was, in fact, only averted by the calling out of the guards, and the many precautions of the magistrates; for Godfrey's body, instead of being speedily deposited in the grave, was carried in public procession to his former habitation, presumably in Green's Lane near Hungerford Market, where he had resided in the neighbourhood of his wharf. Here the doors were thrown open two days, and the populace were invited to gaze on the mangled remains of "the Protestant Martyr." The sight, of course, inflamed their passions, and "prepared their minds to believe in the bloody designs attributed to the Papists." [2] Thus Charing Cross narrowly escaped becoming again the scene of bloodshed.

When Queen Anne's Government thought fit to hobnob with the French Camisards as a means of annoying Louis XIV., it extended a warm welcome to them in London. But they had scarcely become reconciled to the position of refugees before "the lively spirits of the natives of the south began to effervesce in a style extraordinary, even among the numerous sectarians of Great Britain." Their ministers, after remaining in trances or slumbers, such as in these days would have been called mesmeric, gave vent to such wild prophecies that the Government thought fit to interfere, and Charing Cross became the scene of their *dénouement*. Here John Aude and Nicolas Facio, for printing and publishing the writings of Elias Marion, were sentenced to be perched on a scaffold with papers in their hats, signifying their crime, and at Charing Cross they accordingly suffered.[3]

Even so late as Queen Anne's time the populace seem to have sought the neighbourhood of Charing Cross as the most likely source of information as to what was stirring in the political world. The Admiralty, being close by, became a legitimate cradle of the national curiosity as to certain whisperings about abuses in Her Majesty's navy. Accordingly people came this way to see what they could pick up as to the conduct and progress of national affairs. Two citizens, apparently Ned Ward and a friend, issuing from Scotland

[1] Lingard's *Hist. of England*, 1855, vol. ix. p. 180.
[2] *Ibid.* See also *Londinium Redivivum*.
[3] Strickland's *Queens*, 1847, vol. xi. p. 195.

Yard one day, probably from Well's Coffee-House situated there, were much struck by "a merry cobler at Charing Cross," indulging his cheerful humour by singing a piece of his own composition while sitting in his stall. In this act he kept repeating the following words: "The King said to the Queen, and the Queen said to the King." A passenger coming by, who was mighty desirous of knowing what it was the King and the Queen said to each other, stood listening a considerable time, expecting the cobbler would go on with his ditty, and thus satisfy his longing curiosity. The cobbler, however, continued in the same words, till he had tried the patience of his auditor to breaking point —"The King said to the Queen, and the Queen said to the King,"—when the latter feverishly stepped up to the stall and asked the drolling sole-mender what it was the King said to the Queen and the Queen to the King? Upon which Crispin snatched up his strap, and applying it with all his might across the shoulders of the inquirer, said : " How now, Saucebox ! It's a fine Age we Live in, when such Coxcombs as you must be prying into Matters of State ! I'd have you know, Sirrah, I am too loyal a Subject to betray the King's secrets, so pray get you gone, and don't interrupt me in my Lawful Occupation, lest I stick an Awl into ye, and mark ye for a fool that meddles with what ye have nothing to do." [1]

From comedy to tragedy was in those days a transition so frequent that every dweller in London probably had learnt how "every light has its shadow." On November 20, 1727, the unfortunate poet Richard Savage came from Richmond to pursue his studies less interruptedly in London. "Accidentally meeting two gentlemen his acquaintances, whose names were Merchant and Gregory, he went in with them to a neighbouring coffee-house, and sat drinking till it was late, for it was in no time of Savage's life any part of his character to be the first of the company that desired to separate. He would willingly have gone to bed in the same house ; but there was not room for the whole company, and therefore they agreed to ramble about the streets, and divert themselves with such amusements as should offer themselves till morning.

" In this walk they happened unluckily to discover a light in Robinson's Coffee-house, near Charing Cross, and therefore went in. Merchant, with some rudeness, demanded a room, and was told that there was a good fire in the next parlour, which the company were about to leave, being then paying their reckoning. Merchant,

---

[1] The *London Spy*, by Edward Ward, 1709, part ix. pp. 200–1.

not satisfied with this answer, rushed into the room, and was followed by his companions. He then petulantly placed himself between the company and the fire, and soon after kicked down the table. Swords were drawn on both sides, and one, Sinclair, was killed. Savage, having likewise wounded a maid that held him, forced his way with Merchant out of the house ; but being intimidated and confused, without resolution to fly or stay, they were taken in a back court by one of the company, and some soldiers whom he had called to his assistance." The upshot of this was eventually that the poet was set at liberty, through the intercession of the humane Countess of Hertford, but the story is continued with dramatic precision by Dr. Johnson in his "Lives of the Poets." [1]

Charing Cross Post Office now occupies the site of the Hermitage, a chapel from very early times dedicated to St. Catherine. It must have been of considerable dimensions, for it was occasionally used as the lodging for such bishops as came to attend the Court, and had no other residence in London or Westminster. [2] Willis, in his "History of the See of Llandaff," states, on the authority of the Patent Rolls of the forty-seventh year of Henry III., that William de Radnor, the then bishop, had permission from the King to lodge, with all his retainers, within the precincts of the Hermitage of Charing—the mention of which affords further evidence, if need were, that the village existed before the death of Eleanor— whenever he came to London. [3]

Those who would become acquainted with one of the most remarkable views in London, perhaps the *most* remarkable in point of fineness—the vista through Ludgate Hill terminating in Wren's masterpiece, and enhanced by the spire, as Wren intended that it should be, of St. Martin's Church on the Hill, is, viewed from Fleet Street, probably the most picturesque—should take their stand at the south-west corner of Charing Cross Underground railway-station, and looking westward it will, I think, be admitted that on a fine summer's day,—a winter's day preferably, because of the absence of foliage,— the massive architecture of Whitehall Court and the National Liberal Club, overlooking the Gardens, with the Embankment, and its avenue of trees, and the shining river beyond, present one of the finest spectacles to be seen in any capital in Europe. I allude to

[1] Vol. ii. pp. 277–286.
[2] The *Memoirs of Lieut.-Gen. Ludlow*, 1698, iii. 75.
[3] See J. T. Smith's *Streets of London*, 1849, p. 133.

this because the Gardens are probably identical with those which grew the flowers, fruit, vegetables and sweet-herbs supplying the wants of the Hospital of St. Mary Rouncival,[1] and successively the wants of the households of the Earls of Northampton, Suffolk, and Northumberland.

[1] A view of St. Mary Rounceval Chapel, a most interesting contemporary drawing from the Wellesley Collection, was exhibited, among the Gardner Collection of prints relating to London, Westminster, and Southwark, at the opening of the Guildhall Library and Museum in November 1872. In the priory garden was, no doubt, grown the Rounceval Pea (*Pisum majus*), producing a large delicious pea, but possibly the parent institution at the foot of the Pyrenees gave it its name. There was a burial-place attached to the convent. See Mrs. Basil Holmes's *London Burial Grounds*.

CHAPTER II.

A CHARING CROSS REGATTA.

IT is not a matter of common knowledge, I think, that Charing Cross witnessed the first regatta in England. The "Quality" had read and heard of the Venetian *Regattera*, or race of oarsmen, and they determined to have a regatta of their own at a time when the river was still the principal means of locomotion for all classes alike. So, early in the afternoon of Wednesday, June 21, 1775, the river from London Bridge to the Ship Tavern, Millbank, began to swarm with pleasure-seekers. Above 1,200 flags were flying before four o'clock; and such was the public impatience that scores of barges were filled at that time. Even before noon several of the barges belonging to the City Companies, with great numbers of pleasure barges, were moored in the river with their flags flying. Half a guinea was asked for a seat in a common barge. Charing Cross Stairs,[1] well known to Pepys nearly a century before in his water excursions, must have been crowded with intending sight-seers struggling to engage the service of boatmen who had little need for their usual cry of "Oars! Oars!" Those on land had scaffolds erected for them on the banks, while other vessels of every description tried to outdo the land erections by scaffolds of their own. Even Westminster Hall had an erection of this kind, while vessels were also moored for the sale of refreshments.

By six o'clock the Thames was covered with vessels and boats ornamented with divers colours, which began to form themselves into divisions. On the stern of the Director's barge, which was "uncommonly superb," was displayed a blue ensign with the word "Regatta" in large gold characters. It was rowed in great state to its station on the west point of the centre arch of Westminster Bridge a little before seven o'clock. The boats and vessels of the red flag immediately brought up in the line of the four arches on the

---

[1] Not to be confused with Whitehall Stairs, which were the private stairs of royal residents at Whitehall Palace.

Lambeth side ; the blue division being in the direction of the four arches nearest Westminster, while the white was under the two arches on each side of the centre. The grand centre arch was solely appropriated to the race-boats.

The river is said to have presented a splendid scene. A City barge usually carrying ballast was filled on this occasion with the finest ballast London and Charing Cross could produce : to wit, "above a hundred elegant ladies." At half-past seven the Lord Mayor's barge moved, and, falling down the stream, made a circle towards the bridge, on which twenty-one cannon were fired as a salute.

At half-past seven the rivals for the regatta honours began their aquatic sports at Westminster Bridge. In this first effort the red squadron gained the goal first after engaging the white and blue squadrons so far as Watermen's Hall and back. Their prize was a new boat, with furniture complete, coats and badges, and an ensign with the word "Regatta" in gold letters. The second boat had eight guineas each, and the third five guineas ; and to every other candidate who rowed the full distance, half-a-guinea, with permission to be in Ranelagh Gardens (in their uniforms) during the entertainment.

As soon as the winners were declared and their prizes awarded, the whole procession began to move from Westminster Bridge for Ranelagh ; the Director's barge at the head of the whole squadron, with grand bands of music playing in each.

The ladies in general were dressed in white, and the gentlemen in undress frocks of all colours. It was thought that no fewer than 200,000 people witnessed this procession. Minuets and cotillons, &c., were danced after supper in the Temple of Neptune at Ranelagh and other entertainments were patronised, the company consisting of about two thousand persons and personages, among the latter being the Dukes of Gloucester and Cumberland, the Duke of Northumberland, Lords North, Harrington, Stanley, Tyrconnel, Lincoln, Lyttelton, Colerane, Carlisle, March, Melbourne, Cholmondeley, Petersham, &c., and the French, Spanish, Prussian, Russian, and Neapolitan Ambassadors. Mrs. Cornely provided decorations and "an indifferent supper" for seven hundred guineas, and the wine was very scarce presumably in quantity perhaps as well as quality.[1]

Then the scene changes, and those who had disported themselves

---

[1] See Malcolm's *Manner and Customs of London in the Eighteenth Century*, 1800, vol. ii. pp. 293-300.

at the summer regatta are confronted with the open space round the Cross and the pleasure-yielding river clothed in snow and ice. Around the Cross stand the ballad-sellers extracting the ready pence from those on their way to the ice-bound Thames, where, in 1683-4, there was a great frost that lent itself more frequently than in these latter days to the fairs and junketings which we find portrayed in many old engravings ; and this is what the ballad-mongers sang :

> From Westminster Hall to the Temple each day
> The River of Thames, 'twas made a Highway :
> For Footmen and Horsemen and Coaches beside,
> And many brave Gentlemen in them did Ride ;
> But all this great Triumph we justly might fear,
> Might make our sad judgment to fall more severe.
> Then let us be thankful and praise God therefore,
> For He in good time heard the cry of the Poor.[1]

On the occasion of another great frost in the winter of 1739-40, a curious procession might have been seen wending its way past Charing Cross, among sympathetic crowds of people. It consisted of the watermen and fishermen with a peter-boat in mourning, and the carpenters, bricklayers, &c., with their tools and utensils, also in mourning. Their necessities excited pity, and relief was liberally bestowed. This was one of the most intense frosts that had ever been known in this country, known on account of its piercing cold and long continuance as the Great Frost. It commenced on Christmas Day and lasted till February 17.[2] During the great frost of 1814, the spectator at Hungerford Stairs might have witnessed a tragedy of the river in which two young men were the principals. In spite of the warnings of the watermen they ventured on the ice above Westminster Bridge. The large mass on which they stood was loosened by the tide, and gave way, its occupants floating down stream. As they passed under Westminster Bridge they cried out most piteously for help. They had not gone far before they sat down, but both going too near the edge, they overbalanced the mass, and were precipitated into the stream, sinking to rise no more.[3]

Many quips and practical jokes that are popularly supposed to have had their origin at a specific time or in specified circumstances

---

[1] *A Century of Ballads*, by John Ashton. See also Ashton's *Social Life under the Regency*, 1899, pp. 130-1.

[2] *Frostiana*, 1814. This book was printed on a large ice-island between Blackfriars and Westminster, during the Great Frost of 1814. See page 10.

[3] *Ibid*. p. 23.

are, it is well known, traceable to an earlier source. And it seems likely that the whimsical story of the tail-wagging lion which, as the crest of the Percies, adorned the top of Northumberland House, was suggested by a similar story, to be found in Heywood's " Fyrst Hundred of Epigrammes," concerning a fox that stared admiringly at the weathercock of St. Paul's Cathedral. As to the Percy lion, some nameless wag undertook, for a trifling wager, to collect a crowd in the streets of London, upon any pretence, however absurd. He accordingly took his stand opposite, and gazed very earnestly up at the lion. Joined by one or two passers-by, he took out a spy-glass and looked still more intently. A hundred people quickly assembled, and it went round that at a certain hour the lion would wag his tail ! The crowd increased until the Strand was rendered impassable. The greatest curiosity was manifested ; several swore positively that they saw the tail wagging, and long arguments ensued *pro* and *con.* The story adds that the crowds were not dispersed till a smart shower came on, and even then some of the most pertinacious believers ensconced themselves in covered alleys and under doorways to watch the phenomenon. Heywood's story presents, I think, enough resemblance to have suggested the above. The fox thus explains his admiration :

> My noddyng and blyssyng breedth of wonder
> Of the witte of Poules wethercocke yonder
> There is more witte in that cock's onely head,
> Than hath bene in all men's heades that be deade.
> As thus, by common reporte this we fynde,
> All that be dead, did die for lacke of wynde.
> But the wethercock's witte is not so weake
> To lacke wynde : the wynde is ever in his beake.
> So that while any wynde blowth in the skie,
> For lack of winde that wethercocke will not die. [1]

The Percy Lion now occupies a similar position at Sion House, Isleworth, the suburban residence of the Duke of Northumberland. It was at a conference to which Monk was invited by the Earl of Northumberland in Northumberland House that the restoration of Charles II., as yet not openly talked about, was for the first time proposed in direct terms. [2]

Mons. de Monconys, tutor and travelling companion to the young Duke de Chevreuse, on his visit to England in 1663, describes

---

[1] John Heywood's *Woorkes*, 1562 (*Fyrst Hundred of Epigrammes*), " The foxe and the mayde," 10.

[2] J. T. Smith's *Streets of London*, 1849 p. 135.

Northumberland House with brevity and exactness enough to afford a graphic word-picture : "et Nortombelland, qui est de brique, mais plus grande et plus exhaussée que les autres [*i.e.* the other Strand mansions], composée d'un grand corps de logis quarré, accompagné de quatre petites tours, une à chaque coin de Bastiment qu'elles flanquent"[1] There were at first, however, as the House was erected by Bernard Jansen, only three sides of this quadrangle, the fourth having been built towards the river by Algernon Percy, immediately after he came into possession, so that the principal apartments might be removed from the dust and noise of the Strand.

In the immediate neighbourhood of Charing Cross, between where Rounceval Priory stood on the east and Peterborough House, Millbank, on the west, grew, at the beginning of last century, many indigenous plants that would not reward the keenest search to-day : the Ivy-leaved Toad Flax ; the sweet-scented Camomile ; a variety of *Arctium Lappa* called Rose-Burdock ; a variety of flat-horned Clavaria ; Net Conferva ; a variety of Female Fern, or Brakes ; a variety of Arrow-head (*Sagittaria sagittifolia*) ; a variety of the Round-headed Bastard Cyperus ; the Pointed Bulrush ; the Hooded Willow Herb in St. James's Park ; the Bird's-foot Trefoil and the Dwarf Trefoil.[2]

Cockspur Street may be said, approximately, to occupy the site of the three or four houses which up to the middle of the sixteenth century constituted the village of Charing.   This street is a very old one.   Pennant speaks of it in 1572 as filling up the space between the few houses alluded to and Charing Cross.[3]   There does not seem to be any difficulty as to the origin of the street's name, although Cunningham says "why it was so called I am not aware, unless it had some fancied connection with the Mews adjoining." And Mr. Wheatley is disposed to derive it from the Cock Tavern which stood at the end of Suffolk Street.   Perhaps it was so named for neither of these reasons, but because here was first established the trade in artificial cockspurs which supplied the constant demand that must have been created by the frequenters of the cockpits in Whitehall and St. James's Park.   Further reason for thinking that this is so exists in the remarkable fact that steel cockspurs are at

---

[1] " London in the Seventeenth Century," by A. J. Dasent, in the *National Review*, August 1889.

[2] See " Middlesex " in Dugdale's *British Traveller*, iii. 459–466.

[3] *Tour of London.*

the present time still being sold by old-established cutlers in the neighbourhood of Cockspur Street, as I have ascertained by personal inquiry. The sport is not unknown in the recesses of the Cumberland mountains, and ready purchasers of cockspurs are to be found among even our own county gentry. The principal trade, however, I am given to understand, is with the native princes and others of India, and with wealthy citizens of the South American republics. There was a silver-cockspur maker dwelling near here, in the Strand, " near Hungerford Market." He was also a clock-maker, and consequently displayed the sign of the " Dial and Crown." There is a bill to this effect preserved among other curiosities, framed and suspended in the interior of Messrs. Fribourg and Treyer's shop in the Haymarket, the famous old snuff-dealers at the " Crown and Rasp." Similar street names to Cockspur Street occur in Spurriers' Row, Ludgate Hill, and Spurriers' Lane, Tower Street ; Spur Alley in the Strand, and the Spur Inn in Southwark ; but in these instances the rider's spur is meant no doubt. The Cock Tavern, at the end of Suffolk Street, facing Cockspur Street, probably also derived its sign from the circumstance of receiving its chief support from those who had come from a long main or a short main, a Welsh main or a battle-royal, at the Whitehall and Westminster cockpits. Pepys " made merry " over a good soup and a pullet for 4s. 6d. the whole, at the " Cocke," walking in St. James's Park while it was dressing.

" At the Cockpit Royal, the South Side of St. James's Park, on Monday next, being the 4th of this Instant, will be seen the Royal Sport of Cock-Fighting ; and on Tuesday begins the Match for 2 Guineas a Battle, and 20 Guineas the odd Battle ; between the Gentlemen of Middlesex, and the Gentlemen of Surry, and will continue all the Week. To begin exactly at 4 a Clock." [1]

Much larger sums were sometimes staked on the odd battle. A main of cocks was fought on May 11, 12, and 13, 1736, at the George Inn in Alton, Hants, between the Gentlemen of Alton and Petersfield, for five guineas a battle, and one hundred guineas the odd battle.[2]

In Cockspur Street, in 1748, a female dwarf, the " Corsican Fairy," was one of the sights of London. She drew, at half-a-crown a head, crowds almost as numerous as those which in our own day waited on " General Tom Thumb." [3] But we are not told whether

[1] The *Weekly Journal*, December 2, 1721.

[2] *St. James's Evening Post* (London) of April 15 in that year. Cockfighting was so much in vogue in the reign of Charles I. that Vandyck painted a picture of the Court watching a match in the royal pit, Whitehall.

[3] See E. J. Wood's *Giants and Dwarfs*, 1868, pp. 351-2.

this gossamer person, to ensure her safety on a windy day, ever resorted to the expedient favoured by the most famous of the dwarfs of antiquity, Philetus of Cos, who carried leaden weights in his pockets as ballast "to prevent his being blown away."

There were giants in those days, more so than now apparently, and it is questionable whether there is any neighbourhood in the world that has afforded such opportunities for giant-worship as that of Charing Cross. There was the Cambridge giant, the Norfolk giant, the Kentish giant, the Irish and French giants, the Dutch and German giants, at a later period the Italian and the Chinese giants, and many more. The Swedish giant is described as "that Prodigy in Nature the living Colossus or wonderful Giant, from Sweden, now to be seen at the Lottery House next Door to the Green Man, Charing Cross. It is humbly presum'd, that of all the natural Curiosities which have been expos'd to the Publick, nothing has appear'd for many Ages so extraordinary in its Way as this surprising Gentleman. He is much taller than any Person ever yet shewn in Europe, large in Proportion ; and all who have hitherto seen him declare, notwithstanding the prodigious Accounts they have heard, that he far exceeds any Idea they had framed of him.

"Note, He is to be seen as above any Hour of the Day by any Number of Gentlemen and Ladies, from Nine in the Morning till Nine at Night" (poor giant!) "without loss of time." [1] Before this he was exhibited at the "Glass-Shop facing the Mews Wall, Charing Cross," and was then described as a foot taller than "the late famous Saxon, or any ever yet introduced to the World as Giants, and as several learned Gentlemen have declar'd, may justly be call'd the Christian Goliah, no one of human Species having been heard of since that Æra of so monstrous a Size." [2] One spectator fell into poetry over him :

WRITTEN EXTEMPORE BY A GENTLEMAN ON SEEING
THE GIANT AT CHARING CROSS.

Amazing Man ! of such stupendous Size,
As moves, at once, our Wonder and Surprize.
The Son of Kish (being Head and Shoulders taller
Was chose a King, to govern all the smaller :

---

[1] *Daily Advertiser*, January 22, 1742. His name, according to Mr. E. J. Wood in his *Giants and Dwarfs*, was Daniel Cajanico. Some say he was 7 ft. 8 in. and others 8 ft. 4 in. (Swedish).

[2] *Ibid.* March 24, 1741. The Saxon giant was probably Maximilian Christian Miller, who was born at Leipzig in Saxony in 1674, and was exhibited in London in 1728 (George II.) ; another Saxon giant was seen by George I.

Had you been there, the stately Monarch Saul
Had had no Title to that sacred Call.
Repair to Oxford, that sublime Retreat,
The Source of Wisdom, and the Muses' Seat ;
Her learned Sons (who rummage Nature's ways)
Shall come with Pleasure, and with Wonder gaze :
In every Science there each curious Spark,
May mark how Nature has o'er-shot her Mark.[1]

"Last Saturday their Royal Highnesses the three Princesses went to see the surprising Swedish Giant, at Charing Cross, at the sight of whom they express'd the greatest Satisfaction and Astonishment, and made him a very handsome present."[2] There was another remarkable exhibition, which I do not think has been alluded to either by Mr. E. J. Wood in his "Giants and Dwarfs" or by the writer of two excellent illustrated articles entitled "Giants and Dwarfs" in the "Strand Magazine" for October 1894. "We hear that the tall Woman Christian Godwin, from Essex, who has had the honour of being seen by most of the Nobility and Gentry at Charing Cross for some time, designs very speedily to make a Tour round England. She is seven Foot high, and proportionable to her Heighth, tho' but 18 Years of Age. She has had the Pleasure of giving Satisfaction to everybody whose Curiosity has led 'em to see her."[3]

Practical jokes have passed out of vogue nowadays, partly, perhaps, because of the inability of the joker to distinguish between what was offensive and inoffensive in this direction, and partly because we have become too serious. Then there is the ogre who does not believe in fun of any kind. Not so our forefathers, one of whose favourite atticisms was to make the victim of their drollery himself responsible for an act with an unpleasant sequel. This propensity was the origin of the Spring Gardens at Charing Cross, which have been such a considerable asset in London life from the days of Charles I. to those of the County Council. They were so named from a jet of water which was sprung upon anyone who was unwary enough to tread on a pre-arranged spot.[4] Paul Hentzner, in

[1] *Daily Advertiser*, April 24, 1742.

[2] *Ibid.* April 9, 1742.

[3] *St. James's Evening Post*, May 27, 1736.

[4] Perhaps it would be more correct to say that the name was derived from several springs of excellent water which existed here, and probably do still. In fact, Jesse, in his *Literary and Historical Memoirs of London*, Nimmo's edition of 1901, says, "It is remarkable that every house in what is called Spring Gardens Terrace has still a well attached to it."

his "Travels," says : " In a garden joining to this palace (Whitehall) there is a jet d'eau, with a sundial, at which while strangers are looking, a quantity of water forced by a wheel which the gardener turns at a distance through a number of little pipes, plentifully sprinkles those that are standing round."[1] I remember seeing an imitation tree, perhaps a "weeping" willow, at Chatsworth about the year 1880, whose branches were said to "weep" over anyone standing under it at the promptings of the gardener. The branches were nothing but water-pipes : in fact the tree was made of iron. But the ducal joke seems to have been played out, for it did not work when I was there. There was a similar piece of waggery in favour at Mrs. Salmon's waxworks in Fleet Street, visitors to which, upon treading on a certain spring, received an ignominious kick from a figure at the entrance. The late Miss Cuming remembered the gossip about this trap for the unwary, and from her I had it. And another figure, I was told by the late Mr. H. S. Cuming, stood at the top of the stairs. This, when a certain spring was trodden upon, was thrown into a threatening attitude with an uplifted broom.

The behaviour of the public, or of a large portion of it, in old Spring Garden led to the royal privilege being withdrawn, and a new Spring Garden was discovered in Fulke's Hall, Lambeth, which was popularly known as Vauxhall or Fox Hall. The comedy of the "English Monsieur," by James Howard, acted at the Theatre Royal in 1674, was a success of the time, and affords a striking picture of Spring Garden society at Charing Cross. But long after the Garden was built upon it maintained a remnant of its reputation as a corner of London devoted to amusements, although not exclusively so, for here was situated the French Protestant Chapel which on December 2, 1716, was discovered to be on fire, occasioning great alarm in the neighbourhood from its vicinity to several depositories of gunpowder. Disaster was averted, however, by the timely turning to account by the Prince of Wales (afterwards George II.) of his one useful accomplishment, soldiering. Accompanied by a captain of the guard, and having risen between four and five o'clock, he proceeded to the spot and issued directions for subduing the fire. A new chapel was erected in 1731. This chapel seems to have been the one built by an ancestor of Lord Clifford, and which occasioned a dispute, says Cunningham, in 1792 as to the right of presentation, both Lord Clifford and the Vicar of St. Martin's claiming it.[2] So

[1] Hentzner's *Journey into England*, 1757, p. 34.
[2] Malcolm's *Londinium Redivivum*, 1807, iv. 319.

late as 1803 there was exhibited at Spring Gardens, Charing Cross,
Maillardet's Automaton, which consisted of "a musical lady, who
performs most of the functions of animal life, and plays sixteen
several airs upon an organised piano-forte by the actual pressure of
the fingers. Admission one shilling, from ten o'clock in the morning
until ten in the evening."[1]

The Society of Painters in Water Colours, formed in 1804, held
its thirteenth annual exhibition, 1817–18, for the first time apparently
in Spring Gardens,[2] and at Wigley's Promenade Rooms, Spring
Gardens, our wonder-loving ancestors might be entertained with Mr.
Theodon's grand Mechanical and Picturesque Theatre, illustrative of
the effect of art in imitation of nature, in views of the island of St.
Helena, the city of Paris, the passage of Mount St. Bernard, Chinese
artificial fireworks, and a storm at sea. Admission to front seats, 2s.;
second seats, 1s.; with occasional changes of scenes. Or they could
satisfy their curiosity with something that promised, even at that
time, to make good Mother Shipton's prophecy as to carriages going
without horses, for here was to be seen (admittance 1s.) the original
model of a new invented Travelling Automaton, a machine which
can, with ease and accuracy, travel at the rate of six miles an hour,
ascend acclivities, and turn the narrowest corners without the assistance of horse or steam, by machinery, conducted by one of the
persons seated within. There is also a new invented American
stove, for saving fuel.[3] The famous Irish Giant was on show next
door to Cox's Museum in Spring Gardens.[4] Mrs. Harrington
advertises her readiness to undertake miniatures at the Hardware
Shop, next Cox's Museum, Spring Gardens . . . she takes the most

[1] The *Picture of London* for 1803, p. 189.

[2] *Ibid.* for 1818. Close by, in Pall Mall, the Royal Academy held its first
exhibition. In the *Public Advertiser* for Saturday, April 22, 1769, is the following paragraph :

"Royal Academy, Pall Mall, April 21, 1769. The Exhibition will open on
Wednesday next, the 26th instant, at Nine o'clock. Admittance One Shilling
each Person. The Catalogue gratis.—F. M. Newton, Sec."

The origin of the society, however, was with a number of artists who met also
In the neighbourhood of Charing Cross, in St. Peter's Court, St. Martin's Lane,
about 1739, which Hogarth established as the Society of Incorporated Artists,
who held their first exhibition at the Society of Arts, April 21, 1760. From
this sprang the Royal Academy. On the north side of Pall Mall, a little east
of St. James's Street, was Alderman Boydell's Shakespeare Gallery. See
account in Malcolm's *Londinium Redivivum*, 1807, iv. 319.

[3] *Ibid.* for 1803, p. 263.

[4] See E. J. Wood's *Giants and Dwarfs*, 1868, p. 158.

striking likeness in miniature at 2s. 6d. each by virtue of his Majesty's Royal Letters Patent, granted to Mrs. Harrington for her improved and expeditious method of taking the most accurate likenesses ; time of sitting three minutes only : nothing required unless the most perfect likeness is obtained.[1] A relic of these Gardens on the west side of Charing Cross existed so late as the year 1825 in a pleasure resort known as the "Grove." To enter, one had to descend into a cellar of a house surrounded by other houses. This was painted with shrubbery, but the only fragrance inhaled, says the author of "Tavern Anecdotes," was that of the "weed," arising in columns from numerous tubes of clay, rendering the well-painted walls at times invisible. In the "Times" of October 13, 1820, occurs the following obituary notice : "On Thursday, the 5th inst., in the 37th year of his age, Mr. Richard Chapman, of the Grove, Spring Gardens, and late of the British Coffee-house, Cockspur Street." This "Grove" *tavern*, as it appears to have been, was doubtless a survival of the actual grove which rendered Spring Gardens a pleasant rustic resort until, towards the end of the 17th century, it was suppressed in the interests apparently of public morality. Says a writer in 1659,—"the enclosure not disagreeable, for the solemness of the *grove*, the warbling of the birds, and as it opens into the spacious walks at St. James's . . . for it is usual here to find some of the young company till midnight ; and the thickets of the garden seem to be contrived to all advantages of gallantry, after they have refreshed with the collation, which is here seldom omitted, *at a certain cabaret* in the middle of this paradise where the forbidden fruits are certain trifling tarts, neats' tongues, salacious meats, and bad Rhenish.[2] The ladies that have an Inclination to be Private, take Delight in the Close Walks of Spring Garden, where both Sexes meet, and mutually serve one another as Guides to lose their Way, and the Windings and Turnings in the little Wildernesses are so intricate that the most Experienc'd Mothers have often lost themselves in looking for their Daughters."[3] So that, while, after the Restoration, Old Spring Gardens was built upon, a memory of it appears to have survived the ravages of time long afterwards, in the "Grove" tavern. "Admirers of Curiosities" were invited to the Charing Cross Coffee-house, in the corner of Spring Gardens, to see—"arrived from France

---

[1] *Morning Post*, January 28, 1778.
[2] *A Character of England*, 1659, p. 56.
[3] Thomas Brown's *Amusements for the Meridian of London*, 1700, p. 54.

a Man Six and-Forty years old, One Foot Nine Inches high,
yet fathoms Six Foot Five Inches with his Arms.   He walks
naturally upon his Hands, raising his Body One Foot Four Inches
off the Ground : Jumps upon a Table near Three Foot high,
with one Hand, and leaps off without making use of anything but
his Hands, or letting his Body touch the ground.   He shows some
Part of Military Exercise on his Hands, as well as if he stood upon
his legs.   He will go to any gentleman's house if required." [1]   In
1699 there was born a child, afterwards exhibited at the Sign of
Charing Cross, with but one body and two heads. [2]

---

[1] Henry Morley, *Memoirs of Bartholomew Fair*, Warne's ed., p. 249.   [2] *Ibid.*

CHAPTER III.

THE TAVERNS.

LARGELY associated as the immediate neighbourhood of Charing Cross is with the destinies of the Stuarts and with Jacobite intrigue, it is not surprising to find the tavern and the coffee-house in its precincts the scene of many an historic incident. The "Blue Posts" in Spring Gardens was a great resort of the Jacobites during the reign of William III. It was here that Charnock and his gang breakfasted on the day fixed for the murderous ambuscade which they prepared for the King at Turnham Green.[1] "All was ready; the horses were saddled; the pistols were loaded; the swords were sharpened; the orderlies were on the alert; they early sent intelligence from the palace that the King was certainly going a-hunting . . . a party of guards had been sent round by Kingston Bridge to Richmond; the royal coaches, each with six horses, had gone from the stables at Charing Cross to Kensington. The chief murderers assembled in high glee at Porter's lodgings. Pendergrass, who, by the King's command, appeared among them, was greeted with ferocious mirth. 'Pendergrass,' said Porter, 'you are named one of the eight who are to do this business. I have a musquetoon for you that will carry eight balls.' 'Mr. Pendergrass,' said King, 'pray do not be afraid of smashing the glass windows.' From Porter's lodgings the party adjourned to the 'Blue Posts' in Spring Gardens . . . to take some refreshment before they started for Turnham Green. They were at table when a message came from an orderly that the King had changed his mind and would not hunt, and scarcely had they recovered from their first surprise at this ominous news when Keyes, who had been scouting among his old comrades, arrived with news more ominous still. 'The coaches have returned to Charing Cross. The guards that were sent round to Richmond have just come back to Kensington at full gallop, the

---

[1] Macaulay's *History of England*, vol. iv. (1855) pp. 664–665; and vol. v. (1861) p. 298.

flanks of the horses all white with foam. I have had a word with one of the Blues. He told me that strange things are muttered.' Then the countenances of the assassins fell, and their hearts died within them. Porter . . . took up an orange and squeezed it. 'What cannot be done one day may be done another. Come, gentlemen, before we part let us have one glass to the squeezing of the rotten orange.' "[1]

"After breakfast," on May 1, 1852, records Macaulay in the diary, published in his "Life and Letters," "I went to Turnham Green to look at the place. I found it after some search ; the very spot beyond all doubt, and admirably suited for an assassination. The place was a narrow and winding lane leading from the landing-place on the north of the river to Turnham Green. The spot may still easily be found. The ground has since been drained by trenches. But in the seventeenth century it was a quagmire, through which the royal coach was with difficulty tugged at a foot's pace. The time was in the afternoon of Saturday the fifteenth of February." [2]

At the public recognition by the "Grand Monarch," Louis XIV. of France, of the son of James II. as King of England, and when a royal messenger was sent by William of Orange from Kensington to order M. Poussin, the French ambassador, to leave the country without delay, he was found to be supping at the "Blue Posts" in Spring Gardens, along with three of the most prominent Jacobite members of the House of Commons.[3]

No trace remains of the "Bull's Head" tavern in Old Spring Gardens, Charing Cross. During the writing and publishing of "Joannis Philippi Angli Defensio," &c., John Milton lodged at one Thomson's, next door to the "Bull's Head," at Charing Cross, opening into Spring Gardens.[4]

It was outside this "Bull's Head" tavern at Charing Cross that Colonel Blood with five or six of his associates, well mounted and armed, awaited the return home to Clarendon House of the Duke of Ormond. Their design was to carry the Duke to Tyburn and there hang him with a paper pinned to his breast showing why they had done it. Blood had laid a design in

[1] Macaulay's *History of England*, vol. iv. (1855) pp. 664–665, and vol. v. (1861) p. 298.

[2] The *Life and Letters of Lord Macaulay*, by G. O. Trevelyan, 1877, vol. ii. pp. 303–4.

[3] Macaulay's *History*, vol. v. (1861) p. 298.

[4] See Phillips's *Life of Milton*, 12mo. 1694, p. 33. Drummond's Bank is said to occupy the site of both the "Bull's Head" and Lockett's taverns.

Ireland to surprise the Castle of Dublin, and the magazine there, and to usurp the government ; but this being discovered by the Duke of Ormond the night before its intended execution, some of his accomplices were taken and executed as traitors. The deaths of these, Blood and the surviving rogues bound themselves by a solemn oath to revenge upon the person of the Duke.

When the Duke had passed the "Bull's Head" they all took horse and galloped after him, overtaking him near his own gate. They knocked down his footmen, having ascertained beforehand that he was attended by only two or three, took him out of his coach, forced him up behind one of the horsemen, to whom he was tied, and rode away with him. The coachman and servants crying out, the porter reached the spot, and, seeing what was done, pursued them. The Duke strove so violently to free himself that at last he got loose, and threw himself, with the villain he was tied to, off the horse. The rest turned back, and, finding it impossible to carry him away, discharged two pistols at him ; but the night being dark they could not see to take aim properly, missing him both times. And the porter and other assistance coming up, they were glad to make haste away, leaving the noble-man much bruised by his fall. A thousand pounds reward offered by the King did not shake the fidelity of these scoundrels to each other, and they would probably never have been discovered if the failure of the attempt which Blood made on the Crown jewels had not led to his confession of the attempt on the Duke.[1]

Colley Cibber, whilst living in Old Spring Garden, advertised as follows :

" In or near the old Play-house in Drury Lane, on Monday last the 19th of January, a watch was dropp'd having a Tortoiseshell Case inlaid with silver, a silver chain, and a gold seal ring; the arms, a cross wavy and chequer. Whoever brings it to Mr. Cibber, at his house near the Bull-head in Old Spring Garden, shall have three guineas reward." [2] He lived here from 1711 until 1714.[3] In Taylor's "Taverns," 1636, a Bull or Buffle's (Buffalo's) Head is mentioned as being at Charing Cross. It was at his house in Spring Gardens that Prince Rupert breathed his last on November 29, 1684.

[1] Kirby's *Museum*, 1804, vol. ii. pp. 105-6. There was a " Bull Head " or " Bull's Head " Tavern where Pepys was in the habit of calling and dining (*Diary*, 1660), at the corner of Chandos Street. See *Middlesex and Hertfordshire Notes and Queries*, 1897, p. 120.

[2] *Daily Courant*, January 20, 1703.

[3] L. Hutton's *Literary Landmarks*, 1889, p. 52

The name of Spring Gardens has become so closely associated, through their offices being built on the site, with the London County Council, that it bids fair to remain in perpetuity, a memento of other less civilised, if more picturesque times. Its dying depositions, so far as old associations are concerned, were taken in the year 1896, when the new Government Offices absorbed, I think, nearly the whole of New Street, where dwelt Sir Astley Cooper at No. 2 ; Sir James Scarlett (Lord Abinger), at No. 4 ; and Joseph Jekyll, the wit, at No. 22. A curious sodality had its headquarters for some time at No. 10 New Street, Spring Garden. This was the Outinian Society, formed in 1818 at No. 190 Piccadilly by John Penn, a descendant of the founder of Pennsylvania, to whose house, No. 10 New Street, it was afterwards removed. It was a sort of matrimonial society, and its character may be inferred from its descriptive title in 1823 : "A proposal of the Outinian Society for establishing a plan to afford means to any of its members and advocates . . . of entering, on marriage, into a covenant or contract . . . to insure oftener the constant voluntary companionship of husbands and wives."[1] The retaining wall at the end of New Street and along the terrace was a piece, about 225 feet long, of the old Park wall, between which and the Mall was the " Green Walk " where Charles II. stood and talked to Nell Gwynne.

The story of a Spring Gardens crossing-sweeper is a remarkable one. A Mr. Simcox, engaged in the nail-trade in Birmingham, was, on the occasion of one of his visits to London, standing up under an archway out of the rain, when he was agreeably surprised by the opening of the door of a handsome house opposite, and a footman approaching with an umbrella, who presented his master's compliments, saying how he had been observed standing so long under the archway that he feared he might take cold, and therefore would be glad if he would come and take shelter in his house—an invitation which Mr. Simcox gladly accepted. He was ushered into a drawing-room, where the master of the house was sitting, receiving a very kindly welcome. Scarcely, however, had the guest set eyes on his host, than he was struck with a vague remembrance of having seen him before ; but where, or in what circumstances, he was altogether unable to call to mind. His inquiring glances at last conveyed to his host what was passing in his mind. " You seem, sir," said he,

---

[1] See the *Outinian Society*, B. Mus. Cat., Ac. 2265/2. John Penn's house disappeared when the new Admiralty Offices wiped out a large portion of New Street.

"to look at me as though you had seen me before." Mr. Simcox acknowledged that his host was right in his conjectures, but confessed his entire inability to recall the occasion. "You are right, sir," said the old gentleman, "and if you will pledge your word as a man of honour to keep my secret, and not to disclose to anyone what I am now going to tell you, until you have seen the notice of my death in the London papers, I have no objection to remind you where and how you have known me.

"In St. James's Park, near Spring Gardens, you may pass every day an old man, who sweeps a crossing there, and whose begging is attended by this strange peculiarity : that whatever be the amount of the alms bestowed on him, he will retain only a halfpenny, and scrupulously return to the donor all the rest. Such an unusual proceeding naturally excites the curiosity of those who hear of it ; and anyone who has himself made the experiment, when he happens to be walking by with a friend, is almost sure to say to him, 'Do you see that old fellow there ? He is the strangest beggar you ever saw in your life. If you give him sixpence he will be sure to give you fivepence-halfpenny back again.' Of course, his friend makes the experiment, which turns out as predicted ; and as crowds are constantly passing, there are numbers who make the same trial; and thus the old man gets many a halfpenny from the curiosity of passers by, in addition to what he obtains from their compassion. I, sir," continued the old gentleman, "am that beggar. Many years ago I first hit upon this expedient for the relief of my then pressing necessities ; for I was at that time utterly destitute ; but finding the scheme answer beyond my expectations, I was induced to carry it on until I had at last, with the aid of profitable investment, realised a handsome fortune, enabling me to live in the comfort in which you find me this day. And now, sir, such is the force of habit, that though I am no longer under the necessity for continuing this plan, I find myself quite unable to give it up ; and accordingly, every morning, I leave home, apparently for business purposes, and go to a room, where I put on my old beggar's clothes, and continue sweeping my crossing in the park till a certain hour in the afternoon, when I go back to my room, resume my usual dress, and return home in time for dinner, as you see me this day." [1]

Opposite Spring Gardens is the Union Club, at the south-west corner of Trafalgar Square, occupying the site of the famous "Cannon"

[1] See *Notes and Queries*, second series, vol. ix., and the *Romance of London*, by John Timbs.

Coffee-house and Tavern. The architect was Sir Robert Smirke, whose greatest structure is the British Museum, but who was also responsible for the Mint, the General Post Office in St. Martin's-le-Grand, the College of Physicians, Covent Garden Theatre (burnt down in 1856), the extension of King's Bench Walk, and King's College (London). In 1850 the club was chiefly composed of merchants, lawyers, members of Parliament, and, as James Smith, who was a member, writes, "of gentlemen at large." The house is built on ground let by the Crown for 99 years from Oct. 16, 1822.[1]

As the "Cannon" Coffee-house and Tavern it was a popular place of assembly for anniversary and other festivals. "The Independent Electors of the City and Liberty of Westminster, who have agreed to meet Monthly to commemorate the noble Struggle they have so successfully made, are desir'd to meet their Friends at the Cannon Tavern, Charing Cross, Tomorrow, being the 5th instant, at six o'Clock."[2] Here, among other similar resorts, tickets might in 1742 have been had for the "Annual Feast of the Ancient and Honourable Society of Free and Accepted Masons at the Haber-dashers' Hall," whither the Brethren were to proceed after breakfast at the Right Hon. the Lord Ward's, Grand Master elect, at his House in Upper Brook Street, Grosvenor Square, but "No Hackney Coaches were allowed in the procession to the Hall."[3] The "Cannon" is described in the "Epicure's Almanack," 1815, as having for its landlord Mr. Hodges, whose "larder and soups, his waiters and cooks, are, like our hearts of oak, always ready, the Cannon being charged with ammunition for the stomach. The fumes from the cooking stoves are as delightful to the nose of a military affamé as those of gunpowder itself, the incense offered to the god of war." Curran and Sir Jonah Barrington were in the habit of frequenting the Cannon Coffee-house, Charing Cross, where they had a box every day at the end of the room.[4]

The "Cannon," or "Gun" as it is occasionally known, was the cognisance of King Edward VI., of Queen Mary, and of Queen Elizabeth, and it is doubtless to this circumstance that is owing the fact noted in the "Craftsman" newspaper of the eighteenth century,[5] that "nothing is more common in England than the sign of a cannon." The former sign has now entirely disappeared in London,

---

[1] Cunningham's *London*. See also Serjeant Ballantine's *Reminiscences*.
[2] *Daily Advertiser*, February 4, 1742.
[3] *Ibid.* April 10, 1742.
[4] Barrington's *Personal Sketches*.   [5] No. 638.

with the exception of the "Cannon" in Cannon Street, which has a different origin, but the "Gun" survives in numerous instances. The Cannon Brewery, whose site is now covered by Albert Gate, Knightsbridge, doubtless had its origin in a tavern-sign.

Another favourite rendezvous for partisans of the Jacobite interest was the Smyrna Coffee-house, close by in Pall Mall.[1] In 1742 it was known as the "Giles's and Smyrna." The painting in the Royal Scottish Academy by George Ogilby Reid represents the reception by the Jacobites, at the "Smyrna," of the news of Prestonpans. It was a resort of Prior and Swift, and there Thomson received subscriptions for the "Seasons." The house in which Thomson resided in 1725, over the shop of Egerton, a bookseller, is held, on the authority of Jesse and other writers, to be what is now No. 30 Charing Cross, the lower part of which at the present day is a musical instrument maker's shop. His apartments were on the first floor, and we are told that at this time he was "gaping about the town listlessly, and getting his pockets picked, and forced to wait on great persons with his poem of 'Winter' in order to find a patron." A part of his "Summer" is said to have been written here.[2]

Nearer Charing Cross was the British Coffee-house, the site of which, one of the oldest taverns in London, was afterwards occupied by Stanford's, the map-publisher. Of some interest from a structural point of view, as the work of one of the "Adelphi" Adamses, it was a favourite resort of Smollett and was frequented by Dr. Johnson and other literary celebrities. Defoe, in his "Journey through England," says "The Scots go generally to the 'British,' and a mixture of all sorts to the 'Smyrna.'" Under the proprietorship of Messrs. Morley, the "British" was, in 1815, famed for the excellence of its wines. Tickets were to be had at this Coffee-house, in May 1742, for the "Tragedy of *Cato*," followed by a farce, "The Intriguing Chambermaid," presented at the Theatre Royal, Drury Lane. This old landmark was effaced in 1887, and Stanford's premises were acquired by the London County Council

[1] See also the *Tatler*, Nos. 10 and 78 ; the *Spectator*, No. 457 ; Swift's *Journal to Stella* (*Scott*, ii. 49 and 180) ; and Defoe's *Journey through England*, 1722, i. 168. Mr. Austin Dobson, in describing the situation of Dodsley's house, the "Tully's Head," in Pall Mall, says that it was next the passage leading into King Street, or half-way between the site of the old Smyrna Coffee-house (now Messrs. Harrison's) and the old Star and Garter Tavern (*Side-Walk Studies*, 1902, p. 170). See also Mr. G. L. Apperson's *Bygone London Life* where much more will be found concerning the "Smyrna."

[2] Wilmot Harrison's *Memorable London Houses*, 1889, p. 22.

in the latter part of 1899, for the extension of their offices. The Lowtonian Society, so named in honour of its founder and first president, Thomas Lowton, Clerk of the Nisi Prius, met at the British Coffee-house in 1796. It was formed for the association of gentlemen and mutual protection "against insidious attempts to injure their professional reputation." Thomas Lowton was "a highly respected member of the Inner Temple, who was honoured by the confidence of three successive Lord Chief Justices, and held the office of Clerk of the Nisi Prius for forty years." After 1796 the society left the "British," and favoured most of the principal club-taverns with their patronage.[1] An excellent account of this, one of the last, if not the last, of the old tavern-clubs, was given by some extremely well-informed writer in the "Daily Telegraph" for September 19, 1899. One of its earliest visitors was the Hon. James Erskine, one of the Supreme Judges of Scotland, who was so bitterly opposed to Walpole's policy that he gave up his judgeship in order to come to Parliament. During his annual visits to the metropolis he contracted an intimacy with the landlady of the coffee-house— a handsome Scotchwoman named Fanny Lindsay—that did not conduce to his domestic felicity. Accordingly, by the aid of Lord Lovat, the famous plotter whom Hogarth so skilfully depicted, Erskine carried his wife to "St. Kilda's lonely Isle," and there left her in miserable exile for many years.

In 1745—the year of "Bonnie Prince Charlie's" rising—four Scotchmen, all destined to succeed in life, were wont to meet at the "British." These were Tobias Smollett, a struggling surgeon in Downing Street, as yet unknown in the literary way; Alexander Carlyle, afterwards minister of Inveresk, and author of a delightful autobiography; John Blair, a future prebendary of Westminster; and "Bob" Smith, who is believed to have been the successor of Bentley as Master of Trinity College, Cambridge. "Jupiter" Carlyle, so called because he had sat to Gavin Hamilton in that character, had fought under Cope at Prestonpans, and had been an eye-witness of Provost Stuart's neglect to defend Edinburgh, a neglect which nearly brought him to the Tower on a charge of treason. The four, says the writer in the "Daily Telegraph" alluded to, were at the coffee-house when the news of Cumberland's victory at Culloden came. Provost Stuart's son, who was in the room, went out cursing, and Smollett was indignant with the mob for exulting over the savageries of the Duke. Carlyle and he walked from the coffee-house to May-

---

[1] See the *Lowtonian Society, founded* 1793.

fair, through lines of bonfires, and an incessant fusillade of squibs. When next they met at the coffee-house, Smollett read to them the first six stanzas of a poem entitled "The Tears of Scotland." His friends thought it too strongly worded, but he would have no temporising with prudence, and sat down and wrote a seventh stanza.

Another friend whom Carlyle used to meet there was Captain David Cheap, who had sailed with Anson during his famous voyage. The captain was looking out for an author to write the account of the voyage, and came there to make the acquaintance of William Guthrie, then a very popular writer, but was so disgusted with his vapouring, cursing, and swearing that he went away without seeking an introduction.

The writer of this interesting contribution to the literary history of London continues :

"In 1758 John Home came to London with his tragedy of 'Douglas.' He was fortunate enough to secure the patronage of Lord Bute, and soon found himself in the centre of a very pleasant society. Among his daily companions were Wedderburn, afterwards Lord Loughborough, Sir Henry Erskine, Robert Adam, the future architect of the Adelphi, David Garrick, John Douglas (then secretary to the Earl of Bath, and afterwards Bishop of Salisbury), Sir Gilbert Elliot, Dr. Armstrong, Smollett, Dr. Pitcairn, of St. Bartholomew's, and William Hunter, the famous anatomist, and brother of the still more famous John Hunter. These formed themselves into a social club, which met at the 'British.' Several of them belonged to another Scotch club also meeting there, of which Robertson, the historian, was a member. Hunter was a man of brilliant conversation, and his favourite toast was : 'May no English nobleman venture out of the world without a Scottish physician, as I am sure there are none who venture in '—an allusion to the fact that the obstetric practice in London was then almost entirely in the hands of Scotchmen. The coffee-house was then kept by Mrs. Anderson, sister of the John Douglas above-mentioned, and is highly spoken of by Mackenzie, Lord Brougham, and several contemporary writers.

"The house was rebuilt in 1770, the architect being, appropriately enough, Robert Adam ; doubtless he worked *con amore* on the rebuilding of a house in which he had passed so many pleasant hours, and met so many notable people. At all events, its elevation ranked among the most pleasing of his productions.

"Johnson dined at least once in the new house with Boswell, who records that they spent a very agreeable day together. Gibbon also was there, and in very good company, which included Garrick, Colman, Goldsmith, Macpherson, and John Home. They were getting up a claque to launch Colman's ' Man of Business,' and the next day they all went in a body to support it.

" At a later date John Lord Campbell was a member of a Scotch club—The Beeswing—meeting here to uphold the time-honoured institutions of eating and drinking. The latter, says Campbell, was 'tremendous,' but the conversation was as good as any he had ever joined in.

" In 1824 we find the place already described as ' The British Hotel and Coffee-house '; subsequently the words ' and Coffee-house ' disappeared from its style altogether." In Angelo's " Pic-Nic " (1834), the Author says he belonged to a club which used to assemble at the British Coffee-house called the " Keep-the-Line," the greater number of whose members were literary characters. W. S. Fitzgerald, well known for his poetical effusions, was one of the members and was always introduced here after dinner (p. 322).[1] " Deserted by Scotchmen, the hotel became a favoured resort of Americans ; but the clubs of men of wit and learning gave place to the shows of canary fanciers. Though its glory was departed, the hotel business was carried on till 1886, when the place was demolished in order to clear a site for Stanford's new premises."

Near the Horse Guards J. Millan published in 1731 the second edition of " A Compleat Translation of the whole Case of Miss Cadière against the Jesuit Father J. B. Girard, with a Postscript containing several curious Things relating to the said strange and affecting Story." The Jesuit father alluded to was a native of Dôle, and was accused of sorcery, before the Parliament of Aix, by a girl of eighteen named Cadière, who declared that " he had made use of infernal arts to debauch her person." He was, however, acquitted after a long trial, which caused a great sensation at the period all over France.[2]

The " Turk's Head " was a tavern next door to what in 1785 was No. 17 Charing Cross.[3] Mention of it also occurs in 1780 as the Turk's Head Coffee House.[4]

John Millan is described in Mortimer's " Universal Director "

---

[1] See also Reynolds's *Life and Times.*
[2] See *Nouvel Dictionnaire Historique.*
[3] *Morning Chron. and Daily Advt.,* No. 4878.
[4] *London Gazette,* Aug. 12, 1700.

as "buying and selling Libraries, and has a very fine collection of Natural Curiosities." Mortimer also mentions one — Walter, book seller at Charing Cross. This was probably J. Walter who sold "Medical Anecdotes of the last Thirty Years," by B. Dominiceti, M.D. Much concerning this Dominiceti, apparently a "quack," will be found in Lysons's "Collectanea," and in Faulkner's "Chelsea," 1810, vol. ii. p. 427. The "Golden Key and Bible" was the sign of L. Stoke, a bookseller at Charing Cross in 1711, and the "Bible and Crown" was that of Mr. Pratt, near Northumberland House.

King George II. seems to have taken every opportunity to deliver speeches *in propria persona* to his Lords and Commons as the political situations of his stirring reign evoked them. But which occasion it was that suggested the curious sign, for a pamphlet shop, between Charing Cross and Whitehall, of the "King's Speech" one cannot say. It was, however, the sign of John Winbush in 1742 at this spot,[1] and the pamphlets he sold were perhaps largely, if not exclusively, those with which the nation was deluged at the time, and which daringly asserted that every member who voted for the ministry, *i.e.* Walpole's ministry, was a mercenary hireling who bartered his vote for some place which he either enjoyed or expected.[2] On Wednesday, said the "London Daily Post" of February 7, 1737-38, at One o'Clock, "will be burnt by the common Hangman, in New Palace Yard, Westminster, and on Friday at the Royal Exchange, in the Presence of the Sheriffs, a printed Paper which was cried about the Streets on Thursday Evening, under the Title of his Majesty's Most Gracious Speech; the said Paper being a most audacious Forgery, a false scandalous Libel, and a high Contempt of his Majesty, and his Crown and Dignity." The libel, whatever it was, seems to have referred to or reflected upon some passage in the "short speech" with which the King opened Parliament on January 24, 1738.

It is not, I think, generally known that there was a Palace Court, or Court of the Marshalsea of the King's House (abbreviated "Marshalsea"), which was from 1801 to 1849, when it was abolished, held in Old Scotland Yard opposite the Admiralty. It had jurisdiction of all civil suits within twelve miles of the Palace. The process is described in 1818 as short and not expensive, judgment being obtained in three weeks.[3]

---

[1] *Daily Advertiser*, February 4, 1742.
[2] Lyttelton's *Hist. of Eng.*, 1808, vol. ii. p. 199.
[3] The *Picture of London* for 1818, p. 120.

Scotland Yard derived its name from having been erected in the days before the Union of England and Scotland, when the kings of Scotland visited Westminster, and resided here, when they came to do homage for the counties of Cumberland and Huntingdon and other fiefs held by them of the Crown of England. Here resided Margaret Queen of Scots, and sister to King Henry VIII. when she came into England after the death of her daughter.[1] Part of the " Yard," so long the headquarters of the Metropolitan Police until their removal to the Embankment, was formerly the official residence of the surveyor of the works to the Crown. Here lived Inigo Jones ; here died his successor, Sir John Denham, the poet of Cooper's Hill ; and here lived Denham's successor, Sir Christopher Wren. In a fantastic house, immortalised by Swift in some ludicrous lines, lived Sir John Vanbrugh. Van's house was designed and built by himself, says Cunningham, from the ruins of Whitehall destroyed by fire in 1697.[2]

Craig's Court, on the north side of Old Scotland Yard, and on the south side, I think, of Cox's Bank, is more correctly Craggs Court, so called, it is said, after the father of Secretary Craggs, friend of Pope, Addison, &c., but Cunningham says it was named after another Craggs. Here the Sun Fire Office was established in 1726. It was in this court that Speaker Onslow's carriage had an accident when attempting to negotiate the narrow entrance—an accident which hastened through the House the first great metropolitan street reform, the Westminster Paving Act of 1762. One of Sheridan's favourite resorts was the Northumberland Coffee-house, which occupied approximately the site of what was afterwards Wyld's well-known map shop. The umbrella shop at the corner of the court used to boast—perhaps it does still—a fine example of embossed zinc-work of apparently the sixteenth century, in the form of a water-tank, I think. Cox and Greenwood's bank, or, rather, " Army-agency office," stood here, at least as early as 1831.[3]

Charing Cross, with the growth of its importance, naturally became a haunt of the vicious and the reprobate. The horrors of the " Night Cellars " were too repulsive, even for the anything but prudish news-sheets of the time, to particularise, and " Craiggs-Court " inhabitants, used as they were to scenes of violence and dissipation, did not cry out before they were hurt in making an

[1] Stow and Maitland.
[2] *Handbook of London*, 1850.
[3] Elmes's *Topogr. Dict. of London* of that year.

initiatory move in the direction of improvement. They complained and gave information upon oath against a man and his wife for keeping a *very* disorderly Night Cellar, and their harbouring "reputed Thieves, Pickpockets, and other dissolute and wicked Persons, whereby they are frequently disturb'd in the Night-time by Noises, Outcries of Murder," &c. A warrant was granted against the man and his wife by Justice Railton and six other of his Majesty's Justices of the Peace for Westminster. And the said justices committed to Tothill-Fields Bridewell a woman for keeping a disorderly Night-house in Hart Street, Covent Garden, to the great annoyance and disturbance of that neighbourhood. And "several idle and disorderly Fellows and reputed Thieves and Pickpockets, who nightly infest the Streets about Charing Cross, Temple Bar, and the Strand, were also by the said Justices committed to Tothill-Fields Bridewell to hard Labour, several of whom were taken about One o'Clock on Saturday Morning, quarrelling in a Brandy-Shop by Mermaid Court, near Charing Cross, amongst whom was a noted Irish Bagpiper, and Midnight Bully."[1] The neighbourhood also had a notorious and scandalous reputation for its gaming-houses, one of which was the Peacock Tavern at Charing Cross, where one night in May 1756, in consequence of information sent to the magistrates, John Fielding and Saunders Welch, an assembly of gamblers were apprehended by "Mr. Barnes, High Constable of Westminster, and brought before Mr. Fielding, who, in the course of their examination, obtained sufficient evidence to prosecute three other keepers of gaming-houses at the next Westminster Sessions."[2]

Christopher Alley or Hartshorn Lane, afterwards Northumberland Street, Strand, extends, like the present Northumberland Avenue, to the Embankment.[3] Here Ben Jonson lived. King Charles I. is said to have sent the poet a very tardy and a very small sum when the latter was in poverty and sickness, and the recipient is *said* to have remarked, " I suppose he sends me this because I live in an alley—tell him his soul lives in an alley ! " This ridiculous story is believed to be purely a malicious invention. It must have originated in some wilful perversion of a line of Jonson's contained in a poem on Sir

---

[1] *London Evening Post*, June 17, 1732.
[2] *Whitehall Evening Post*, May 8, 1756.
[3] Hartshorne Lane or Alley was pulled down about the year 1761, and Northumberland Street built in its place (Dodsley's *London and its Environs*, 1761).

Kenelm Digby, whom he calls "prudent, valiant, just, and temperate," and adds quaintly :

> His heart is a brave palace, a broad street,
> Where all heroic ample thoughts do meet,
> When Nature such a large survey hath ta'en,
> As others' souls to *his dwelt in a lane*.[1]

But, according to Fuller, Jonson in his childhood dwelt in the same lane. "Though I cannot," he says, "with all my industrious inquiry, find him in his cradle, I can fetch him from his long coats. When a little child he lived in Hartshorn Lane, near Charing Cross, where his mother married a bricklayer for her second husband."[2] A house in George Street, York Buildings, is advertised in 1742 to be let, and inquiries are to be made of Mr. Rowle, bricklayer, in Hartshorn Lane, near Charing Cross.[3]

It was at No. 16 Northumberland Street that a most desperate fight for life and death took place between Major Murray and Mr. Roberts, a solicitor and bill-discounter ; the latter attempted the life of the former for the sake of getting possession of his mistress, to whom he had lent money. Under pretext of advancing a loan to the Grosvenor Hotel Company, of which the major was a promoter, he decoyed him into a back room on the first floor of No. 16, then shot him in the back of the neck, and immediately after in the right temple. The major, feigning to be dead, waited till Roberts's back was turned, then springing to his feet attacked him with a pair of tongs, which he broke to pieces over his assailant's head. He then knocked him down with a bottle which lay near, and escaped through the window, and from thence by a water-pipe to the ground. Roberts died soon afterwards, but Major Murray recovered, and the jury returning a verdict of justifiable homicide, he was released. The papers described Roberts's rooms as crowded with dusty buhl cabinets, inlaid tables, statuettes, and drawings. These were smeared with blood and wine, while on the glass shades of the ornaments a rain of blood seemed to have fallen.

See Thornbury's *Haunted London*.

[2] *Worthies*, 1662, p. 243. A bricklayer was, of course, a "tradesman" whose social status was, in those days, far higher than that imputed to his descendant of to-day, when hardly anything is done in the building way without brickwork. There is still an ale-house in King Street, Hammersmith, with the sign of the "Tradesman" or the "Tradesman's Arms," which probably existed long before the "Bricklayers' Arms."

[3] *Daily Advertiser*, February 11, 1742.

In Northumberland Court Nelson lodged when a young lieu-tenant.[1] Sir Edmondbury Godfrey was not a wool merchant as stated in "Old and New London," but a *wood* merchant, whose wharf was at the bottom of Northumberland Street. He himself, however, dwelt in Green's Lane, the site of which was absorbed by the South-Eastern Railway annexes. The Northumberland Arms—now, I think, the Northumberland Hotel, at the bottom of North-umberland Street—was a favourite resort for those connected with the wharves and the coal trade, and probably also with the wood trade established here time out of mind.[2]

The exact situation of what was presumably a tavern with the sign of the "Red Cross" is not apparent, but there was a Cross Lane, leading out of Spur Alley (Craven Street) into Hartshorn Lane (Northumberland Street) which Stow describes as "a place of small account."[3] This may therefore have received its name from the "Red Cross" at Charing Cross.[4]

At the "Lamb," Charing Cross, the sign of Mr. J. Beighton, linen-draper, was to be sold a drawing of one of Wren's masterpieces —it could hardly have been the exterior—of St. Stephen's Church, Walbrook. Subscriptions were taken in at the "Lamb," and by the proprietor, G. Marshall, at Mr. Vardy's, near Kensington Palace. Possibly the drawing was of the interior, which Cunningham describes as "all elegance and even grandeur. Never was so sweet a kernel in so rough a shell—so rich a jewel in so poor a setting. The cupola is a little St. Paul's, and the lights are admirably disposed throughout . . . the oval openings are somewhat ungrace-ful." Sir Christopher Wren is said to have lived in a house close by in Walbrook, subsequently No. 5.[5] There was a "Lamb's Ordinary" at Charing Cross. See Collection of Signs in St. Martin's Library, Charing Cross, No. 2,790.

Opposite the "Ship" tavern, for some time known as the "Rummer," near the Admiralty, was a perfume shop with the usual sign of the "Civet Cat." The proprietor's advertisement testifies, with many other instances, to the fashionable demand, in the middle of the eighteenth century, for Italian toilet waters and requisites :[6]

---

[1] *Old and New London.*
[2] *London Saturday Journal*, vol. ii. p. 104.
[3] Strype's *Stow*, 1755, vol. ii. book vi. ch. iv. p. 651.
[4] Collection in St. Martin's Library, No. 957.
[5] Cunningham.
[6] *Whitehall Evening Post*, October 15, 1756.

"To the Ladies, &c.

" 1. The Italian Lotion or Fluid invariably takes off Sunburn, Brownness, or Heats, from the Face, Neck, or Hands.

" 2. The Venetian Cream repels Pimples, removes Scruff or Morphew, and soon after causes the Skin to become most delicate plump ; fair, soft, and smooth.

" 3. The Original and only true Royal Chymical Wash-Ball, whose Virtues for many Years past need no Encomium.

" N.B.—At the above shop may be had in any Quantities, The Genuine Delescot's Opiate and Tinctures, so famous for the Teeth, Breath, and Gums, Likewise, an excellent Pomatum to strengthen, thicken, and nourish the Hair, with a Liquid that will change the Red, Grey, &c. into a beautiful Brown or Black."

At Charing Cross, one of the most extraordinary characters of the earlier part of the Stuart period, Lord Herbert of Cherbury, met with an attempt at his assassination which was foiled only by a more than ordinary effort of courage and dexterity. His gallantry towards a court lady, which, however, he asserts to have been without criminality, produced a desperate attempt on the part of the lady's husband, Sir John Ayres, to imbrue his hands in Lord Herbert's blood. It is also said that the Lady Ayres in question, who was one of the ladies-in-waiting upon Anne, Queen of James I., was indiscreet enough to entertain a most unmatronly regard for Lord Herbert. Lady Ayres, finding some means to get a copy of Lord Herbert's portrait, gave it to Isaac Oliver, the famous miniature-painter, to copy. This being done she caused it to be set in gold and enamel, and so wore it about her neck that " it was hidden under her breasts." This came to the knowledge of Sir John Ayres, and, in the words of Lord Herbert, " gave him more cause of jealousy than needed, had he known how innocent I was from pretending to anything which might wrong him or his lady ; since I could not so much as imagine that either she had my picture, or that she bore more than ordinary affection to me. . . . Little more than common civility ever passed betwixt us, though I confess, I think no man was welcomer to her when I came, for which I shall allege this passage :—

" Coming one day into her chamber,[1] I saw her through the

[1] This was customary. See Wright's *Domestic Manners &c. of the Middle Ages.*

curtains lying upon her bed with a wax candle in one hand and the picture I formerly mentioned in the other. I coming thereupon somewhat boldly to her, she blew out the candle, and hid the picture from me ; myself thereupon being curious to know what that was she held in her hand, got the candle to be lighted again, by means whereof I found it was my picture she looked upon with more earnestness and passion than I could easily have believed, especially since myself was not engaged in any affection towards her. I could willingly have omitted this passage, but that it was the beginning of a bloody history which followed. Howsoever, yet I must before the Eternal God clear her honour. And now in court a great person [Queen Anne, wife of James I.] sent for me divers times to attend her, which summons though I obeyed, yet God knoweth I declined coming to her as much as conveniently I could, without incurring her displeasure ; and this I did not only for very honest reasons, but, to speak ingenuously, because that affection passed betwixt me and another lady (who I believe was the fairest of her time) [1] as nothing could divert it. I had not been long in London when a violent burning fever seized upon me, which brought me almost to my death, though at last I did by slow degrees recover my health ; being thus upon my amendment, the Lord Lisle, afterwards Earl of Leicester, sent me word that Sir John Ayres intended to kill me in my bed, and wished me to keep a guard upon my chamber and person ; the same advertisement was confirmed by Lucy Countess of Bedford, and the Lady Hoby shortly after. Hereupon I thought fit to entreat Sir William Herbert, now Lord Powis, to go to Sir John Ayres, and tell him that I marvelled much at the information given me by these great persons, and that I could not imagine any sufficient ground hereof ; howbeit, if he had anything to say to me in a fair and noble way, I would give him the meeting as soon as I had got strength enough to stand upon my legs. Sir William hereupon brought me so ambiguous and doubtful an answer from him, that whatsoever he meant, he would not declare yet his intention, which was really, as I found afterwards, to kill me any way that he could, since as he said, though falsely, I had w—d his wife. Finding no means thus to surprise me, he sent me a letter to this effect ; that he desired to meet me somewhere, and that it might so fall out as I might return quietly again. To this I replied that if he desired to fight with me upon equal terms, I should, upon assurance of the field and fair play, give him meeting when he did any way specify

[1] This lady has not been identified.

the cause, and that I did not think fit to come to him on any other terms, having been sufficiently informed of his plots to assassinate me.

" After this, finding he could not take advantage against me, then in a treacherous way he resolved to assassinate me. . . . Hearing I was to come to Whitehall on horseback with two lackeys only, he attended my coming back in a place called Scotland Yard, at the hither end of Whitehall, as you come to it from the Strand, hiding himself here with four men armed on purpose to kill me." As he was nearing Charing Cross,[1] Sir John rushed upon him with a sword and dagger, and one of his lackeys, a great fellow with courage *nil*, ran away and left him to his fate. In this first encounter, Lord Herbert's horse received several wounds, and kicked and plunged so violently as to keep the assassins at bay some minutes. Lord Herbert, aiming a blow at Sir John Ayres, unfortunately broke his sword at the hilt, and with no other defence than the remnant of his weapon, defended himself most valiantly. Alighting from his horse his foot caught in the stirrup, and he was thrown violently on the ground ; but being extricated from that position by his other lackey, a little Shropshire boy, he managed to regain his feet and get his back against a wall, waging thus an unequal warfare with the whole of his assailants. In a few minutes he was surrounded by upwards of thirty persons, friends and adherents of Sir John, who encouraged the assassins by their shouts to make short work of him. Two gentlemen, seeing so many men set against one, came to the rescue, and Sir John Ayres was twice thrown to the ground ; he got up a third time, and making a more furious assault, stuck his dagger into Lord Herbert's side, where it remained sticking for a minute or two, until pulled out by Henry Cary, afterwards Lord Falkland. Lord Herbert, in the meantime, wrestling with his assailant, Sir John was thrown a third time, when Lord Herbert, kneeling upon his body, wounded him in four places with his sword remnant, and nearly cut his hand off. The desperate combat was then ended, Sir John's friends carrying him away senseless to a boat that was waiting for him at Whitehall Stairs. Lord Herbert recovered of his wounds in ten days, and sent a challenge to Sir John Ayres to meet him in equal combat in the field, with his sword in hand, but received for answer that Sir John would not meet him, but would kill him with a musket from an open window.

Sir John Ayres was afterwards arrested by order of the Privy

[1] The *Autobiography of Edward Lord Herbert of Cherbury*, by Sidney L. Lee, B.A., 1886, pp. 128-136.

Council, and several times examined : he expressed great contrition for his offence, alleging his wife's confession of criminality as a palliation. This, however, his wife afterwards recanted. His father disinherited him for his conduct, and he became, as the Duke of Lennox told Lord Herbert, "the most miserable man living." By the desire of the King he was discharged from custody, and Lord Herbert was commanded neither to send to him, nor receive from him, any challenge, nor to pursue the matter further.

One of the most famous taverns at Charing Cross was the "Rummer," of which the present well-known "Ship" at No. 35 Charing Cross is a direct descendant. It is now, I think, the Ship Restauraunt (Pratti Rugero's) and is numbered 45, not, as formerly, 35 Charing Cross. No trace of the "Rummer" exists. It is described as being two doors from another well-known restaurant, to wit, Lockitt's, the site of which is now occupied by Drummond's bank. Cunningham, in his "London," says, without stating his authority, that the "Rummer" was removed to the waterside (by which he means merely the river side of the street) of Charing Cross in 1710, and was burnt down November 7, 1750. But he must be in error as to this, for in an advertisement given below, relating to the exhibition of a wonderful "Luminous Ampitheatre" of 200 fountains at the "Rummer" in 1742, it will be seen that, at the end, it is plainly stated that "There is a back door" (from the tavern) "into Spring Gardens," Spring Gardens being of course on the south-west side of Charing Cross, or on the right as we should now proceed down Whitehall from Trafalgar Square.

The hospitality of the "Ship," by which sign the tavern was known at least as early as 1731, must have been extended to many who underwent the sanguinary discipline of the various tortures associated with the "wooden peccadilloes," as the pillory was called,[1] or of even the milder correction of the whipping-post, which may to

---

[1] In allusion to the ruff or collar known as the "peccadillo," also known as the "wooden ruff." The hurdle on which felons were drawn to the place of execution was the "wooden chariot." See *Dialogue on Oxford Parl.*, 1681 (*Harl. Misc.* ii. 125). Ralpho, the supposed sprite in Butler's *Hudibras*, allowing that the devil and the Independents had engaged in the Covenant, says :

> " Sir . . . tis true, I grant
> We made and took the Covenant :
> But that no more concerns the Cause
> Than other perj'ries do the laws,
> Which, when they're proved in open court,
> Wear wooden peccadilloes for't."—(Part III. canto i. line 1449.)

this day be seen preserved in the crypt of the church of St. Martin's-in-the-Fields.   Branding, nose-slitting, and ear-lopping were the least noteworthy of his congenial duties, and the common hangman, sooth to say, found merely his pastime therein, compared with what he had to perform until public indignation was aroused.   On June 10, 1731, Joseph Crook, *alias* Sir Peter Stranger, stood on the pillory for one hour, after which he was seated in an elbow-chair, and the common hangman cut both his ears off with an incision knife, and showed them to the spectators ; afterwards delivered them to Mr. Watson, a sheriff's officer, then slit both his nostrils with a pair of scissors, and seared them with a hot iron, pursuant to his sentence.   He had a surgeon to attend him on the pillory, who immediately applied things necessary to prevent the effusion of blood.   He underwent it all with undaunted courage ; afterwards went to the Ship Tavern, at Charing Cross, where he stayed some time, then was carried to the King's Bench Prison, to be confined there for life.   " During the time he was on the pillory he laughed and deny'd the fact to the last."[1] In 1742 the contents of the "Ship" were for sale.   "To be Sold by Hand, On Monday next, and the following Days, till all are sold, The genuine Household Furniture of Thomas Giles, at the Ship Tavern, Charing Cross ; consisting of all sorts of clean Household Furniture, and all sorts of Kitchen Furniture.   Note, There is a Parcel of neat Wines to be dispos'd of at the same Place."[2]   The tavern, however, merely changed hands, and in 1815 it is described in the " Epicure's Almanack " as follows : " Until of late this concern was considered merely in the light of a public house.   The present proprietor has removed the tap to the back premises, and in its former space has fitted up a Coffee-room, with a larder displaying steaks, chops, and other light dishes.   He has done this purely for the accommodation of persons going or coming by the numerous short stages which draw up at the door."   He also takes care to have an outlet into Spring Gardens.   In the reign of Charles II., the " Ship," then known as the " Rummer," was kept by Samuel Prior, uncle of Matthew Prior, the poet, the family connection ceasing in 1702.   It was here that Jack Sheppard committed his first crime by stealing two silver spoons.   In Hogarth's " Night " the sign of the " Rummer " hangs outside, and a skit on the Salisbury *Flying* Coach consists in that expeditious vehicle being overturned, with passengers inside, when it had only just started from the doors

---

[1] *Daily Advertiser*, June 11, 1731.

[2] *Ibid.* May 1, 1742.

of the tavern, whose original situation, on the south-west side of Charing Cross, may be seen by comparing the site of Rummer Court in an old map dated 1734, and published in Smith's "Antiquities of Westminster," where it will be found that the court was situated between Buckingham Court and Cromwell Place. Rummer Court survived the tavern on this site at least as late as 1761.[1] Next door to the "Ship" was the "Fleece." Charles Thom, of the Fleece Eating-house in the Strand, near Northumberland House, advertises that he "is remov'd to the Fleece next Door to the Ship Tavern at Charing Cross, where all Gentlemen may depend on good Entertainment and Attendance."[2] If you had been a patron, in 1742, of the multifarious amusements which made Charing Cross at that time pre-eminently the great centre for London pleasure-seekers, your company would have been "humbly desir'd by Hugh Roberts, Engineer, to be Spectators of his Models, and other curious Plans, to shew the Nature of the Country in regard to Mines, and to answer what he laid down before both Houses of Parliament, at the New Theatre in James Street, near the Hay-Market, where a Lecture will be repeated to justify his Proposals for draining Mines and other Mechanical Arts of great Use. Note, Some Tickets having been deliver'd, and the Place therein mention'd being the Long Room at the Rummer by Charing Cross; this is humbly to give Notice, that the Place is occasionally chang'd, and the said Theatre taken for that Purpose, which will begin by the 26th instant, at five o'clock in the Afternoon. Boxes, 2s. 6d., Pit, 1s. 6d. ; Gallery, 1s."[3]

There was also "to be seen at the Rummer Tavern, Charing-Cross, by any single person, or any Number of Persons, from Ten in the Morning till Nine at Night, at 1s. each, the celebrated Luminous Ampitheatre, constructed of Silver, polish'd Steel, and cut Glass, exhibiting at one View upwards of two hundred Fountains, curiously playing at one and the same Time, which, with the Infinity of Lustres (exceeding beyond Comparison the greatest Splendour ever yet beheld, even at the most magnificent and costly Entertainment), so strongly affect every Beholder with Delight and Surprise, that it renders them as it were lost in Ecstasy and Thought. It is not possible to declare the Splendour and Beauties of this noble Structure by Words ; a true Idea thereof cannot be communicated but by the Sight only. There is not Room here to insert all the Figures the several Fountains form themselves into, but each of them is agree-

---

[1] See *London and its Environs Described*, 1761.
[2] *Daily Advertiser*, Oct. 29, 1741. [3] *Ibid.* June 26, 1742.

E

able and entertaining, representing a Star, a Fan, a Globe and Cross, transversed fifty-four different Ways, &c. Note, the Company are allow'd to walk round the Fountains, that they may have ocular Demonstration that they are not amused with any trifling Perform-ance. There is a back door into Spring-Gardens. Note, It has given great Satisfaction to His Royal Highness the Duke, and to several of the Nobility and Gentry." [1]

Something similar to these luminous fountains, if not the very same thing, has been " invented " by M. A. Adamoff, and is described in " La Nature " of about May 25, 1896.

In the engraving by Hogarth alluded to, of " Night," the sign has a bunch of grapes also appended. So that I think the tavern must be identical with the " Rummer and Grapes," Westminster. At the "Apple Tree" Tavern, in Charles Street, Covent Garden, four of the London Freemasons' lodges, considering themselves neglected by Sir Christopher Wren in 1716, met and chose a grand master, *pro tem.*, until they should be able to place a noble brother at the head, which they did the year following, electing the Duke of Montague. Sir Christopher had been chosen in 1698. The three lodges that joined with the Apple Tree Lodge used to meet respectively at the " Goose and Gridiron," St. Paul's Churchyard; the " Crown," Parker's Lane; and at the " Rummer and Grapes " Tavern, West-minster. [2]

At a later period George Morland's painful life-story is not unassociated with the " Rummer " Tavern, through an incident which occurred here. Morland appears to have had an aversion to persons of high rank, even when they were on a level with himself in vulgar propensities. An instance in point occurred at the " Rummer " Tavern, Charing Cross, at which house he, with Bob Packer, the pugilist, had made an appointment to meet some of their boxing companions. The party disappointed them, but as they sat drinking by themselves the late Duke of Hamilton entered, and, seeing the artist, said to Packer, " Who is he?" Bob replied, "Morland the painter." "Can he spar?" "Yes, your Grace." The Duke then bade him stand up, and Morland obeyed; but the first blow knocked Morland across the room, and, as he afterwards declared, he was so awed by the mere name of a nobleman that, had he possessed the utmost skill, he could not have employed it. His Grace next ordered a coach, and, after inquiring of Morland where he was going, desired him to get into it with Packer, and said he

---

[1] *Daily Advertiser*, February 15, 1742.   [2] *History of Signboards.*

would set them down. The Duke then mounted the box, and the coachman got behind. When they arrived near Morland's house, the Duke stopped and asked which house it was; on being told it was three doors further, he abruptly bade the painter get out, and in a manner that did not a little hurt his pride; for he often observed, when speaking of this incident, that he never was so chagrined at any insult he had ever received. In fact, Morland had a considerable share of pride, which was exceedingly mortified when, from being treated disrespectfully, he felt the consequence of his dereliction of character.[1]

Besides the " Ship " Restaurant, sometime the " Rummer and Grapes," there was another "Ship" at Charing Cross, the sign of Mr. Rhodes, bookseller, who had been formerly wardrobe-keeper at the Blackfriars Theatre, and in 1659 opened the Cockpit Theatre in Drury Lane. In the same year Betterton the actor was apprenticed to him, and here Kynaston, a fellow apprentice, played a woman's part under Rhodes's direction.

[1] George Dawe's *Life of George Morland*, 1807, pp. 112–113.

CHAPTER IV.

THE TAVERNS—*continued.*

A DAM LOCKET was the landlord of a famous " ordinary " tavern close to Buckingham Court, Spring Gardens, which is often mentioned in the plays of Cibber and Vanbrugh, and which catered for the Horse-guard.   The site is now occupied by Drummond's bank. It was much frequented by Sir George Etheridge until he had run up a bill that he was unable to pay, when he began to absent himself. Mrs. Locket thereupon sent a man to dun him, and threaten him with a prosecution if he did not pay.   Sir George, an utter *poco-curante,* sent back word to Mrs. Locket that if she stirred a step in the matter he would kiss her.   On receiving this answer, the good lady, much exasperated, called for her hood and scarf, and told her husband, who interposed, that "she would see if there was any fellow alive who would have the impudence."   "Prithee ! my dear, don't be so rash," said her husband; "there is no telling what a man may do in his passion ! " [1]   The original Locket was dead in 1688, but an Edward Locket inhabited the same house till 1702. In the "London Gazette" for 1693,[2] notice is given by the latter that he had taken the Bowling Green House on Putney Heath, "where all gentlemen may be entertained."   This seems to be identical with the bowling-green attached to the picturesque "Green Man" tavern on the right as one emerges from Putney on to the Heath, and which is still standing.

> *Bellair.*—Where do you dine ?
> *Dorimant.*—At Long's,[3] or Locket's.
> *Medley.*—At Long's let it be.
> *The Man of Mode; or, Sir Fopling Flutter,* 4to, 1676.

---

[1] *A Ramble in the Streets of London,* by J. T. Smith, 1849, p. 88.

[2] No. 2965.

[3] Long's was another famous " ordinary " then in the Haymarket (Cunning-ham's *London*).   An " ordinary " is defined in *Bailey's Dictionary,* 1740, as "a victualling-house where persons may eat at so much per meal."   Johnson also says it is "a place of eating established at a certain price."

The wits who, in the words of Mr. Thornbury, buzzed about Charing Cross like bees round May flowers, were doubtless not so aggressive in their public behaviour as another asset in the social life of the time, the pot-valiant libertine or the " disguised " reprobate, who possessed neither wit nor even ordinary conversational talent, but who, with sword by his side, was for ever trying to compensate for his social deficiencies by seeking an opportunity for a tavern-brawl, when, if an expert bully, he would in a moment, and without rhyme or reason, pink an opponent whom he had never set eyes on before. For instance, a Croatian captain under the Earl of Essex, " who had a world of cuts about his body with swords, and was very quarrelsome and a great ravisher," was coming out of a tavern, when a lieutenant of Colonel Rossiter, who had great jingling spurs on, was passing. Said the captain, " The noise of your spurrs doe offend me ; you must come over the kennel and give me satisfaction." Thereupon they drew and passed at each other. The lieutenant was run through the body and died in an hour or two, and it was not known who killed him.[1] And at a later period Lord Mohun, Lord Warwick, and three army officers were drinking together at " Lockit's " when angry words arose between Captain Coote and Captain French, whom Lord Mohun and the Earl of Warwick and Holland[2] endeavoured to pacify. Lord Warwick was an intimate friend of Captain Coote, and had lent him a hundred pounds to buy his commission in the Guards. Also, when the captain was arrested on one occasion by his tailor for a debt of £13, Lord Warwick lent him £5 5s., and he often paid his reckoning and showed other offices of friendship. On the evening in question the disputant's friend and Coote, being separated while they were upstairs, unluckily stopped to drink ale again at the bar of Lockit's. The row began afresh, Coote lunged at French over the bar, and at last all six called for chairs, and went to Leicester Fields, where they fell to. Their lordships engaged on the side of Captain Coote. Lord Warwick was severely wounded in the hand, and French was stabbed, but honest Captain Coote got a couple of wounds, one especially " a wound on the left side just under the short ribs, and piercing through the diaphragma," which, in the words of the narrator, " did for Captain Coote." [3]

Drummond's is said to have gained its fame as a bank by

---

[1] *Anecdotes and Traditions*, p. 3.
[2] Step-father, I think, of Addison.
[3] Thackeray's *English Humourists*, 1869, " Steele," p. 215.

advancing money secretly to the Pretender. Upon this being known
the Court withdrew all their deposits. The result was that the
Scotch noblemen rallied round the firm, and brought in so much
money that the bank soon became a leading one. It is older than
Coutts's. Here Pope banked. The following advertisement seems
to bear some relation to the early history of the firm, whose offices
were originally so small that a sailor, who had an order upon them
for £20 prize money, generously offered to take £5 on account,
and to call for the residue in a month or two—Jack being most
solicitous not to overstrain their resources :

" MONEY on BOND.

NOBLEMEN and Gentlemen may have sums of Money advanced on
Bond Security, by application to B. D. at the Westminster Coffee-
house, Charing Cross. Clergymen having Livings, Officers on
Half Pay, and all persons holding estates of incomes for life, accommodated on the same security. To prevent trouble to parties
applying, it is requested that particulars of income, sum wanted, &c.,
be stated in a letter to the above address, to which a speedy answer
will be given."

The extension of the Mall for the formation of the Processional-
road through Spring Gardens into Trafalgar Square was first mooted,
like so many other public-spirited proposals, in the columns of the
" Builder " so long ago as the year 1858,[1] by Mr. William Bardwell.
Mr. Bardwell pointed out that the proper communication from
Charing Cross to the Park should be made by pulling down two
houses in Spring Gardens then in Government possession, and the
shoemaker's shop at the corner opposite Drummond's. The astonished eye, he remarked, would then perceive an uninterrupted view
from the centre of the Strand direct to Buckingham Palace—a most
beautiful vista, perfectly unmatched by any other in the metropolis,
and decidedly one of the finest improvements yet to be carried out.
The suggestion appears to have fallen flat on official ears, for it is
not until 1882 that it again crops up ; and yet again in 1885 that a
public roadway is advocated in the " Builder " in a direct line with
the Strand to the Mall.[2] The scheme is now in a pretty fair way of
being realised ; but the space in 1905, added to the width of the
road by the demolition of the two wedge-shaped houses opposite

---

[1] *Builder*, July 31, 1858.
[2] *Ibid.* June 1882, and Dec. 1885, p. 877.

Drummond's, is an utterly inadequate termination to such an ambitious design.

Other places of public resort on this spot besides the " Rummer " had convenient back entrances into Spring Gardens. The " Green Man " at Charing Cross, next door to which was the Lottery Office where the Swedish Giant was exhibited,[1] was known earlier, in the reign of William III., as " Young Man's Coffee-house " in Buckingham Court.[2] It had a backdoor into Spring Gardens, and was much frequented by "officers."[3] At "Young Man's" was exhibited "a Little Man, Fifty Years of Age, Two Feet Nine Inches high, and the Father of Eight Children," who, " when he sleeps, puts his Head between his two Feet, to rest on by way of a Pillow, and his great Toes one in each Ear."[4] This " Young Man's Coffee-house " was set up in opposition to " Old Man's," over the way, near Scotland Yard. " Old Man's " was so called after the proprietor, Alexander Man, " Coffee, tea, and chocolate maker " to William III. It was sometimes also known as " Man's," or the " Royal Coffee-house," and was a favourite resort of " Stock-jobbers, Paymasters and Courtiers."[5]

"To be Lett or Sold. Almost opposite to the Admiralty, near Charing Cross, A Large new-built Brick House, late Old Man's Coffee-House, five Stories high, elegantly finish'd. Also a back House and Kitchen, commodiously fitted up, with good Cellaring, and other Conveniences, fit for a Tavern, Coffee-House, or other publick Business, and with a little Alteration may be fitted up for a private Family. Enquire at Mr. Millan's, Bookseller, near the said House."[6] The " Old Man's " Coffee-house probably had its origin in an earlier Coffee-house known as the " Royal," which is always described as being situated either "at Charing Cross" or " near Whitehall." This was about 1684-7, as will be seen by the references given to the " London Gazette" of those years. The " Royal " appears to have been a well-known resort ; for tickets for the County

---

[1] *Daily Advertiser*, February 4, 1742.

[2] *London Daily Post*, February 7, 1737-8.

[3] Macky's *Journey*, 1722, i. 168.

[4] Henry Morley, *Memoirs of Bartholomew Fair*, 8vo., p. 251.

[5] Macky's *Journey*, ibid. Ned Ward, in his *London Spy*, describes " Man's Coffee-house " as the "most Eminent Coffee-House at the end of the Town " (Part IX. p. 201). This was in 1709. "On Monday last died Mr. Edmund Man, Master of Old Man's Coffee-house at Charing Cross, a very noted and reputable Person of the Profession. He succeeded his Father in the said Coffee-house, which was the Second that was set up in the Cities of London and Westminster " (*Daily Post*, May 15, 1728).

[6] *Daily Advertiser*, December 21, 1741.

Feasts, so much in vogue through the seventeenth and eighteenth centuries, were frequently advertised as obtainable there:

"All persons Born in the County of Warwick and the City of Coventry, are desired to take notice that there will be held a County Feast on Tuesday the 25th inst. November, at Merchant Taylors' Hall. Tickets to be had at the Royal Coffee House, Charing Cross, &c."[1]

Tickets might also be had here for the Annual Wiltshire Feast at the Merchant Taylors' Hall,[2] as well as for the Gloucester County and City Feast.[3] Probably no connection with the "Feasts," but "True" Dr. Anderson's (or Scott's) Pills were to be had at the Royal Coffee-house, Charing Cross.[4] Anderson's Pills are described in Dr. Paris's "Pharmacologia" as consisting of the Barbadoes Aloes, with a proportion of Jalap and Oil of Aniseed. Thomas Herbert (or Hubert), His Majesty's Watchmaker, dwelt over against the "Royal" Coffee-house, near Whitehall. Perhaps the first servants' registry was that known as "The Intelligence Office for Servants," first established under a patent granted by Charles II. in the year 1676. The patentees had appointed three places where masters and mistresses and servants might mutually accommodate themselves, opposite to the Assurance Office, within the Royal Exchange, next door to the "Royal" Coffee-house, near Whitehall, and at the Three Cranes, near the Meal Market, Southwark.

There was another Coffee-house at Charing Cross, known as "Jenny Man's," but whether identical with either of the other "Man's" one cannot say. Addison, however, alluding to the current report of the death of the King of France, says: "Upon my arrival at Jenny Man's, I saw an alert young fellow that cocked his hat upon a friend of his who enter'd just at the same time with myself, and accosted him after the following manner :—'Well, Jack, the old prig's dead at last. Sharp's the word. Now or never, boy. Up to the walls of Paris directly.' With several other deep reflections of the same nature."[5] In the year preceding the battle of Preston (in Lancashire) the following mysterious announcement appeared in the "Post-Boy" of June 3–5, 1714: "There are lately arrived here the Dublin Plenipo's. All persons that have any business concerning the GOOD OLD CAUSE, let 'em repair to Jenny Man's Coffee House

---

[1] *Lond. Gaz.* Oct. 30, 1684.   [2] *Ibid.* Nov. 6.
[3] Oct. 30, 1684 (erroneously quoted, I think, from the *Gentleman's Magazine*).
[4] *Lond. Gaz.* Mar. 8, 1687.   [5] *Spectator*, 403, vol. iii. p. 444.

at Charing Cross, where they may meet with the said Plenipo's every day of the week except Sundays, and every evening of those days they are to be spoke with at the Kit-Cat Club." [1]

Next door to " Young Man's " was " Tom's " Coffee-house, whence are advertised " Masquerade Habits to be Let, at Five Shillings per Habit, the greatest Variety of any Place soever, being very Curious and Comick, at Tom's Coffee-house, next door to Young Man's Coffee-house, Charing Cross." [2]

Opposite " Young Man's " was the "Orange Tree," the sign of a snuff-dealer apparently : " Whereas the late Anthony Rodrigues (famous in his Life-time for preparing Snuff) did for valuable Considerations impart his Secret of mixing and preparing the said Snuffs to Mr. James Puech : These are therefore to give Notice That all the said sorts of Snuff are carefully and exactly prepared by the said James Puech, and sold by him at the House [? called the] Orange Tree, opposite Young Man's Coffee-house at Charing Cross." [3]

At Mr. Evans's, Glover, over against "Young Man's" Coffee-house at Charing Cross, were sold Cornaro's Drops,[4] not mentioned in Paris's "Pharmacologia." All manner of virtues are attributed to them, the inventor probably trading on the famous name of Lewis Cornaro, the noble Venetian, who, having lived freely in his youth to the injury of his health, determined to re-establish it by strict temperance. This he succeeded in doing by reducing himself to twelve ounces of food and fourteen of wine a day. At the same time, by exerting his reason and philosophy, he also conquered his temper, which was naturally impatient and bad. He died in his ninety-eighth year, but did not recommend to all the severities of diet which he practised himself.[5]

Francis Place, the " Radical Tailor of Charing Cross," dwelt first at No. 16, and later at No. 29, Charing Cross.[6]

A spot associated with the name of the immortal Wren was Buckingham Court, on the west side of Charing Cross. Wren was "Surveyor of their Majesties' Works" when this court was "a nest of vice and dirt," and, worse than all in those days, it possessed a coffee-house that harboured meetings of those who were sworn to

[1] *Notes and Queries*, October 29, 1853, p. 421.
[2] *Daily Post*, February, 1725.
[3] *London Gazette*, April 24, 1704.
[4] *Weekly Journal*, Oct. 21, 1721.
[5] See Haller's *Bibliotheca Medicinæ Practicæ*, 1776–1788, 4 vols. 4to.
[6] *Life of Francis Place*, by Graham Wallas ; and also *Eccentric Biography*, p. 77.

further the interests of the old religion.[1] " Whereas information hath been given to this Board that there is a great and numerous concourse of Papists and other persons disaffected to the Government that resort to the Coffee House of one Bromefield, in Buckingham Court, near Wallingford House, and to other houses there : And whereas there is a Door lately opened out of that court into the lower part of the Spring Garden that leads into S[t]. James's Park, where the said Papists and disaffected persons meet and consult, w[ch] may be of dangerous consequence. These are, therefore, to pray and require you to cause the said Door to be forthwith bricked or otherwise so closed up as you shall judge most fit for the security of their Majesties' Palace of Whitehall, and the said Park and the avenues of the same. And for so doing this shall be your warrant, given at their Majesties' Board of Green Cloth at Hampton Court the 9th day of September, in the first year of their Majesties' reign, 1689.   DEVONSHIRE, NEWPORT.

" To Sir Christopher Wren, Knt.,
    Surveyor of their Majesties' Works." [2]

Mr. Hilton-Price says that the " Devil " tavern in the Strand was formerly known as Shuttleworth's Coffee-house, i.e. in 1698.[3] If so, it seems to have been removed from Buckingham Court, Charing Cross, for in the " London Gazette " for April 11, 1689,[4] is advertised as stolen from Mrs. Cramer " at Shuttleworth's Coffee-house at Charing Cross," by Tobias Cramer, a smooth-faced proper man, about twenty-one years of Age, a considerable Parcel of Broad Gold and Guineas, about o 1 (?) in Spanish Money and Cross Dollars, and three Pieces of Bullion ; he had on a dark Olive colour'd Cloth coat, and a blew Rateen Wastcoat with Silver Brede. Whoever secures him and gives Notice to . . . Mr. Cramer . . . shall have ten guineas Reward."

Within three doors of Young Man's Coffee-house, " against the horse," i.e. the statue of Charles I., dwelt a " man-milliner " exhibiting in 1709 a sign of the " Olive Tree and Still." He advertised " the goods of a person who had failed, consisting of Men's Mourn-

---

[1] Possibly Bromefield's Coffee-house was identical with that which was known later as Young Man's Coffee-house, q. v., p. 189.

[2] Letter Book in Lord Steward's Office, quoted by Cunningham.

[3] Signs of the Strand, in Middlesex and Herts Notes and Queries, 1897, p. 196. Devil Tavern Yard at Charing Cross derived its name from a tavern with that sign (Dodsley's London and its Environs, 1761).

[4] See also London Gazette, November 2, 1691.

ing Gowns of rich silks, Stuffs, Calicoes," &c. His sign indicated two branches of trade,—the " Olive Tree " showing that not only the goods usually supplied by a man-milliner were sold, but articles generally of Italian millinery also, such as artificial flowers, Genoa velvet, Leghorn hats, &c. Dr. Johnson derives the word " milliner " from Milan, a Milaner being one who dealt originally in Milanese and Italian finery generally. Professor Skeat says that, although this is disputed, it means " almost certainly a dealer in goods brought from Milan." The Haberdashers were originally called " hurers " and " milaners," *i.e.* cap-makers and dealers in Milan wares.[1] The Still stands for a perfumer's, both these trades having been dependent on Italy for a supply of scents and toilet-waters. The popinjay described by Hotspur was " perfumed like a milliner," [2] and for a long time after Shakespeare in the flesh there is a sugges-tion of a close connection between the two trades. Evelyn says in his " Diary " that the shops of milliners and perfumers were noted places of assignation. The milliners' shops in the New Exchange, Strand, were notorious for this. Attended by the most showy young women who could be procured, they were the haunts of beaux and profligates, who spent their time and money there in frivolous con-versation.

The perplexity that often arises from such combinations on the signboard as the " Three Nuns and Hare " would not exist if it were remembered that such compound signs were often, especially when there is some striking incongruity in the two objects composing the sign, the result of one sign being added to another when its owner came into another's business, or, as pointed out by the " Spectator," when an apprentice on setting up trade united the sign of his master with his own. It would be otherwise absurd to attempt the attributing of any propriety to such a conjunction as the repose of a nun and the wild haste of a hare. Mrs. Piozzi mentions the sign of the " Hare running over the heads of Three Nuns," which used to stand at Charing Cross.[3] Originally the lace-maker's sign, from the lace-work produced by the nuns who thus employed their time, it became later apparently a fur-dealer's cognizance : " Lost on Saturday last, between the Hours of Twelve and One at Noon, between the Palace at St. James's and the Earl of Thomond's House in Dover Street, a Lady's sable Muff. Whoever will bring the said Muff to Mr. Goodchild's, the Three Nuns and Hare at Charing Cross, or to the

---

[1] Herbert's *Twelve Great Companies.*   [2] 1 *Hen. IV.* i. 3.
[3] *British Symphony*, vol. ii. p. 50.

Bar of the Horn Tavern in New Palace Yard, Westminster, shall receive a Guinea Reward. No greater Reward will be offer'd." [1]

The Straits of Gibraltar, it is well known, were at one time believed to be the end of the world, and the terminus of human adventure and aspiration, and the classical appellation of the Pillars of Hercules was given to them in consequence of a fiction that Hercules, in his travels to find the oxen of Geryon, raised the two mountains known as Calpe (now the Rock of Gibraltar) and Abyla (now Jebel Zatout), as monuments of his journey, placing on them the inscription "NE PLUS ULTRA." So Charing Cross, being the utmost limit of town life in the seventeenth century, had its tavern-sign of the "Hercules Pillars," beyond which was the rusticity of St. James's Park, St. James's Fields, the Five Fields, and Hyde Park, where, as London extended still further west, there was another "Hercules Pillars" which is mentioned by Wycherley in his "Plain Dealer," 1676, as being in Piccadilly. Apsley House now occupies its site, I think, but the Charing Cross tavern was in Pall Mall, and was kept by one William Penck.[2] The arms of the "Rock" are azure, between two pillars a castle argent, from the gate a golden key, pendant,[3] but the sign generally represented the demigod standing between the pillars, or pulling the pillars down—a strange cross between the Biblical and pagan Hercules.[4] At the "Chequer" near Charing Cross the carriers from Blanvile (? Blandford) in Dorsetshire used to lodge. If Blandford be meant, no doubt the carriers supplied London with the shirt-buttons and thread in which, especially the former, the town had an extensive trade.[5] This tavern is perhaps identical with that which Hogarth supplies as a background for his first plate of the "Harlot's Progress," where a young country girl is just being launched upon the town from the York stage-waggon which stands by. In the clutches of the woman who receives her with smiles, she begins her career of wretchedness to a premature death. The Bell also appears as a sign outside, but the Chequers are plainly represented over the entrance to the tavern. The house appears to have been situated "by the end of St. Martin's Lane, at Charing Cross."[6] Saunders and Drew's coach to and from Bath and Bristol came to the "Chequer" on Mondays, leaving on

---

[1] *Daily Advertiser*, June 25, 1742.
[2] See the Bagford Ballads, Harl. Coll. 5996, fol. 88, No. 247.   [3] Burke.
[4] *Hist. of Signboards*, 1884, p. 71.
[5] Taylor's *Carriers' Cosmography*, and Hutchinson's *Dorsetshire*.
[6] *New View of London*, vol. i. p. 17.

Tuesdays.[1]   Coaches also left the "Chequer" at Charing Cross for Brentford, Chertsey, Hammersmith, Hampton Court (when the Court is there), Kingston-on-Thames, and Twickenham.[2]   Pepys records having "put up his own dull jade, and there saddled a delicate stone horse of Captain Ferrers at the 'Chequer,' and with it rid in state to the Park."

A remarkable place catering for the amusement of the public in the middle of the eighteenth century, when, as Ned Ward speaks of Charing Cross in 1709, it was still practically "the end of the town," was the "Mitre" tavern "opposite Craig's Court."   So far as I can ascertain, it has not been noticed by any writer upon this once *ne plus ultra* quarter of Cockaigne.   Here all kinds of curiosities were exhibited for the edification of the gaping country cousin, no less than for the homespun cockney, and not the least noteworthy was a prototype apparently of the modern motor-car:

"This is to acquaint all Lovers of Ingenuity, that there is lately arriv'd from the Canton of Bern in Switzerland, and to be seen at the *Mitre Tavern*, Charing-Cross, from Nine in the Morning till Nine at Night, a most curious Chaise That travels without Horses. This beautiful convenient Machine is so simply contriv'd, and easily manag'd, as to travel upwards of forty Miles a Day, with very little Trouble to the Rider, or Danger of being put out of Order.   The whole Thing, though capable of carrying three Persons, weighs less than Two Hundred Weight."[3]

A few days later the public are informed that "the curious three-wheeled Chaise, that travels without Horses, which has given so universal a Satisfaction to all the Nobility and Gentry, while shown at the Mitre Tavern, Charing Cross, is now remov'd to the Great Booth near the Steps in Middle Moorfields."[4]

Neither do I find that the following wonderful structure has ever been noticed by writers like Chambers, Hone, and Timbs :

"To be Seen, by four, five, or more, at One Shilling each, in a large Room *at the Mitre*, near Charing Cross, opposite Craigg's Court, The Microcosm : or, The World in Miniature.   Lately made by Mr. Henry Bridges, after ten Years close Study and

---

[1] *Present State of London*, 1690, p. 403.

[2] *Complete Guide to London*, 1840, pp. 71, 73, 78, 80, and 101.   See also a valuable Collection relating to the signs of London and the Home Counties, in St. Martin's Library, Charing Cross.

[3] *Daily Advertiser*, April 6, 1742.

[4] *Ibid*. April 19, 1742.   See also the "Microcosm, or the World in Miniature," exhibited at the "Mitre," *ibid*. Dec. 23, 1741.

Application ; and when exhibited to publick View, was honour'd with the Presence of the Royal Family, as well as the Nobility and Gentry, and receiv'd the Approbation and Applause of the ingenious Professors of the several Arts and Sciences that compose it.

" The Author, having thus succeeded beyond his Expectation in his first Attempt, has since, with the utmost Assiduity, made considerable Additions and Improvements ; so that the Piece is now completely finish'd, and humbly offer'd to the Curious for their further Approbation.

" This Machine, for the Magnificence of its Structures, the Beauty of its Painting and Sculpture, the Excellency of its Musick, the vast Variety and Justness of its moving Figures, is esteem'd one of the most curious Pieces of Mechanism that ever appear'd in Europe.

" Among many other Improvements, in the Astronomical Part, are added, two Planetariums, never before exhibited. The first represents the Solar System, with the Orbits and their proper Excentricities, in Proportion to each other ; in which, the Planets, in their like Proportion, perform their respective annual and diurnal Motion by Clock-Work, with a Velocity of ten Months Motion in ten Minutes. The second is a System of Jupiter and his four Satellites, in like Proportion, performing their proper Revolutions with the Solar System ; exhibiting their Immersions into, and Emersions out of Jupiter's Shadow ; with their Occultations by, and Transits over the Body of that Planet ; as also their mutual Transits amongst each other ; with many more Astronomical Phænomena than can be well express'd in the Compass of an Advertisement.

" This Work is judg'd by all who have seen it worthy to adorn the Palace of a Prince, as it exceeds whatever has been done of this kind. And as it will bear seeing more than once, 'tis hoped no Person will take it amiss if not admitted to see it a second time gratis.

" Note, Mr. Bridges being engag'd in much Business at home, would be willing to dispose of this Machine, either wholly, or in Partnership." [1]

" The two Gentlemen that had the Misfortune to quarrel and fight on Monday Morning at the Mitre Tavern, Charing Cross, were Mr. Lewis, late a Cornet in Major-General Evans's Regiment of Dragoons, and Mr. Oliphant, now a Cornet in the said Regiment. The former was run through the Body, and since died." [2]

" Professor " Sheard, of Hoxton, claims to be the only monstrosity

---

[1] *Daily Advertiser*, Dec. 23, 1741.
[2] *Daily Post*, Dec. 9, 1724

manufacturer in Europe. He might have been an eighteenth-century Barnum, reigning supreme over the amusement world of Charing Cross, if he had only shed his effulgence on that period, for Londoners and their country cousins appear to have gone monster mad. What a moral force might not a great showman be—what an influence he probably is—that is, if he heed the wingèd words of Schiller : "Live with thy century, but be not its creature ; produce for thy contemporaries, however, what they need, not what they applaud." And surely "monsters," as well as automata and waxwork replicas, have their lessons to teach. The word "monster" as applied to the marvels in favour with the curious of this century, of course, means nothing more than what was out of the common order of nature, as indeed it did in Shakespeare's time—witness Trinculo in *The Tempest :*

"A strange fish ! Were I in England now (as once I was), and had but this fish painted, not a holiday fool there but would give a piece of silver : there would this monster make a man [1] ; when they will not give a doit to relieve a lame beggar, they will lay out ten to see a dead Indian." [2]

Almost any abnormally shaped or sized animal was exhibited and drew its thousands. But what could the following have been ? As some fishermen "near Exeter drew their Net to shore, to their great Surprize, a Creature of a Human Shape, having two Legs, leaped out of the Net and ran away with great Swiftness ; and they not being able to overtake it, knocked it down by throwing Sticks after it. At their coming up to it, it was dying and groaned like a human Creature. Its Feet were webbed like a Duck's, it had Eyes, Nose, and Mouth, resembling those of a Man, only the nose somewhat depressed ; it had a Tail not unlike that of a Salmon, turning up towards its Back ; it is four Feet in Height, and now publickly shown at Exeter." [3] The wily suggestion of the mermaid, in the "Tail not unlike that of a Salmon, turning up towards its Back," leads one to suspect that this was an ingenious "plant " on the part of the artless fishermen,[4] aided, consciously or unconsciously, by the local Professor Sheard. But a "strange fish " attracted, in the year 1742, crowds of "holiday fools " to the "Mitre ":

[1] *I.e.* would be the making of a man, with regard to what was a common eighteenth-century expression, "getting an estate."

[2] Act ii. scene 2.   [3] *St. James's Evening Post*, November 5, 1737.

[4] Unless, as is quite possible, it was an animal of the seal tribe which thus assisted an imagination egged on by the commercial instincts of its captors.

"To be seen, at the *Mitre Tavern*, Charing-Cross. The largest Thames-Monster, or miraculous man-eater, that was ever in the World, taken on the 26th of April last, just above London-Bridge, in the River Thames. As a Boy was washing his Mop, this surprising Monster caught hold of it in his Mouth, and had very like to pull the Boy into the River, but he calling out for Help, several Men came to his Assistance, and with great Difficulty dragg'd this Monster out, and he liv'd four Hours after on shore. He is near four Foot long, full three Foot round in the Body, and two Foot and a half round his Mouth ; his Neck is like a Bull, and Belly like a Bag ; he has sixteen Rows of Teeth, has two Rows of Teeth in his Back and Breast inwards twelve Inches from his Mouth, and just double the Number of Teeth as Days in the Year ; he has two very plain Hands, eight Fingers and two Thumbs, and Nails on each like a Christian ; he has four Horns on his Head, and other Weapons on his Back ; his Flesh is very fat and white, and has monstrous large Fins ; he had neither Heart, Tongue, nor Lights, but all the Entrails he had are to be seen with him. All the Gentlemen and Sailors that have seen him, that have been in most Parts abroad for many Years, and all the Accounts, Books, or Prints of Fishes, that have been produced, cannot shew the like, it being neither like the Shark, Porpus, Aligator, or Grampus. Great Numbers of the Curious daily resort to see it, and acknowledge it to be the most surprising uncommon Fish that ever they saw.

"Also a Dog-Fish, lately taken off of Billingsgate ; and the curious Lock of Hair cut off a Gentlewoman's Head, so much approv'd of, that the whole World is challeng'd for Five Hundred Guineas to produce the like."[1]

As might be supposed in these times, the wonder-wistful were confined to no particular class. All who could afford the necessary " piece of silver " were as inextricably caught in the showman's net as the fish that he had landed. The showman's chief patronage, in fact—at a time when the mermaid's existence was an unshaken article of popular belief—was derived from " the nobility and gentry," and often even the reigning monarch. The majority of the objects exhibited, however, seem to have been genuine monstrosities, monstrous births having, about the middle of the eighteenth century, when they were the vogue, especially enjoyed the attention of the learned physician and antiquary, Dr. James Parsons, who lectured upon them.

[1] *Daily Advertiser*, May 22, 1742.

"On Tuesday last one Clowsely of Oxford Road had a Sow pigg'd a Monster; its Head, Neck, and Skin resembling a Child, and all the rest of the Body. Legs and Tail like a Pig."[1] "On Thursday last a large Sea-Monster, of an extraordinary Magnitude, struck itself ashore above Rumley River in Glamorganshire, and was immediately taken by a Fisherman. It had Hands and Wrist Joints like a human Creature."[2]

Abnormal productions of the animal world were from early times known as "monsters." In the thirteenth century a *lusus naturæ* was regarded as an omen of evil import; in our own time it becomes a lucrative exhibition. A bi-corporal lamb and a two-headed female are described in a MS. entitled "Liber de Antiquis Legibus," and a facsimile engraving of the first is presented in Bentley's "Excerpta Historica." They happened in the time of Henry III. Larwood and Hotten, in their "History of Signboards," suppose the "Monster" tavern at Pimlico to be a corruption of "Monastery," a sign which "may have been put up" on account of the land having been leased to the Abbot and Monastery of Westminster. But a close acquaintance with the news-sheets of the seventeenth and eighteenth centuries would, I think, have led them to alter their opinion ; for, as in the case of the "Mitre," curiosities of all kinds, including "Monsters," were exhibited for the benefit, and to attract the custom, of tavern frequenters and others, whence, it seems almost beyond doubt, the Pimlico hostelry derived its sign. Separate chapters, however, might well be written on both "Mermaids" and "Monsters."

There were other applications of the term "monster," such as to the *living* wonders that aired their beauty and accomplishments at both Charing Cross and Bartholomew Fair. The dog Toby, the dogs that danced the morrice, the black wolf, the bull with five legs, and especially the hare that played the tabor,[3] were all described as monsters, by which the true sense of the word was intended : that is, a "show" (Lat. "*monstro*"). Other objects that were shows, yet not "monsters," were the mechanical figures in which our forefathers delighted no less than do we, to-day, in a good automatic penny-in-the-slot affair, and the neighbourhood of Charing Cross was a

[1] *St. James's Evening Post*, October 21, 1736.
[2] *Daily Advertiser*, April 27, 1742.
[3] A sketch of this ancient "monster" appears in an illuminated MS. of Hours of the Virgin, painted three centuries before Ben Jonson depicted the humours of the Fair at Smithfield (*Bartholomew Fair*, Act v. sc. 3). The copy in Morley's *Bartholomew Fair* was taken direct from the MS. alluded to.

F

nursery of this improved taste.   The celebrated mechanician
Vaucanson, for instance, exhibited at the " Long Room " of the
Haymarket Opera-house a figure which performed complete airs on
the pipe and tabor, "excelling the most esteemed performers on
those instruments," and also a man with a German flute, who played
several tunes "with all the Delicacy and Perfection, depending on
the various Motions of the Tongue, the Fingers, and the Instrument
itself, swelling the Notes like a natural Performer, to the great
Astonishment of all that are present."   And if this " produced the
greatest sensation wherever it was exhibited," it was even surpassed
by Vaucanson's celebrated mechanical duck, which excited the
interest of all Europe.   No less an authority in natural philosophy
than Sir David Brewster himself says, indeed, that it " was perhaps
the most wonderful piece of mechanism that was ever made."   It
has, however, been excelled in marvellousness by Mr. Maskelyne's
" Psycho."   This duck exactly resembled the living animal in appearance and size.   It swam, quacked, waved its wings, preened its
feathers, accepted barley from the hand, and digested its food, an
operation performed by placing in the interior of the automaton
certain substances which made a solution of the food.[1]   " Last
week," says a newspaper paragraph of the time, " the Prince of Saxe-
Gotha, several of the Nobility, and Persons of Distinction, were
[? went] to see the Performance of the three Mechanical Figures, at
the Long Room at the Opera House in the Hay-Market, which so
far exceeded their expectations, that they thought it impossible so
much could be done by artificial Figures." [2]

The following are some of the Coffee-houses and Taverns at

[1] For further information as to this most wonderful automaton, see Sir David
Brewster's *Letters on Natural Magic*.   In an advertisement relating to these contrivances in the *Daily Advertiser* of May 30, 1742, " those who desire a more
particular account of these figures " are invited " to peruse a Memoir . . .
presented to the Royal Academy of Sciences, containing a full Description of
their Construction and Performance.   This Memoir is translated into English by
Dr. Desaguliers, with the Addition of a Letter from Mr. Vaucanson, giving a
particular Account of the Duck, and the other figure playing on the Tabor and
Pipe."   See also Beckmann's *History of Inventions*, 1846, ii. 136–7–8, and
Account of Mechanism of Automaton playing on the German Flute, by Desaguliers,
B. Mus. Lib. Catalogue, 538, i. 38.   See also, for an account of some wonderful
objects exhibited at Cox's Museum in Spring Gardens, a full description of much
interest in Mr. G. L. Apperson's *Bygone London Life*, 1903, pp. 110–118.

[2] *Daily Advertiser*, February 22, 1742.   *Cf.* also Roger Bacon's Brazen
Head, &c., in *Some Mediæval Mechanisms*, by Sidney H. Hollands in the
Antiquary.

Charing Cross, omitted in the usual course, either because their exact locality is enigmatical, or because in a few instances one is not sure that the references are correct. Mr. F. G. Hilton Price in "Middlesex and Herts Notes and Queries," 1897 (vol. iii. pp. 196–7–8–9), gives a valuable list of no fewer than sixty-six instances of these public resorts in the neighbourhood of Charing Cross, a list which possibly includes some of the following :

The "Harp and Ball," Charing Cross. See "Illustrations of the Life and Neighbourhood of the New Post Office, St. Martin's-le-Grand," p. 65.

Madame Rochford's Chocolate House was "by Charing Cross." See the "Englishman," No. 31 (Saturday, December 12, 1713).

The "Feathers" Tavern, Charing Cross. (Johnson's "Lives of the Highwaymen," earliest ed., p. 387.)

The "Jockey" Tavern at Charing Cross in 1688. ("Lond. Gaz." Ap. 19 of that year.)

Salopian Coffee-house, Charing Cross. See "Life and Letters of the Rev. Richard Harris Barham, 1870, vol. i. p. 93. Also Collection in St. Martin's Library (2481).

The "Devil" Tavern. See Devil Tavern Yard ("London and its Environs," 1761, vol. ii. p. 224).

The "Speaking Man" at Spring Gardens. (Lysons' "Collectanea"), 5 vols. (vol. i. p. 132.)

The "Buffalo's Head," Charing Cross. See "Collection of Trials," vol. iii. p. 552, and Caulfield's "Portraits," 1819, vol ii. p. 26, &c. Also "History of Signboards."

The "Goat" at Charing Cross was a resort of Pepys. So was the "Three Tuns," perhaps the inn of that name which stood on the site of No. 66 Bedford Street, Strand, near the corner of Chandos Street.

Thornbury, in his "Haunted London," refers to the "Elephant," the "Sugar Loaf," the "Old Vine," the "Three Flower-de-Luces," and the "Three Queens," which stood somewhere at Charing Cross between the years 1680 and 1730. There was also a "White Lion."

Brown's Coffee-house. "This is to acquaint Gentlemen, That there are to be sold at Brown's Coffee-house in Spring Gardens:

"All Sorts of the newest fashion'd Tye Perukes, made of fresh string, Humane Hair, far exceeding any Country Work, at the following Prices, viz. from a fine Grey to a fine Grizzle, from four

F 2

Guineas to three Guineas, and all other Colours down to forty
Shillings " (" Daily Post," May 1725 (? or 1728).

" Mrs. Ebeall, who kept the Charing Cross Coffee-house, the
corner of Spring Gardens, leading to the Park, now keeps the Bell
Tavern or New Crown Bagnio, the bottom of St. Martin's Lane,
near the Church. . . . Bathing, Sweeting, and Cupping at the lowest
Prices, also good Attendance and neat Wines, &c." (" Daily Advertiser," Nov. 7, 1741).

The " Little Rummer below Charing Cross " (" Lond. Gaz.,"
Nov. 25, 1686).

CHAPTER V.

THE ELEANOR CROSS.

THE sumptuous, if unfortunately placed, monument within the gigantic *grille-de-fer* enclosing the forecourt of Charing Cross Hotel, is believed to be a fair representation, as to its general outline, of the original Eleanor Cross. The not unreasonable though elaborate embellishments were suggested by a study of the other Eleanor memorials—notably, I think, the Northampton cross, which it resembles more closely than any of the others—that mark the course of the funeral *cortège* on its way from Lincolnshire to Westminster. But the *grille* which hides it is as great a nuisance from artistic considerations as ever was Middle Row, Holborn, Holywell Street, Strand, or the late block of buildings at the entrance to Tottenham Court Road, for *practical* reasons. The Chatham and South-Eastern Railway Company build a beautiful monument, and forthwith elaborate as close a time for it as for partridge in August, and it would be considered by the cabmen surrounding it quite an eccentric act to attempt a closer acquaintance with it than that which is afforded by a casual passing through the forecourt.

The present cross was erected at the expense of the railway company from the designs of Edward Middleton Barry, third son of the distinguished architect of the Houses of Parliament. Barry's designs were founded on the traditions of the old structure, and with some regard to the only drawings, three in number, that are known to exist. One of these is in the British Museum, another in the Bodleian Library, and a third in the possession of the Society of Antiquaries. The modern trophy is built of Portland stone, but the panels and shields of the upper story are of red Mansfield. In this upper story are eight crowned statues, four of which represent Eleanor as queen, while the other four depict her in the exercise of charity.[1] In one of the latter four she is in the act of giving alms

[1] The suggestion of the eight figures is derived from Pennant, who, in his last edition of *London*, describes the cross as octagonal, and he especially states that the Charing Cross had *eight* figures, double the number of any of the other crosses.

from a purse ; in another she is distributing bread, while in the two others she is represented as the foundress of churches and religious houses. The statues have at their feet the figures of eight kneeling angels, with wings outstretched, and hands clasped as in prayer. The shields in the lower stage are accurately copied from those existing on the surviving crosses of Waltham and Northampton, and on the Abbey tomb, and consist of three varieties. On a dingy day an opera-glass will aid in the scrutiny of the details, but the first shield displays three lions passant gardant, first assumed as the royal arms of England by Henry II. in 1154, and which still form part of the royal arms as borne by King Edward VII. The second is that of Ponthieu, which Queen Eleanor bore in right of her mother, and simply consists of three bendlets within a bordure. The third shield represents the arms of Castile and Leon, arranged quarterly ; and this is especially interesting as being a representation of the earliest quartering of arms. The order of the shields accords with the arrangement at Northampton, Waltham, and Westminster. This monument suggested the erection, at the instance of the late Queen Victoria, of the Albert Memorial, to the memory of her exemplary consort.

It is not to be supposed, because the village of Charing's existence was antecedent to the erection of the Eleanor Cross, that therefore the spot was necessarily unknown as Charing Cross before the more famous memorial was raised by Edward I. It is highly probable that it was the pre-existence of a roadside or " weeping " cross at this spot that suggested to the king the site for such a commemorative landmark.[1] Such a cross stood near Stafford, where the road turns off to Walsall, and has given to the spot the name, which survives to-day, of " Weeping Cross," and several writers, among whom is the Rev. Edgar Sheppard, in his " Whitehall Palace," allude to a wooden cross that existed here before the stone edifice. One must say, however, that, whatever the probabilities, the statements to this effect appear to remain unsubstantiated.

The exact site of the cross is said to be occupied by the very interesting statue of Charles I., close to the western exterior of the Grand Hotel. The opening to the thoroughfare now known as Whitehall, the upper part of which, right and left, is known as Charing Cross, was, in the seventeenth century, of much narrower dimensions, and the statue was then consequently more noticeable,

[1] See Viollet-le-Duc, *Dictionnaire de l'Architecture.*

although it still occupied a position midway between each side of the street now known as Whitehall.

The cross took three years to build, and whilst the Waltham Cross cost only £95, that at Charing cost £650, which, allowing for the vast difference in the value of money, was a very large sum. The stone was brought from Caen, and the marble for the steps from Corfe, in Dorsetshire, for which a considerable sum was paid. The "architects" were Hubert de Corfe, Richard and Roger de Crundale, Richard de Stowe, John de Bells, Ralph de Chichester, Dymenge de Legeri, Michael de Canterbury, and the sculpture was the work of William de Ireland and Alexander de Abingdon.[1]

The hazardous statement is made by J. T. Smith, in his " Streets of London," that " a stone cross, from the design of Cavalini (sic), afterwards replaced the wooden one." Now Cavallini was born in 1279, and according to the accounts, by her executors, of Queen Eleanor's expenses, the process of building had already begun in 1291—in fact it occupied the three years up to 1294. So that Pietro Cavallini must have been but twelve years of age when he was entrusted with such an important commission, and one cannot think that they humoured the infant prodigy in those days as we do now, even allowing for the fact that the original cross was, compared with Barry's design, of a crude character, with no especial richness discernible in the ornamental parts.[2]

When the Puritan tyranny, represented by the Long Parliament and a Roundhead mob of fanatics, abolished the cross in 1647, its appetite had already been whetted for destruction by the demolition of the Westminster Clock-house, four years previously,[3] the sign of the " Golden Cross " which distinguished the tavern of that name, and of the Cheapside Cross in the same year as the " Golden Cross " sign, namely 1643. There is an amusing ballad entitled " The Downfall of Charing Cross," which the music antiquary, Dr. Rimbault, says is printed with the music for three voices by " Mr. F. Farmeloe," in " The Second Book of the Pleasant Musical Companion," 1687 :

[1] J. Abel's *Memorials of Queen Eleanor*, 1864.

[2] That is, judging from a likeness of it which appears in Aggas's map of Queen Elizabeth's time. Prints of both the old and the modern cross may be seen in the *Hartridge Collection* (Guildhall Library), vol. xxxv.

[3] Strickland's *Queens of England*. This was the first clock in England to be set up in a clock tower, which was opposite to Westminster Palace. *Ibid.*, 1840, vol. ii. p. 197. Ned Ward alludes to it.

Undone, undone, the lawyers are,
    They wander about the towne,
Nor can find the way to Westminster,
    Now Charing Cross is downe :
At the end of the Strand they make a stand,
    Swearing they are at a loss,
And chaffing say, that's not the way,
    They must go by Charing-cross.

The parliament to vote it down
    Conceived it very fitting,
For fear it should fall and kill them all,
    In the house, as they were sitting.
They were told, god-wot, it had a plot,
    Which made them so hard-hearted,
To give command, it should not stand,
    But be taken down and carted.

Men talk of plots, this might have been worse
    For anything I know,
Than that Tomkins, and Chaloner,
    Were hang'd for long agoe.[1]
Our parliament did that prevent,
    And wisely them defended,
For plots they will discover still,
    Before they were intended.

But neither man, woman, nor child,
    Will say, I'm confident,
They ever heard it speak one word
    Against the parliament.
An informer swore, it letters bore,
    Or else it had been freed ;
I'll take, in troth, my Bible oath,
    It could neither write nor read.

The committee said, that verily
    To popery it was bent ;
For ought I know, it might be so,
    For to church it never went.
What with excise, and such device,
    The kingdom doth begin
To think you'll leave them ne'er a cross,
    Without doors nor within.

---

[1] For their share in Waller's plot to surprise the City. Tomkins, however, was not hanged at Charing Cross, but at the Holborn end of Fetter Lane, near his own house in Holborn, while Chaloner was hanged also by his own house in Cornhill, by the Royal Exchange. (Allen's *London*, 1827, vol. i. p. 365.)

Methinks the common-council shou'd
    Of it have taken pity,
'Cause, good old cross, it always stood
    So firmly to the city.
Since crosses you so much disdain,
    Faith, if I were as you,
For fear the King should rule again
    I'd pull down Tiburn too.[1]

Speed thus sums up the character of Queen Eleanor: "To our Nation she was a loving mother, and (saith Walsingham) the columne and pillar as it were of the whole Realme. In her honour the King her husband (who loved her above all worldly creatures) caused these many famous trophies or crosses to be erected, wheresoever her noble Coarse did rest, as it was conveyed from Lincolnshire to buriall in Westminster. Nor could anything but the respect to other weightie matters, now presently in hand, withhold our pen from paying to her memory a far more copious commendation. . . . She was a godly and modest princess, full of pity, and one that shewed much favour to the English nation, ready to relieve every man's grief that sustained wrong, and to make them friends that were at discord."[2] But although historians have done her full justice in this respect, the tongue of slander will run on pattens in the presence of even the noblest virtues, and the flawless character of Eleanor was assailed in a popular ballad entitled "A warning against Pride, being the Fall of Queen Eleanora, Wife to Edward I. of England," who for her pride sank into the earth at Queenhithe, and rose again at Charing Cross, after killing the Lady Mayoress. The ballad-writer, says Miss Agnes Strickland, had evidently found some faint traces of the quarrels between the City of London and Eleanor of Provence, Eleanor of Castile's mother-in-law, regarding Queenhithe, and confounded her with the latter through her name being associated with Charing Cross.

THE KING CHARLES STATUE.

The statue of the eminently virtuous monarch Charles I., which occupies the site of the old Eleanor Cross, commemorates a good if not an especially wise man, whose high theoretical notions of

---

[1] Percy's *Reliques of Ancient Poetry*, ed. by H. B. Wheatley, 1886, vol. ii. p. 323.

[2] Speed's *History of Great Britain*, 1632, bk. ix. ch. 10, p. 635.

kingly prerogative were, however, but such as had been fondly held by predecessors on the throne as good as, though perhaps greater than, himself. And a characteristic of these predecessors was certainly not, any more than in Charles's case, a philosophical appreciation of the rights as well as the duties of the people. It was not considered necessary, even in the case of such a worthless monarch as King John, to cut his head off to secure Magna Charta, and one has reason to know that many a foreign revolutionary points to England, and to the murder of the most amiable of the Stuarts, for a precedent as to the necessity for such violence in the attainment of representative government.

Divided as opinion may be as to the artistic merits of Hubert le Sœur's effort in equestrian statuary, there can hardly be two opinions as to the famous landmark it has become in occupying the spot upon which stood the cross—a monument the name of which is destined, as it passes from the lips of one generation to another, to perpetuate the memory of Queen Eleanor apparently for all time.

And now in its place, more liable to impairment, it is true, than a good name of either king or queen, stands the almost imperishable statue of the First Charles, looking towards the very spot where :

> While round the armèd bands
> Did clap their bloody hands,
> He nothing common did, or mean,
> Upon that memorable scene ;
> But with his keener eye
> The axe's edge did try :
> Nor call'd the Gods with vulgar spight
> To vindicate his helpless right,
> But bow'd his comely head
> Down, as upon a bed.[1]

There appears to have been an equestrian statue of George I. put up in Hanover Square soon after the laying out of the " street " as it was called about the year 1719.[2] Whether the Pitt statue superseded it and what became of it one cannot say. It could hardly have been identical with that by Van Nost in Grosvenor Square. It was, however, the subject of an amusing Jacobite broadside, entitled—

---

[1] Marvell.

[2] In the St. Martin's Rate-books it is called Hanover-square-street in honour of the reigning King George I.

A Dialogue between the Old Black Horse at Charing Cross, and the New One, with a Figure on it in H—— Square.

I.

In London late happen'd a pleasant discourse,
Twixt an Old English Nagg and a Ha—— er Horse
No wonder my Friends, if plain English they speak,
For in (old) Æsops time, Horses spoke Heathen Greek.
Derry Derry down.

II.

King Charles's black Nagg being tir'd of the Town,
From fair Charing Cross, one fine Evening stole down,
And trotting along t'wards the Fields for fresh Air,
He Spy'd a strange Beast up in H——er Square.
Derry, &c.

III.

Marching up, he most Civilly greeted the Steed,
But soon found, he was not of true English breed,
And the Rider he thought, a much more Aukward thing,
For he look't like a Lout, and was dress'd like a King.
Derry, &c.

IV.

The Charing Cross Nagg, thus began ; Brother Pad,
Tis enough sure to make any mortal Horse mad,
To see such a Rider bestride a poor Horse,
Were you Hag-ridden, sure you'd scarce be rid worse.
Derry, &c.

V.

Quoth the poor harmless beast, my hard Lot I must bear,
And I but the Lot of these Three Kingdoms share ;
For this Wretch on my Back has a Proverb on's side
Set a Begger on Horse back, to the D——l he'll ride.
Derry, &c.

VI.

You seem to have brought him Sr. many a long Mile
But *Englishmen* sure, will ne're think it worth while ;
For this Creature to rule them, to send very far,
When my good Old Master, they never would bear.
Derry, &c.

VII.

We came from a poor little Town call'd Ha——er,
But Oh ! had you seen us before we came over,
You'd say times mend with me, and this stupid Thief,
Since, I've eat good Oats, and his Worship good Beef.
Derry, &c.

VIII.

H——er ! O Pox, I remember that Name,
His Grandsire I think was King at Boheme,
My good natur'd Master, poor Man was undone,
By helping that Beggarly House to a Throne.

Derry, &c.

IX.

To a throne they were mounted, then as they desir'd
But all the whole Crew of them fairly retyr'd,
And tho' these poor Palatines, seem settled here,
Their Grand-fathers Fortune, 'tis hop'd they may share.

Derry, &c.

X.

Says Charles's Black-Nagg, be ruled by me,
To Tyburn you now, being in the right Way,
Then carry him thither, and there let him Swing,
Or else pack him home, like a Dog on a string.

Derry, &c.

XI.

Put on his Bob-Wigg, Piss-burnt with the Weathe
And his Grogerum Coat, in which he came hither,
With his Hoe in his hand, he will look very smart,
And so drive him back in an old Turnip Cart.

Derry, &c.

XII.

From fam'd *Charing-Cross*, they wou'd fain have me down,
In room of a *Hero*, they'd put up a Clown ;
But still my old Master, I hope, will me stride,
When the *Devil* away with that Cuckold does ride.

Derry, &c.

XIII.

So saying, in Wrath he march'd back to his station,
And left this advice, for the good of the Nation,
Since this H——er beast you'll not find worth your care
Let him go to Grass, and the man have his Mare.

FINIS.

In considering an unjust aspersion on the symmetry and proportions of the animal which the statuary has appropriated to Charles
—namely, that of its resemblance to a dray-horse—it should be
remembered that in those days the statuary and the painter mounted
their subjects upon a charger, and a charger of the prevailing breed,
which was closely related to the dray-horse, as is now also the undertaker's horse and that of the Household Cavalry. Youatt, in his

book on the horse, says that the horses of the household troops are not so large and so heavy, probably, as formerly. It would be an equally cheap and unfair criticism to call it an "undertaker's" as a "dray" horse. Hubert le Sœur's production was the first equestrian statue ever erected in Great Britain. At the Restoration it was re-erected on its present pedestal, the design for which is said, with some uncertainty, however, to have been the work of Grinling Gibbons, a circumstance perhaps as little known as that the pedestal of James II.'s statue, now erected in front of the Admiralty, is another reputed example of Gibbons's designing powers.[1] The Charing Cross pedestal is 17 feet high, and enriched with the arms of England, trophies, cupids, palm-branches, &c. Hypercritical persons affect to have discovered that the horse is without a girth, but anyone who will take the trouble to look carefully will find that there is a girth passing over a very strong rein on the right of the animal.[2] The king's sword, however, with buckler and straps, disappeared mysteriously from the statue on the night of April 13, 1810.[3] Few people are aware, too, that the George pendant from the ribbon has vanished. The hole in the ribbon whence the decoration hung may be seen if the part be closely scrutinised, and on the left forefoot of the horse—though it cannot be seen unless one is in an elevated position—is the inscription of the sculptor, thus :

HVBER(T) LESVER

(FE)CIT * 1633 (? or 1638)

I believe, too, that a close scrutiny of the half-closed right hand will show that it formerly grasped a bâton.

The statue measures 7 feet 8 inches from the foot to the top of

---

[1] The statue itself, in bronze, is known to be by him. Gibbons was also responsible for the pedestal of Charles II.'s statue at Windsor, the statues of Charles II. at the Royal Exchange and at Chelsea Hospital. Gibbons employed numerous carvers to carry out his designs. The pedestal of the Charing Cross, although believed to have been designed by him, was executed in marble by Joshua Marshall.—*Dict. Nat. Biog.*

[2] J. T. Smith's *Streets of London.*

[3] This was when scaffolding was erected on some public occasion. See also Viscount Dillon on "Charles I.'s Statue at Charing Cross" (The *Middlesex and Hertfordshire Notes and Queries*, 1898, vol. iv. pp. 1–4, with a superb illustration of the statue). It is stated in the *Gentleman's Magazine*, April 1810 (p. 377, col. ii.), that they were picked up by a porter of the name of Moxam, at the "Golden Cross," and deposited in the care of Mr. Eyre, trunkmaker, who apprised the Board of Green Cloth of the circumstance. The sword and appendages were of copper, of which metal the statue is formed.

the horse's head ; 9 feet 2½ inches from the plinth to the top of the figure ; 6 feet from the plinth to the neck of the horse ; 5 feet 10 inches is the height from the plinth to the top of the hind quarters ; it is 7 feet 9 inches from head to tail ; 8 feet 2 inches is the circumference of the horse measured from the back of the saddle-cloth, and 16 feet is the measurement of the horse round the chest and hind quarters.

In the winter of 1855–6, Sir G. G. Scott repaired the pedestal, and found that fractures in the black marble slab had been pieced with Portland stone. The fastenings of three feet of the horse had also become insecure owing to the strain caused by the attitude of the horse. Scott inserted a copper chain round the stones of the cornice below a new and thicker slab of granite, securing the latter to the pedestal and the horse's feet to the slab with copper bolts.[1]

Probably while Le Sœur was modelling his famous masterpiece in the narrow purlieus of Bartholomew Close he had little thought of becoming the object of that sincere form of flattery which imitation bespeaks. On June 15, 1719, a warrant was issued at the request of the Lord Mayor and magistrates of Dublin, giving leave to Mr. John Hoest, statuary, to take a model of the horse at Charing Cross, with the intention of placing his Majesty, presumably George I., on horseback in their city.[2]

The taking of the cast of the pedestal and statue by Mr. Brucciani for the Sculpture Court at the Crystal Palace, Sydenham, as one of the illustrative examples of seventeenth-century sculpture, and as companion to Marcus Aurelius, required three tons of plaster and ten cwts. of iron. It was calculated that in making the moulds and cast, and erecting the latter, twenty-two tons of plaster and fifteen tons of iron were used.

When the statue was rehabilitated in its original situation after its brief sojourn in the backyard of Revett, the brazier, Edmund Waller, the poet, produced the following lines, in reference to the circumstance :

That the First Charles does here in triumph ride :
See his son reign, where he a martyr died ;
And people pay that reverence as they pass
(Which then he wanted !) to the sacred brass ;
Is not the effect of gratitude alone,
To which we owe the statue and the stone.

---

[1] *Builder*, Jan. 7, 1905.
[2] *Home Counties Magazine*, 1899, vol. i. p. 84.

But heaven this lasting monument has wrought,
That mortals may eternally be taught,
Rebellion, though successful, is but vain ;
And kings, so killed, rise conquerors again.
This truth the royal image does proclaim,
Loud as the trumpet of surviving fame.[1]

The statue was rendered more picturesque in its associations in the old days by reason of its being so well known as a landmark. Indeed it served all the purposes of a signboard. At Harrison's warehouse " Against the King on Horseback " were to be had men's morning gowns made of the following silks :

" Rich Brocaded Silks	Thread Sattins
Rich Damasks	Scotch Plods
Half-Yard ditto	Callimancoes
Flower'd Sattins	Flowered Russels
Lutestrings	Norwich Russels
Turkey Mantuas	Norwich Crapes

Banyan Gowns after the newest Fashion."[2]

It does not seem to be known what has become of a curious statue in fine marble which workmen discovered in 1729, while making a new sewer at Charing Cross. The workmanship was said to be "surprisingly beautiful . . . and was generally said to be St. Sebastian tied to a tree, who was shot to death by arrows. The dying passions expressed by distorted muscles and agonizing pangs are beautifully fine, and it is looked upon as a very great curiosity."[3] "St. Swithin" points out, however, in "Notes and Queries," that the Saint was not "shot to death by arrows," but that he survived the attack of the bowmen, and was actually convalescent when he was beaten to death with clubs.[4]

"The Oldest State Lottery Office" had business at Charing Cross, "behind the King on Horseback," in 1756. "Behind," "over against," and "facing" the King on Horseback are directions constantly encountered in old newspapers. The widow Cressett "facing the King on Horseback" dwelt at the "Two Golden Sugar Loaves," and has the following notice : "By Order of the Master of

---

[1] Waller's *Poems*, 1792 (*Epigrams*, etc.), p. 496.

[2] *Craftsman*, August 24, 1728.

[3] *St. James's Evening Post*, July 19, 1729, ; and *Notes and Queries*, Dec. 3, 1904, p. 448.

[4] *Notes and Queries*, Dec. 24, 1904, p. 518.

the Bath and Pumper and also of the Master of the Hot Well of the Bristol Waters, that she hath them fresh every Wednesday and Saturday. She also sells the true German Spaw and all other Mineral Waters."[1] It was also the rendezvous for the unemployed before Sir Robert Peel's days, and here was a stand for the sedan chairs. In a coloured drawing of about 1740, a sedan rests on the pavement surrounding the statue, and country-looking carts stand around with horses attached, which feed from receptacles provided with fodder. The statue must have been a serious obstacle in the way of traffic during the darkness, and it was not till the year 1767 that lamps were affixed to the railings. A memorandum dated Monday, February 5, 1767, says: "The Board of Works having given orders for six globe lamps to be fixed on the irons round the statue of King Charles I. at Charing Cross, for the safety of carriages, they were lighted up last night for the first time." A drawing in the Crace Collection represents a countryman standing by the statue, and a cockney says to him, "You have been standing here a long while, my lad; whom are you waiting for?" To which the countryman replies, "I ha' gotten a Letter for one Charles Stuart, and they tell I thic be he, so I be waiting for'n till he gets off his Horse." A similar story is told of Tony Lumpkin in connection with the Golden Cross Inn.

On July 3, 1810, a small loaf, fastened by a string, was suspended from the statue, to which was attached a placard, stating that it was purchased from a baker, and was extremely deficient in weight, being one of a numerous batch. The notice concluded by simply observing, "Does this not deserve the *aid* of parliament?" This exhibition attracted a great crowd of people, until the whole of the loaf was nearly washed away by subsequent heavy rain.

When James Elmes wrote his valuable contribution to London topography entitled "Metropolitan Improvements," in 1827, a pump[2] stood at the south side of the pavement surrounding the statue, and an old woman has come for a pail of water. The old oil-lamps, which rendered the darkness more visible, have disappeared, and two tall gas-lamps have taken their place.

---

[1] See Mr. F. G. Hilton Price in *Middlesex and Hertfordshire Notes and Queries*, 1897, p. 199.

[2] There was a Pump Court, Charing Cross, in the eighteenth century. See *Environs of London*, 1761, vol. v. p. 173. This, however, may have been so named after another of the several pumps in the neighbourhood. There is one still in working order in the basement of No. 119 Pall Mall, S.W., which Mr. Dixon Gibbs, the very old-established tea-dealer, informs me is supplied from a spring at the back.

" Over against the Watch House, Charing Cross," was the " Unicorn," the sign of Thomas Bant at the " White Periwig." [1] This watch·house—the " favourite resort of the Georgian nobility and gentry," as Mr. Austin Dobson describes it—was " not far from the turnpike " at the end of St. Martin's Lane.[2]

THE PILLORY.

Public opinion, in spite of the partiality of the populace towards it in the cruel sport which its victims afforded, began, though tardily, to be strongly antagonistic to the pillory as a means of punishment. But it was not abolished until so late as 1837, when it was found that the " babes in the wood " were not infrequently, when unpopular, pelted to death. It is well known, on the other hand, how Daniel Defoe's lot was an exception, how the pillory was hung with garlands, and how his health was drunk by the sympathising mob. There were many popular terms for this instrument of torture, among which was that of a " pair of spectacles." " These are to give notice that Peter Pinch, baker, dwelling in Light-loaf Lane, intends, at the next sessions, to sell his share in a pair of spectacles, which are made of substantial two-inch board, not to be worn upon the nose, but the neck and wrists, through which a man may clearly see his faults, and his enemies, and be made feelingly sensible of the swift flight of goslings, ducklings, and chickens, while they are yet in the cloister of the egg-shell ; they are fit for all ages from 18 to 60, and teach such as use them the most difficult distinction between good and evil." [3]

If they do some things better in France, the abolition of the pillory in that country in 1832, five years before it was suppressed by statute in Britain, was one of them. The Paris pillory, however, was a more complex affair. It stood in the middle of a round tower with openings on every side, and was movable on an axis, or arbor, round which the executioner gave the criminal the number of turns appointed in court, stopping him at each opening to show him to the people. It was intended for several kinds of criminals, particularly for fraudulent bankrupts, and all those who made a cession or surrender of their effects to their creditors were obliged

[1] *Middlesex and Hertfordshire Notes and Queries*, vol. iii. pp. 196–9.
[2] *A Paladin of Philanthropy*, by Austin Dobson, 1899, p. 314.
[3] *Poor Robin's Intelligencer*, 1675.

to take some turns round the pillory on foot, with a green cap on.[1] With us the pillory consisted of a wooden frame or screen, raised several feet from the ground, behind which the culprit stood, supported on a platform, his head and hands being thrust through holes in the screen so as to be exposed in front. The exposure the sufferers endured at the hands of a volatile and unreasoning mob was often of the cruellest character. The punishment has been in use in most countries in Europe, and it may be supposed that it was introduced into this country by the Romans, *collistrigium*, however (as if from *collum stringens*), being but a pseudo-Latin form, apparently, for the contrivance used by the Romans was known as a *columbar*, from a resemblance of the apertures to the holes in a dovecot (*columbarium*). It was employed for the punishment of slaves, and in all probability resembled the " wooden collar " of the Chinese, as represented by a drawing in Staunton's " China." The pillory at Charing Cross, as elsewhere in England, seems to have. been intended especially for the correction of fraudulent butchers, poulterers, bakers, perjurers, and libellers. By a statute, 51 Hen. III., A.D. 1266, dishonest bakers are to be suspended by the *collistrigium*, or stretch-neck. Representative and numerous instances of the crimes thus punishable will be found in Riley's " Memorials of London Life in the Thirteenth, Fourteenth, and Fifteenth Centuries." Defoe stood in the pillory at Charing Cross on the 29th, 30th, and 31st of July, 1703. The people formed a guard, covered the pillory with flowers, and drank the author of " Robinson Crusoe's " health. His " Hymn to the Pillory," which was sold among the crowd in large numbers, may be seen in any complete edition of his works, notably Nimmo's. His biographer in the " Dictionary of National Biography " calls attention to the fine lines :

> Tell them the men that placed him here
> Are scandals to the times ;
> Are at a loss to find his guilt,
> And can't commit his crimes.

The last person who stood in the pillory in London was Peter James Bossy, for perjury, not however at Charing Cross, but in the Old Bailey, on June 22, 1830. Edmund Curll, the notorious book-seller, was pilloried at Charing Cross for selling obscene books. He was first tossed in a blanket by the boys of Westminster. A

---

[1] Several illustrations of the different forms of the pillory may be seen in Douce's *Illustrations of Shakespeare.*

school oration on Dr. South was pirated by Curll in 1716, and printed with false Latin. The boys accordingly invited him to the school to get a corrected copy. Falling into the trap, he was first whipped, and then tossed in a blanket or rug.[1] Another delinquent, Parsons, the author of the well-known imposition, the " Cock Lane Ghost," was exposed in the Charing Cross pillory.

In 1730, or thereabouts, Thomas Hayes, commander of a merchantman, stood on the pillory at Charing Cross from the hour of twelve to one, when a surgeon, attended by the proper officer, got upon the pillory, where the victim sat in a chair, and the surgeon with an incision knife cut his left ear off, delivering it to Hayes with his own hands. Then the officer took it from him, and held it up between finger and thumb to the view of the spectators. This was pursuant to a sentence at the Court of King's Bench, for forging a bond of £560 upon Mr. Edmond Longbotham, also formerly commander of a merchantman. He was a plain elderly man with grey hair, and was not pelted by the populace, which was very numerous. The situation of the pillory close to the statue is shown in a coloured print in the Crace Collection.

A farcical course of pillory punishment was undergone at Charing Cross when the political writer, Dr. Shebbeare, launched upon an appreciative public his " Sixth Letter to the People of England." Although orders had been given for his arrest on the appearance of the " Third Letter," it was not till the "Sixth" that he was taken into custody. The leading idea of these " Letters " was the then not unpopular one, that the grandeur of France and the misfortunes of England were wholly attributable to the undue influence of Hanover in the British council-chamber. And in allusion to the White Horse being the armorial ensign of the House of Hanover, Shebbeare's motto prefixed to his " Letters " was the well-known verse from the Apocalypse—" And I looked and beheld a pale horse ; and his name that sat upon him was Death, and Hell followed." The headstrong doctor, however, had too many eggs in his basket, and being tried for libel, was convicted, and sentenced to pay a fine of £5, be imprisoned for three years, and to stand in the pillory. The last part of his sentence was not altogether a success from the Crown's point of view, for the under sheriff at the time, a Mr. Beardmore, happened to be of exactly the same political opinions as Shebbeare. The consequence of this was that the latter was taken to Charing Cross in a state coach and was merely placed beside the pillory, not in it,

[1] See also the " Ship " tavern, Charing Cross.

with an Irish chairman acting as footman, clothed in appropriate livery, and holding an umbrella over the delinquent.[1]

I do not know why it was omitted at the accession to the throne of King Edward VII., but royal proclamations were customarily made at Charing Cross, serving presumably for Westminster. I think I am right in saying that Charing Cross, too, besides its historic associations with the cross and the statue, is the most elevated spot in Westminster. In the " Times " of January 24, 1901, it is stated that " no proclamation is to be made either at Charing Cross or at Wood Street." Temple Bar and the Royal Exchange were the only two spots chosen on that august occasion. The late Queen Victoria, however, was proclaimed at Charing Cross, in Chancery Lane, in Wood Street, Cheapside—on the spot where the cross formerly stood, and at the Royal Exchange. The procession for the purpose, having passed the north side of the statue of King Charles I., halted opposite Northumberland House, when the heralds, being uncovered, proclaimed Her Majesty Queen Victoria, who would have been proclaimed Alexandrine Victoria, but that the first name was omitted by accident in her signature.[2] Here, according to W. H. Pyne in one of his gossiping books, Hogarth stood at a window of the Golden Cross, making sketches of the heralds and the sergeant-trumpeter's band, and the Yeoman Guard, who rendezvoused at Charing Cross, purposing to make a picture of the ceremony of proclaiming George III. king; nothing, however, came of it but an inflammatory cold which the artist contracted. When Lord North resigned, and Fox formed a Whig ministry which declared America independent, peace was proclaimed at Charing Cross in 1783, and again in 1802 the proclamation of peace was read on this spot by the Norroy King-at-Arms, when the definitive treaty known as the Peace of Amiens was subscribed on March 27 in that year by the Marquis of Cornwallis for England.

On the failure of Czar Nicholas's attempt to add Turkey to his dominions as he had annexed Poland, and the close of the Russian war to which it led, peace was again proclaimed at Charing Cross on May 10, 1856.

Near the statue of Charles I., but the exact spot in the Strand is not known, Peter the Great was one day walking with the Marquis of Carmarthen, who had been selected to be his *cicerone*, when a porter,

[1] See Lemprière's *Universal Biography*, and Chambers's *Book of Days*, vol. ii. p. 661.

[2] Wm. J. Thoms, *Book of the Court*, 1844, p. 59.

bearing a heavy weight upon his back, pushed against His Majesty with so much violence as to overturn the Czar of All the Russias in the kennel. In the highest degree irritated, the Czar, immediately he recovered his legs, made a rush for the offender, with the intention of striking him. Lord Carmarthen, however, apprehending that in a pugilistic encounter the porter would in all probability have the advantage, interfered with so much promptitude as to prevent further hostilities. Turning angrily to the porter, "Do you know," said the Marquis, "that this is the Czar?" Whereupon the man's countenance lighted up with an impudent grin : "Czar !" he said, " we're all Czars here." [1]

In 1685–6, William Penn, the great legislator of Pennsylvania, dated his letters from "Charing Cross." Penn dwelt in Norfolk Street, Strand, but whether he considered this "Charing Cross," as is quite possible however, one cannot say. Peter the Great lived in Buckingham Street, which was of course, as now, much nearer Charing Cross.

Around the time-honoured statue converged a varied assortment of street-vendors. Whether Lord Beaconsfield ever really expressed any partiality for the primrose above other flowers I do not know, but certain it is that the street-cry "Primroses, two bunches a penny," was heard in the neighbourhood of the "Horse" long before Benjamin Disraeli was of an age at which he could look back on his teens.[2] Mingled with the flower-seller's cry was that of the match-seller :—

> I cry my matches at Charing Cross,
> Where sits a black man upon a black horse ;

and from a sturdier throat came the familiar invitation, "Clean yer honour's shoes !"

> Go, thrive : at some frequented corner stand ;
> This brush I give thee, grasp it in thy hand ;
> Temper the foot within this vase of oil,
> And let the little tripod aid thy toil ;
> On this methinks I see the walking crew,
> At thy request, support the miry shoe ;
> The foot grows black that was with dirt embrowned,
> And in thy pocket jingling halfpence sound.
> The goddess plunges swift beneath the flood,
> And dashes all around her showers of mud :

---

[1] Jesse's *London and its Celebrities*, 1901, vol. iii. p. 78.
[2] See *Ackermann's Repository*, circa 1823.

> The youth straight chose his post ; the labour ply'd
> Where branching streets from Charing Cross divide ;
> His treble voice resounds along the Mews ;
> And Whitehall echoes—" Clean your Honour's shoes ! "[1]

But the street-cries would suddenly cease, and the shoe-cleaner would pick up his three-legged stool or cricket,[2] which served the purpose of his modern box-block, and hasten towards the quarter whence were heard the nasal accents of Punchinello, or the sound of his horn, and his Pandean pipes.

The earliest authentic references to Punchinello occur in the overseer's books of St. Martin's-in-the-Fields. Charing Cross, in-deed, seems to have been the first part of London which echoed with the nasal drolleries of the hardened old wife-beater. In the books alluded to for the years 1666 and 1667 there are four entries relating to Punchinello, " Y\ :c Italian popet player," who paid in one instance as much as £2. 12s. 6d. for his booth at Charing Cross, but what length of time this charge covered is not clear. With the waning of out-door amusements, however, Punch may be seen in the vanishing crowd, though fighting his ground inch by inch, and naughty boys no longer spend the money, like Jem Trifle's friend, on Punch and Judy, that had been entrusted to him to buy a new pair of shoes with, " and when he got in the crowd he lost his money," a whole five-shillings. But the wanton course of Punch is nearing its end, following hard on the heels, with "Guy Fawkes" and "Please remember the Grotto," of the Maypole and Jack-in-the-Green.

> Thou *lignum-vitæ* Roscius, who
> Dost the old vagrant stage renew,
>   Peerless, inimitable Punchinello !
> The queen of smiles is quite undone
> By thee, all glorious king of fun,
>   Thou grinning, giggling, laugh-extorting fellow.[3]

According to Gallani, in his "Vocabolario del Dialetto Napole-tano," "Punchinello" was derived from Puccio d'Aniello, a peasant, whose humorous eccentricities were, in the seventeenth century,

---

[1] Gay's *Trivia*, Bk. ii.

[2] The streets of London were over-run with the shoe-black boys. They carried, in addition to a small stool under the arm, a tin pail with slippers, brushes, and blacking.

[3] Quoted, with several other verses, in the *Mirror*, vol. iii. p. 364, from the *New Monthly Magazine*.

transferred to the Neapolitan stage, where he has continued to be the medium of local and political satire, and a favourite conventional character in the Italian exhibitions of *fantoccini*, or puppet-shows. The " business " card of one of the latest exponents of the reckless liar and profligate, whose one redeeming point was that he was anything but hypocritical, read in 1870 :

" Professor Manley and Brewer [*sic*]. Proprietors of the Royal Punch and Judy, Late of the Crystal Palace and Forrester's Fêtes. Private Parties and Schools punctually attended. Address—Royal George, Tower Street, Westminster Road, S." I am informed by " Professor " Davis, who earns a living that can only be called precarious, in the West End, that there are but six Punch and Judy men, all told, in London, and they are thus located (this was in the year of grace 1904) : One at Poplar, one at Kennington, one in Marylebone, one in Curtain Road, Shoreditch, one in Notting Hill, and another in Portobello Road. Poor Punch ! There is a touch of sadness perceptible in his conversation, the reflex doubtless of great hardships, which is certainly not discernible in the wicked jovial character he personates. Even as one was speaking to him in Sackville Street after the curtain was down, a "gentleman " emerged from a fine house under whose windows the performance had taken place, and with quite unnecessary heat—for this Punch is an amiable, quiet-spoken man—ordered him away. When Mayhew wrote his " London Labour and London Poor," about 1850, there were eight Punch showmen in London, or, counting two men to each frame, sixteen.

CHAPTER VI.

CRAVEN STREET.

THE Rate-books of St. Martin's-in-the-Fields reveal the fact of Craven Street having been known, until 1742, as Spur Alley. The old "Globe" tavern, a favourite meeting-place for the parishioners and vestries of the parishes of Westminster for the regulation of parish affairs, appears to have stood at the corner of Craven Street, Strand, part of the site being now occupied by the Craven Hotel, 44 and 46 Craven Street.[1] It was evidently next door to this "Globe" that a Mr. Campbell established the banking business which was afterwards known by the style of Campbell and Coutts. This was in 1692 ; but when the New Exchange was pulled down in 1737 the business appears to have been removed to the premises so long occupied in the Strand up to the year 1904 ; the house on the south side of the Strand was erected by Mr. Middleton, who also, I believe, became a partner in the earlier history of the firm of Coutts & Co.

The "Globe" was not behind the other Charing Cross taverns in being a recognised "show" resort.   A most remarkable character exhibited his prowess here.   This was the "Lythophagus," or Stone-eater, an eccentric being who actually cracked flints between his teeth like nuts, and then gnawed, crunched, and reduced them to the smallest pieces.   By striking him on the stomach, the stones would resound as in a sack.   Such stones as marbles, pebbles, &c., which he was able to reduce to powder, he made up into a paste which was to him a most agreeable food.   This is, perhaps, the less surprising part of his performance, since earth or clay-eating is known to be a depraved taste among the Javanese, Sumatrans, and the Indians of Venezuela.   The gullet of the "Globe" lithophagus was very large, his teeth extremely strong, his saliva very corrosive, and his stomach lower than the ordinary human stomach.   This was an accomplishment which appears to have been, beyond doubt, a

[1] See Lysons's *Collectanea.*

scientific fact.   It is described by Father Paulin in the " Dictionnaire Physique," and Mr. Charles Boyle speaks of a private soldier very famous for digesting stones.[1]   J. O'Keefe, the Irish dramatist, wrote " The Stone-eater's Song " :

> Make room for a jolly Stone-eater,
>   For stones of all kinds I can crunch,
> A nice bit of Marble is sweeter
>   To me than a Turtle or Haunch.
> A street that's well-paved is my larder—
>   A Stone you will say is hard meat,
> But, neighbours, I think 'tis much harder,
>   Where I can get nothing to eat !
>   *Chorus :*—With my crackledy mash, ha ! ha !
>   And a jolly Stone-eater am I.
> London Bridge shall serve for a luncheon—
>   Don't fear—I won't make it a job :
> The Monument next I will munch on,
>   For fear it should fall on my nob ;
> Ye Strand folks, as I am a sinner,
>   Two nuisances I will eat up ;
> Temple Bar will make me a good dinner,
>   And then on St. Clement's I'll sup.
>
> I think, if my mind does not alter,
>   The Spaniards some trouble I'll save :
> I'll eat up the Rock of Gibraltar,
>   And still if my stomach should crave,
> I'll eat up Pitt's diamond at Paris,
>   I'm told 'tis the rarest of stones—
> If Monsieur inclin'd then for war is,
>   At Cherbourg I'll eat up the Cones.
>
> The Ostrich, Sir, I can beat hollow,
>   Though smartly he gobbles horse shoes !
> So, cut out in stone, and I'll swallow
>   An Ostrich for Michaelmas Goose !
> Though with Stones I came here to be treated,
>   Whilst Liberty Britons enjoy,
> The Rock where the Goddess is seated
>   May no Stone-eater ever destroy.
>   With my crackledy mash, ha ! ha !
>   And a jolly Stone-eater am I.[2]

In 1767 a number of subalterns of the army and mariners on half-pay assembled at the " Globe " tavern in the Strand, and deputed Lieutenant Carroll to wait on the Marquis of Granby and General

[1] See the *London Evening Post*, March 27, 1788, and print by Hollar, 1641.
[2] The *Morning Herald*, Aug. 7, 1788.

Conway to return thanks for their gracious reception of the application for an augmentation of their allowances.[1]

In 1785 the house was known as the Globe Tavern, Coffee-house and Royal Hummums, in which year, or in 1784, it was thus styled when opened by Daniel King.[2]

A Mr. Eaton, a Leicestershire gentleman staying at the "Globe" on the business of the Ashby-de-la-Zouch canal, was attacked by a gang of ruffians in Panton Street, Haymarket, and robbed, and beaten so terribly that he died before he could be conveyed to his lodging.[3]

The only mention of a landlord connected with the "Globe" that I have encountered is that of George Pack, the actor. He appeared on the stage when very young, as a singer, having received his instruction from Richard Leveridge. He left in the meridian of life to keep the "Globe" tavern at Charing Cross.[4]

In Craven Street lived Mr. Denis O'Brien, who wrote in the "Morning Post" the impassioned appeal in behalf of his distressed friend, Sheridan, then upon his death-bed, ending with "Life and succour against Westminster Abbey and a splendid funeral." O'Brien held a colonial appointment, and was employed in secret political service; but fell into the common fate of secret service men, and was at length deserted by the party whom he had actively served; he died in great distress.[5]

An incident associated with Craven Street was a remarkable marriage which Horace Walpole mentions in a letter to George Montague, of the 3rd of September, 1748. A handsome fellow named Tracy was walking in the park and overtook three girls. Having some of his acquaintance with him, they followed them. The girls, however, ran away, and the company grew tired of pursuing them, all but Tracy. He followed them to Whitehall Gate, where he gave a porter a crown to dog them. He told the pretty one she must go with him, and kept her talking till Tracy arrived, quite out of breath and exceedingly in love. He insisted on knowing where she lived, which she refused to tell him : and after much disputing went to the house of one of her companions, and Tracy with them. He there made her discover her family, that of a butterwoman in Craven Street, and engaged her to meet him the next morning in the park ;

¹ *Gentleman's Magazine*, May 18, 1767.
² *Morn. Chron. and Daily Advert.*, Jan. 8, 1785.
³ *Gentleman's Magazine*, May 15, 1793.
⁴ *Notes and Queries*, 2nd Series, vol. v. p. 235.
⁵ The *Romance of London*, by John Timbs, F.S.A.

but before night he wrote four love-letters, and in the last offered two hundred pounds a year to her, and a hundred a year to Signora la Madre. Griselda made a confidence to a staymaker's wife, who told her that the swain was certainly in love enough to marry her if she could determine to be virtuous and refuse his offers. "Ay," says she, "but if I should, and should lose him by it." However, the measures of the cabinet council were decided for virtue; and when she met Tracy the next morning in the park, she was convoyed by her sister and brother-in-law, and stuck close to the letter of her reputation. She would do nothing, she would go nowhere. At last, as an instance of prodigious compliance, she told him that if he would accept such a dinner as a butterwoman's daughter could give him he should be welcome. Away they walked to Craven Street; the mother borrowed some silver to buy a leg of mutton, and they kept the eager lover drinking till twelve at night, when with a chosen committee the faithful pair waited on the minister of Mayfair. The doctor was in bed, and swore he would not get up to marry the king, but that he had a brother over the way who perhaps would, and who did. "The mother borrowed a pair of sheets, and they consummated at her house; and the next day they went to their own palace." [1]

When the "Globe" became the "Craven," it shared with the "Standard," in Leicester Fields, the distinction of being the only tavern remaining in the parish of St. Martin's-in-the-Fields which could boast of a large room capacious enough for parochial and election feasts. This was at the beginning of the nineteenth century. The Duke of Northumberland was accustomed annually to entertain munificently at the "Craven" his fellow parishioners—the fat bucks of Chevy forming, no doubt, part of the feast, since venison was the chief article in the *menu.* "Buck" was a cant name for a club or society about the period alluded to. Hence the "Craven" was perhaps somewhat appropriately a meeting-place for the festivities held there by the "Senior Bucks' Lodge," whatever that might have been. [2] Such Lodges are described as spurious offshoots

[1] Jesse's *Memorials of London,* Nimmo, 1901.

[2] A "buck" was also a cant name for a "cuckold." See Bailey's *English Dialect Words of the 18th Century.* "BUCKS. To be sold a compleat Regalia, and other useful and ornamental Appendages of a Bucks' Lodge, in perfect Condition, which may be viewed from the Hours of Ten till One on Tuesday next, the 7th inst., by applying at the Pewter Platter, in Charles Street, Hatton Garden, where any Person wishing to become a Purchaser is requested to leave a Proposal in Writing, with Name and Address, and the Committee appointed to dispose thereof will send an Answer thereto."—*Daily Advertiser,* Jan. 4, 1794.

of the freemasons. Ten years later we read that "the famous and noble Order of Bucks held its meetings at the Thatched House Tavern, St. James's Street, but formerly they were held at the ' Sun ' in Monkwell Street." Increasing, however, in numbers and respectability, the order removed nearer the court, " for the accommodation of the nobility and gentry of which it is composed." [1]

The " Craven Arms," No. 3 Craven Court, Craven Street, Strand, was formerly the " Ship and Shovel," a change to be regretted, since the latter sign was, without doubt, reminiscent of the thirsty stevedores who took out the ballast, coal, or corn from the barges at the wharves in this part of the Thames, which received sea-borne coal, before the introduction of railways. We find the baker's " Peel " employed as a sign in a similar way.

No. 7 Craven Street has a mural tablet outside, informing the passer-by that the great Benjamin Franklin lived there, when he represented the American colonists. The house is further remarkable for having been the place of meeting for the " Society for the Relief of Persons imprisoned for Small Debts." This charitable effort had its origin in the well-meant endeavours of the Rev. Dr. Dodd, who himself was hanged at Charing Cross for a forgery by which he hoped to escape the responsibility for *large* debts.

Grinling Gibbons, the producer of so many exquisite examples of the wood-carver's art, is said to have been born in this street about the middle of the 17th century, when the thoroughfare was known as Spur Alley ; but if a statement of his sister's, among the Ashmole MSS., be more worthy of acceptance, he was born at Rotterdam. Here also dwelt the Rev. Mr. Hackman, the infatuated lover who shot Miss Reay. The story is, perhaps, not so well known as to be unworthy of repetition. " It was on the evening of the 7th of April, 1779, that a handsome well-dressed woman was seen to be about to enter her coach on emerging from Covent Garden Theatre. As she was doing so a young man in the garb of a clergyman moved abruptly towards her, fired a pistol at her head, so receiving the bullet that she fell dead on the spot. Another report showed that he had turned another on himself with suicidal intent, but without fatal effect, upon which he proceeded to beat his brains out with the butt-end, as if eager to deprive himself of life. But he was secured, and, bespattered with his own blood and with that of his victim, he was immediately carried before a magistrate. The dead body was taken to a neighbouring tavern to await a coroner's inquest.

[1] *Tavern Anecdotes*, by Christopher Brown, 1825, p. 109.

"No more romantic story broke the dull tenor of English aristocratic life in the eighteenth century. The lady was Miss Reay, well known as the mistress of the Earl of Sandwich, an elderly statesman of great ability, who conducted the whole of the naval affairs of England during the war with the American colonies. Miss Reay was of humble origin, but possessed beauty, intelligence, and an amiable character. She had borne four children to the Earl, who treated her with the greatest tenderness and affection.

" Rather more than three years before the above date, a young military officer named Hackman, in quarters at Huntingdon, was, in the course of an ordinary hospitality, invited by Lord Sandwich to Hitchinbroke, his lordship's country residence. Though the time was little more than a century before our own, it was different in some of the essentials of good taste, if not of morals ; and we learn with some little surprise that this distinguished statesman had Miss Reay established as the mistress of his house, for the reception of such society as visited him. The young man, who was of an enthusiastic temperament, fell violently in love with Miss Reay, and sought to win her affections with a view to matrimony. The poor girl, who had the grace to wish she was not what she was, opened her heart to his addresses. They corresponded, they met ; the young man was permitted to believe that the most cherished hope of his heart would be realised. To fit himself the better to maintain her as his wife, he studied for holy orders, and actually entered upon a curacy (Wiveton, in Norfolk). Miss Reay's situation became always more and more embarrassing, as the number of her children increased. Well disposed to Hackman, she was yet bound by strong ties of gratitude to Lord Sandwich. In short, she could not summon sufficient moral courage to break through her bondage. She seems to have striven to temper the violent transports of her lover, but his was not a constitution to bear with such a disappointment. His letters, afterwards published, fully show how his love for this unfortunate woman fixed itself as a morbid idea in his mind. For some weeks before the fatal day, he dwells in his letters on suicide, and cases of madmen who murdered the objects of their affections. The story of Chatterton seems to have had a fascination for him. He tells a friend, on March 20, that he did not believe he could exist without Miss Reay. He then, and for some time further, appears to have contemplated only his own death as the inevitable consequence of his blighted passion. On the morning of April 7 he was employed in reading Blair's 'Sermons,' but afterwards, having traced Miss Reay to the theatre, he went back to his lodging for a brace of pistols, which he employed in the manner described.

" The wretchedness of the unhappy man during the few days left to him on earth was extreme. He woke to a just view of his atrocious act, but only to condemn himself, and the more eagerly to long for death. After his condemnation, the following note reached him :

" ' April 17, 1779.

" ' To Mr. Hackman, in Newgate.—If the murderer of Miss Reay wishes to live, the man he has most injured will use all his interest to procure his life.'

" His answer was :

" ' Condemned Cell, Newgate, April 17, 1779.

" ' The murderer of her whom he preferred, far preferred to life, suspects the hand from which he has such an offer as he neither desires nor deserves. His wishes are for death, not for life. One wish he has : could he be pardoned in this world by the man he has most injured ? Oh, my lord, when I meet her in another world, enable me to tell her (if departed spirits are not ignorant of earthly things) that you forgive us both, and that you will be a father to her dear infants ! J. H.'

" Two days after this date Hackman expiated his offence at Tyburn.

" The surviving children of Miss Reay were well educated by their father ; and the fourth, under the name of Basil Montagu, attained the rank of Queen's Counsel, and distinguished himself by a ' Life of Bacon,' and other works." [1]

At No. 27 Craven Street, now, I think, a private hotel, lived and died James Smith, Solicitor to the Ordnance, and one of the authors of the "Rejected Addresses." Not that he lived here always, however, for he was born in the house of his father in Basinghall Street, No. 26, and afterwards lived at No. 18 Broad Street, Austin Friars, where an amusing incident happened in which he was concerned. A second James Smith came to the

[1] " The correspondence of Hackman with Miss Reay was published by Mr. Herbert Croft, under the appropriate title of *Love and Madness*. The book has become extremely rare, but the bulk of the letters are reprinted in a collection of *Criminal Trials*, 6 vols., Knight and Lacy, 1829 " (Chambers's *Book of Days*, i. 486-7).

place after he had been for many years a resident, producing so much confusion to both that the last comer waited on the author and suggested, to prevent future inconvenience, that one or other had better leave, hinting at the same time that he should like to stay. "No," said the wit, "I am James the First; you are James the Second; you must abdicate." And as James the First he was appropriately buried in the royal parish of St. Martin-in-the-Fields, having died at his Craven Street residence in 1839, on December 24. The part-author of the "Rejected Addresses" was not the only lawyer who dwelt in this street, for many others found it conveniently in the neighbourhood of Westminster Hall, before the new Palace of Justice was built at Temple Bar, a circumstance which provoked the following *jeu d'esprit* :

> In Craven Street, Strand, ten attorneys find place,
> And ten dark coal-barges are moored at its base ;
> Fly, Honesty, fly ! seek some safer retreat,
> For there's *craft* in the river, and *craft* in the street.[1]

which elicited :

> Why should Honesty fly to some safer retreat,
> From attorneys and barges, 'od rot 'em ?
> For the lawyers are *just* at the top of the street,
> And the barges are *just* at the bottom.[2]

Sir Joshua Reynolds enters in his "Note Book," January 22, 1761, an engagement with "Akenside, Craven Street."[3]

During the rage for mineral waters, those of the West Ashton Mineral Well, near Trowbridge in Wilts, discovered in the year 1731, were to be had of the sole vendor in London, Daniel Gach, druggist, at the "King's Arms" against Craven Street in the Strand : "By drinking and washing with this Water, more than 100 persons have been already cured of Wounds, from one to upwards of twenty years standing, of Scorbutical Eruptions, of sore Eyes, sore Breasts, the Leprosy, and the King's Evil.

"N.B.—Lodgings may be had at the same Place, and in the town of Trowbridge, within one Mile and a half Distance.

"The water is also sold in Bristol by Mr. Grip, Printer ; in Salisbury, by Mr. Carent and Mr. Light ; in Bath, by Mr. Horton, Apothecary, near the Abbey. No other correspondence is ye settled."[4]

---

[1] James Smith, *Comic Miscellanies*, 1841, vol. ii. p. 171.
[2] Sir George Rose.   [3] Wheatley's *Cunningham*.
[4] *London Evening Post*, May 10, 1733.

VILLIERS STREET.

It is well known that George Street, Villiers Street, Duke Street, Of Alley (about four houses down Villiers Street, on the left, going from the Strand), and Buckingham Street, preserve every word in the name and title of George Villiers, the second and last Duke of Buckingham, whose death is recorded in a brief entry in the parish register of Kirby Moorside, Yorkshire, as having occurred on April 17, 1687 : " George Vilaus, lord dooke of bookingham." If this be correct, Cunningham is wrong in giving the year in the index to his " London " as 1688. James I. conferred a part of the lordship of Kirby Moorside upon his favourite " Steenie," the first Duke. These streets occupy the site of York House, a palace of the Archbishop of York, of which a relic survives in Inigo Jones's beautiful Water-gate at the bottom of Buckingham Street,[1] and in the street name of York Buildings. Elmes, in his " Topographical Dictionary of London," is in error when he says that it was *John*, Duke of Buckingham, who gave its name to John Street, Adelphi, for this street was named after John, one of the Adelphi or " brothers " Adam, the eminent architects, a fact, one would have thought, of which a fellow architect would have been cognisant. Evelyn notes in his " Memoirs " how he " took a house in Villiers Streete, York Buildings, for the winter, having many important concernes to dispatch, and for the Education of my daughters."[2] The street was built about the year 1674. Sir Richard Steele lived here from 1721 to 1724. " In 1725," says Cunningham, " I find, in the rate-books of St. Martin's, the word ' gone ' against his name." He died in Wales in 1729.[3] One of Steele's unfortunate enterprises was associated with this part of London. Here, in York Buildings, he fitted up a sort of nursery for the stage. On one occasion he gave to some two hundred guests a sumptuous entertainment, with dramatic recitations. Addison assisted, and wrote an epilogue for the occasion, in which occur these lines of quiet humour :

> The sage, whose guests you are to-night, is known
> To watch the public weal, but not his own.

And here Steele was outwitted by his stage-carpenter refusing to drive another nail until he was paid ; when the essayist said his

---

[1] The motto of the Villierses, *Fidei coticula Crux*, which is still that, I believe, of the Earls of Jersey and Clarendon, could be seen, and possibly can still be seen, on the side of the gate which faces the street.

[2] Vol. i. p. 530 (November 17, 1683).   [3] *London Past and Present*, 1850.

friend's elocution was perfect, though he didn't like his subject much.[1] In St. Martin's Library is a water-colour drawing of the shops of Richardson, the celebrated printseller, then at the N.W. corner of Villiers Street, No. 31 Strand, now part of the forecourt of Charing Cross Railway Station.

There seems to have been a street between Villiers Street and Buckingham Street, known as Charles Court, which Elmes, in his "Topographical Dictionary," describes as being the fifth turning from Charing Cross, counting apparently from Northumberland Street. It is mentioned in the "General Evening Post" as the "next turning to Villiers Street,"[2] and in the "Stranger's Guide to London" it is said to be "by Hungerford Market. Heere is a Plying place for Watermen."[3] The latter gives a Brewer's Yard in the Strand. Perhaps this is identical with a narrow entrance-way on the west side of the railway forecourt, which is now known as Brewer's Lane. This Brewer's Lane as well as Green's Lane, "near Hungerford Market," may have derived their names from the circumstance of John *Green*, of Westminster, *brewer*, having been with three others the purchasers of York House, the site of which they, about the year 1672, converted into the present George, Duke, Villiers, and Buckingham Streets.[4] Any nobleman or gentleman who wanted his Red or Fallow Deer removed from forest, chase, park, or paddock only had to apply to Mr. Barker (occasional, not universal provider), at the Apple Tree and Bell Inn, in Brewer's Yard, near Hungerford Market, who had "the best and safest method of removing Deer : He . . . was Yeoman of the Tents and Toils, and was brought up in that Business under his Father, who enjoyed that Place under King Charles II., King James II., and King William III. to the Reign of the late Queen Anne," &c.[5] There was a " Clark's Coffee-house " in Villiers Street, in York Buildings.[6]

The Music Room in Villiers Street, perhaps the same with the " Great Room " and the " Duke's Theatre " mentioned further as in York Buildings, was almost as celebrated in its day as the Hanover Square Rooms at a later period. Among Aaron Hill's " Miscellanies "[7] is " A Prologue for the third night of Zara, when first played at the Great Musick Room in Villars Street, York Buildings," 1735. About three years previous to Mr. Garrick's appearing at the theatre

---

[1] Timbs's *Romance of London.*
[2] September 1796.   [3] 1721.   [4] Cunningham's *London.*
[5] *Weekly Journal*, January 5, 1723.
[6] *Daily Post*, February 1726.   [7] Vol. iv. p. 106.

H

in Goodman's Fields, he performed Chamont in the "Tragedy of the Orphan," at a small house called the Duke's Theatre in Villars Street, which was situated within a few doors of the bottom of the street, on the right-hand side. The play was got up by the scholars of Eton College. The ladies who were present at Garrick's professional *début* were so fascinated by his splendid powers that they offered him their purses and trinkets from the boxes.[1]

Edmund Kean, the tragedian, was uncertain in his temper, and the associates of his lower carousals were always doubtful whether he would be offended or pleased with their familiarity. Higman, a bass-singer and an acquaintance of Kean's, took a public-house in Villiers Street, Strand, and changed the sign to "Richard the Third." This house was much frequented at one time by the tragedian, who on several occasions noticed the presence of one Fuller, a ventriloquist and mimic. Kean was told that Fuller imitated him, among others, admirably, but the mimic—bearing in mind probably the story of Henderson and Garrick—always omitted the actor's portraiture when he saw the great original present. One evening, however, Kean came into the room after Fuller had begun his imitations, which were announced in a sort of concert-bill, to be of Matthews, Emery, Knight, Bannister, Young, Kemble and Kean ! The tragedian took his seat, and Fuller proceeded ; Kean tapping the table ever and anon in token of approbation. Fuller paused before he attempted the last imitation, but Kean looked approval, and he essayed. Before, however, Fuller had enunciated five lines, Kean threw a glass of wine in his face, and a scuffle ensued, in the course of which Kean said that if he thought he was such a wretch as Fuller depicted he would hang himself. [2]

Judging by the position of the famous Water-gate at the bottom, Buckingham Street may be said to occupy the centre of the site of York House where Lord Chancellor Bacon, the son of Sir Nicholas Bacon, Lord Keeper, was born in 1560–1.[3] Being in the garden one day watching the peter-boat men casting their net, as they did often very successfully in those days, he asked them what they would take for their draught. "They answered so much : his Lordship would offer them no more but so much. They drew up their nett, and in it were only two or three little fishes ; his Lordship then told them, it had been better for them to have taken his offer. They replied,

---

[1] Wheatley's *London*.   [2] Diprose's *Book of the Stage.*

[3] A fragment of the old palace is said to be still standing at No. 15, the lower portion of which is the office of the Charity Organisation Society.

they hoped to have had a better draught, but, said his Lordship, 'Hope is a good breakfast, but an ill supper.'"[1]   Samuel Pepys, the diarist, lived in this street, though the house has since been rebuilt, and is now numbered 14, the last on the west side, overlooking both the Thames and "the most perfect gem of architecture in London." Opposite Pepys's house, "in a large house at the bottom of York Buildings," lodged Peter the Great, during his famous sojourn in this country, and here he used to spend his evenings with his *cicerone* Lord Carmarthen, drinking undiluted (so it is said) hot brandy with pepper in it.   Hence, too, the Czar, in accordance with his aquatic instincts, was fond of travelling by the river.   Readers of Smollett's "Roderick Random" will be interested to know that the Water-Gate Lodge was tenanted by the Hugh Hewson who was the original of Hugh Strap, the simple, generous, and faithful friend of the ingrate hero, Random.   Hewson, for forty years, kept a hairdresser's shop in St. Martin's-in-the-Fields, and was fond of pointing out to his customers and acquaintances scenes in "Roderick Random" which had their origin, not in the author's fancy, but in actual truth. Hewson left an underlined copy of "Roderick Random," showing how far he was indebted to the genius of the Doctor, and to what extent the incidents are founded in reality.   Hewson died in 1809.   In Gilchrist's "Life of Etty" the painter, we are told that the artist's rooms looked on to a terrace (Etty's house having been No. 14 in Buckingham Street, formerly Pepys's), with a small cottage at one end, and that the keeper was a man named Hewson, supposed to be the original Strap of "Roderick Random." At No. 14 Etty dwelt from 1824 till within a few months of his death in 1849.   He first took the ground floor (afterwards occupied by Mr. Stanfield), then the top floor ; the special object of his ambition being to watch sunsets over the river, which he loved with a love like Turner's, who frequently said, "There is finer scenery on its banks than on those of any river in Italy."   Its ebb and flow, Etty used to say, was like life, and "the view from Lambeth to the Abbey not unlike Venice." In those riverside rooms artists of two generations have assembled, Fuseli, Flaxman, Holland, Constable, and Hilton—then Turner, Maclise, Dyce, Herbert, and all the newer men.[2]

It was also for the sake of chambers commanding a view of the river that David Copperfield and his aunt came and dwelt in this

---

[1] *Aubrey's Lives*, ii. 224.

[2] Gilchrist's *Life of Etty*, vol. i. p. 221.   See also Thornbury's *Haunted London*.

street. They were at the top of the house, "very near the fire-escape, with a half-blind entry, and a stone-blind pantry." Two of the most interesting features in the street are the two doorways forming the entrances to two houses now numbered 17 and 18, on the east side, near the lower or river end. No. 17 is said to have been a house built for one of the Duchesses of Newcastle. On the first floor is a good deal of panelling, a carved fireplace in the front room, and a boudoir or closet leading out of the smaller room at the back. No. 18 used to be and perhaps is still—as is the case with most houses in this street—used as offices, and has a much more elaborate door-way, with a flat coffered hood, supported on two carved brackets of excellent design. Many of the mouldings and some of the carving have been destroyed and obliterated by successive coats of paint. There is some bold ironwork on each side of the doorway, and good cast terminals to the railings. No. 19, next door, has a lamp bracket, but is not otherwise noteworthy.[1]

No. 22 Buckingham Street was the house of Power, the publisher of the "Irish Melodies," to whom Moore wrote so many letters.[2]

In Buckingham Street dwelt Dr. Potts, the inventor of the hydraulic pile-driving process and other mechanical contrivances, and here he expired on March 23, 1850. Dr. Potts belonged originally to the medical profession, but, by inclination, even from school-boy days, and while a class-fellow with Lord John Russell, the Premier at the time of his death, and the Duke of Bedford, he appears to have devoted himself to mechanical and engineering pursuits. His name, however, will be most closely associated with the ingenious process for driving piles.[3]

Humphrey Wanley, who formed a catalogue of Saxon manuscripts for Dr. Hickes's "Thesaurus of the Northern Languages," wrote from his lodgings over against the "Blew Posts" in Duke Street, York Buildings, to Sir Hans Sloane, May 6, 1707.

It is not generally known that the great Napoleon Bonaparte lodged in a house in George Street, a thoroughfare preserving the Duke's Christian name, which extends from Duke Street to the Em-bankment. Old Mr. Matthews the bookseller, of the Strand, used to relate that he remembered the Corsican ogre residing here for five weeks in 1791 or 1792, and that he occasionally took his cup of chocolate at the Northumberland Coffee-house, opposite Northumber-land House; that he there read much, and preserved a provoking

---

[1] Roland Paul's *Vanishing London*, plate vii.
[2] Wheatley's *London*.   [3] The *Builder*, April 6, 1850, p. 165.

taciturnity towards the frequenters of the coffee-room ; though his manner was stern, his deportment was that of a gentleman. Near his lodgings in the Adelphi was a place much resorted to by another ruler of France, Louis Philippe, who, between 1848 and 1850, was a frequent visitor at the Lowther Bazaar in the Strand.[1]

We are left in uncertainty as to where the Long Room in York Buildings was, since " York Buildings " was a general name for the streets and houses erected on the site of York House, but it was perhaps identical with what was known as the Duke's Theatre in Villiers Street, York Buildings (see " Villiers Street "). A benefit was given at the " Great Room," as it was then called, in York Buildings for " Mr. Gordon "—probably the professor of music at Gresham College of that name, who died in 1739. " On Monday next will be perform'd, a Consort [*sic*] of Vocal and Instrumental Music. The first Violin by Mr. Dubourg, who will likewise perform several Solo's and Sonato's. Tickets to be had at the British and Smirna Coffee-houses, and at the door, at half-a-guinea each."[2] Matthew Dubourg, the violinist and soloist referred to, was an eminent pupil of Geminiani, having led the violins for Handel when in Dublin. One night, having a solo part in a song, and a close to make *ad libitum*, he wandered about a great while, and seemed a little bewildered and uncertain of his *original* key ; but at length coming to the shake which was to terminate this long close, Handel, to the great delight of the audience and augmentation of applause, cried out loud enough to be heard in the most remote part of the theatre, " Won't you come home, Mr. Dubourg ? " or rather, to give the exact words, " You are welcome home, Mr. Dubourg " Geminiani died in Dubourg's house, aged 96.

Here, on the site of old York House, was established in the 27th of Charles II. the York Waterworks to supply the inhabitants of St. James's. In a MS. list of patents granted in the reign of Charles II. in my possession is the following :

" Water house to supply St. James's { R. vij die May con Ralph Bucknall and Ralph Waine to sett upp a Water house upon the River of Thames upon parte of the Ground belonging to Yorke house to serve the Inhabitants of St. James's with water for 99 years."

[1] The *Romance of London*.
[2] This was in 1721. See a collection of material relating to the Signs of London and the Home Counties, in the Library of St. Martin's-in-the-Fields, No. 132.

The works are described in the " Foreigner's Guide to London," 1720 ; but the Company took to purchasing estates, granting annuities, and assuring lives, and proved to be one of the bubbles of that year of wild speculation. The fire-engine ceased to be worked in 1731 ; but it was afterwards shown for several years as a curiosity. " Its working by sea-coal was attended with so much smoke, that it not only must pollute the air thereabouts, but spoil the furniture." [1]

The confused affairs of the Company, and the consequent dis-putes and lawsuits with its creditors and debtors, gave rise to a host of pamphlets and even a political novel. The last of the property was sold in 1783. However, the spirit of the York Buildings Waterworks lingered here until a later time ; for in Buckingham Street, in 1818, were " the Sea-water Baths," which were supplied by a vessel with water below Southend. [2]

The limits of these excursions eastward are reached at George Court, a court eleven doors east of Buckingham Street, and opposite Agar Street. The site of the minor structures—the courts and gardens of Durham House—was bounded on the west side by this George Court and York Buildings.

An interesting account of the Adelphi arches, extending from York Buildings under the whole of the Adelphi, will be found in " The Adelphi," by Mr. H. B. Wheatley, 1885, p. 17.

[1] *London Daily Post,* 1741.

[2] *Romance of London.* An interesting engraving by Boydell of a view of London taken off the Thames, near York Buildings, where the tower-spire arrangement of these waterworks is a conspicuous object, is exhibited (No. 53 in the catalogue) in St. Martin's Library.

CHAPTER VII.

THE GOLDEN CROSS HOTEL.

ONE of the most interesting spots in this historic neighbourhood is the Golden Cross Hotel. Not that the present house is identical exactly, in its situation, with the old inn bearing that sign, but in that it perpetuates the memory of an old hostelry the antiquity of which is probably traceable to the kind of half-way house between London and Westminster that existed here in the earliest known history of the village of Charing. The probabilities have already been pointed to of a cross—a wooden cross, it is said—having stood here before that erected to the memory of Queen Eleanor, and it is reasonable to assume that the tavern depicted in early engravings was, from its associations, distinguished by the sign of the Golden Cross. The old inn figures prominently in Canaletti's well-known view of Charing Cross in the Northumberland Collection ; but it was pulled down when the Trafalgar Square improvements took place in 1830. The purchase of the inn at the time of these improvements was by far the largest that the Commissioners had to make. It was concluded on December 28, 1827, when the extensive premises, with three houses in St. Martin's Lane and two houses and workshops in Frontier Court, were bought of George Howard and others for the sum of £30,000. The " Golden Cross " was the " Bull and Mouth " of the west, and one of the most extensive coaching centres in England, whose fame, as a writer in the year 1815 remarks, had spread from the Pillars of Hercules to the Ganges, from Nova Zembla to New Zealand, and from Siam to California.[1] It may, of course, have escaped one's notice, but in the course of a comprehensive study of the mid-eighteenth century news-sheets I do not remember having encountered an advertisement that related to coaches *regularly* departing from the " Golden Cross." A Chaise and Pair for Portsmouth is announced which

---

[1] The *Epicure's Almanack*, 1815, a curious and valuable guide to the hostels of that time.

"will set out on Monday next, or *if requir'd*, a Coach and four Horses, either on Monday or Tuesday next." [1]   In cases where they were needed only occasionally, notice was probably given to the drivers of coaches that started from the older-established coaching centres citywards.

Mr. G. Boulton of Leatherhead, described as a man of powerful understanding and considerable acquirements, and of a very kindly, hospitable disposition, was proprietor of the " Golden Cross " at the beginning of the last century.   His advertisements are of interest as showing the time occupied in the journey, and the rates to which travellers were subject.   The proprietors, Messrs. Tilt, Hicks, Baulcomb, Boulton, and Co., of the Coach from Lewes to London and from London to Lewes, "respectfully inform the public that their fares, either way, are : inside 13*s*. o*d*., outside 8*s*. 6*d*.   And that they set out from the Star and White Hart Inns, Lewes, every Morning, precisely at half-past eight, and arrive at the Golden Cross, Charing Cross, at six in the evening ; which is to the full as early as any Coach from Brighton through Cuckfield arrives in the Metropolis at this season of the year." [2]   " Died at Charing Cross, October 29, 1814, G. Boulton Esq., of Leatherhead, formerly proprietor of the Golden Cross, Charing Cross, a man of powerful understanding and considerable acquirements, and of a very kindly, hospitable disposition." [3]   The " Eclipse," in 1821, set out from the " Golden Cross " daily at 7.30 A.M., for Exeter, going by Salisbury, Blandford, Dorchester, and Bridport.   A Mr. Stratton was the proprietor of the inn in 1814.

Mr. Horne, another proprietor, and one of the largest coach-owners in England, died in the prime of life August 8, 1828.   A relative, however, must have succeeded him, for B. W. Horne and Co. are described as the proprietors, in the " Globe " of July 24, 1834, where they " respectfully inform the public that the speed of the Chester Mail has very much increased, rendering it decidedly the best conveyance to Chester (in twenty hours only), through Lichfield, Stafford, and Eccleshall, which sets out every evening at half-past seven o'clock, from the Golden Cross, leaving the Cross Keys, Wood Street, Cheapside, punctually at a quarter before eight, at very reduced fares. . . N.B.—'Liverpool Umpire,' from the above inns every afternoon (in twenty-three hours) ; only one

---

[1] *Daily Advertiser*, March 27, 1742.
[2] The *Sussex Weekly Advertiser*, Nov. 29, 1802.
[3] *Gentleman's Magazine*, Nov. 1814.

guard and one coach throughout the journey; arrives in time for the Irish Government packets." [1]   In 1833 the late Duke of Beaufort's father took a house at Brighton and had occasion frequently to run up to London to attend the House of Commons, of which he was a member.   The best coach then was the "Times," which plied between Castle Square, Brighton, and the "Golden Cross," Charing Cross.   It was driven by Goodman, a surly cross-grained fellow, who would not let the then Marquis of Worcester touch the reins. Vexed at this discourtesy, Lord Worcester repaired to a large coach proprietor in the Borough, and within a fortnight a rival to Goodman's coach was running at greatly augmented speed. [2]

"An Excellent New Ballad ; being entitled ' A Lamentation over the Golden Cross, Charing Cross,' " which is attributed to Maginn, the Irish satirical writer, bemoans the change wrought in this locality :

> No more the coaches shall I see
>   Come trundling from the yard,
> Nor hear the horn blown cheerily
>   By brandy-bibbing guard.
>
> King Charles, I think, must sorrow sore,
>   E'en were he made of stone,
> When left by all his friends of yore
>   (Like Tom Moore's rose) alone.
>
>   .   .   .   .   .
>
> O ! London won't be London long,
>   For 'twill be all pulled down ;
> And I shall sing a funeral song
>   O'er that time-honoured town.

In the days when this breathing-space for Londoners had to cater for the appetites of those whom an enthusiasm for "taking the air " had brought so far west, the tavern-keepers in the neighbourhood were, no doubt, alive to the opportunity afforded for *victualling* as well as drinking.   And although the Malt Duty may have been, as indeed Ned Ward says it was, nowhere better promoted than in the parish of St. Martin-in-the-Fields, yet the taverners were actually licensed victuallers in those days, and it is not impossible that the Carrier, in "King Henry IV.," had the "Golden Cross " in his mind's eye when he recalled a certain duty he had to perform of delivering "a gammon of bacon and two razes of ginger at Charing Cross." [3]   And, like the other surrounding pleasure resorts,

---

[1] *Globe*, July 24, 1834.   [2] *Daily Telegraph*, August 1892.
[3] Part I. Act II. sc. I.

it was at a later time an attractive spot for those who were bitten with the "Monster" and curiosity mania. In January 1742 was to be seen at the "Golden Cross" an exhibition testifying to the influence of Dean Swift's works upon the popular imagination. Dr. Johnson thought that, in "Gulliver's Travels," "that which gave most disgust must be the history of the Houyhnhnms,"[1] but fifteen years after that strange production's appearance, visitors to the "Golden Cross" were delighting in "the Houyhnhnm, or the most beautiful Harlequin Mare, foal'd on the Mountains in Wales, whose spots by far exceeded the Leopard, and, for its excellency in Make and Shape, is the greatest Curiosity of its Kind in the whole World."[2]

"To be Seen at the Sign of the Golden Cross. The Great Rhinoceros or real Unicorn, that was taken in the Great Mogul's Dominions, after a Journey of a thousand Leagues by Land to Patna, was shipp'd on board the Lyell, Capt. Acton, and brought to London in June 1740. To be seen at 1s. each.

"This extraordinary Animal is but four Years old; his Body is covered with Folds like a Coat of Mail, and scaled all over; so as to defend itself from the Injuries of all other Animals; besides a large Horn on its Nose, with which he attacks the Elephant, his sworn Enemy. Before he enters into Engagement with the Elephant he whets his Horn on a Stone, and then aims at the Elephant's Belly, knowing it to be the tenderest Part, and in this Manner destroys the Elephant. There has never been one in England since he Memory of Man. He is next in growth to the Elephant

"A great Number of the Nobility and Gentry daily resort to see him."[3]

The proprietor's repertory exhibits a remarkable *penchant* for zoological curiosities. Here he produced "The largest Horse in England (to be Sold cheap), being nineteen Hands an Inch and a half high, and every way proportionable, which has been shewn at the Golden Cross for some time past, to the general Satisfaction of the Nobility, Gentry, and others, that have had the Curiosity of beholding such a Prodigy in Nature."[4]

Another *rara avis* reputed to be seen at the "Golden Cross," but of a more phantom character, was the "Pretender." Many a Tony Lumpkin arrived fresh and raw in London, hoaxed with a letter of recommendation to Charles Stuart at the "Golden Cross," only, of course, to find his quest of an even less encouraging nature than the

---

[1] *Lives of the Poets.*   [2] *Daily Advertiser*, Jan. 2, 1742.
[3] *Daily Advertiser*, Feb. 22, 1742.   [4] *Ibid.* April 3.

"Devil's Lontun" of his own "sheer." This joke probably occupied the same shelf in the brain of the perpetrator with that of sending a poor boy to the chemist for a penn'orth of pigeon's milk, to the cobbler for strap-oil, to the bookseller's for the "Life of Eve's Grandmother," or to the Tower to see the lions washed,[1] fools' errands all sacred to the hoary custom of the First of April.

In November 1742 there was shown at the "Golden Cross" "a Wonderfull Young Man, Aged 22, who never had the use of Hands, Arms, Legs, or Feet, 4 st. 2 lbs. in weight, and 2 ft. long; as comely in the face as most men. He was received by Sir Hans Sloane, writes with his mouth much better than others pretend to with their hands. . . . He has neither Stump, nor any other instrument to perform with, and is justly esteemed the Wonder of the World. He does everything with his Mouth."[2]

It was to the "Golden Cross" that the notorious gambler and card-sharper "Captain" England was accustomed to resort. Here he was constantly on the watch for the unplucked who came to town by coach. His nefarious operations were so successful that he was able to support an "elegant" house in St. Alban's Street, where he engaged various masters to teach him the polite arts, and gained a slight knowledge of the French language. In the years 1779 to 1783 he was probably at the height of his prosperity, for he then kept a good house and table, and would give eighty or ninety guineas for a horse, a price supposed to be equal to 200 guineas at the present time. His conduct among men of rank and family, with whom he happened to associate in the way of his profession, was so polite and guarded, that he gained general respect; but he was resolute in enforcing payment of sums he had won. One evening he met a young tradesman at a house in Leicester Fields, to have an hour's diversion at "the babes in the wood,"[3] where he contrived to lose a few score pounds, for which he gave a draft upon Haulrey's; but requested to have his revenge in a few more throws, when he soon regained what he had lost, and as much in addition. Upon which, being late, he proposed for both to retire, being then past three in the morning; but the tradesman, conceiving himself tricked, refused payment of what he had lost. England then tripped up his heels, rolled him in the carpet, took a case-knife from the sideboard, which he flourished over him, and, using menacing language, at last

---

[1] See Peter Lombard in the *Church Times*, 1893.
[2] *Daily Advertiser*, Nov. 13, 1742.   [3] Dice.

cut the young citizen's long hair off close to his scalp. Dreading worse proceedings, the youth, on being allowed to regain an erect posture, gave a cheque for the amount, wished the captain a civil good morning, and although he frequently saw England subsequently he never spoke of the circumstance. At Newmarket England quarrelled with a "gentleman blackleg," whom he accused of having loaded dice always with him, and received the answer that "if he had, he knew who made them for England." England fought a duel at Cranford Bridge, June 18, 1784, with a Mr. Le Rowles, a brewer at Kingston, from whom he had won a large sum, for which a bond had been given ; and not being paid, he arrested his late friend. A duel ensued, which proved fatal to Mr. Le Rowles. England fled to Paris and was outlawed. It is said that in the early period of the Revolution he furnished some useful intelligence to our army in the campaign in Flanders, for which he was remunerated by the British Cabinet. Another of England's favourite resorts was Munday's Coffee-house in New Round Court, close by, but removed later to Maiden Lane.

In Duncannon Street, which extends from No. 449 West Strand to Trafalgar Square, may be seen the old archway through which the Pickwick coach trundled to the inn, the site of which is now partially occupied by a railway office. It was in front of the hotel or inn that Mr. Pickwick was assailed by the hackney coachman, and thereupon taken under the protection of Mr. Jingle. And when the Pickwick pilgrims set out hence on their journey it was the archway of the "Golden Cross" that elicited more disjointed remarks from Mr. Jingle. "Terrible place—dangerous work—other day—five children—mother —tall lady, eating sandwiches—forgot the arch—crash—knock— children look round—mother's head off—shocking, shocking ! Looking at Whitehall, sir ?—fine place—little window—somebody else's head off there, eh, sir ?—he didn't keep a sharp look-out enough either—eh, sir, eh ? "

Here, too, David Copperfield was introduced by the chambermaid to a bedroom that " smelt like a hackney coach, and shut up like a family vault." And anon he had a shrewd suspicion that the " half a pint of sherry that he had ordered was being concocted by the waiter, behind a partition, of the dregs from the glasses of previous imbibers. At all events it was flat, and had more English crumbs in it than David was accustomed to expect in foreign wine."

When, in 1643, puritanical bigotry was at its height, the " Golden Cross " sign was taken down as superstitious and idolatrous, " by order of the Commission or Committee appointed by the House."[1]

The Restoration of the second Charles was commemorated at Charing Cross by the sign of the "Pageant," which represented the triumphal arch erected at that place on the occasion of the entry of the King. It remained standing for one year. The house which it distinguished is evidently the same with that called by Pepys the "Triumph." It seems to have been a fashionable place, for the diarist went there on May 25, 1662, to see the Portuguese ladies of Queen Catherine. "They are not handsome," he says, "and their fardingales a strange dress. Many ladies and persons of quality came to see them. I find nothing in them that is pleasing; and I see they have learned to kiss and look freely up and down already, and I believe will soon forget the recluse practice of their own country. They complain much for lack of good water to drink." Mr. Stephen Jones, in his edition of the "Biographica Dramatica," has drawn up a list of printed descriptions of the London "Triumphs" or Lord Mayor's Shows, whence it seems that the first account of this annual exhibition known to have been published was written by George Peele for the inauguration of Sir Wolstone Dixie, Knight, on October 29, 1585, when children personified the City, Magnanimity, Loyalty, Science, the Country, and the river Thames, &c. But of the royal processions that passed by Charing Cross to Westminster before Lord Mayor Norman took to going by water, interesting accounts will be found in J. G. Nichols's "London Pageants." It seems to have been the fashion to leave the erection of these "pageants" or "triumphs," as the arches were called, to the alien merchants. At the marriage of the Prince of Brazil in Lisbon in 1729, of the twenty-four triumphal arches erected by foreigners "the English arch will be the finest, and will cost at least 20,000 crusadoes; the Hamburghers' about 15,000."[2]

---

[1] Timbs's *Curiosities of London*, 1876, p. 84.

[2] *Whitehall Evening Post*, Feb. 22, 1728–9. A crusado was a coin stamped with a cross: value, three shillings.

"Believe me, I had rather have lost my purse
Full of crusadoes."—*Othello*, iii. 4.

See the "Pageant," Beaufoy's *Tokens*, No. 304, and Boyne's *Tokens*, p. 207.

CHAPTER VIII.

ROUND COURT

CUNNINGHAM, in his invaluable " London," does not mention
New Round Court; but New Round Court, although it was
connected with Round Court by a passage-way, was quite distinct
from the latter, and there was even another distinct place at the
back of both, called the " Back of Round Court," as may be seen in
Strype's Stow.[1]   One has seen it stated somewhere that New Round
Court was so named to distinguish it from the old Round Court in
St. Martin's-le-Grand, but this hardly seems to have been the case.
In a useful little topographical work on London by W. Stow, dated
1721, *Round* Court in the Strand is described as "noted for mercers,"
and there is no mention of a *New* Round Court at that time, which
seems to have come into existence, in name if not in fact, soon after
the taking down of the New Exchange (which had itself taken the
place of the Old Exchange in the City) in 1737.   New Round
Court has long surrendered its site to Charing Cross Hospital.   It
was partly in the Bermudas and partly in Porridge Island, and was
opposite York Buildings, extending back to the present short
thoroughfare known as King William Street; but it was effaced
during the improvements which were carried out under the Strand
Improvement Act of 1829.   It had little right to be called "Round,"
however, for it had more corners than any "court" in London.   But
it is remarkable for having billeted quite an assemblage of mid-
eighteenth century booksellers, as well as dealers in fashionable
fripperies, fans, gloves, toilet wares, millinery, &c., an association to
be accounted for probably in the pulling down of the New Exchange
opposite and the consequent removal of its stall-keepers.

At the " Cicero's Head," in Round Court, the sign of Charles
Marsh, bookseller, was published " A Poetical Epistle : Humbly
inscribed to any Body."

> May none but Patriots in the Senate meet ;
> No servilé Wretch, with base, unhallow'd Feet,

---

[1] 1755. Plan of St. Martin's Parish.

Who hangs upon a Statesman for support,
Presume to tread St. Stephen's sacred Court ;
Yet have we left, as with the Jews of old,
Numbers that bow not to that Baal, Gold :
Souls full of Honour, who, like Curtius brave,
Tho' Self-devoted, would their Country save.   (P. 15.)

'The Author humbly hopes the Transition of the Measure from Lyric to Heroic, at this Line (*Rome saw, indeed, her Consuls War for Fame*) will be pardoned ; for though these Verses were begun in a joking Humour, yet he could not help growing grave, when he consider'd that Corruption was lately grown to such an height, it might in Time have destroyed the Liberties of his Country."[1] Marsh also advertises a "Catalogue of the Libraries of Mr. Mackay, Mathematician, and the Lady Kincaid, both being lately deceased," &c.[2]

The "Horace's Head" in Round Court, Strand, was the sign of Oliver Payne, brother of "honest Tom Payne," who was one of the first second-hand booksellers to issue catalogues, and succeeded his brother Oliver at this sign. He advertises the catalogue of a small but curious collection of books, "in most Faculties, Lately purchas'd, in Greek, Latin, and English, French, and Italian . . . in excellent condition. Among which are the following :

"FOLIO.

Buxtorfi Bib. Hebraica, 2 tom.
—do— Concordantiæ Heb.
Dict. de Bayle, 3 tom. Rot. 1702.
Athenæus, Gr. Lat. a Casauboni.
Dryden's Works, 4 vols.
Burnet's Own Time, 2 v.
Rushworth's Collect. 8 v. best Edit.
Tillotson's Works, 3 v.
Hook's Micrographia
Bib. Frat. Polon. 8 tom.
Atlas Maritimus
Scapulæ Lex. Elz.

QUARTO.

Addison's Works, 4 vols. l.p.
Diog. Laertius a Meibomius, 2 tom.
Poetae Lat. Minores a Burmanni, 2 v.

Cellarii Geog. Edit. opt. 2 tom.
Aulus Gellius a Gronovius.
Philosoph. Transact. abridged, 7 v.
Corpus Juris Civilis, 2 tom. 1735.
Le Pois sur les Medailles Antiq.
Pomel of Drugs, best.
Virgilius Delph.
Terentius Delph.

OCTAVO AND TWELVES.

Virgilii Opera varior. 3 tom.
Polybius a Gronovii, 3 tom.
Livii varior. Edit. opt. 3 tom.
Ovidii Opera varior. 3 tom.
Plutarch's Lives, 5 vol.
Gordon's Tacitus, 4 v.
Jones's Synopsis Pal.
Tanner's Notitia Monast.

---

[1] *Daily Advertiser*, July 14, 1742.
[2] *Ibid.* March 15, 1742. See other catalogue advertisements, *Ibid.* July 15 and December 18, 1741.

Vies de Plutarque, par Dacier, 9 tom.   Seneca, 4 tom. Elz. 1 l.
Horace de Dacier, 10 tom.   Livius, 3 tom. Elz.
Horatius, Elz.   Opere di Redi, 6 tom." [1]

"STANDING ARMIES.

This Day is Published

"A Short History of Standing Armies in England, written by that eminent Patriot, Tho. Trenchard, Esq.

> Captique Dolis Donisque coacti,
> Quos neque Tydides, nec Larissaeus Achilles,
> Non Anni domuere decem non mille Carinæ. — *Virg. Æn. II.*

"What are we to expect if in a future Age an ambitious Prince should arise with a dissolute and debauch'd Army, a flattering Clergy, prostitute Ministry, a Bankrupt House of L——s, a Pensioner House of C——ns, and a slavish and corrupted Nation?   Vide Page 24.

"N.B.   This is the Book so particularly recommended by the two last Craftsmen, wherein he wishes the whole People of England would read it at this Juncture.

"Sold by Oliver Payne, Bookseller, in Round Court in the Strand, and the Booksellers and Pamphlet Shops in London and Westminster. (Price One Shilling)." [2]

Oliver Payne also published the "Memoirs of Count Bonneval; Or a complete History of the late War in Italy; containing a particular Account of all the Battles, Sieges &c.   Likewise a true Relation of the most secret Intrigues and Negotiations of the courts of France, Spain, Germany and Savoy.   Interspersed with Variety of entertaining Amours and Original Letters of the several princes concerned.   Also the political Intrigues of the late King of Sardinia, containing an Account of the ill Treatment of Mr. Phelippeaux the French Ambassador at the Court of Turin.   Translated from the French, by J. Sparrow, Gent.   With a new Map, explaining the Seat of the last and present War in Italy.   Price, neatly bound, gilt and letter'd, five Shillings." [3]   This was dedicated to the Duke of Marlborough.   Johnson's "Lives of the Highwaymen," a once very popular book, was printed for and sold by Oliver Payne in Round

---

[1] *Daily Advertiser*, Dec. 18, 1741.   In 1742 the style was W. and T. Payne, *Ibid.*, July 17.

[2] *Craftsman*, Jan. 6, 1732.

[3] *Grub Street Journal*, Feb. 13, 1735, and *St. James's Evening Post*, June 11, 1734.

Court.[1] There is a portrait of Thomas Payne in Dibdin's "Decameron," 1817, vol. iii. p. 435. From 1750 to 1790 he was in "Castle Street, next the Upper Mews Gate, near St. Martin's Church," at the bottom, says Mr. Dobson, of what is now Charing Cross Road.

Next door to the "Horace's Head" was the "Cambden's Head," or "Camden's Head," the sign of T. Woodman[2] in New Round Court, who advertises Sir Isaac Newton's "Treatise of the Method of Fluxions and Infinite Series, with its Application to the Geometry of Curve Lines. Translated from the Latin Original not yet published. Designed by the Author for the Use of Learners."

Also Crawford's "Lives and Characters of the Crown and State of Scotland. Collected from the Original Charters, &c., and the most approved Histories."

"The Deposing and Death of Queen Gin, with the Ruin, of the Duke of Rum, Marquis of Nantz, Lord Sugar-Cane, &c. Price 6d. As it was acted on Monday last at the New Theatre in the Haymarket."

"Thomson's 'Four Seasons,' with curious Copper-Plates. Quarto and Octavo."[3]

Another long announcement relates to the publication, "This Day," of "The Law and Lawyers laid open. In Twelve VISIONS, setting forth the Grievances of the Law, and the Remedies pro-pos'd, &c., &c.

"'Corruptissima in Respublica [sic], plurimae leges.'—Tac. Ann. III. c. 27."

This was also printed for J. Chrichley, at the London Gazette, Charing Cross.[4]

At the "Plato's Head," near Round Court, in the Strand, Dr. William Smellie's "Treatise on the Theory and Practise of Mid-wifery" first saw the light. Dr. Smellie's numerous improvements in the art that he professed gave him a permanent claim to the grati-tude of posterity. He states in one of his publications that he had educated nearly one thousand students, who had, while attending his lectures, afforded assistance to eleven hundred and fifty poor women, such patients being supported during their confinement by a sub-scription raised among the pupils.[5]

---

[1] Wheatley's *London*, and *Eighteenth Century Vignettes*, 2nd series, by Austin Dobson, 1894, p. 192.

[2] In 1722 the lower part of Will's Coffee-house, in Covent Garden, was occupied by a bookseller, "*James* Woodman, at Camden's Head."

[3] *St. James's Evening Post*, Sept. 14, 1736.   [4] *Ibid.*, Feb. 24, 1737.

[5] Hutchinson's *Biog. Med.* and *Lond. Daily Post*, July 24, 1751.

I

In the same year, 1751, "Peregrine Pickle" was "Printed for the Author at Plato's Head, near Round Court, in the Strand."

"Plato's Head" was on the north side of the Strand, nearly opposite Buckingham Street.[1]

It was in Round Court, in the centre of the key shops, herb shops, and furniture warehouses of Bedfordbury, that, in 1836, Robson the actor was apprenticed to a Mr. Smellie, a copper-plate engraver, and the printer of the humorous caricatures by Mr. George Cruikshank,[2] who was a little too late to ridicule the exacting absurdities of the Stamp Act. In 1798 one Williams, the keeper of a reading-room in Round Court, was convicted of lending a news-paper to read, and taking a penny for the use of it, for which, by 29 George III. c. ix., he was fined £5.[3]

In the eighteenth century, when no woman was complete without a fan at her girdle, J. Pinchbeck, at the "Fan and Crown" in New Round Court, "publish'd" on a fan-mount "A Curious and correct perspective View of the South Front of the new grand Amphitheatre at Chelsea, as also of Chelsea-College, and the Parts adjacent, as the same was taken from a commodious Situation near the Thames."[4] Pinchbeck must have been established here for at least nine years, for in 1732 he was advertising : "The Ladies' Historical and Political Fan ; or, the European Race. Curiously done on a Fan-mount, which is executed in a new and beautiful Taste by Encouragement from several polite Ladies. To be had at Pinchbeck's Fan Ware-house in New Round Court. . . .

"N.B.—Although this Fan had no Meaning annex'd to it, yet the Oddness of the Figures makes so beautiful a Picture that nothing of the Kind hath ever been done in this Way so entertaining to the Publick."[5] Silks consisting of Brocades, Tissues, Damasks, "strip'd" and plain corded Tabbies, flowered and plain Sattin Tobines, "strip'd," flowered, and plain Mantuas, &c., with great choice of black Silk Crapes, and Bombazeens were "selling off considerably under Prime Cost at Benj. Willmot's, at the Seven Stars in Round Court, Chandois Street."[6] And at the "Two

---

[1] L. Hutton's *Literary Landmarks*, 1888.
[2] *Robson: a Sketch* (Hotten), quoted in *Haunted London*, 1880, p. 236.
[3] Timbs's *Walks and Talks about London*, 1865, p. 249.
[4] *Daily Advertiser*, May 20–25, 1742.
[5] *London Evening Post*, Nov. 2, 1732.
[6] *Public Advertiser*, March 18, 1768.

Golden Sugar-Loaves " in the same fashionable court might be obtained the following :

	£	s.	d.			£	s.	d.
Scarlet Cloaks . . .	0	10	6	Half-Ell Black ⎫				
Mantelets trim'd . . .	0	14	0	Callimanco Coats ⎭	.	1	1	0
Velvet Hoods . . .		4	6	Black Russel ditto .	. .	1	8	0
Long ditto		13	0	Callimanco Gowns	.	0	18	0
Velvet Manteels . . .	1	1	0	Scotch Plad ditto .	. .	1	4	0
Silk Quilted Coats . . .	1	4	0	Stuff Damask ditto .	. .	1	7	0

"Note, Rich brocaded Silk Gowns, Damasks, Turky Silk, Floretta's, Thread Sattins, Tukytees, Velvet Caps, and Women's Silk Hats ; likewise Banjans of all Sorts, at as reasonable rates as above." [1] A house with a unique sign, that of the " Turkey-Cock," stood "over against New Round Court in the Strand," where inquiries were to be made concerning a " Good House to be Lett, at a reasonable Rent, with an Oven and other Conveniences, fit for an Eating House." [2]

Munday's Coffee House, a favourite resort of that clever scoundrel Dick England, but removed later to Maiden Lane, was in New Round Court, where five pounds reward was to be had for the recovery—stolen from a linen-draper's in the Strand—of a " Piece of spotted Lawn and a Piece of flower'd Lawn, . . . no Questions ask'd ; if pawn'd or sold, your Money again with Thanks. No greater reward will be offer'd, and if cut, the Reward in Proportion." [3]

A curious side-light upon the life in Round Court is afforded by a communication of Steele's to the " Spectator," purporting to be "the humble petition of Bartholomew Ladylove in the parish of St. Martin's-in-the-Fields, on behalf of himself and neighbours :

" That your petitioners have, with great industry and application, arrived at the most exact art of invitation or entreaty : that by a beseeching air and persuasive address, they have for many years last past peaceably drawn in every tenth passenger, whether they intended or not to call at their shops, to come in and buy ; and from that softness of behaviour, have arrived, among tradesmen, at the gentle appellation of ' The Fawners.'

" That there have of late set up amongst us certain persons from Monmouth-street and Long-lane, who by the strength of their arms, and loudness of their throats, draw off the regard of all

---

[1] *London Evening Post*, Nov. 4–7, 1738.

[2] *Daily Advertiser*, March 15, 1742. The sign also occurs among the Banks Bills (1765).   [3] *Ibid.* July 13, 1742.

passengers from your said petitioners ; from which violence they are distinguished by the name of ' The Worriers.'

" That while your petitioners stand ready to receive passengers with a submissive bow, and repeat with a gentle voice, ' Ladies, what do you want? pray look in here;' the Worriers reach out their hands at pistol-shot, and seize the customers at arm's length.

"That while the Fawners strain and relax the muscles of their faces in making distinction between a spinster in a coloured scarf, and an husband in a straw hat, the Worriers use the same roughness to both, and prevail upon the easiness of the passengers, to the impoverishment of your petitioners.

" Your petitioners therefore most humbly pray that the Worriers may not be permitted to inhabit the politer parts of the town ; and that Round-court may remain a receptacle for buyers of a more soft education.

" And your petitioners, &c." [1]

Heathcock Court, Strand, is comparatively too far removed from what we should now perhaps consider the " immediate neighbourhood " of Charing Cross, and would consequently be outside our notice but for the fact that the " Heathcock " tavern, after which the court is named, was always spoken of as the " Heathcock, Charing Cross," in accordance with the usual latitude allowed in such descriptive directions, before the abolition of house-signs. The idea seems to have been to get people to come so far as some well-known spot in London, when further inquiries would make the rest of the journey easy. We can imagine the men waiting round the " Horse " for employment being glad to direct the anxious sight-seer the way to the " Heathcock," where he wished to see " a surprising young mermaid taken on the coast of Aquapulca . . . allowed to be the greatest curiosity ever exposed to public view." [2]   This " Heathcock " is one of the many London signs which must have necessarily been found to be outside the scope of such a comprehensive work as Larwood and Hotten's " History of Signboards." The tavern, however, certainly existed so late, at least, as 1787. [3]   A heathcock with wings expanded, and holding in his beak a flower, is the crest of the Coopers' Company, [4] whence probably the sign,

[1] *Spectator*, No. 304.

[2] Frost's *London Showmen*.

[3] The Banks " Collection of Admission Tickets," portfolio I.

[4] There is an heraldic illustration of the heathcock in Berry's *Encyclopædia Heraldica*, plate xi. (or ? xl.), 9.

which appears to have survived over the entrance to the court as late as 1844. In July of that year it was removed, in spite of the remonstrance of Mr. Peter Cunningham, and lost sight of. Mr. Philip Norman, with his ever keen eye for the ancient and picturesque in domestic architecture, calls attention to two old houses fronting Heathcock Court, which were remaining in 1893.[1]

[1] *London Signs and Inscriptions.*

CHAPTER IX.

SOME OF THE STREETS.

AGAR STREET was probably so named after the amiable and accomplished George James Agar-Ellis, the editor of Walpole's "Letters," whose motion in the House of Commons for a grant to purchase the Angerstein collection of pictures [1] led to the formation of the National Gallery, of which he became a trustee. He was created Lord Dover on June 20, 1831, but previously, in 1830, he had been appointed Chief Commissioner of Woods and Forests, the year whence Agar Street probably dates, since he was compelled to resign that office on account of ill-health, when he was succeeded by Viscount Duncannon on February 11, 1831. The latter gave his name to Duncannon Street, about the time, in 1837, that the street was built during the improvements in Trafalgar Square. Another Chief Commissioner, Lord Lowther, gave his name to the Lowther Arcade, the site of which is now occupied by the great bank of Coutts's. [2] The fair was originally served by German, French, and Swiss toy dealers; indeed, the idea of such passages adapted to trade seems to have been borrowed from France, for about the time the Lowther Arcade first became a wonderland for children, Paris had its *Passage des Panoramas*, the *Passage Delorme*, the *Passage d'Artois*, the *Passage Feydeau*, the *Passage de Caire*, and the *Passage Montesquieu*, while sometimes such passages were called by the French "Galeries." The Lowther Arcade excelled the "Burlington" in certain architectural daintinesses. The ceiling of small pendentive domes was much admired, the arcade itself having been nearly 250 feet in length. Many a fond parent must regret its effacement—recalling the joys they experienced in contributing to the happiness of their open-eyed offspring the many delightful

---

[1] *Parliamentary Debates*, new series, ix. 1359.

[2] The proprietors of Coutts's Bank purchased the Crown lease of Lowther Arcade when it was placed in the market about the year 1898 by the trustees under the will of the late Mr. William Bird, and was withdrawn from the sale at auction at £30,000.

surprises the place afforded. A country friend of Mr. Joseph Hatton's well expresses this feeling of disappointment in one whose scarce visits to London always included a turn through this toy fair. " 'Almost the last time I was in London,' he says, ' I spent an hour or two in the Lowther Arcade. It was the eve of my little son Dick's birthday, and I wanted to take him a suitable present. . . . I can taste, in my mind, the very smell of the delightful place, something between sawdust and lavender. And the hum and music of it ; the toy trumpets, the accordions, the strips of melodious glass that you played upon with a little hammer ! And the youngsters with their parents and guardians on the self-same errand as my own, to buy something for a boy or a girl, and the difficulty of choosing the right thing. It was a much easier task for me to select a wedding present for my dear Dick's mother when she was Miss ——. But that is neither here nor there. You know I am a bit of a sentimentalist, and by Jove, yesterday when I found that wondershop was gone ! ' . . . He sighed, and mopped his face." [1]

Nearly opposite the Lowther Arcade was the Lowther Bazaar, and both the former and the latter appear to have been in a way the successors of the New Exchange and of the frivol shops there and in Round Court. The Lowther Bazaar was celebrated for its show of fancy goods, Magic Cave, and other exhibitions. Louis Philippe used frequently to drop in from his residence behind in York Buildings.

"LOWTHER BAZAAR,

PUBLIC LOUNGE,

35 Strand,

PATRONISED BY THE ROYAL FAMILY.

" Messrs. Graves and Young, in gratefully acknowledging the very extensive patronage they have hitherto enjoyed (having the unparalleled number of between five and six thousand visitors daily), beg leave to announce that in addition to the beautiful Fountain of Real Water constantly turning various Wheels and Pyramids, and an Illuminated Chinese Pagoda, they have just added a novel and splendid Parisian Saloon, with Patent Revolving Ceiling, representing the Signs of the Zodiac, Chinese Transparencies, Cosmoramic Views, and a Grand Musical Cabinet constantly playing various popular airs ; the whole fitted up in a style of elegance entirely original.

[1] " Cigarette Papers " in the *People*, Aug. 14, 1904.

"This was the First Bazaar in England to introduce the French System of having each Stand lotted off with articles all at the same price, commencing from sixpence upwards.

" ☞   Importers of French Jewellery, China, Perfumery, Combs, and Foreign Toys of every description.

" N.B.—Visitors admitted to the Saloon & Cosmoramic Views, by purchasing any article to the amount of One Shilling, and children Sixpence."[1]

At the Adelaide Gallery (named after Queen Adelaide), now Gatti's Restaurant, a "Grand Exhibition of Art" was held in 1854, and the place was once known as the Adelaide Gallery of Practical Science, where Jacob Perkins exhibited his steam gun. Between the years 1838 and 1843, a living electric eel was exhibited, and a variety of exhibitions, concerts, &c., were subsequently held here.[2]   King William Street is named after William IV., who took some interest in the Trafalgar Square improvement scheme, being said to have suggested "the name for the square, as well as the erection of the monument to Nelson, while one of his last appearances in public was in 1837, before the opening of the first Academy Exhibition here in May of that year."[3]   Adelaide Street, too, is named after the Queen of William IV., daughter of the Duke of Saxe-Meiningen.

In King William Street, Toole's Theatre, and the famed "Beefsteak Club" above it, whose members removed their gridiron to Green Street, Leicester Square, were pulled down between the years 1896 and 1900, to make room for the extension of Charing Cross Hospital. Originally a whisky store, it became in 1849 the first home in London of the Oratorian Fathers under the direction of Cardinal Newman, until in 1852 the Oratory of St. Philip Neri was removed to its present quarters in South Kensington.   Here it was that the learned and saintly Father Faber, with others of the brethren, used to electrify Catholic and Protestant alike with the force of their preaching.   After an interval of disuse the building became the Polygraphic Hall, and passed into the hands, I think, of a Mr.

---

[1] A Handbill of the time with no date.

[2] Mr. George Clinch in *Harmsworth's Magazine*, April 1899 : "The Arcades and Bazaars of London."   There is a drawing by T. H. Shepherd of the Adelaide Gallery, and also an engraving of the interior, on the walls of St. Martin's Library, Charing Cross.

[3] *Haunted London*, by Walter Thornbury, 1880, p. 220.

Woodin, who produced an entertainment called "Woodin's Carpet-bag and Sketch-book," in which the author is said to have exhibited amusing quick changes of character, and ventriloquism. Then it became the Charing Cross Theatre, and was finally taken over by Mr. Toole and called the "Folly Theatre" from 1880 to 1895, when the popular actor's chief successes were "The Don," "Walker, London," and "Thoroughbred," he having opened it in 1879 or 1880 with H. J. Byron's "A Fool and his Money." After his first season it was again overhauled and redecorated, and was opened again as Toole's Theatre on February 16, 1883.

Chandos Street owes its name to William Brydges, Lord Chandos, the ancestor of the magnificent owner of "Canons." It runs from Bedford Street to St. Martin's Lane, where there is said to have been an ancient turnpike, to which Mr. Austin Dobson thinks that Steele alludes in his "Ramble from Richmond to London," where he relates how, out of pure idleness, he diverted himself by following in "an Hack" the track of a handsome young lady with a mask and a maid. The damsel's chariot was travelling "through Long Acre towards St. James's." "Thereupon," says the vivacious essayist, "we drove for King Street, to save the Pass at St. Martin's Lane." At the end of Newport Street and Long Acre the vehicles become entangled, and for a moment he gets a glimpse of his charmer "with her Mask off." The chase continues "in all Parts of the Town" for an hour and a half, when the quarry is discovered to be a "Silk-worm," which is your hackney-coachman's term for those profitable fares "who ramble twice or thrice a Week from Shop to Shop, to turn over all the Goods . . without buying anything."[1]

Between Chandos Street and St. Martin's Church, and leading into Church Lane, was Moor's Yard,[2] a space of ground which, tradition has it, was in early times a place of execution for male-factors. The turnpike-house mentioned by the Bishop of Rochester was stated by many of the oldest inhabitants in Smith's time to have been removed, owing to a compromise which the Earl of Salisbury effected with the parish, on account of its being deemed so great a nuisance to the Earl, whose house stood nearly opposite.[3]

So that the Chandos Tavern, which appears to have succeeded

---

[1] *A Paladin of Philanthropy*, by Austin Dobson ("The Grub Street of the Arts"), 1899, pp. 294–5.

[2] R. Horwood's *Plan of the Cities of London and Westminster*, 1799.

[3] J. T. Smith, *Nollekens and his Times*, vol. ii. p. 237.

Pullen's wine-vaults, is thought to occupy the scene of this turnpike at what is now No. 28 St. Martin's Lane at the corner of Chandos Street, and opposite to the shop of Meriade Gibus, the famous inventor of the opera-hat.[1] In case this ingenious contrivance in head-gear should ever be superseded and the New Zealander should ever discover its ruins outside some dismantled theatre, it may perhaps be as well to place on record a description of it. The sides are made of merino or some similar material, and the crown and brim, which are stiff as in an ordinary hat, are connected by a set of springs, so that the hat can be flattened or expanded at pleasure. The original perpetrator of the ordinary tall silk hat of to-day also dwelt near here, by name Mr. Hetherington, a Strand " haberdasher of hats." He was, it is said, brought before the Lord Mayor, charged with a breach of the peace, and inciting to riot, in that he had, on the morning of January 15, 1797, walked down the public highway wearing "a tall structure having a shiny lustre, calculated to frighten timid people." This antipathy to the " topper " is by no means extinct among the proletariat. I remember witnessing, outside the Grand Hotel at Charing Cross, on some public occasion of rejoicing, the unprovoked assault of two roughs upon the tall hat of a passer-by. This peaceable-looking young citizen, however, happened to be an expert amateur boxer, and although the hat that he wore was not a beautiful object to look at when his assailants had done with it, the owner laid them both low before they could finish their sarcasms.

---

[1] Although another hatter, of the name of Cuthbertson, has succeeded to the business, the name of Gibus is still retained. An example of the original Gibus may be seen within.

CHAPTER X.

MORE OF THE STREETS.

THE erection of a very notable addition to the architecture of London, the Coliseum in St. Martin's Lane, has considerably diminished the width of a court situated between Bedfordbury and the Lane, called Taylor's Buildings. At the Bedfordbury end of this court is the side elevation of the Hole-in-the-Wall Tavern, now known as the "Marquis of Granby," Nos. 51 and 52 Chandos Street. Under the former sign the tavern had once been kept by a certain Mother Maberley, who had been honoured, or dishonoured, by the protection of the licentious George, Duke of Buckingham. And here it was that the famous highwayman Claude Duval was caught napping—in plainer English, *drunk*—by the bailiff: "Duvall was taken drunk at the Hole-in-the-Wall in Chandos Street, and well it was for the bailiff and his men that he was drunk, otherwise they had tasted his prowess; for he had in his pocket three pistols, one whereof would shoot twice, and by his side an excellent sword, which, managed by such a hand and heart, must without doubt have done wonders." [1]

Rawlins, the engraver of the fine and much coveted Oxford Crown, with a view of the city under the horse, dates a quaint supplicatory letter to John Evelyn from the Hole-in-the-Wall in St. Martin's.

The Marquis of Granby, for his many virtues, military and private, deservedly took the place on the signboard, not only of the Hole-in-the-Wall in Chandos Street, but of many other tavern-signs in London. The following is one of many instances that served to strengthen the people's affection for the gallant Marquis. It also illustrates the prevalence of a taste for the "muffles," as boxing-gloves were then called, taking us back to the days when Vauxhall was in the height of its splendour. Old Tyers, the proprietor of the Gardens, had commissioned Hayman, the painter, to panel the

---

[1] *Harleian Miscellany*, vol. vii. p. 398.

" Hall of British Worthies " with portraits of the heroes of our land. The gallant and good-natured Marquis of Granby was waited upon by Tyers with a request that he would honour Hayman with a sitting. In consequence, the hero of Minden dropped in at the artist's studio in St. Martin's Lane. " But, Frank," said the peer, " before I sit to you, I insist on having a set-to with you." Hayman, astonished at the oddity of the observation, affected not to understand his visitor, whereupon the Marquis exclaimed, " I have been told that you are one of the last boxers of the school of Broughton, and I flatter myself I am not altogether deficient in the pugilistic art, but since I have been in Germany I have got out of practice, therefore I want a little trial of your skill." Hayman pleaded age and gout as obstacles to his consent. To the first the Marquis replied " there was very little difference between them ; and to the second, that he considered exercise as a specific remedy," adding, laughing, " besides, a few rounds will cause a glow of countenance that will give animation to the canvas." Hayman no longer resisted, the gloves were donned, and to it they went. After a good display of strength and science, Hayman delivered such a straight hit in the " breadbasket " that down they both went with a tremendous crash. This brought upstairs the affrighted Mrs. Hayman, who found the Academician and the Commander-in-Chief rolling over each other on the carpet like two unchained bears. Frank, who was a humourist and *bon-vivant*, often narrated this anecdote of the nobleman—

Who filled our sign-posts then as Wellesley now,

over a social glass at his own and his friends' merry meetings.[1]

In Chandos Street the most gorgeously decked popinjay could preen his feathers at Tom Joyce's, the lace-cleaner, who hung out his sign of the " Crown and Golden Letters," and undertook to clean " all sorts of Silver and Gold Lace Shapes, Stars, Buttons, Brocades, Stuffs, and Fringes, and all sorts of Embroidery, in the best Manner, without doing any Detriment, if it be on the finest Cloth, Silk, or Velvet. I have liv'd here fifteen Years, and there never was any other Lace-Cleaner liv'd here but me and my Wife. I have perform'd the like in foreign Countries, to the great Satisfaction of all Gentlemen and Ladies : and there is no one in England knows this Art, or can perform it, like myself." [2]

At the " One Tun " tavern in Chandos Street, of which he had

[1] Henry Downes Miles's *Pugilistica*, 1880, vol. i. p. 91.
[2] *Daily Advertiser*, January 9, 1742.

become the proprietor, died, in 1844, Ruthven, the famous Bow Street runner, aged fifty-two years. He was for thirty years attached to the police force, having entered it at the age of seventeen, and retired with a pension of £220 per annum from the British Government. It was he who, among many other notorious captures, accomplished that of Thistlewood, for the Cato Street conspiracy, in which daring enterprise Smithers was killed; of Thurtell, the murderer of Mr. Weare; and he also was responsible for the discovery of bank robberies and forgeries on Government to an enormous amount. He was a most eccentric character, and had written a history of his life, but would on no account allow it to meet the public eye.[1] In the year 1750 Dr. Arne and Dr. Boyce frequently invited to the "One Tun" tavern a boy of vulgar manners, who, having drunk freely of geneva, played on the harpsichord without method, and produced such beautiful wild harmony as quite delighted those great professors of music.[2]

Much as to fashions in mid-eighteenth century dress may be gathered from the newspaper announcements of the "man-mercers" and the "man-milliners." Joseph More, at the Wheatsheaf, No. 3, Chandos Street, betrays a "haste to be rich" by adopting "a different way of business," and wishes to dispose of "an elegant assortment of Tissues, Brocades, Satins, Armozeens, Lustrings, &c. . . . Variety of Poplins, Queen's Stuffs, Bombazeens, together with a general assortment of mourning Black Satins, and Florentines, for Gentlemen's wearing. The lowest price at a word."[3] The last silk-mercer in Chandos Street disappeared about the year 1865, where a large fortune was made from the famous mazarine-blue silk, the colour of the cardinal's robes. The father of John Thelwall, the political writer and elocutionist, was a silk-mercer in this street, where John was born in 1764. There, too, Humfrey Wanley the antiquary, and librarian to Robert Harley, Earl of Oxford, lodged, as we gather from a letter in the Harleian MSS., from the Rev. Thomas Baker, Cambridge (Oct. 16, 1718), addressed "To the worthy Mr. Wanley at the Riding-Hood Shop, the corner of Chandois and Bedford Streets, Covent Garden."

In an "improvement" clearance about the year 1830 was taken down, on the north side of Chandos Street, the large hotel known as the "Key," mentioned in the scandalous chronicles of the eighteenth

---

[1] The *Gentleman's Magazine*, obituary notice, May 1844 (vol. xxi. p. 552).
[2] Creed Collection of Tavern Signs.
[3] *Morning Herald* and *Daily Advertiser*, December 15, 1783.

century as the resort of rakes, royal and noble, and their companions, for whose privacy coaches drove under the gateway, close to the hotel door. [1]

On the night of January 5, 1751, at about 11 of the clock, "three young Gentlemen of the Law, going along Chandos Street in their Merriments, thought fit to break a Lamp at the Door of Mr. Brown, a Butcher, whereupon his Servant stept after them to know the Reason, which they explain'd by several blows on his Head, and drove him back again into his Master's Shop, which was soon filled with People in a tumultuous Manner; Mr. Brown being at that Time with some Friends at the Swan, Word was brought of a Riot at his House, and that his Wife was frightened, his Servants beat, and his Goods like to be thrown into the Street; the poor Man immediately ran over the Way to protect his Family, and being told which were the Offenders, he seizes two of them, and being a stout Man tumbles them Neck and Heels out of his Shop, a Watchman hauls out a third, so they were carried to the Round House. The next Morning, on a Hearing before the Justice, the Parties were all dismissed." [2]

The St. Martin's Round House seems to have been abolished long before that appertaining to the neighbouring parish of St. Giles. In Ainsworth's "Jack Sheppard" the latter, probably one of the last that remained, is described as having stood in an angle of Kendrick Yard, its back windows looking upon the burial-ground of St. Giles's Church; it was built in a cylindrical form, like a martello tower, though, from bulging, it resembled an enormous tusk set on its end: it was two stories high, and had a flat roof, surmounted by a gilt vane in the shape of a key. The St. Martin's Round House, which Mr. Austin Dobson describes as "a favourite resort of the Georgian nobility and gentry," was a means of inflicting much cruelty even upon turbulent "night-birds," to say nothing of the innocent that were often bundled into it indiscriminately. The writer has a note from a newspaper of the middle of the eighteenth century, without any precise date, which tells how one Thursday night the Westminster constables made a general search "and took up a great Number of People, and so many Women were crowded into St. Martin's Round House, that four of them were suffocated and found dead the next Morning, for which some Persons were Yesterday taken up and committed to the Gatehouse, great Barbarity appearing in the Affair."

[1] Timbs's *Walks and Talks*, 1865, p. 182.
[2] Newspaper of January 6, 1751.

There was a sign of the "Ship" appertaining apparently to a tavern in Chandos Street, where the creditors of "Messrs. William and Gilbert Gordon, Perriwig-Makers, late Partners in Suffolk Street, of St. Martin's-in-the-Fields, were desired to meet . . . in order to receive their Dividend of the Money now got in of the aforesaid Gordon's Debts." [1]

This Chandos Street seems to have excelled all others in the neighbourhood of Charing Cross in its qualifications for the title of "Queer Street." On an unfortunate Thursday in December 1718, four highwaymen were drinking at the "One Tun" tavern, "near Hungerford Market," when, as usual, they must find something to fall out about, and, without having far to go in search of an excuse, they found it in the division of their booty. But the drawer overheard them, and sent for a constable, when they were secured and committed to Newgate, soon after, probably, dying of a "hempen fever." [2] A complete arsenal was found upon them, viz. two blunderbusses, one loaded with fifteen balls, the other with seven, and five pistols loaded with powder and shot. [3]

Some years later the "One Tun" appears to have become the "One Tun and King's Arms," and the creditors of Mr. Charles Mist, "late of Wardour Street, Old Soho, in the Parish of St. Ann, Westminster, Paviour, are desir'd to meet the said Mr. Mist's Friends, at the One Tun and King's Arms in the Strand, the 19th of this instant July, at Four o'Clock in the Afternoon of the same Day; at which time the Creditors are desir'd to bring with them their respective Demands upon the said Charles Mist." [4]

Matthew Blakiston, grocer, opposite the "One Tun," in the Strand, *i.e.* in Chandos Street, expresses a touching solicitude to confer upon the public the benefits of his "best double-refin'd Loaf-Sugar, commonly call'd treble-refin'd, at $8\frac{3}{4}d.$ per Pound; also the finest Hyson Tea at 14*s.* per Pound, and so, in Proportion, all Sorts of Tea, Coffee, Chocolate, and Caracca Cocoa Nuts, and other Grocery Wares cheaper than now sold by any Grocer in London. He likewise sells all Sorts of Teas, Coffee, Sago, &c. for Exportation; and to prevent any Imposition, he delivers a Catalogue of the Prices of all his Goods, which for Goodness he submits to the Judgment of

[1] *Daily Advertiser*, March 18, 1742.
[2] *Weekly Journal*, December 6, 1718.
[3] *History of Signboards.*
[4] *Daily Advertiser*, July 10, 1742.

every one that is pleased to deal with him. Also Arrack cheaper than any where else in Town : No less Quantity than five Gallons.

"N.B.—He gives all Servants who are sent to him a Ticket,

> Mr. Blakiston,
> Grocer, in the Strand.

printed (as in the Margin) by Way of Certificate to Masters or Mistresses, that they have not mistook his Shop, which has too often happened, to his Prejudice and their Disappointment." [1]

Late in the eighteenth century there met at a tavern kept by one Fulham, in Chandos Street, Covent Garden, a convivial club called the "Eccentrics," which was an offshoot of the "Brilliants." They next moved to Tom Ree's, May's Buildings, St. Martin's Lane, and here they were flourishing at all hours. The club afterwards met at the "Green Dragon" tavern in Fleet Street, and it comprised at one time many celebrities of the literary and political world. From its commencement the club numbered upwards of 40,000 members of the *bons vivants* of the metropolis, many of whom held high social position ; among others were Fox, Sheridan, Lords Melbourne and Brougham. On the same memorable night that Sheridan and Lord Petersham were admitted, Hook was enrolled ; and through this club membership Theodore is believed to have obtained some of his high connections. [2]

It would be remarkable if the arms of the Vintners' Company had been neglected on the signboards of this neighbourhood, for the commercial dealings of the Vintners with tavern-keepers here must have been enormous. So we find the "Three Tuns" in Chandos Street a tavern-haunt of Pepys the diarist, when he came so far west to "take the air." It was at the "Three Tuns" that Sally Pridden, *alias* Sally Salisbury, from her resemblance to the Countess, in a fit of jealousy, stabbed the Hon. John Finch in 1723. Her story will be found in the Newgate Calendar, [3] and—unique coincidence probably—her portrait was painted by Sir Godfrey Kneller.

In company of several neighbours in Covent Garden one Monday night in 1679, Robert Taylor, a dancing-master, *upon occasion of some words*, as usual, killed one Mr. Price of the same place at the "Three Tuns" in Shandois Street. "The said R. Taylor is a person

---

[1] *St. James's Evening Post*, January 31, 1738.

[2] John Timbs's *Lives of Wits and Humourists*, 1862, vol. ii. p. 303.

[3] Vol. i. pp. 260–62. According to Mr. Laurence Hutton, the "Three Tuns" stood on the site of No. 66 Bedford Street, *near* the corner of Chandos Street, but it is evident from the above and from what follows that it was partially, at all events, in Chandos Street.

of middle stature, hath a cut across his chin, a scar in his left cheek, having two fingers and a thumb of one hand burnt at the ends shorter than the other, round visaged, thick lipt, his own hair being of a light brown under a periwig ; he lived in James Street, in Covent Garden. Whoever apprehends him, and gives notice thereof to Mr. Reynolds, bookseller, in Henrietta Street, Covent Garden, shall have 10 pound reward. And whereas it was printed in last week's 'Intelligence' that he was taken, you are to take notice that it is most notoriously false." [1] Again, on a certain Monday in February 1725, two officers in the Guards, who were reputed good friends, could find nothing better to do than to set to quarrelling. So Captain Turtle of the 3rd Regiment and Brigadier Wilson of the 1st Troop went to the "Three Tuns" in Chandos Street, called for a room to drink in, and immediately fought a duel, in which the captain was so dangerously wounded that he died next day. But it was said that before his death he acknowledged himself the aggressor before several witnesses. [2]

Although it would be difficult to find one now, Chandos Street possesses the distinction of having been one of the first streets, if not the very first, not only in London but in England, in which a balcony was erected. This was in the middle of the 17th century ; and it was Lord Arundel who was responsible for the innovation, one which led to its being adopted as a distinctive house-sign : " He [Lord Arundel] also was the first that invented balconies ; ye first was in Covent Garden, and in Chandos Street at the corner was Ye Sign of a Balcony, which country folks were wont much to gaze on." Six blank lottery tickets having been dropped, John Cox, upholsterer, requests that they may be brought to his sign of the " Iron Balcony " in " Druery " Lane, next door to the Lord Craven's. [3] Quacks were authors in those days, not indeed in a literary way exactly, but as the inventors of some medicine to which they were anxious to call the attention of the public. One J. Manton, surgeon, advertises himself at the Balcony-House, next to the Crown and Sceptre Tavern in Old Bailey, where might be had a " pleasant alterative Diet-Drink," of which he was the " Author," " whose specifick Qualities, in changing and sweetning the whole Mass of Humours, are so surprizing, etc." [4] It was in the fashionable days of

---

[1] Chambers's *Book of Days*, vol. ii. p. 92.
[2] *Daily Post*, February 11, 1725.
[3] *Post-Boy*, August 15–18, 1718.
[4] *Weekly Journal*, December 2, 1721.

Covent Garden that the Balcony, as something more than a "nine days' wonder," fairly took that quarter by storm. Richard Brome, in his "Covent Garden Weeded, or The Middlesex Justice of Peace," 1658, says : "That's the Bellconey she stands on, that jets out so on the forepart of the house ; every house here has one of them." "Shandois Street" was so contiguously situated to Covent Garden that it was probably embraced in the name of that historic quarter. For instance, the "Anchor and Crown" is advertised as at "the lower-end of Shandois Street, near Covent Garden," next door to which was sold "the Water that cures the King's Evil" and innumerable other evils incidental to the King's subjects who favoured town-life. This town-life rendered those who adopted it liable to another evil curable only through the wearing, by those who promoted it, of the Anodyne Necklace, as the hangman's rope was called. And not exempt from the molestation of the footpad and the highway robber were the highest in the land, among whom on one occasion was the "magnificent" Duke of Chandos, grandson of George Brydges, Lord Chandos, after whom the street under notice was named. In December 1720 four men, Thomas Phillips, William Heater, William Spickett, and Joseph Lindsey, were apprehended at the Black Horse in the Broad Way, Westminster, on suspicion of robbing on the highway, carried before the Justice at St. Margaret's, who committed them to the Gatehouse. They violently resisted when taken, and one of them shot at a Mr. Rowlet, a constable, the bullet grazing his shoulder. It was said that two of these men were concerned in the robbery committed some time before upon his Grace the Duke of Chandois. [1]

A very noted resort in Chandos Street in the 18th century was the "Lebeck's Head." It was at the north-west corner of Half Moon Passage, a passage since merged in Bedford Street, not *Bradford* Street as in the "History of Signboards." [2] Of this Lebeck, who was a famous cook of the latter part of the 17th and the beginning of the 18th century, there is a fine mezzotint—I think, if I remember rightly, it is a mezzotint—in the Creed Collection of Tavern Signs in the British Museum Library. Perhaps this is the engraving executed by Andrew Miller in 1739 from a painting by Sir Godfrey Kneller. "The Lebeck's Head" had its imitators in both London and the provinces. It was the favourite headquarters for

---

[1] *Weekly Journal*, December 24, 1720.
[2] This, however, is probably a mere printer's error.

meetings of a commercial nature. For instance, the butchers, fish-mongers, poulterers &c. of Westminster that kept shops in the markets within the Liberty are requested to meet here at six o'clock to consult how to apply to Parliament to have their leases made void, "that they may be at the Liberty of following their Customers into the New Building, and not to be confin'd to the Markets, and starv'd whilst a Handful of Forestallers run away with their Bread." [1] Again, the "Creditors of Charles Pitfield, Esq., deceas'd, are desir'd to meet at the Lebeck's Head Tavern in Chandos Street, Covent Garden, tomorrow, the 16th instant, at six o'clock in the Evening, to consider of a proper Remedy to be taken for the Recovery of their respective Debts." [2]

The landlord of the "Bell and Dragon" in Chandos Street, among twenty-one other alehouse keepers, avowedly expresses himself, in 1756, as being in sympathy with the Master-Taylors and Staymakers, who were "much concerned at the unhappy Combinations that a few evil-minded Journeymen have raised among the rest. And having now tried every Method to convince them of their Errors, and dissuade them from an Opposition to Laws so much in their Favour, are now resolved (if we should be put to the disagreeable Necessity by a Continuation of their Obstinacy), to punish all who shall offend against the aforesaid Laws : But as we would rather choose to live in Harmony with our Journeymen, and as the several Alehouse Keepers whose Names and Signs are hereunto annexed, have given publick Testimony of their Dislike to all Combinations, and have expressed a Desire of serving both Masters and Journeymen, we do hereby give Notice to all Journeymen Taylors and Staymakers, who are willing to submit to the Wages and Hours prescribed by the Law, that if they will use any of the following Alehouses as Houses of Call, without Slates or Articles, that he will apply for them at the said Houses in Preference to any other." Here follows the list alluded to. [3]

From a trades token it appears that there was a sign of the "Three Elms" in Chandos Street, appertaining to Edward Boswell in 1667. The Civil Service Supply Association, at the eastern end of Chandos Street, is said to have had its origin about twenty or thirty years ago

---

[1] *Daily Advertiser*, April 6, 1742.
[2] *Ibid.* October 15, 1742.
[3] Vide *Collection of Material relating to the Signs of London and Home Counties in the St. Martin's Library, Charing Cross* (No. 219).

in the purchase by a few clerks, at wholesale price for division among themselves, of a chest of tea. They "struck ile" when the idea was enterprisingly adopted by them on an extended scale.

The "Rhenish Wine House," Charing Cross, seems to have been situated, like the "Canary House," somewhere in the vicinity of Bedford Street. There was another in Channel Row, Westminster :

> What wretch would nibble on a hanging shelf,
> When at Pontack's he may regale himself?
> Or to the house of cleanly Rhenish go,
> Or that at Charing Cross, or that in Channel Row?[1]

[1] *The Hind and the Panther Transversed.*

CHAPTER XI.

THE "LEMON TREE."

BEDFORDBURY, running parallel to and eastward of St. Martin's Lane, and leading northward from Chandos Street, had fallen, in Cunningham's time, from a once decently inhabited place to a nest of low alleys and streets. With the extension of Metropolitan London, however, on all sides, it is assuming, like St. Martin's Lane, something of renewed life, owing, no doubt, to contiguity to Covent Garden Market and other important districts. The sign of the "Lemon Tree" in this street, a few doors from the "Marquis of Granby," is probably owing in its origin to being in the immediate neighbourhood of the market. The first sign of the "Lemon Tree" seems, indeed, to have been in the Market itself, for Charles Ogle advertises for sale in a vault under the "Lemon Tree" in Covent Garden Market, at seven shillings a gallon, "A Large and curious Parcel of Brandy and Rum Orange Shrub, made with true Seville Oranges of this Season, when they were in their best Perfection. Note, Those who buy five Gallons or a greater Quantity shall be abated Six Pence a Gallon." [1]

I believe the lemon tree was introduced into this country at the extreme latter end of the fifteenth century, but the sign arose when the fruit, and perhaps the tree, was first sold at Covent Garden. The author of the valuable little "Epicure's Almanack" of 1815 says, "Almost all the principal market gardeners within ten or twelve miles of the metropolis rent a stand in Covent Garden, where every esculent vegetable, in or out of season, indigenous or exotic, natural or forced, may be purchased. Among the superior fruiterers we notice Mr. Cook at the 'Lemon Tree,' Mr. Moulder, Mr. Bunting, Mr. Grange, Mr. Mabbot, Messrs. Best and Strudwicke." [2]

[1] *Daily Advertiser*, Dec. 12 and 22, 1741.

[2] The *Epicure's Almanack*, 1815, p. 294. That the lemon tree was cultivated in the neighbourhood of London before is evident from the following : "Just brought over from Holland, a fine Collection of Orange and Lemon Trees, both

It is not every day that one meets with an advertisement by a publican of a chapel to let. Yet inquiries were to be made of Mr. Collin Donaldson, of the "Lemon Tree " in Bedfordbury, concerning the letting (" to be enter'd upon immediately ") of " A Meeting Place, in Great Queen Street, Lincoln's Inn Fields, with new Pulpit and Cushion, new Pews, Window-Curtains, Brass Branches, &c., all complete, and fit for any congregation of Protestant Dissenters. To be had on very easy Terms."[1]

Sir Francis Kynaston, one of King Charles I.'s esquires of the body, dwelt in Bedfordbury, or, at least, he is described on the rate-books of St. Martin's as living in Covent Garden, in 1636 (meaning probably, as was customary, the *district* of Covent Garden) " on the east side of the street towards Berrie."

It was in Bedfordbury apparently that the Museum Minervæ, of which Sir Francis Kynaston was the " Regent " or president, was "established at a house in Covent Garden." The constitutions of this academy for the " nobility and gentry " were published in London in 1636, in quarto. It was instituted in the eleventh year of the reign of Charles I. at a house in Covent Garden purchased for the purpose by Kynaston, and furnished by him with books, manuscripts, paintings, statues, musical and mathematical instruments, &c., and every requisite for a polite and liberal education. Only the nobility and gentry were admissible, and professors were appointed to teach the various arts and sciences. When the plague was raging Kynaston obtained permission of the King to use King James's College at Chelsea, both as a refuge from the violence of the contagion and as a retirement in which the education of the young men might be continued uninterrupted. The Provost, however, of the Chelsea College objected, and the Museum Minervæ had to put up with accommodation at Little Chelsea.[2]

Two Lions rampant supporting a crown, and a " Half Moon, were two signs in Bedfordbury, as trade tokens testify.

plain, and variegated with the finest Cream and Yellow Colours, of the Sorts, full of Fruit and Flowers, of all Sizes fit for the Orangery, or to adorn Ladies' Chambers : to be sold very cheap by James Lesley, at Mr. Frazier's, next door to Beaufort House, near the Waterside at Chelsea ; where all Gentlemen and Ladies may be furnished with the most curious of Bulbous Roots from Holland and other parts of Europe, at the lowest prices" (*London Journal*, July 29, 1721).

[1] *Daily Advertiser*, April 6, 1742. This, of course, may not have been a tavern at that time.

[2] Faulkner's *Chelsea*, 1829, vol. i. p. 227.

Mr. James Payne, a bookseller of Bedfordbury (perhaps the son of Thomas Payne), died in Paris in 1809. Mr. Burnet describes him as remarkable for his amenity as for probity and learning. Repeated journeys to Italy, France, and Germany had enabled him to collect a great number of precious MSS. and rare editions, most of which went to enrich Lord Spencer's Library—the most splendid collection ever made by a private person.[1]

Before Bedfordbury had quite fallen from its high estate the following curiosities in textile fabrics, the stock in trade of Robert Davidson, Woollen Draper and Man's Mercer, No. 2, Bedfordbury, were announced for sale : Jeans, Jeanets, Thicksets, Corduroys, Cordereens, Sattinets, Cantoons, Ribb'd Delures, Velverets, Velveteens, Prunellas, Velvets, Lastings, Silkeens, Printing Jeanets, Damascuses, Florentines, Princess Stuffs, Stripe Linseys, Flannels, Baizes, Superfine Cloths, Seconds, Liveries, &c.[2] And at Mr. Arrowsmith's, Turner's Court, Bedfordbury, next Chandois Street, was to be sold A REAL INDIA SHAUL " for the Prime Cost, Sixteen Guineas." It is again described as " a very beautiful Shaul Hand-kerchief." [3]

There is, it must be confessed, something of an air of slum-land still in parts of Bedfordbury, with its narrow and devious courts and alleys.   Part of it, however, was swept away with the larger portion of the pestilential rookery consisting of the Caribbee Islands, formerly known as the Bermudas, in 1830. And in 1880–1 a further improvement was made by the erection of large blocks of model lodging-houses, occupying nearly all the space between Bedford Street and Bedfordbury.

New Street is a continuation of King Street, Covent Garden, to St. Martin's Lane, with Bedfordbury leading south to Chandos Street.   The landlord of the " Swan " tavern in this street, now, I think, known as the White Swan Hotel, No. 14, could justly claim at the beginning of last century to be a licensed *victualler*, for in the " Epicure's Almanack " we read that it was in 1815 " a long established house, well known for the excellence of its fish, flesh, and fowl, which are served up in the best style of cookery by bill of fare daily, to a respectable and numerous company of guests."   At the " Coffee House in New Street " dwelt in 1671 Joseph Howard, whose token bore the half-length figure of a man holding a cup with a hand

[1] *Notes and Queries*, 2nd series, vol. viii. p. 122.
[2] *Morning Chronicle and London Advertiser*, March 3,ʳ1780.
[3] *Ibid.*

issuing from a cloud, and pouring into it from a coffee-pot. On a table are three pipes.[1]

"Painful as it is to relate," writes one who was a *persona grata* with the great and learned Samuel Johnson, to wit Richard Cumberland, "I have heard that illustrious scholar assert (and he never varied from the truth of fact) that he subsisted himself for a considerable space of time upon the scanty pittance of fourpence halfpenny per day."[2] And on one occasion Johnson relates how at the "Pine Apple" in New Street he "dined very well for eightpence, with very good company. Several of them had travelled. They expected to meet every day, but did not know one another's names. It used to cost the rest a shilling, for they drank wine ; but I had a cut of meat for sixpence, and bread for a penny, and gave the waiter a penny ; so that I was quite well served, nay, better than the rest, for they gave the waiter nothing."[3] This was when he occupied his first lodgings in London at a stay-maker's in Exeter Street, close by.

Benjamin Cooke, the father of the celebrated English musician Dr. Benjamin Cooke, was a music-seller at the sign of the "Golden Harp" in New Street, Covent Garden. Here he published Corelli's Twelve Grand Concertos and his Four Operas, or Sonatas, all in Score. "Corrected and recommended by the learned Dr. Pepusch, to all students of Musick" &c. ;[4] the "Favourite SONGS in the Opera of Operas ; or TOM THUMB the Great, as they were perform'd at the Theatre in the Haymarket," &c. ;[5] William Corbett's "Thirty-five Concertos or Universal Bizzaries for four Violins, Tenor Violin, Violoncello, and thorough Bass for Organ or Harpsichord, in seven Parts ;[6] the compositions of John Humphries, a violinist and composer, for his instrument in London, who died in 1730 ;[7] and "The AMUSEMENT : Being a Collection of twelve English Songs (one of which is *Hail! Windsor*, as sung by Mr. Lowe, at the Theatre in Drury Lane), all compos'd by Mr. J. Travers."[8] Also Six Concertos by Sig. Alex. Scarlatti ; Twelve ditto by Mr. De Fesch ; Six ditto by Mr. Avison ; two Volumes of

---

[1] Akerman's *Account of Tradesmen's Tokens*, 1849, p. 144.

[2] *Memoirs of Richard Cumberland*, 1806, p. 261. Cumberland was always treated with great courtesy by Dr. Johnson, who in his *Letters to Mrs. Thrale*, vol. ii. p. 68, thus speaks of him : "The want of company is an inconvenience, but Mr. Cumberland is a million."

[3] Boswell's *Johnson*, ed. by J. W. Croker, 1831.

[4] *Craftsman*, April 29, 1733.   [5] *Ibid.* September 8, 1733.

[6] *Daily Advertiser*, April 6, 1742.   [7] *Ibid.* October 15, 1742.

[8] *Ibid.* February 4, 1742.

Lessons for the Harpsichord, compos'd (expressly for the Princess of Asturia) by Sig. Domenico Scarlatti; six Solos for two Violoncellos, by Sig. Lanzetti, for the practise of his Royal Highness the Prince of Wales; and Twenty Canzonettas, or Italian Ballads, by "Mr. De Fesch." Cooke's distinguished son was the composer of the glees "In the merry month of May," "Hark the lark," "How sleep the brave," &c., and the vocal duets "Let Rubinelli charm the ear," and "Thyrsis when he left me." Dr. Cooke had the character of a most amiable and agreeable man. Miss Hawkins, in her anecdotes, says, "No one was ever less vain of superior excellence in an art, or rather, less sensible of it, than Dr. Cooke; he certainly supposed that every body could do what he did, 'if they would but try.'" He died in 1793.

In New Street art was represented, as regards residents, by Flaxman's father, who kept there a shop for the sale of plaster casts, at the sign of the "Golden Head," whence Flaxman *fils* sent his first contribution to the Royal Academy Exhibition in 1770. It was a "Portrait of a Gentleman," a model.

New Street was one of the numerous streets in this part of the West-end that became fashionable under the Stuarts owing to their proximity to "the joyous neighbourhood of Covent Garden;" and till about 1860 it was the chief carriage-way to Covent Garden, when Garrick Street was formed to give a good western approach thereto.[1] Cunningham says that the Countess of Chesterfield, with whom Van Dyck was in love, occupied a house on the south side in 1660. To this day it retains a much older aspect than the streets by which it is surrounded.

Having taken a furnished cottage a short time ago in a certain remote part of Essex, which may as well be nameless, we, my wife and myself, were considerably surprised to find that it was customary for the landlord to insert advertisements in the newspapers intended for the notice of a kind of people whose presence was strongly resented by the estimable vicar of the parish—so much so, indeed, that he threatened, I believe, to buy up the property, several houses, in question. But while the modern advertisement does not excite suspicion in the ordinary reader, the brazen advertiser of the eighteenth century seems to have had no fear of the law before his eyes, for he thus announces himself: "To the Ladies. Any lady whose situation requires a temporary retirement, may be accommodated agreeable to her wishes in the house of a gentleman eminent in his profession,

---

[1] Wheatley's *Cunningham.*

whose honour and secrecy may be depended upon, and every vestige of pregnancy obliterated, so as to elude the scrutiny of the most sagacious. Letters directed to A.B. at Mr. Conn's, tobacconist, No. 20, New Street, Covent Garden, will immediately be transmitted as addressed." [1]

Nothing exhibits more forcibly the sad aspect of urban life than the number of hospitals that the purse-strings of the not altogether selfish rich have opened to the unfortunate poor. The increase in the number of these hospitals during nearly a century has been most remarkable, and therefore of infinite credit to the charitable who are responsible for so much development—not forgetting the indispensable and devoted servants of Æsculapius who spend their lives largely in re-doing what other people have undone, either by inadvertence, neglect, or downright crime. In the year 1818 there were but twenty-three hospitals, as we understand the word now, including those for " lying-in." [2] But " Whitaker's Almanack " gives a list, to-day, of no fewer than *ninety-one*, including, besides the great general hospitals, those for consumption and chest diseases, for children, women, nervous diseases (epilepsy, paralysis, &c.), fever, skin, cancer, orthopædic, dental, throat and ear, and others of a miscellaneous character. We recall the divine words, " Faith, Hope, Charity ; but the greatest of these is Charity." And it was in the real spirit of Christ that the vigorous Dr. Benjamin Golding, by his virile philanthropy, forwarded the foundation, in the year 1818, of the West London Infirmary, afterwards known as the Charing Cross Hospital. It is not generally known that under the former designation it was established, in the first instance, in Villiers Street. How appropriate the simple lines of Dr. Golding himself to the occasion :

> How happy they who, blest by fortune's store,
> Enjoy the means to comfort the distressed ;
> T'assuage the sufferings of the lowly poor,
> And soothe the anguish of the aching breast !

The first stone of the present building was laid by the Duke of Sussex, with Masonic ceremonies, on September 15, 1831. At its completion it differed in its exterior from the present building in that it has received the addition of the whole of the top story. Dr. Golding contemplated, by the establishment of this hospital, the hitherto untried combination of a Dispensary for supplying attendance and medicine to the sick poor at their own homes, with a Hospital

[1] The *Evening Mail*, May 25, 1789.   [2] The *Picture of London*, 1818.

for receiving and providing with clean domestic comforts the more dangerous cases—as indoor patients. Its first patrons were the Princesses Augusta and Sophia, and the Dukes of York and Kent. The sufferings of the poor which this beneficent institution has been instrumental in alleviating, even during the twelve or fourteen years anterior to the present site being occupied, may be gauged by the fact that during that time there were admitted for relief as out-patients upwards of 30,000 poor sick persons. This, however, it must be remembered, was at a time when Porridge Island, the Bermudas, and the C'ribbee Islands, upon the site of which the hospital now stands, constituted a series of the most awful slums, swarming with the wrack of Modern Babylon. This at the time, 1831, formed the eighth casualty hospital for the metropolis, the others being St. Bartholomew's, Guy's, St. Thomas's, St. George's, the London, Westminster, and Middlesex. On account of the enormous traffic of the neighbourhood, and in a less degree owing to its proximity to Charing Cross Railway Station, and to the area between that station and Waterloo Junction, it has as many accidents as any hospital in London, sometimes as many as eight in one day.

Bedford Street, leading from nearly opposite the Adelphi into King Street, on the west side of Covent Garden, is described by Strype as being favoured by mercers, drapers, and lacemen. Of these, the son of Kynaston the actor was an opulent mercer here in the fashionable days of Covent Garden, and here the actor in his old age lived and died. *Dick Kynaston*, as he was familiarly known, was, I think, the first impersonator on the stage of female characters, and on one occasion Davenant, the manager, when King Charles II. expressed impatience for the lifting of the curtain, answered—" Sire, the scene will commence as soon as the queen is shaved." Garrick and his friend Dr. Arne were of the opinion that these male actors of female parts were selected from amongst the counter-tenors, and even that they spoke in *falsetto*. In the prologue written for the performance of Kynaston's Desdemona were the following lines :

> Our women are defective, and so sized
> You'd think they were some of the Guard disguised ;
> For to speak truth, men act, that are between
> Forty and fifty, wenches of fifteen ;
> With bones so large, and nerve so uncompliant,
> When you call *Desdemona*—enter giant.

Shop-bills relating to the tradesmen in this street may be seen in the Banks Collection (from 1785 to 1789), notably one relating to the "Three Crowns." This house, No. 26, is still, I think, a gold-lace manufacturer's and retained its old sign of the "Three Crowns" until the house was pulled down in 1875. As a laceman's sign the "Three Crowns" is probably in allusion to the arms of the Drapers' Company, which consist of three golden crowns, in their turn allusive to the crowns of the three kings of Cologne.

"Turkey Coffee 6s. 4d., with allowance to them that buy Quantities. Bohee from 12s. to 24s. All sorts of Green, the lowest 12s. Chocolate with sugar 2s. 2d. All Nuts 3s. 6d. The finest Brazils 48s., and 3s. 4d. an Ounce. Portugal 18s., and 1s. 4d. an ounce, Right Amazona, Barcelona, and Port St. Lucar. Sold very cheap by Wholesale or Retail; and Orange-flower water : at the 'Star' in Bedford Court, near Bedford Street, Covent Garden." This advertisement, exhibiting the high price of tea even fifty years after its more general introduction about 1657, appertained to Robert Tate, druggist, who in 1711 describes himself as "against York Buildings in the Strand." Green tea is said to have first begun to be used in 1715, but Tate in Bedford Court advertises it as early as 1709.[1] Bedford Court was nearly opposite to Henrietta Street, in Bedford Street, and leading into Chandos Street. In this court was White's Coffee-house, where the sale is announced to all "Connoisseurs in Musick," of a large collection of MS. music in Italian.[2] And at the "Cæsar's Head" in Bedford Court, near Covent Garden, William Sare was a bookseller who published a catalogue of "valuable and curious Libraries, lately purchas'd, in most Languages and Faculties, viz. History, Divinity, Law, Poetry, Travels, Voyages, Agriculture, Mathematics, Antiquity, Dictionaries, Lexicons, &c. in Greek, Latin, Italian, Spanish, French, English, &c." Catalogues, among other places, might be had at Slater's Coffee-house in St. Martin's Lane.[3]

The "Constitution" tavern, which survived in Bedford Street as late, at least, as 1879, seems to have given place to the premises of the Institute of Builders, and the Builders' Accident Insurance Company, at Nos. 31 and 32. At all events 32 was the number of the house in 1879. It is described in 1815 as having its sign painted symbolically to represent the Church and State, the former by Westminster Abbey and the latter by Westminster Hall. "Be that as

---

[1] See the *Tatler*, Dec. 20, 27, 1709; Dec. 10, 1710; and the *Postman*, Nov. 24–27, 1711.

[2] *Daily Advertiser*, Dec. 18, 1741.

[3] *Ibid.* Oct. 15, 1742.

it may, the constitution of John Bull will never be in jeopardy while he has money and appetite for the good things offered to him at this house, especially if he take moderately a plentiful potation of the peerless punch for which the 'Constitution' is renowned." [1]

The difficulties created for wayfarers by the abolition of the sign-boards must have led to the use of many words not to be found in the ordinary dictionary until "custom," which, according to Burke, "reconciles everything," had forced upon the recognition of the public the new system of numbering, and one consequence of their removal was elaborated advertisements for use in the dark such as that of "Doctor James Tilbrough, a German doctor," who resided "over against the New Exchange, in Bedford Street, at the sign of the Peacock, where you shall see at night two candles burning within one of the chambers before the balcony." [2]   The "Cross Keys," a man dipping candles, "Three Birds," and a "Sugar Loaf" were four signs in Bedford Street in the seventeenth century. [3]   Instead of stone pavement, the customary posts were placed at intervals to distinguish the footway from the road, and when Sheridan lived in this street he and the author of "Miscellanea Nova," S. Whyte, were standing together at the drawing-room window expecting Johnson, who was to dine there.   Sheridan asked Whyte whether he could see the length of the Garden.   "No, Sir!"   "Take out your opera-glass; Johnson is coming; you may know him by his gait."   "I perceived him," says Whyte, whose narrative occurs in the little work alluded to, "at a good distance, working along with a peculiar solemnity of deportment, and an awkward sort of measured step. . . . And upon every post as he passed along I could observe he deliberately laid his hand, but missing one of them; when he got at some distance he seemed suddenly to recollect himself, and immediately returning, carefully performed the accustomed ceremony, and resumed his former course, not omitting one till he gained the crossing."   This, Sheridan assured Whyte, however odd it might appear, was his constant practice; "but why or wherefore he could not inform me." [4]   The house in which Chief Justice Richardson lived, No. 15, which, with Nos. 14 and 16, was pulled down in 1863, was tenanted latterly by Mr. Joseph Lilly, the well-known bookseller, who removed thence

---

[1] *Epicure's Almanack*, 1815, p. 158.
[2] See *Old and New London*, vol. iii. p. 267.
[3] Akerman's *Account of Tradesmen's Tokens*, 1849, pp. 27–8.
[4] *Miscellanea Nova*, 1801 (Addenda to Remarks on Boswell's *Johnson*, p. 49).

to Nos. 17 and 18 New Street, Covent Garden, his large stock of old books, particularly rich in early English literature, and black-letter books in general.[1]

The lower end of Bedford Street, formerly known as Half Moon Street, is in the parish of St. Martin's-in-the-Fields, while the upper end appertains to St. Paul's, Covent Garden. The "Half Moon" tavern stood at the Strand end of the street, "opposite the New Exchange Buildings."

In the overseers' accounts of St. Martin's-in-the-Fields, under the date July 1, 1655, is an entry that must do the heart of the supererogatory section of the "Lord's Day Observance Society" good. The society has, or had some few years ago, offices in Bedford Street, and it seems natural to suppose that the reason the Half Moon tavern, which formerly stood at the bottom of what was Half Moon Street, disappeared is because the society detected a man in the "Moon" in question, gathering sticks on Sunday. Whether "John Stro," as the Scotch fisher-folk call the hermit in the moon, was an abstainer is open to question, since he was wicked enough to worry about fagots on the Sabbath ; but certain it is that two men in the "Moon" tavern, to wit, Coll Corbit and Mr. Hill, were, according to the St. Martin's accounts alluded to, fined £1 for drinking therein "on the Lord's Day."[2]   From 1648 to 1660, when Puritanism was at its red-hottest, people were fined for the commonest offences committed on Sunday. Entries occur in the accounts alluded to, of fines received for "riding in a coach," "carrying linen," "a barber for trimming" (the High Wycombe barber can no doubt sympathise), "carrying a haunch of venison," "carrying a pair of shoes," and one person "for his wife swearing an oath." Sir Charles Sedley and the Duke of Buckingham were frequently fined, in 1657 and 1658, for riding in their coaches on the "Lord's Day."[3]   But the "Man in the Moon" must have found the temperature in the neighbourhood of the "Observance Society" very high, for Christopher Deane, "at the Half Moon in the Strand, opposite the New Exchange Buildings," advertises in 1742 the sale by auction of all his "Household Goods, Plate, Linen, China, some pictures, and a great variety of good Kitchen Furniture."[4]

At the south-eastern corner of Bedford Street was the house,

[1] Timbs's *Walks and Talks about London*, 1865, p. 178.
[2] Wheatley's *Cunningham*.
[3] *Ibid*.
[4] *Daily Advertiser*, May 20, 1742.

now long since taken down, where Clay, who first applied papier-mâché to tea-trays in 1760, made thereby a fortune of £80,000. Some of his finest trays were painted by early members of the Royal Academy, among whom was Wheatley.

Possibly the blue colour with which many of the London signs were invested by their owners was an arbitrary selection with no special symbolism, excepting in cases, of course, like the " Blue Lion," the crest of the Percies, &c., but the adoption of the cerulean colour was so frequent that it gives one pause to wonder whether its adoption did not arise from more than mere fancy, or from the necessity merely of distinguishing a certain sign from others that represented similar objects in other varieties of the prismatic spectrum.   It seems possible that the colour of the sky, sacred in ancient mythologies, like red as that of the sun, has come down to us on the signboard no less certainly than in the folk-lore of the provinces, where a superstitious belief in it survives to the present day.   The young mothers, for instance, by Teviotside, wear a twist of plaited blue thread about their necks until their babies are weaned, and the mischievous west-country fairy hates the sight of blue flowers.   King Richard exclaims, " The lights burn blue ! " and among the Slavs, if the candle burns blue, there is said to be an angel in the room.   According to Randle Holme, "the pure azure sky signifieth piety and sincerity."   According to one's own observation, the colour of the sign depicted was never fanciful and arbitrary, but was in accordance with the rules invariably—at all events in the actual signboard days—associated with heraldic symbolism.   And such was the origin, no doubt, of the sign of the *Blue* Bible in Bedford Street which occurs in the Luttrell Collection in the British Museum (1683).   It distinguished the shop of William Sheares, Junior, in 1656, for whom was printed " Men, Miracles," &c.   The Blew Bible occurs again in Green Arbour Court, Little Old Bailey, as the sign of Michael Sparke in 1633, for whom was printed Prynne's " Histrio-Mastix." The name of the " Bermudas " probably dates from about the year 1609, when Sir George Somers was cast away upon them and claimed them for the Virginia Company.   The Virginia Company sold them to another company, to which a charter was granted by James I., June 29, 1615, when a settlement was formed.   The accounts which adventurers gave of the intricacies of these islands, accentuated by a poetical description of them by Waller the poet, while resident as an exile there during the Civil Wars, no doubt suggested this curious name for a congeries of courts and alleys remarkable for their labyrinthine nature. Their turbulent character is alluded to by Ben Jonson :—

"*Justice Overdo.* Look into any angle of the town, the Streights or the Bermudas, where the quarrelling lesson is read, and how do they entertain the time, but with bottle-ale and tobacco. The lecturer is o' one side, and his pupils o' the other, but the seconds are still bottle-ale and tobacco, for which the lecturer reads and the novices pay. Thirty pound a week in bottle-ale ! forty in tobacco ! and ten more in ale again." [1]

The "Caribbee Islands" too seems at a later period to have been suggested as a name for these rookeries by the fact of those islands being the easternmost of the West Indies, as Charing Cross was then the westernmost part of the town.

The trail of the cook's shop was all over Porridge Island, whence it was so named. The Trafalgar Square improvements led to the effacement of this spot also. In the "World" of November 29, 1753, is described "the fine gentleman, whose lodgings no one is acquainted with ; whose dinner is served up under cover of a pewter plate, from the Cook's shop in Porridge Island ; and whose annuity of a hundred pounds is made to supply a laced suit every year, and a chair every evening to a rout ; returns to his bedroom on foot, and goes shivering and supperless to rest, for the pleasure of appearing among people of real importance with the Quality of Brentford."

Henrietta Street, another once fashionable thoroughfare, is a continuation westward of the south side of Covent Garden Market, terminating at the north-east corner of Bedford Street. It was built in 1637, and named after *la reine malheureuse*, Henrietta Maria, the beautiful daughter of the most illustrious sovereign in Europe, Henry of Navarre (and Marie de Médicis), and Queen of Charles I. Strictly speaking, the street should have been called Mary Street, for Mary was the name by which her husband and her court chose to speak of her. [2] As a complement of Henrietta Street being so named, King Street, also built in 1637, was called after the King. King Street, running parallel with Henrietta Street, is at the north-west corner of Covent Garden, and leads into New Street and St. Martin's Lane. From a house in Henrietta Street, the beautiful Georgiana, Duchess of Devonshire, and the other fair and high-born women who canvassed for Charles James Fox, used to watch the humours of the Westminster election. Hannah More, on one

---

[1] *Bartholomew Fair*, II. i.
[2] Strickland's *Queens*, 1852, vol. viii. p. 33.

of these occasions, appears to have been staying in Henrietta Street. " I had like," she writes to one of her sisters, " to have got into a fine scrape the other night. I was going to pass the evening at Mrs. Coles's in Lincoln's Inn Fields. I went in a chair. They carried me through Covent Garden. A number of people, as I went along, desired the men not to go through the garden, as there was an hundred armed men, who suspected every chairman belonged to Brooks's, and would fall upon us. In spite of my entreaties, the men would have persisted, but a stranger, out of humanity, made them set me down, and the shrieks of the wounded, for there was a terrible battle, intimidated the chairmen, who were at last prevailed on to carry me another way. A vast number of people followed me, crying out, ' It is Mrs. Fox: none but Mr. Fox's wife would dare to come into Covent Garden in a chair : she is going to canvass in the dark !' Though not a little frightened, I laughed heartily at this, but shall stir out no more in a chair for some time." [1]

The most eminent of the English miniaturists, Samuel Cooper, the " Vandyck in little," whom his friend Pepys, in his " Diary," calls the "great limner in little," dwelt for many years in Henrietta Street. Whether it is legible now one cannot say, but his epitaph in Latin in St. Pancras Churchyard styles him "the Apelles of his age." His wife was the sister of the poet Pope's mother.

A famous latter-day tavern was " Offley's," at No. 23 Henrietta Street. Offley was originally at Bellamy's. But whereas the House of Commons chop was small and thin, honourable members some-times eating a dozen at a sitting, Offley's was thick and substantial, and, served with shred shalots, warmed in gravy with its accompaniment of nips of Burton, was a delicious after-theatre supper. There was singing one evening of the week in the great room, where Francis Crew sang Moore's melodies, then in their zenith. A higher class of men attended than were encountered later, and among them were a few well-to-do, substantial tradesmen from the neighbourhood. Hither came the renowned surgical-instrument maker from the Strand, who had the sagacity to buy the iron from off the piles of Old London Bridge after it had lain for centuries under water, and convert it into some of the finest surgical instruments ever made. [2] But Offley's declined in popularity with the departure of the merry old host, and the house was let to the Cambridge publishers, the

[1] Jesse's *London: Its Celebrated Characters, &c.* (Bentley, 1871).
[2] Timbs's *Walks and Talks about London*, 1865, p. 181.

L

Macmillans, who afterwards went to Bedford Street.   In two houses opposite Offley's, Mr. Bohn, *père*, assembled his immense stock of books, outnumbered, however, by his eldest son, Mr. Henry Bohn, in York Street.[1]

The Royalist, Sir Lewis Dyve, dwelt on the south side of Henrietta Street in 1637, as did also Strafford in 1640.   The south seems to have been the more fashionable side, for Samuel Cooper, the miniaturist, was living here when a rate was made for raising £250 for payment of the rector and repairs of the church of St. Paul, Covent Garden, according to an ordinance of January 7, 1645 ; and he was still here when Pepys visited him on March 30, 1668, to arrange about the portrait of his wife.   His price was then £30.   Kitty Clive lived here in March 1756, when she advertised her benefit.   When McArdell, the engraver, hung out his sign of the " Golden Ball " in this street, Walpole wrote to Grosvenor Bedford in 1759 : " I shall be much obliged to you if you will call as soon as you can at McArdell's in Henrietta Street, and take my picture from him.   I am extremely angry, for I hear he has told people of the print.   If the plate is finished, be so good as to take it away, and all the impressions he has taken off, for I will not let him have one." [2]   When, in 1764, he engraved and sold his fine print of Garrick and Mrs. Cibber as Jaffier and Belvidera, he lived "at the corner of Henrietta Street in Covent Garden."   Sir Robert Walpole was chairman of a small social club which met at the house of Samuel Scott, the marine painter.   Captain Laroon (well known in the artistic and social circles of his day) was deputy-chairman, under Sir Robert.   The club consisted of only six gentlemen, who met at stated times in the drawing-room of Scott, and it was unanimously agreed by the members that they should be attended by Scott's wife only, who was a remarkably witty woman.   Captain Laroon made a most beautiful drawing of the members of the club in conversation.[3]   Jane Austen lived in this street for a time, at the house of her brother, who was a partner in the bank close by.[4] Catherine Clive, the celebrated comic actress, resided for some time in this street, and here died one who was aforetime a poet of some

---

[1] Timbs's *Walks and Talks about London*, 1865, p. 181.   See also " Horæ Offleana " in *Bentley's Miscellany*, March 1841.

[2] Wheatley's *London*.

[3] Smith's *Nollekens and his Times*, vol. ii. p. 273.

[4] *Fortnightly Review*, n.s., vol. xxxvii. (1885), p. 263, quoted in Wheatley's *London*.

celebrity—Paul Whitehead—the social companion of Frederick, Prince of Wales.[1] His poetical squibs exercised a considerable influence over the politics of the day. He was one of the depraved brotherhood who assembled at Medmenham Abbey. By his last will, says Jesse, Paul Whitehead bequeathed his heart, enclosed in a marble urn, to his friend, Lord Le Despencer, with a request that it might be placed in his lordship's mausoleum at High Wycombe. The fantastic wish was complied with, but what has since become of the heart and the urn we know not.[2] He died on December 20, 1774, in his lodgings in this street, having, during the course of a protracted illness, burnt all his manuscripts within reach.

At Rawthmell's Coffee-house in Henrietta Street, the Society of Arts was formed in 1754. And at the "Castle" tavern Sheridan fought his second duel, the first having been interrupted at Hyde Park, near the Hercules Pillars.[3] It was at the "Castle" tavern that the gallant feat was performed of a young blood taking one of her shoes from the foot of a noted toast, filling it with wine, and drinking her health, after which it was consigned to the cook, who prepared from it an excellent ragout, which was eaten with great relish by the lady's admirers.[4] We are told that John Pierce, the Soyer of his day, was the cook.

At the "Golden Head" in Henrietta Street, Sir Robert Strange, the eminent engraver, was living in 1756, when he published his proposals for engraving, by subscription, three historical prints—two from Pietro da Cortona, and one from Salvator Rosa.[5]

There was a celebrated tavern with the sign of the "Key" at the corner of Henrietta Street, *circa* 1690 (query, "Cross Keys" *infra*).

A "Lady dress'd in yellow Damask, that spoke to a Gentleman in a Hackney coach about 6 o'clock at Night on Saturday last in Henrietta Street, Covent Garden," is requested to send "a Letter directed for Mr. Jeffreys at Rochford's Coffee-house, Charing Cross, letting the said Mr. Jeffreys know where she may be heard of, when she will be inform'd of something much to her Advantage. N.B. The Gentleman order'd the Coach to carry him to the Lodge in Hyde Park."[6]

---

[1] Jesse's *London: Its Celebrated Characters and Remarkable Places* (Bentley, 1871), p. 358.

[2] *Ibid.*

[3] *Literary Landmarks*, by L. Hutton, 1889, p. 273.

[4] *History of Signboards*, 1884.

[5] Wheatley's *London*.

[6] *Daily\Post*, July 1725.

The " Constitution " tavern in Bedford Street, No. 32 in 1879, seems to be identical with the "Cross Keys" at an earlier period, which is described in Burn's "Beaufoy Tokens" as between Henrietta and King Streets in Bedford Street, and of which two tokens are extant.   The " Cross Keys " was certainly at the corner of Henrietta Street, and a place of some note to judge from the following :

" The Independent Electors of the City and Liberty of Westminster are desir'd to meet tomorrow at seven o'clock at the Cross Keys Tavern, the Corner of Henrietta Street, Covent Garden, on special affairs." [1]

John Partridge, the mountebank almanac-maker, out of whom Swift and the " Tatler " extracted some fun, had, according to Jesse, a shop in Henrietta Street.   His fame, too, will live as long as a halo of due appreciativeness encircles one of the most pleasing poems in the English language—Pope's " Rape of the Lock."   Partridge was brought up to the trade of a shoemaker, which he practised in Covent Garden in 1680 ; but having acquired some knowledge of Latin, astronomy, and astrology, he published an almanac.   Swift began his humorous attacks by " Predictions for the Year 1708, wherein the Month and the Day of the Month are set down, the Persons named, and the Great Actions and Events of Next Year particularly related as they will come to pass.   Written to prevent the People of England from being further imposed upon by the Vulgar Almanac-makers."   After discussing with much gravity the subject of almanac-making, and censuring the almanac-makers for their methods, he continues as follows :   " But now it is time to proceed to my predictions, which I have begun to calculate from the time the sun enters Aries, and this I take to be properly the beginning of the natural year.   I pursue them to the time when he enters Libra, or somewhat more, which is the busy time of the year ; the remainder I have not yet adjusted " &c.   " My first prediction is but a trifle, yet I will mention it to shew how ignorant those sottish pretenders to astrology are in their own concerns.   It relates to Partridge the almanac-maker.   I have consulted the star of his nativity by my own rules, and find he will infallibly die on the 29th of March next, about eleven at night, of a raging fever ; therefore I advise him to consider of it, and settle his affairs in time."   Partridge, after the 29th of March, publicly denied that he had died, which increased the fun, and the game was kept up by the " Tatler."

---

[1] *Daily Advertiser*, March 15, 1742.

Then Swift wrote "An Elegy on the Supposed Death of Partridge, the Almanac-maker," followed by :

THE EPITAPH.

Here, five foot deep, lies on his back
A cobbler, starmonger, and quack,
Who to the stars, in pure good-will,
Does to his best look upward still.
Weep, all ye customers, that use
His pills, his almanacs, or shoes ;
And you that did your fortunes seek ;
Step to his grave but once a week.
This earth, which bears his body's print,
You'll find has so much virtue in 't,
That I durst pawn my ears, 'twill tell
Whate'er concerns you full as well,
In physic, stolen goods, or love,
As he himself could when above.

In the "Rape of the Lock," after the robbery of Belinda's "wavy curl," Pope proceeds to place the stolen object among the constellations :

This the beau-monde shall from the Mall survey,
And hail with music its propitious ray ;
This the blest lover shall for Venus take,
And send up prayers from Rosamonda's lake ;
This Partridge soon shall view in cloudless skies,
When next he looks through Galileo's eyes ;
And hence th' egregious wizard shall foredoom
The fate of Louis and the fall of Rome.[1]

---

[1] Pope's *Poetical Works*, 1866 : " Rape of the Lock," canto v.

CHAPTER XII.

ST. MARTIN'S LANE.

WHEN migratory London, in its restless desire to dissociate domestic life from the hustling highways of commerce, first began "throwing bricks and mortar at haystacks," St. Martin's Lane was one of the earliest localities, at the end of the sixteenth century, to capitulate. The traveller through the Lane might still pause and listen to the nightingale in Spring Gardens, but by the year 1600 both sides were built upon, says Pennant,[1] who is in this instance perhaps more entitled to credence than the usually accurate Cunningham who says that it was built about 1613 ; for James Howel in his " Londinopolis," 1657, alludes to one side at least having been occupied by private dwellings before the year given by Cunningham. "On the west side of St. Martin's Church and Lane," he says, "are many gentile fair Houses in a row built by the same Earl of Salisbury who built Britain's Burse, but somewhat before." That is, the houses on the west side of the Lane were built before 1608, which was the year in which the first stone of the New Exchange or Britain's Burse was laid. Although the word " Lane " does not necessarily imply a passage-way between hedgerows only, yet in this case the street certainly does retain evidence, in its name, of former rural environments. And we are reminded of this rusticity, not only in the name of the thoroughfare, known until, at least, 1613 as West Church Lane, but in that of a court between numbers 49 and 50 called the Hop Gardens, though incorrectly, for its old name was the " Hop Garden," in the singular, albeit in Strype's Stow it is called the Hop Yard—"The Hop Yard," he says, "indifferent good for Stabling, and has an open passage into Bedfordbury." This Hop Yard, as we may on such high authority speak of it, possibly appertained originally to Sir Hugh Platt, the horticulturist, who was the third son of a London brewer named Richard Plat or Platt. He maintained experimental gardens both in Bethnal Green and

---

[1] *London*, 1793, p. 141.

St. Martin's Lane. The last of five tracts by him which appeared under the title of " The Jewell House of Art and Nature, conteining sundry new Experiments in the Art of Husbandry," in 1594, deals with miscellaneous topics like " the brewing of beer without hops." A Mr. George Fenner, in the middle of the eighteenth century, announces a theft, apparently from the stables alluded to by Stow, of " a bright Bay-Mare, fourteen hands high, nine years old, with a small Star in her Forehead, a cut Tail, and an ' R ' or ' H ' or ' S ' clipped on her near Hip ; several white Saddle-spots, an old Fire-brand of an ' S ' on her near shoulder, the Hair rubbed off both her Fillets." Twenty shillings reward is offered by Mr. Fenner at the Hop Garden in St. Martin's Lane. A pamphlet published about the same time (1736) by D. Browne, at the Black Swan without Temple Bar, sets forth " The Riches of a Hop-Garden, from the several Improvements arising by that Beneficial Plant, as well to the private Cultivators of it as to the Publick. With the Observations and Remarks of the most celebrated Hop-Planters in Britain. Wherein such Rules are laid down for the Management of the Hop as may improve the most barren Ground, from one Shilling to thirty or forty Pounds an Acre per Annum. In which is particularly explained, the whole Culture from the first breaking up of the Ground, the Planting etc., to the Kilning, or Drying of the Hop. Rendred familiar to every Capacity. By R. Bradley, Professor of Botany in the University of Cambridge, and F.R.S. The Second Edition. Price 1s. 6d." [1] Also another pamphlet, " Instructions for Planting and Managing of Hops, and for raising of Hop Poles. Drawn up and published by Order of the Dublin Society. Price 1s." [2]

The progress of science has rendered Dr. Richard Bradley's works obsolete. He is chiefly noteworthy in having forestalled, so it was said, Dr. Brewster in the discovery of the kaleidoscope. But the contrivance proposed by Bradley for producing combinations of coloured surfaces depends on principles totally different from those on which the kaleidoscope is constructed, and are calculated to produce a very inferior effect. [3] Whether Sir Hugh Platt was the planter or not, there is every probability that the Hop Garden in St. Martin's Lane dates from the very limited cultivation of the hop at the beginning of the seventeenth century, when England certainly did not produce a quantity sufficient for her own consumption. [4] The

[1] *St. James's Evening Post*, December 11, 1736.   [2] *Ibid.*
[3] See preface to Martyn's *Dissertation on the Æneis*.
[4] Beckmann's *History of Inventions*, 1846, vol. ii. p. 385.

garden must almost necessarily have been devoted to a very limited amateur cultivation of the hop, *i.e.* the English hop, " Hop-Scotch," among the children of the court, being at a later period more in evidence. It occupied ground south of the White Horse Livery Stables. In J. T. Smith's " Nollekens and his Times," we are told that these stables were originally Tea Gardens, and that the house overhanging the gateway was supposed then to be the oldest build- ing in the Lane. This was in 1828, but the house has long since vanished. The White Horse stables were well known as "Hornby's livery and private stables," whence in 1820 are advertised a Pony, Gig and Harness, to be Sold, together or separately ; the pony is sound, fast, and quiet in harness or to ride ; the gig is handsomely and tastily built in the Stanhope style, with drop box and low steps —very little used." [1] A similar advertisement relates to a " Horse, *Dennet*, and Harness." [2] A dennet was, I believe, a two-wheeled travelling carriage.

The house in St. Martin's Lane which Thomas Coutts made his urban home is not apparently known. Betty Starky, a housemaid in Coutts's Strand office, must have already been aware of what her future, as "a most respectable, modest, handsome young woman" was to be, when, on a certain occasion, she was scouring her master's stairs. Possibly she asked too much when a clerk approached, wearing dirty boots, and was requested to remove them. The clerk snappishly refused, whereupon Betty remarked : " Before long I'll make you put off your shoes and your stockings too, if I choose it." On the death of Mr. Campbell, about 1760, James Coutts took his brother Thomas as a partner and changed the name of the firm to James and Thomas Coutts. James was very angry with his brother for what he considered this *mésalliance* with the housemaid. Yet Thomas's sterling qualities as a man, and his exceptional abilities as a banker, were such that James never thought of dissolving the partnership. So Thomas took his "clean and industrious" bride home to his house in St. Martin's Lane. The number in the Lane is not mentioned, but here Lord Dundonald and his brothers often visited them, and it was remarked that Mrs. Thomas Coutts's good sense, amiable disposition, and exemplary conduct endeared her to all her husband's family, and commanded the respect of everyone who knew her. [3]

---

[1] *Times*, October 10, 1820, first page.   [2] *Ibid.*
[3] Vide *Coutts and Co., Bankers*, by Ralph Richardson, F.R.S.E., F.S.A. Scot., 1900, pp. 67–8.

Goethe, says the author of "Coutts and Co.," contracted a decided *mésalliance* when he married Christiane Vulpius, a beautiful girl of humble life. Thomas Coutts, however, acted more honourably to his humble partner than Goethe did to his, for Coutts married Betty Starky at once, whereas the German philosopher allowed many years to pass before he had the courage or sense of honour to wed Christiane Vulpius.

While alluding to old houses, there was in St. Martin's Lane a fine example of the better-class London shop which, sixty years ago, had even then retained all its essential features through many changes. The richly carved private door-case told of the well-to-do trader who had either himself erected it or had converted the place from a private dwelling into a shop, which was that of an Italian warehouse. The window was curiously constructed, carrying out the traditional form of the old open shop with its projecting stall on brackets, and its slight window above, but effecting a compromise for security and comfort by enclosing the whole in a sort of glass box, above which the trade of the occupant was shown more distinctly in the small oil-barrels placed upon it, as well as by the models of candles which hung in bunches from the canopy above. The whole of this framework was of timber, richly carved throughout with foliated ornament, and was unique as a surviving example of the better class of shops of the last century.

The growth of the vine also in the more suburban parts of London, and the good and strong wine, generally of a Burgundy character, that was the result, is really remarkable. At Lee's Nursery, Hammersmith, and at Parson's Green, the production was copious, and the groves of Charing were not behind the more outlying parts in their offerings to Bacchus. Even so late as the beginning of the last century No. 96 St. Martin's Lane possessed a tenant of the name of Powell, whose mother had, for many years, made "a pipe of wine" from a vine nearly a hundred feet long which was attached to the establishment.[1]

Perhaps it is worthy of mention that, during the excavations for the foundation of the present St. Martin's Library, I went over a very old house just then receiving the attentions of the "house-

---

[1] *A Paladin of Philanthropy*, by Austin Dobson, 1899 (The *Grub Street of the Arts*, pp. 303–4). The extensive cultivation of the vine in the neighbourhood immediately surrounding *old* London, and the survival of the place-names in which "Vine" occurs, forms a subject meriting particular attention from some future London historian. "The Royal Vineyard" in St. James's Park survived apparently so late as 1742 (see *Daily Advertiser* for April 22 of that year).

breaker," which, in the early days of the "Cradle of English Art,"[1] had evidently belonged to some well-to-do and possibly distinguished person.   Behind a pilastered canopy in one of the bedrooms, where the bed would have been, was a secret door which one could even then open without the slightest perceptible noise.   In the ground at the side of the house I found a portion of a beautifully carved stone representation of the royal arms which I had reason to assume had appertained to the old Royal Mews before its dismantling.   Near it I obtained also a cornelian-handled razor of the seventeenth century.   During the excavations for the new St. Martin's Vestry in Charing Cross Road the old pond re-appeared, which I was told, erroneously however, by an antiquary at the time is mentioned in Hearne's unpublished Diary in the Bodleian Library, as having been the pond into which Nell Gwynn's mother fell whilst in a state of inebriety, and was drowned.[2]   Possibly this pond was identical with that mentioned in a paragraph relating to what occurred in a crowd which had collected to observe the ruins, after a fire apparently, at the end of the Lane.   Several gentlemen and others one Sunday were standing looking on, when a woman attempted to pick a gentleman's pocket.   But he apprehended her in the fact, and "laid her on with his Cane, pretty heartily, which drew the Resentment of the Mobb upon him, as not being acquainted with the Reason ; but being acquainted therewith the Offender was hurried away to the Pond in the Meuse,[3] and underwent the Discipline usual in such Cases."

But everything should have a beginning, so that it will be as well to revert to the end of St. Martin's Lane, which debouched, until the formation of Trafalgar Square and the effacement of the Mews, upon that part of the Strand exactly opposite what is now Northumberland Avenue.   The millions that pass Charing Cross in the yearly routine of their avocations and pleasures are happily leavened, doubtless, by a fair proportion of great men and women—both the known and the

---

[1] Thus Mr. Ashby-Sterry describes St. Martin's Lane, and it certainly sounds better than the *Grub Street of the Arts* of Allan Cunningham, which is not quite accurate.

[2] Faulkner, in his *History of Chelsea*, 1810, quotes " a paragraph in a newspaper of the day " as follows : " We hear that Madam Ellen Gwynn's mother, sitting lately by the water-side, at her house by the Neat Houses, near Chelsey, fell accidentally into the water and was drowned " (*Domestic Intelligence*, August 5, 1679).

[3] Probably meaning in the vicinity of the Mews ; or could there have been a pond within the Mews walls for watering the horses ?   See Appendix.

unknown great. And if these in the flesh were absent, there would be the shadows of Nelson, Napier, Gordon, Havelock, and King Charles, to remind us of Emerson's not very graceful simile, that " without great men great crowds of people in a nation are disgusting ; like moving cheese, like hills of ants or of fleas—the more the worse." But among these crowds of great, little, and ordinary folk, how many are aware that just beyond where the Havelock statue, at the south-east corner of the Square, stands—opposite the Grand Hotel—was the entrance to St. Martin's Lane. And a few feet to the west of this threshold of the nursery of English art stood a famous coaching inn known as the " Checker." At what precise time the Chequer Inn disappeared is not apparent, but it seems to have vanished after giving its name to the court, and the growth in the public patronage of coaches for travelling appears to have converted it into the " Coach and Horses," whence the Epsom Coach set out every day in 1740, and the Windsor Coach every day in summer, Tuesdays, Thursdays, and Saturdays in winter.[1] It is this inn that has, I think, been immortalised by Hogarth,[2] as a background for his first plate of the " Harlot's Progress."

On the east side of the Charing Cross entrance to St. Martin's Lane was the Star Inn. Star Court is thus situated in Strype's plan of St. Martin's parish. The King's Head Inn, situated in a small court next, eastward, to Star Court, was exactly opposite Hartshorn Lane, now Northumberland Street. This was in the Strand. There was an Hermaphrodite exhibited at the King's Head " over against the Mews Gate, Charing Cross."[3] This was in 1700, and it was considered a " monster." After the publication of Prynne's " Retractation of his Book against Stage Plays, called Histrio-mastix," a large posting bill dated " From the King's Head in the Strand," signed " William Prynne," and headed " The Vindication," recites the title of the pamphlet and declares it " to be a mere forgery and imposture." The style of this " Retractation " so thoroughly imitates Prynne's that nothing in it but the stultification of his general opinions could occasion a doubt of its genuineness ; and the imposition might still pass pretty current if one of Prynne's bills were not in existence. A copy of this fierce denial is in Mr. J. P. Collier's " Poetical Decameron," vol. ii. p. 322.[4]

[1] *Complete Guide to London*, 1740, pp. 76-103.
[2] See also p. 60.
[3] Morley's *Bartholomew Fair*, ch. xvi. p. 251.
Hone's *Ancient Mysteries*, 1823, p. 216.

On the west side of St. Martin's Lane, mention has been omitted of Woodstock Court, opposite the statue of King Charles, and between the entrance to the Lane and the Great Mews. I have been unable to ascertain why this court was so named, but possibly it was in some way owing to the traffic between London and Woodstock in Oxfordshire, in the fine wash-leather gloves and polished steel watch-chains for which the town of Woodstock was famous. The Woodstock trade in polished steel chains has, however, been killed by Birmingham and Sheffield. The work of the Woodstock artificers was so famous that two ounces of polished steel chain sold in France for 172*l.* John Marston, in "Certain Satyres" (London, 1598) thus describes the ruff of a beau :

> His ruffe did eate more time in neatest setting,
> Than Woodstock-work in painfull perfecting.

" The comparison of the workmanship of a laced and plaited ruff," says Warton, " to the laboured nicety of the steel-work of Woodstock is just."

But it is equally probable that Woodstock Court derived its name from some association with King Charles I.'s manor of Woodstock, where he was a frequent visitor, as were also his sons, Kings Charles and James.[1] It is worthy of remark, too, that Woodstock Church was dedicated in the name of the same saint as St. Martin's-in-the-Fields, St. Martin, Bishop of Tours.

For many years subsequent to 1733, there was a crossing westward to the " Checker " between the Mews Gate and Spring Gardens, which was swept assiduously—as beggars will sweep crossings if they find it worth their while—by a one-legged man named Ambrose Gwinett. This Gwinett had been hanged, and afterwards hanged in chains, near Deal, as the murderer, on circumstantial evidence, of one Richard Collins, in reality kidnapped by privateers. Being discovered to be alive, Gwinett was taken down by his relatives, recovered, went to sea, and at Havannah fell in with his supposed victim. In 1768 his story was printed from his own narrative, with a frontispiece evidently based (in part) upon the Execution plate of Hogarth's " Apprentice " series. It is but fair

---

[1] Woodstock, the great hunting park for game, about eight miles from Oxford, established by Henry I., became an important royal residence, much frequented by Queen Eleanor of Guienne, and equally celebrated for her husband's Fair Rosamond Clifford, whose semi-mythical biography still clings to the park and neighbourhood (*Journal of British Archæological Association*, vol. xlvii. part 3, p. 251).

to add that from a manuscript note in a copy of the "Life and Adventures" at the British Museum, it would seem that Bishop Percy regarded the whole thing as a concoction of Bickerstaffe the dramatist.[1] While speaking of crossings, in a Scotch magazine for January 1866, there was an article under the title of "Grandfather and I," which described some of the phases of metropolitan life and manners in the year 1800. The pavements, such as they were, must have been in a queer condition to have rendered necessary the tactics of which a lady of considerable distinction was the surprised witness, her companion having alighted, when their carriage stopped at a jeweller's near Charing Cross. The coach stood across the cause-way, and some gentlemen, wanting to cross to the other side, desired the coachman to move on a little. The fellow was surly and refused, and during the altercation the lady came to the shop door, and foolishly ordered her coachman not to stir from his place. On this one of the gentlemen, without any hesitation, opened the coach-door and, with boots and spurs on, went through the carriage ; he was followed by his companions, to the extreme discomposure of the lady within. To complete the jest, a party of sailors, coming up, observed that "if this was a thoroughfare they had as much right to go through it as the gemmen " ; and they accordingly went through the coach also.

Sir William Davenant the poet's indulgence in licentious dissipation subjected him to a disease which so injured his nose as to furnish the sarcastic spirits of the age with a never-failing topic for coarse jests and allusions. Some years after the loss of this both useful and ornamental appendage he was passing by the Mews at Charing Cross, when he was followed by a beggar-woman, who prayed God to preserve his eyesight. Davenant, who had nothing whatever the matter with his eyes, inquired, with some curiosity, what on earth could induce her to pray for his eyesight, for, he said, " I am not purblind as yet." " No, your honour," she said, " but if ever you should be, I was thinking you would have no place to hang your spectacles on." [2]

As one came up St. Martin's Lane from the Strand, the first turning on the left, before the Trafalgar Square fountains began discharging their columns of green water, was Duke's Court. The court

[1] *A Paladin of Philanthropy*, by Austin Dobson, 1899, p. 246. The story, however, does not read like an invention, and survival from the rope on the part of the victim is known to have happened in several instances.

[2] Jesse's *Memorials of London*, 2nd series, 1901, p. 152.

was here in 1831, and probably later, for even the preliminary preparations for the laying out of the Square were of a leisurely character. This Duke's Court is not mentioned either by Cunningham or by Wheatley, but it was here that the celebrated bookbinder, Roger Payne, dwelt, whose *chef-d'œuvre* was the binding, at a cost of fifteen guineas, of the *Æschylus*[1] in Lord Spencer's library. Payne was a native of Windsor Forest, and was born in 1739. His talents as an artist, particularly in the finishing department, were of the first order, and such as, up to his time, had not been developed by any other of his countrymen. " Roger Payne," says Dr. Dibdin, " rose like a star, diffusing lustre on all sides, and rejoicing the hearts of all true sons of bibliomania." He bound with such artistic taste as to command the admiration and patronage of many noblemen, but owing to his excessive indulgence in strong ale, he was in person a deplorable specimen of humanity. During the latter part of his life he was the victim of poverty and disease. He closed his earthly career in Duke's Court, November 20, 1787, and was interred a few yards away from his residence, in the burial-ground of St. Martin's-in-the-Fields, at the expense of his worthy patron, Mr. Thomas Payne.[2] In this court was one of the toy-shops where Boydell was in the habit of exhibiting his etchings for sale, and which displayed the sign of the " Cricket Bat."

At the " Crown " in Duke's Court the journeymen tailors and staymakers formed a combination in 1756 against their masters.[3] In a daily newspaper of November 1762 it is stated that " the signs in Duke's Court are all taken down and fixed to the front of the houses." J. Davies was a bookseller and publisher in this court in 1742.[4]

Crown Court must have been somewhere immediately in the neighbourhood, although I cannot ascertain where.[5] One Saturday in April, 1764, three persons were coming to town on horseback from Deptford. One of these, the master of the Thistle and Crown Alehouse in Crown Court, near St. Martin's Church, rode furiously against a post and dashed his brains out. How they managed it we are not told, but another was thrown, had his leg broken,

---

[1] Thomas Stanley, the editor of *Æschylus*, who died in 1678, was buried in St. Martin's churchyard.

[2] Thornbury's *Haunted London*, 1880, p. 458.

[3] Collection in St. Martin's Library of material relating to the signs of this part, No. 2, 888.

[4] He advertises the *Confessions of Count * * ***, translated from the French : *Daily Advertiser*, Feb. 18, 1742.

[5] Possibly Crown Court, Soho.

and was taken up for dead, while the third was dismounted and very much bruised.[1]

Mr. J. W. Harrison, whose extensive acquaintance with this neighbourhood is very remarkable, informs me that Duke's Court was called Duke Street when King James granted an acre of land for the graveyard, workhouse, &c.

---

[1] Collection of Newspaper Cuttings, &c., in St. Martin's Library, Charing Cross (April 14, 1764).

CHAPTER XIII.

ST. MARTIN'S LANE—*continued.*

PERHAPS one of the most extraordinary artifices ever resorted to by a bailiff (in the *exigeant* eighteenth century), on the scent of a debtor, was that of the famous " Jack " Faringdon. He had an action against Richard Bush, a joiner and coffin-maker in St. Martin's Lane, Strand. This person, being a " shy cock," as the " shoulder-dabbers " styled a wary evader of his pecuniary responsibilities, was found to be a difficult bird to snare. However, the bailiff and his " follower " went to an ale-house in St. Martin's Lane near where he dwelt, and, confiding their plan to the victualler, called for a pack of cards and played at cribbage until high words arose about cheating, when, in their pretended passion, they drew their swords. Now the bailiff's follower had a lamb's bladder filled with blood in his pocket, the contents of which, being pricked by the bailiff's sword, ran about the floor. The bogus victim dropped his sword and fell, as if dead. There was a cry of " Murder ! " which flew from one end of the Lane to the other. The victualler shut his door, swearing he would let nobody in till the corpse was laid out. Accordingly the " follower " lay stretched out on a " shuffle-board table " with a clean sheet spread over him, and the tapster was sent to Richard Bush to take measure of the supposed deceased for a coffin, who accordingly came, and, pulling out the rule that he wore tucked into his apron-strings, fell to measuring the supposed corpse without taking off the sheet, saying that he was full 6 feet 3 inches long, and that his coffin must be 1 foot 8 inches in depth. Upon which up jumped the corpse swearing it would be too large for him any way, and Faringdon, taking hold of the joiner, said he had an action for £12 against him, which the poor joiner was forced to discharge before they would dismiss him.[1]

Before we come to the *present* lower end of St. Martin's Lane,

---

[1] *The Comical and Tragical History of the Lives and Adventures of the most noted Bayliffs in and about London and Westminster,* by Captain Alexander Smith, 1723, p. 59.

there was, on the west side, Red Lion Court, which was between Duke's Court and Grant's Court; and Ellis Court, between Grant's Court [1] and Hemming's Row or Rents. And just about here, "near the Stocks," which were near the wall of the Watchhouse in front of St. Martin's Church, was a place of resort very popular with chess-players, mostly City men, in such leisure time as their business circumstances afforded. But it attracted all the most famous chess and draught players, as Simpson's did at a later period. When Nathaniel Smith the engraver, father of J. T. Smith, Keeper of the Prints and Drawings in the British Museum, lodged with Roubiliac the sculptor, in St. Martin's Lane, Smith was introduced by Roubiliac—in consequence of a bet made at Old Slaughter's—to the famous Parry, to play at draughts with him. Parry, although blind, was one of the first draught-players in England. The game lasted about half an hour. Smith, perceiving the venerable blind man to be much agitated, would most willingly have lost the game; but as there were bets depending on it, his integrity overpowered his inclination, and he won. This circumstance being made known to the other famous players, Sturges, Batridge, &c., the engraver was soon annoyed with challenges. The Dons at the "Barn" invited him to become a member; but all these temptations he withstood for the Arts, which he then studied with avidity. The "Barn," sometimes called the "Barn Meuse," was for many years frequented by all the noted players of chess and draughts, and it was there they often decided games of the first importance, played between persons of the highest rank, living in different parts of the world. [2]

An extremely sad case of self-destruction was that of James Sutherland, Esq., a judge-advocate of the Court of Admiralty, at Minorca and Gibraltar, whose tragic death became accidentally associated with the "Barn" tavern, and the immediately neighbouring St. Martin's Workhouse. While, one day in August 1791, King George III. was passing from the Queen's house to the *levée* at St. James's about one o'clock in the afternoon, this eminent naval adviser placed himself close to the rails of the Green Park, and shot himself in the breast with a pistol, in the hearing, and almost in the presence, of His Majesty. . . . A green silk purse containing two pence in coppers, a sixpence, a snuff-box, and a white pocket-handkerchief were all that were found in his pockets. The body was conveyed to St. Martin's Workhouse, and the coroner's

---

[1] Strype's *Stow* (1755) alludes to these as "three small ordinary courts."
[2] John T. Smith's *Nollekens and his Times*, 1828, vol. ii. p. 215.

inquest was taken at the "Barn Meuse," where, after a sitting of four hours, the jury humanely brought in a verdict of lunacy.

In the evidence he was stated to be a man of the strictest honour and most inflexible integrity, but he conceived that he had been treated with neglect at the hands apparently of the King, at the instigation of General Murray, and poverty was the chief cause. Expenses and privation were incurred in an important mission with despatches from Lord Weymouth to the Governor of Minorca. The mission failed, and in addition to his troubles he suffered, for many months, the horrors of a French prison.[1]

In December 1864 the Vestry of St. Martin's-in-the-Fields received notice from the Office of Woods and Forests that the Government would require the whole of the workhouse alluded to and its site " for the purpose of the National Gallery." [2]

The turnings that have already been noticed on the left side of St. Martin's Lane, coming up from Charing Cross, were all footways, rather than thoroughfares for vehicular traffic, which took its course through Hemming's Row, described by Elmes as the " first coach-turning on the left hand, going from the Strand." This Hemming's Row, or " Rents," although practically destroyed at the formation, in 1889, of Charing Cross Road, really occupied the present site of St. Martin's Place West with Parr's Bank and St. Martin's Library on the west side, a continuation, in fact, across St. Martin's Lane of Chandos Street. The library and offices of the Royal Society of Literature (No. 4 St. Martin's Place), of which the architect was Decimus Burton in 1830–1, were demolished for the laying out of the south end of Charing Cross Road, after the passing of the National Gallery Enlargement Act, followed by the removal of the workhouse, and Hemming's Row. The Provident Institution and Savings Bank, founded in 1816, stood at the present south-west corner of St. Martin's Lane. It closed its doors on the transfer of the accounts to the Post Office Savings Bank in January 1896, when the building was occupied by Parr's Bank.

I think it is Stow who says that " Hemming's Rents, opposite to Chandos Street, hath a great passage into Leicester Fields both for Horse and Foot. The buildings are on the North side, having the

---

[1] *Gentleman's Magazine*, August 17, 1791 (Deaths), and September 1791, pp. 868–70. St. Martin's Workhouse was situated between Duke's Court and Hemming's Row. See Horwood's *Plan of the Cities of London and Westminster,* 1799.

[2] *Builder*, December 3, 1864, p. 891.

Wall of St. Martin's churchyard, and the Trouble that the Carts and Coaches make in their frequent Passage occasions it not to be over well inhabited." Perhaps it was on account of this churning of the roadway by the heavy traffic of the time that it was unequivocally known as Dirty Lane,[1] a name from which it appears to have been redeemed by one John Hemings, apothecary, who probably built or owned houses here since the street was known as Heming's Rents. In the overseers' accounts of St. Martin's, £12 is stated to have been received in 1679 of John Hemings by way of a fine for not serving as overseer.[2] The "Ring and Pearl" was the sign of Denis Pere, jeweller and silversmith in Hemming's Row.[3]

The parish burying-ground adjoining the church of St. Martin was destroyed in 1829, when a new site was found in Camden Town. The custom of "waking" the dead, of which one could narrate instances occurring only lately among the Boers and in Italy, as well as among the Irish, is alluded to as having been prevalent in St. Martin's parish, in 1698, by Misson, in his "Mémoires par un Voyageur en Angleterre." Butler, the keeper of the Crown and Sceptre tavern in St. Martin's Lane, he says, told him there was a tun of rich port drunk at his wife's funeral. . . . and that "No men ever goe to women's burials, nor women to men's, so that there were none but women drinking of Butler's wine. Such women in England will hold it out with the men, when they have a bottle before them, as well as upon the other occasions, and tattle infinitely better than they."

There was another popular resort, described sometimes as "at Charing Cross," and at others as "near St. Martin's Church," known as the Rainbow Coffee-house, in Lancaster Court. This Lancaster Court does not appear to have derived its name from the Duchy of Lancaster—which extended west only so far as Cecil Street—but from a former beneficent vicar of St. Martin's, Dr. Lancaster, of whom there is a half-length portrait on the walls of the vestry-room, which vestry-room, according to Waters's plan of the parish in 1799, stood at the top, on the east side, of Lancaster Court, and at the south-eastern corner of the church. Dr. Lancaster was

---

[1] Hatton's *New View of London*.

[2] Cunningham. Upon an old wooden house at the west end of the Rents, near the second-floor window, was a stone tablet with the inscription, "Heming Row, 1680" or 1685.

[3] *Daily Advertiser*, Feb. 18, 1742. There are two views of houses at different periods at the corner of Hemming's Row and St. Martin's Lane, drawn by T. H. Shepherd, in St. Martin's Library.

Provost of Queen's College, Oxford (of which University he had been Vice-Chancellor), and Archdeacon of Middlesex, and died in 1717, when he left a considerable sum by will towards completing his college, previously benefited by his munificence.[1]   In Lancaster Court John Williams advertises that he " has had the Honour to be employ'd by the greatest Nobility, Gentry, and others in Town to destroy Bugs out of Palaces and other large and antient Buildings in which I have succeeded and effectually cleansed, by an infallible liquid (not to be parallel'd in England) which is endu'd with such exquisite Qualities that it kills them instantly, and is in no wise offensive to the Smell, or destructive to the finest Furniture," &c.[2] Another advertisement in the " Craftsman " ten years earlier[3] is embellished with an elegant cut representing six of the animals in question, in detestation of which an owner of the good old Scandinavian name of "Bugg," a word of entirely different etymology, advertised in the " Times " that he would in future be known by the name of " Norfolk Howard."   Fifteen yards of looped Mechlin lace between two and three fingers broad, and a piece of " grounded " lace of the same length, for which five and four guineas reward are offered respectively, are advertised from the Rainbow Coffee-house in Lancaster Court, by St. Martin's Church.[4]   This Lancaster Court ran from the centre of the south side of the church, in a south-eastward direction, to the Strand.[5]

From Mr. Barrett's at the Golden Anchor and Baptist's Head at the upper end of Church Court near St. Martin's Church is advertised the loss of a " Dimity Pocket, with a little Pocket in the inside, containing two Snuff-boxes, one black, and the other Iron japann'd," &c. . . . " Half a Guinea Reward, or in proportion for any part, and no Questions ask'd."[6]   This Church Court was at the bottom of St. Martin's Lane, between what was afterwards Agar Street and Duncannon Street, and "over against Hungerford Market."   Elmes says it was at No. 446 Strand.   The houses, among which was Allen's Coffee-house, abutted on Lancaster Court.

---

[1] *Londinium Redivivum*, 1803, vol. iv. p. 193.

[2] *Daily Advertiser*, June 15, 1742.

[3] The *Craftsman* of September 8, 1733.   In the winter of 1905 I encountered a respected instance of the name of Bugg in East Anglia, its native home.

[4] *Daily Advertiser*, Oct. 15, 1742.

[5] R. Horwood's *Plan of the Cities of London and Westminster*, 1799.   The ancestors of the Trees lived in Lancaster Court (Mr. J. W. Harrison), and here was Dr. Lancaster's vicarage.

[6] *Daily Advertiser*, April 3, 1742.

On October 27, 1737, " Allen's " was the scene of a fire which broke out about four o'clock A.M.   The Coffee-house was consumed before the contents could be removed ; the proprietor's mother, aged about seventy, who was ill in bed, perished in the flames, and was found in the ruins about eight o'clock.   The house adjoining towards the church was gutted, and another beyond was very much damaged. In Lancaster Court Mr. Tovey's " Compting-house " took fire, but now came the " perpetual Stream Hand-Engine belonging to their Office "—presumably the Westminster Fire Assurance Office, incorporated in 1717 and originally located close by in Tom's Coffee-house, St. Martin's Lane,[1]—which played out of the King's Arms Yard, and not only extinguished the fire at Mr. Tovey's, " but 'tis thought greatly contributed to the Preservation of the King's Arms Tavern, for a Closet belonging to an Alehouse next to the Strand, and adjoining to the Tavern, was also extinguished by the said Engine. 'Tis said the fire began in a Stove-Chimney, and there is good Reason to believe it, because the Smell of Burning Soot was taken Notice of by several of the Neighbours about Eleven o'clock on Thursday Night, which caused an Enquiry not only to be made at Mr. Allen's, but at several other Places in the Neighbourhood." [2]

The above testifies pretty accurately to the site of the King's Arms Tavern at Charing Cross.   It was probably near the south-west corner of St. Martin's Church and on the east side of St. Martin's Lane, which, it must be remembered, extended, before the Trafalgar Square Improvements, almost up to the portals of Northumberland House, as may be seen in Stow's plan of St. Martin's parish.

How happy those who preside at the Government Offices would be if they could put troublesome deputations in a bag !   Yet half-a-crown reward is offered to whomsoever shall bring " a black-Leather Letter-Case, in which was a Deputation from the Stamp-Office," to the King's Arms in St. Martin's Lane, "and no Questions ask'd."[3] It must, however, have been a different kind of deputation.

Being near the Mews—where the abuses that were practised by the King's servants in their " buying and selling horses and chaises, harness and carriages, by which means the Mews had been made a

---

[1] See Elmes's *Topographical Dictionary of London* (Westminster).   An extract from the parish books says : " July 2, 1728, expended at Tom's Coffee-house in St. Martin's Lane when the churchwardens of the severell parishes mett about the pest-fields, 1s. 6d."

[2] *St. James's Evening Post*, Oct. 27, 1737 (possibly 1734).

[3] *Daily Advertiser*, Feb. 19, 1742.

kind of trading place, to the great dishonour of the King," had become notorious [1]—the King's Arms Tavern naturally acquired a flavour of horse-dealing, such as, I believe, is associated to this day with taverns in the neighbourhood of Tattersall's and Aldridge's.   Many are the advertisements, for instance, like the following :

" To be SOLD,

" At the King's Arms Inn in St. Martin's Lane,

" A Very beautiful strong bay Gelding, fifteen Hands high, eight Years old, with a swish Tail, well mark'd, fit for the Road, a Hunter, or for an Officer, Master of sixteen Stone, and warranted sound." [2]

Again at the same mart :

" A Chesnut Gelding, fifteen Hands high, six Years old, with a star and small Blaze ; walks, trots, and gallops well ; fit both for the Road and Hunting, has two Years Meat in his Belly, never was abus'd, and warranted sound." [3]

The trade in horses which the King's stables here seem to have created drew large numbers of the rougher element in the population towards the spot, of whose riotous behaviour in this part Charing Cross had its more than fair share of experience.   At the King's Arms occurred one among many instances of how a riot was brought about in the streets of London, owing occasionally to the just anger of the mob, but more frequently through the malice of some individual. About the middle of July 1795 a fifer named John Lewis, having been refused liquor at the King's Arms, Charing Cross (then deprived of its license), and turned out of the house for his insulting behaviour, attracted an immense crowd round the door by falsely asserting that his companion had just been kidnapped, and was then chained down in the cellar with three others, whence they were to be conveyed away by a secret door that communicated with the Thames.   This tale was so fully credited by the people that, although the house was submitted to search and nothing of the kind discovered, all the furniture was destroyed or carried off, &c., before the military could disperse the rioters.   Lewis, however, was taken into custody by some persons who had witnessed his improper conduct.   But this was not the end of the matter.

[1] The Earl of Cork and Orrery, " Concerning the Office of the Master of the Horse," in the *Pall Mall Magazine*, Jan. 1896.
[2] *Daily Advertiser*, March 1, 1742.   [3] *Ibid.* June 26.

On the two following days a mob assembled both at Charing Cross and in St. George's Fields, where they partly demolished the Recruiting Offices, and made bonfires of the furniture. They were at last dispersed by the Horse Guards, who, after enduring a great deal of insult, were forced to ride their horses among them, by which several were trampled on and severely wounded, and some of the more active rioters were apprehended. On the succeeding morning another great multitude collected, and several parts of the town were threatened with disturbances, but the judicious distribution of the soldiery had the effect of intimidation, and the tumult ceased without the necessity for using particular violence. The instigator of these disorders was capitally convicted for the offence, and was hanged at Newgate in November ; some other persons also suffered for participating in them.[1]

When the excavator ploughed his cross-furrows of Shaftesbury Avenue and Charing Cross Road through the slums of St. Giles— there are not so many beggars now for the saint to extend his tutelage to—the writer attended the diggings in many cases, and many were the interesting mementoes of seventeenth-century life that he acquired in the wake of the labourer. Among these are especially noteworthy the small collection he formed of Venetian wineglass stems, many of them beautiful in themselves, but all possessing an added beauty of opalesque iridescence through long contact with the earth. Generally they resembled the more simple examples represented in the Catalogue of the Collection of Glass formed by Felix Slade, Esq., F.S.A.,[2] but the writer never encountered a perfect glass with bowl and stem intact, always the stem alone, reminding one of James Howell's quaint saying that "a good name is like Venice glass, quickly cracked, never to be mended ; patched it may be." Whether these Venetian wineglasses, found in a peculiar abundance in this neighbourhood,[3] as I can testify, were purchased at the glass-shop at the corner of St. Martin's Lane, in Glasshouse Street, or in Crutched Friars one cannot say, but there is reason to suppose that the glass-shop at the corner of St. Martin's Lane was coeval in its origin with the fashionable residential quarter where the wine-glass stems alluded to were found, and that the owner of the shop was a wholesale purchaser of one of the glasshouses where, as Stow

---

[1] Brayley's " London and Middlesex " (*Beauties of England and Wales*, vol. x.) part I., and Allen's *History of London*, 1828, vol. ii. p. 121.

[2] Ed. 1871, pp. 82–88 (plates b, c, d, &c.).

[3] In the years 1890–91.

says of the factory in Crutched Friars, "was made glass of divers
sorts to drink in."[1] The "Glass-Shop facing the Mews Wall" was so
well known as to become a landmark, and there the living Swedish
Colossus was exhibited.   They called him the "Christian Goliah,"
but his admirers at a shilling a head must have had some misgivings as to the accommodation which a glass-shop afforded for a
giant, than whom "no one of human species had been heard of
since that Æra of so monstrous a size," the "Æra" alluded to
being that of the Saxon giant, than whom the Swedish "Goliah"
was a foot taller.[2]   This Saxon giant was Maximilian Christian
Miller, born at "Leipzig" in Saxony in 1674.   There is a handbill
relating to him in the British Museum as follows :

"G.R. This is to give notice to all gentlemen, ladies, and others.
That there is just arrived from France, and is seen at the Two
Blue Posts and Rummer near Charing Cross, a giant born in
Saxony, almost eight feet in height, and every way proportionable ;
the like has not been seen in any part of the World for many
years : he has had the honour to shew himself to most princes
in Europe, particularly to his late Majesty the King of France, who
presented him with a noble scymiter, and a silver mace."   The
King of France referred to was Louis XIV., who died in 1715.
James Paris, in his manuscript book in the British Museum, says
that Miller was exhibited at the Blue Post, Charing Cross, about the
beginning of November 1732.   Thoresby the antiquary, in his
"Ducatus Leodiensis," 1714, says that he had it under the giant's
own hand that the latter was seven feet five inches, but he had
increased several inches by 1728.

The real business of Jerrom Johnson of the Glasshouse was not
exploiting giants, but that of satisfying the prevalent taste for cut
glass, lustres, &c. : "The right and most curious Lustres, new-

---

[1] Their delicate fabric is again alluded to by James Howell, in a letter written
to his brother from Venice in 1621, who says, "When I saw so many curious
glasses made here, I thought upon the compliment which a gentleman put upon
a lady in England, who, having five or six comely daughters, said he never saw
in his life such a dainty cupboard of crystal glasses.   The compliment proceeds,
it seems, from a saying they have here, that the first handsome woman that
ever was made was made of Venice glass ; which implies beauty, but brittleness
withal (and Venice is not unfurnished with some of that mould, for no place
abounds more with lasses and glasses)."

[2] *Daily Advertiser*, March 15, 1742. The giant probably had a room to himself either at the back or upstairs.   For the Saxon giant see E. J. Wood's *Giants
and Dwarfs*, 1868, p. 115, where, however, no mention is, I think, made of the
Swedish giant.

fashion Salts, Diamond cut and scallop'd Candlesticks, Decanters, Plates, Dishes, Bowls, Basons, Cups, Saucers, Middle-Stands, Desart Glasses, all cut, scallop'd, and flower'd Glasses, shall always be sold cheapest by the Maker." [1] Johnson himself was a Glass Scalloper, [2] whose shop appears to have occupied the site of what is now the "Chandos" tavern, at the south-eastern corner of St. Martin's Lane.

Described as near St. Martin's Lane, so presumably not far from the "Glass Shop," was the "Tea-Pot," the sign of a china-shop, where inquiries were to be made concerning the letting of "an hand-some Gentleman's Seat at Shackleford in Surrey—four Miles from Guilford, six from Farnham, and two from Godalming " . . . "enquire also at the Reverend Mr. Swift's at Putenham, near Guilford." [3]

The old St. Martin's round-house, which has already been alluded to, stood at the present bottom of St. Martin's Lane, exactly opposite the centre of the portico of St. Martin's Church, [4] and I think it has been mentioned that the parish whipping-post may still be seen in the crypt of the church.   Mr. Walter Thornbury mentions another riot here which is represented in a rare etching exhibiting the front of the round-house while the row is in progress. [5] In one of Walpole's "Letters" to Sir Horace Mann [6] he relates how there had lately been the most shocking scene of murder imaginable. "A parcel of *drunken* constables took it into their heads to put the laws in execution against *disorderly* persons, and so took up every woman they met, till they had collected five or six and twenty, all of whom they thrust into St. Martin's round-house, where they kept them all night with doors and windows closed. The poor creatures, who could not stir or breathe, screamed as long as they had any breath left, begging at least for water ; one poor creature said she was worth eighteen-pence, and would gladly give it for a draught of water, but in vain ! So well did they keep them there that in the morning four were found stifled to death, two died soon after, and a dozen more are in a shocking way. In short, it is horrid to think what the poor creatures suffered ; several of them were beggars, who, from having

[1] *Daily Advertiser*, Feb. 4, 1742.

[2] *i.e.* one who indented the edges either with scallop or shell-like curves or in other ways, as in the gadrooning of the edges of china or earthenware plates and dishes.

[3] *Mist's Weekly Journal*, Sept. 3, 1726.

[4] *Nollekens and his Times*, vol. i. pp. 93–94.

[5] *Haunted London*, 1880, p. 256.

[6] The *Letters of Horace Walpole*, 1840, vol. i. pp. 215–16.

no lodgings, were necessarily found in the street, and others honest labouring women. One of the dead was a poor washerwoman, big with child, who was returning home late from washing. One of the constables was taken, and others absconded ; but I question if any of them will suffer death, though the greatest criminals in this town are the officers of justice ; there is no tyranny they do not exercise, or villainy of which they do not partake. These same men, the same night, broke into a bagnio in Covent Garden, and took up Jack Spencer,[1] Mr. Stewart, and Lord George Graham, and would have thrust them into the round-house with the poor women, if they had not been worth more than eighteen-pence ! "[2]

The removal of what Malcolm calls "the execrable watch-house and sheds in front of the church" seems to have led to the opening up of the view past the Mews which we now enjoy, looking from Pall Mall East, a betterment which Elmes, as will, I think, be seen in his "London Improvements," was still further instrumental in promoting. In his "Topographical Dictionary" he says that Pall Mall East is a new street, recently formed from the eastward of Pall Mall to the portico of St. Martin's Church. Even from Waterloo Place the view embraces a part of the portico of the church, its spire, and the National Gallery, as may be seen on the cover of the new (1905) series of the "Pall Mall Magazine."

When Hogarth engraved his "Two Plates from a Paviour's Sign" the roads, and, but for the posts separating them therefrom, the footways also, were in a chaotic condition, and the Pavement in St. Martin's Lane was spoken of almost with bated breath. So much admiration did the comparative novelty evoke, indeed, that such spots as had undergone this improvement were spoken of as the Pav'd Alley or Court, the Pav'd Entry, Paviour's Alley or Court, of which varying forms of nomenclature there were in 1761 not more than fifteen or sixteen known instances throughout London.[3] A relic of this eighteenth century stone-worship survives to this day in Finsbury Pavement, while in 1761 there was a Pavement Row in Moorfields. It was not till a year later, in 1762, that this deplorable state of things was remedied by an Act for new

---

[1] "Jack" Spencer was the favourite grandson of old Sarah, Duchess or Marlborough, who left him a vast fortune (Walpole's *Letters*, i. 215-16).

[2] There is a description of the disgusting and barbarous interior of a watch-house at a late date, drawn from the personal experience of one who was on a certain occasion thus immured by mistake—Henry Angelo. See his *Reminiscences*, 1830, vol. ii. pp. 214-18.

[3] The *Environs of London*, 1761, vol. v.

paving in the City and Liberties of Westminster. Cobbles were abolished and their place taken by blocks of Scotch granite.[1] Until then every inhabitant acted according to his fancy, some "doors" consequently being "superbly paved, some indifferently, some very badly, and others totally neglected, according to the wealth, avarice, and caprice of the inhabitants. And a proof of the filth and nastiness which prevailed is detailed in the 'London Chronicle' of that time."[2] With regard to the plan for a new pavement it was stated that "all sorts of dirt and ashes, oyster shells, and the offals of dead poultry and other animals, will no longer be suffered to be thrown into the streets, but must be kept until the dustman comes ; nor will the annoyances erected by coachmakers be permitted ; and when a house is pulled down the rubbish must be carried to a proper place and not left in the streets."[3] The pavement[4] was considered so remarkable that it served by way of a street sign up to a later period. At the "lower end of the paved stones, St. Martin's Lane," a cabinet-maker hung out his sign of a "Crown and Looking Glass." As printed on his bill-heads the sign consisted of a modern mirror surmounted by a fan.[5] Again, "at the Golden Fleece *on the Pavement* in St. Martin's Lane, near Charing Cross," inquiries were to be made of a Mr. Siddall as to the "Letting . . . of the Turret House on Brooke Green, near Hammersmith, late in the possession of Richard Jackson, Esq. . . . a good Garden wall'd all round and planted with the best of Fruit, Coach-House, Stables, and all other Offices . . . very convenient for fifteen or sixteen in Family."[6] Advertisements for the "Daily Advertiser" were, again, taken in at S. Harding's, the Bible and Anchor, *on the Pavement* in St. Martin's Lane.[7] This Harding seems to have been the author of a little book on the "Monograms of Old Engravers," and here he sold old prints. It was to this shop that Wilson, the sergeant

---

[1] According to the Rev. John Entick, in his *History of London*, the Strand in 1766 was considered "one of the finest streets in Europe for length, breadth, buildings, trade, and the goodness of the pavement lately performed with Scotch stone in the modern taste" (vol. iv. p. 409).

[2] Allen's *History of London*, 1828, vol. iv. p. 346.   [3] *Ibid.* p. 346.

[4] The west side of the street from Beard's Court to St. Martin's Court was called the Pavement ; but the road has since been heightened three feet (Thornbury's *Haunted London*, 1880, p. 252).

[5] Banks Collection, Brit. Mus.

[6] *Daily Advertiser*, April 13, 1742. A Beaufoy token (No. 798) relates to a "Golden Fleece" tavern in St. Martin's Lane.

[7] *Ibid.* April 3.

painter, took an etching of his own, which was sold to Hudson as a genuine Rembrandt. That same night, by agreement, Wilson invited Hogarth and Hudson to supper. When the cold sirloin came in, Scott, the marine painter, called out, " A sail, a sail ! " for the beef was stuck with skewers bearing impressions of the new Rembrandt, of which Hudson was so proud.[1] In the " Cellar under the Hand and Pen on the Pav'd Stones in St. Martin's Lane (the Cellar and Vault to be Lett) " were for sale " extraordinary good Anchovies for 6*d.* the Pound or 1 0*s.* the Barrel ; and fine Florence Oil at 1 0*s.* the Gallon, and very good Florence Oils for 7, 8, or 9 Shillings the Gallon." [2] Later, twenty-eight years later, the Hand and Pen house itself apparently was " to be Lett " . . . " having been a School or Office many Years for the boarding and qualifying Persons for Business in Writing and Accounts, &c. . . . with a pleasant Garden," &c.[3] At the " lower end of the Lane," which may have been anywhere between New Street and the south-eastern extremity of Trafalgar Square, dwelt the King's Chairman, John Williams, as No. 2680 in Boyne's "Trades Tokens" testifies. Paul Savigne, a cutler, dwelt at the sign of the " Halbert and Crown," in St. Martin's Churchyard, in 1791. " Whereas several Sets of Synopsis of Mineralogy were left with Mr. Haywood of St. Martin's Churchyard, St. Martin's Lane, Charing Cross, by Mr. James Miller : Notice is hereby given that unless the said Mr. James Miller takes them away within fourteen Days from the Date hereof they will be sold to defray Expenses." [4]

The lower part of St. Martin's Lane has been largely devoted for some years past to the exacting art of dentistry. Dentists who do not advertise, says a writer in the " Globe," are to be found among the doctors. And dentists who *do* advertise regard the National Portrait Gallery as a pleasant waiting-room for their guests. Another specialised part of London has been made by molar-molesters on Ludgate Hill.

[1] Smith, *Nollekens and his Times*, vol. ii. p. 224.
[2] *Post Boy*, April 28, 1714.
[3] *Daily Advertiser*, April 28, 1742.   *Ibid.* Jan. 4, 1794.

CHAPTER XIV.

ST. MARTIN'S LANE—*continued.*

WHEN Admiral Vernon, familiarly known among his sailors as " Old Grogram," leapt into fame by his capture of the fort of Portobello with only six ships in 1739, his portrait "dangled from every signpost"[1] and his name was on every lip, while Peter Monamy painted the hero's ship for a famous tavern of the day, as a sign. This was the " Portobello," a few doors north of the church in St. Martin's Lane. The Admiral obtained his nickname through wearing a grogram (*étoffe à gros grains*) cloak in foul weather. The British tar of the time afterwards transferred the abbreviated term "grog" to a mixture of rum or of gin or other spirituous liquor with water—because such a beverage was first introduced by the Admiral on board ship. The word has since attained an evil sense in being applied to a system by which the Inland Revenue is defrauded. The whisky bonder puts hot water into the empty cask and allows it to remain until all the alcohol has been extracted from the wood.

Tom's Coffee-house in St. Martin's Lane seems to have stood between Chandos Street and May's Buildings, on the east or less fashionable side. At all events Elmes describes the Westminster Fire Assurance Office as having been originally started at Tom's Coffee-house in St. Martin's Lane,[2] and Mr. J. T. Smith, in his " Nollekens and his Times,"[3] says that the Westminster Fire Office was first

[1] The *Mirror* (No. 82), Sat., Feb. 19, 1780.

[2] *Topographical Dictionary*, 1831.

[3] Two vols. 1828, vol. ii. p. 237. Mr. Austin Dobson, however, says it was either in St. Peter's Court or at its entrance. This would, of course, still be between the thoroughfares named by Smith, but on the opposite side. The Westminster Fire Office, one of the oldest offices for insurance against damage by fire now existing, was founded in 1717. It is consequently 188 years old. Possibly it had a still remoter origin in the society described in the following from the *Postman* of March 14, 1702 :

" The Amicable Contributors for Insuring Houses from loss by Fire, at their

established " between Chandos Street and May's Buildings." To the office of the " Merchants' Waterworks " for raising water belonged three engines, one of which was a windmill in Tottenham Court Road fields, and later (in 1761) two water-mills turned by the common sewer, one at Tom's Coffee-house in St. Martin's Lane, and the other in Northumberland Street, then spoken of as "late Hartshorn Lane, in the Strand." From these three engines issued three main pipes of six and seven inch bore, from which the neighbourhood of the places indicated was supplied with water.[1] At Tom's Coffee-house were sold by auction by James Levi " several curious and useful Books ; consisting of Greek, Latin, English, French, Italian, Spanish, &c., Books in Divinity, Philosophy, Philology, Physick, Anatomy, Chirurgery, Geography, History, Voyages, Mathematicks, Architecture, several Classicks in Usum Delphini and cum Notis variorum, and some of the French Journals," which were catalogued under the title of " Bibliotheca Schelta." [2]

The court on the south side of the new Coliseum, formerly known as Taylor's Buildings, leading into Bedfordbury, has been much narrowed by the encroachments of the monster pleasure resort. In Stow's time it was known as Dawson's Alley.

The huge building known as the Coliseum is one of the most extraordinary edifices, in point of both exterior and interior, in London. It covers about an acre and a quarter of ground, that is the circus and music-hall combined, and its erection has led to alterations in the aspect of both what was at one time Taylor's Buildings and May's Buildings, and to the erasement of the Star and Garter, Black Horse, and other buildings. It is claimed for the stage that it is the largest and most perfectly equipped ever built.

Office at Tom's Coffee-house in St. Martin's Lane, near Charing Cross, Insure £100 for 7 years for 12s., 5s. of which will be returned at the end of the Term, and a Dividend of profits yearly, with other advantages.

" NOTE.—Those whose Policies are expired, may at the Office receive their deposite Money and Dividends on Demand.

" If any Persons who have any Interest in the Joint Stock of the Play-house in Drury Lane, by any grant or purchase, under the Patents granted from the Crown to Sir William Davenant, or Mr. Killigrew, are willing to sell their said interest, whether Shares or part of Shares, arising by Profits of Acting in the said Play-house, this is to desire all such Persons to enter their Names, their Lodgings, what share they have, and the lowest price they will sell at, with Mr. Thomas Hoy near the Pump in Chancery Lane, and they shall be treated with for the same."

[1] *London and its Environs*, 1761, vol. iv., p. 321.

[2] *Daily Advertiser*, March 18, 1742.

Charles Buildings, the second court on the right, disappeared at this time, but Turner's Court, on the north side of the Coliseum, I think, remains. When Isaac Ware was a chimney-sweep in Charles Court, he must have had only his own pluck to console him with the possibilities of becoming proficient in the most exacting art of the architect. He was seen one day, by a gentleman who was passing, to be chalking houses on the front of Whitehall. This gentleman became his patron, educated him, and sent him to Italy. Then he edited "Palladio," and built the house, No. 6 Bloomsbury Square, where D'Israeli *père* compiled his "Curiosities of Literature." He also built the town-house of the Earl of Chesterfield (since rebuilt) in South Audley Street, Grosvenor Square. In this magnificent mansion, the architect of which retained the stain of soot in his skin to the day of his death, might still be seen, until its pulling down, the favourite apartments of the Earl, furnished and decorated as he left them—and among the rest, what he had boasted of as "the finest room in London." His spacious and beautiful library overlooked the finest private garden in London. The walls were covered halfway up with rich and classical stores of literature; above the cases were, in close series, the portraits of eminent authors, French and English, with most of whom he had conversed; over these, and immediately under the massive cornice, extended all round in foot-long capitals the Horatian line :

NUNC · VETERUM · LIBRIS · NUNC · SOMNO · ET · INERTIBUS · HORIS
DUCERE · SOLICITÆ · JUCUNDA · OBLIVIA · VITÆ.

On the mantelpieces and cabinets stood busts of the ancient orators, interspersed with voluptuous vases and bronzes, antique or Italian, and airy statuettes in marble or alabaster, of nude or semi-nude opera nymphs.[1]

At the "White Peruke," three doors from May's Buildings, John Vere, Corncutter, gives notice of attendance at the Rainbow Coffee-house, Cornhill, on Mondays, Wednesdays and Fridays, for "cutting and curing of Corns, cutting of Nails, and also infallibly cures Warts of any kind, having great Skill therein."[2]

May's Buildings, between Nos. 40 and 41 St. Martin's Lane, was built by one of the name of May in 1739. May himself, according to Smith's "Nollekens," dwelt at No. 43, which, with the front ornamented with two pilasters supporting a cornice, Smith con-

---

[1] The *Quarterly Review*, No. 152, p. 484.   [2] *Ibid.* July 15, 1742.

sidered one of the neatest specimens of architectural brickwork in London.[1] The Sutherland Arms, in May's (afterward Great May's) Buildings, was at the beginning of the century the favourite meeting-place of the Illustrious Society of Eccentrics, for whom an exclusive apartment was provided. Here they met " at least three hundred and sixty-five nights in the year." Of this club, which met first at a tavern in Chandos Street (*q. v.*), and then at the Crown in Vinegar Yard, Drury Lane, Sheridan was a member, and Tom Rees was the landlord. The club is stated to have flourished so late as the middle of the nineteenth century. In 1815 it was a house, according to the " Epicure's Almanack," of a decidedly superior class, and noted for possessing the best waiter in London. It was much frequented by the eloquent Richard Lalor Sheil, by William Mudford, the editor of the " Courier," a man of logical and sarcastic power, and by " Pope Davis," an artist, who, in later years, was a great friend of the unfortunate Haydon. " Pope Davis " was so called from having painted, when in Rome, a large picture of the " Presentation of the Shrewsbury family to the Pope."

It is hardly a just aspersion on the part of Allan Cunningham—reiterated by Mr. Austin Dobson in his " Paladin of Philanthropy "—to designate St. Martin's Lane the " Grub Street of the Arts," and I am sure that the latter's namesake, "the English Vandyck," would disapprove, for, if he did not live in the Lane, he was buried in St. Martin's Churchyard, and must have known Mytens and others who did. At all events it could hardly be applicable to the time when Reynolds, Roubiliac, Raimbach, Hone, Fuseli, &c., dwelt there. More accurately might May's Buildings have been so designated, for it was here that the " pot-boilers " were produced by those whose avocation was the equivalent of that of the literary hacks in what is now Milton Street, City. And on Mr. Dobson's own showing there was in May's Buildings a manufactory, according to Foote's " Taste," of sham Rembrandts and Ostades, " which deceived the opulent amateur, and filled the pockets of the Puffs and Carmines of the day."[2]

One of the most remarkable business firms in London is that of Messrs. J. W. Harrison and Sons at Nos. 45, 46 and 47 St. Martin's Lane, and possibly, nay probably, it is a unique circumstance among the greater commercial houses of London that this establishment has been in the hands of the same family, from father to son, for six

---

[1] Smith's *Nollekens and his Times*, 1828, vol. ii. p. 237.
[2] *A Paladin of Philanthropy*, by Austin Dobson, 1899, p. 314.

successive generations, having originated about the year 1745.[1] Messrs. Harrison were in Lancaster Court, on the south side of St. Martin's Church, until 1828, and before settling in St. Martin's Lane removed from Lancaster Court to Orchard Street. The printing of the Government newspaper, the famous "London Gazette," has been in the hands of the family for practically one hundred and thirty years. On the day when the news of the battle of the Alma reached England, September 30, 1854, the present head of the firm sat in his office in the afternoon when a messenger arrived from the Duke of Newcastle, the First Secretary of State for War, asking him to hasten to Downing Street, where the Duke was in temporary occupation of the Chancellor of the Exchequer's rooms.

Hastening back with the messenger, Mr. Harrison found the Duke in a state of great excitement. " We have such glorious news," said the Duke, explaining the nature of it. But the puzzle was how to make it known. Of course, it would be printed in the " Gazette " ; but it was Saturday evening, and there were no papers until Sunday. It was, however, important that the public anxiety should be allayed by the widest possible circulation of such a piece of news. " Nobody knows it, and I don't know how to communicate it," the Duke went on. The news had found him almost alone in his office—there were only two messengers in the place—and it seemed impossible that the news of the Alma could be circulated that night. Mr. Harrison was equal to the occasion. He immediately thought of the theatres. There were three of them open : why not have the telegram read out there? The plan was thought excellent, and Mr. Harrison returned to St. Martin's Lane, set up the news with his own hands, and sent men round to the theatres with early copies of the " Gazette." " See the manager " were the instructions to the messengers. " Take no refusal. Insist on having the performance stopped by order of the Duke while this news is read out." The men obeyed the orders to the letter, and at Drury Lane and other theatres the scenes were historic. A paragraph in the " Greville Memoirs " tells how the writer was passing the Adelphi Theatre when the play suddenly ceased and the people rushed out, shouting and cheering wildly over the victory.

While the theatres were cheering themselves hoarse, Mr. Harrison

---

[1] Messrs. Bayley & Co., the perfumers opposite, at No. 94, are older, their date going back to before 1739, but they cannot claim this *lineal* descent of the name from father to son. There is, in fact, no Bayley now, I think, in the firm. See further " Cockspur Street."

with a bundle of "Gazettes" was making his way to the Mansion House in a hansom cab. It was eight o'clock at night, and Lord Mayor Sydney came down half dressed, and in slippers. The telegram woke him up. Seizing the paper, his lordship rushed upstairs, shouting the good news all over the house.

But all the world was not at the Mansion House, and some means must be found of making the glad news known to the citizens. The Sheriffs were dining at the London Tavern, then in Bishopsgate, and thither Mr. Harrison, the Lord Mayor's chaplain, and the Lord Mayor himself in slippers, flew as fast as a hansom cab could go with them. Rushing upstairs, the Lord Mayor pushed to the front. The dinner was half over, and one of the Sheriffs was speaking. The Lord Mayor took possession of the chair and read out the news. "It was an extraordinary sight," says Mr. Harrison, "such as I have never seen since. The guests left the table and went away, and soon the news was everywhere."

The telegram had been despatched at seven o'clock in the morning from Belgrade, and at nine o'clock at night it was known, without the aid of newspapers, all over London. The news was the occasion of the only Sunday opening of Messrs. W. H. Smith's book-stalls which has ever been known. The telegram ran as follows :—

"The entrenched camp of the Russians, containing 50,000 men, with a numerous artillery and cavalry on the heights of Alma, was attacked on the 20th inst. at 1 P.M. by the allied troops and carried by the bayonet at half-past three, with a loss on our side of about 1,400 killed and wounded, and an equal loss on the side of the French. The Russian army was forced to put itself in full retreat."[1]

The site of Kynaston's—corrupted to Chemister's—Alley may be seen at the back of Messrs. Harrison's premises. It is now occupied by their workshops. May's Buildings are to the right. The Alley was named after Sir Francis Kynaston the poet, who dwelt in Bedfordbury.

In the profusion of latter-day literature relating to the honoured name of Chippendale, I do not think it has ever been noted that he dwelt at the sign of the "Chair" in St. Martin's Lane. This was doubtless the "Covered Chair," as the "Sedan" was sometimes called, and he appears to not only have *made* this popular convey-ance, but to have upholstered it to boot, for in the advertisement of

---

[1] See also the *Gazette*, October 1, 1854, and the *Strand Magazine*, July 1903, where there is a very interesting account by Mr. Arthur Hill of "The Govern-ment's Newspaper."

his second edition of "The Gentleman and Cabinet Maker's Director," he directs "All Commissions for Household Furniture, or Drawing thereof, to be sent to the Cabinet and *Upholstery* Warehouse, at the Chair in St. Martin's Lane," his colleague at the time (1756) being J. Rannie.[1] A copy of this second edition was sold in 1894 for £18 18s., and another was advertised for sale in 1896 for £12 12s.[2] Chippendale's extensive premises, No. 60 in the Lane, were, in Smith's time, occupied by a Mr. Stutely, builder. Mr. J. T. Smith prophesied the return of the public taste to Chippendale. No. 63, in Roubiliac's time, accommodated Rysbrach's rival with a distinct passage through to his premises, and in his studio here Roubiliac took refuge after he had quitted Peter's Court. The site of his new premises was held in Smith's time by three persons, one of whom was the printer of a Sunday paper, entitled "The Watchman."[3] It must have been here, in the sculptor's time, thinks the author of "Haunted London," that Garrick, coming to see how his Shakespeare statue progressed, drew out a two-foot rule, and put on a tragic and threatening face to frighten a great red-headed Yorkshireman, who was sawing marble for Roubiliac; but who, to his surprise, merely rolled his quid, and coolly said, "What trick are you after next, my little master?"

When Roubiliac died, one of his pupils, a conceited pretender, took the premises in 1762, and advertised himself as "Mr. Roubiliac's successor." His master used to say to Read when he was bragging, "Ven you do de monument, den de varld vill see vot von d—— ting you vill make." Of Read's wretched monument of Admiral Tyrrell in Westminster Abbey Nollekens used to say, "That figure going to heaven out of the sea looks for all the world as if it were hanging from a gallows with a rope round its neck."[4]

A combination of signs not mentioned in the "History of Signboards"—the "Cow and Still" near New Street, the lower end of St. Martin's Lane—is suggestive of the early workman's favourite beverage of "Rum and Milk." In a vault under this "Cow and Still" attendance was given from nine in the morning till nine at night, for the sale of "Red Port, 4s. per Gallon; White Port, 5s. 4d.;

[1] The *Whitehall Evening Post*, December 4, 1756. The sign of the "Three Chairs" in St. Paul's Churchyard is also spoken of as that of the "Three Covered Chairs" (*Daily Advertiser*, December 21, 1741).

[2] The Quaritch *Catalogues*.

[3] *Nollekens and his Times*, 1828, vol. ii. p. 239.

[4] *Ibid.* p. 241.

Canary, 9s. a Gallon, French Brandy, 11s. per Gallon, all new neat from the Grape." [1]

The Camisard refugees appear to have had a coffee-house of their own in the days of their patron Queen Anne. "The Printed Planks (?) of the Lottery, with the Prizes, are to be seen every day at the Camisars Coffee-house the middle of St. Martin's Lane." [2] And here no doubt these Calvinists of the Cevennes discussed plans for the future, and awaited the return to life of Dr. Emms, who died on Dec. 22, 1707. For the English Camisards had staked their reputation that he would so return on the 25th of May. Guards were set over his grave; but it is needless to add that Dr. Emms slept on the sleep which knows no waking.

In 1818 there was an "Army and Navy" Coffee-house in St. Martin's Lane,[3] and also, in 1742, a "Slater's Coffee-house." [4]

At No. 70 Nathaniel Hone exhibited his picture of "The Pictorial Conjuror displaying the whole Art of Optical Deception." This was in ridicule of Sir Joshua Reynolds as a plagiarist, and also designed to insult Miss Angelica Kaufmann. On these grounds it was refused admittance at Somerset House. Hone was an Irishman, and an eminent miniaturist in enamel, in which he was reckoned inferior to no artist of his time except Zincke.

The corner house of Long Acre, formerly No. 72 St. Martin's Lane, formed part of the extensive premises of Mr. Cobb, George III.'s upholsterer—a proud, pompous man, who always strutted about his workshops in full dress. It was Dance's portrait of Mr. Cobb, given in exchange for a table, that led to Dance's acquaintance with Garrick. One day, in the library of Buckingham House, old King George asked Cobb to hand him a certain book. Instead of doing so, mistaken Cobb called to a man who was at work on a ladder, and said, "Fellow, give me that book." The King instantly rose and asked the man's name. "Jenkins," replied the astonished upholsterer. "Then," observed the good old King, "Jenkins shall hand me the book." [5]

"The Terrace" was the earliest designation of what is now Upper St. Martin's Lane; [6] then it was called "Little" St. Martin's Lane. Here dwelt Dr. Golding before he took up his residence at

---

[1] *Postman*, November 24–27, 1711.   [2] *Ibid.* October 11, 1711.
[3] *Picture of London* for that year, p. 414.
[4] See "Bedford Court," off Bedford Street, Covent Garden.
[5] Smith's *Nollekens*, vol. ii. p. 250.
[6] Cunningham's *London*.

Charing Cross Hospital, of which he was practically the founder. While alluding to Dr. Golding it is perhaps worthy of record that it was he, with the aid of Mr. Robb, who established the reputation of the present biscuit-bakers' firm by inventing what was well-known to London's childhood as " Robb's Biscuits," of which it is not necessary to say more than that the " Lancet " [1] speaks highly of them. A. Robb & Co. have been at No. 79 St. Martin's Lane for about sixty-five years, but before settling here they had a place somewhere in the lower part of the Lane, "near Chandos Street." Altogether, I am told by the present representative of the firm, they have been in St. Martin's Lane for almost a hundred years. So have Aldridge's.

Aldridge's was a great horse repository so early at least as 1779. In the " Morning Post " of August 11 for that year is an advertisement exhibiting the different conditions of sale then from now : " By Mr. Aldridge at the original repository in St. Martin's Lane. This day at twelve o'clock. A number of carriages as usual, some clever pairs of coach geldings and odd ditto, several bony useful good geldings and mares come off long journeys, three seasoned hunters (masters of high weights), a great number of post-chaises, machine cart geldings ; in all upwards of 160 lots. To be viewed and a trial had."

Some particular attention is paid to pedigree in the following : " By Mr. Aldridge at the original repository in St. Martin's Lane, a bay filly, three years old, got by Eclipse, her dam by Omnium, her granddam by Sterling, her great-granddam by Godolphin, her great-great-granddam by Stranger's Arabian, her great-great-great-granddam by Pelham's Barb, her great-great-great-great-granddam by Old Shot, her great-great-great-great-great-granddam by the white-legged Lowther Barb out of the Old Vintner mare. *N.B.*—This filly is the property of two gentlemen, and will be sold to the best bidder." [2]

In 1847 "the whole of the houses on the east side of Upper St. Martin's Lane, vested in the Mercers' Company, were being demolished for the formation of the new street from the west end of Long Acre to be carried into King Street, Covent Garden, and ultimately extended to the point of junction of Holborn, New and Old Oxford Streets, and Tottenham Court Road." [3]

[1] August 7, 1897. Dr. Golding lived on the west side of Upper St. Martin's Lane.

[2] *Country Life*, November 23, 1901, where there is an interesting account of " New Aldridge's."

[3] The *Globe*, 1847.

The coat of arms representing the three Fleurs-de-lys over the entrance to a bird-dealer's at the corner of West Street, Upper St. Martin's Lane, was put up in honour of " S.A.R. le Comte de Paris," who appears to have patronised this well-known dealer in sporting dogs, established here in 1831. Upper St. Martin's Lane was even up to Elmes's time known as *Little* St. Martin's Lane in contradistinction to *Great* St. Martin's Lane, of which it is a continuation. The Cross Keys Inn formerly stood at the first court on the left from Long Acre, and is described by Stow as " large and of good resort." It seems to have become effaced during the improvements that caused the disappearance of Slaughter's. It was, however, here in 1742, for Thomas Thomson, tailor, who dwelt "at a Chandler's Shop near the Cross-Keys in St. Martin's Lane in the Fields," is invited to hear " something very much to his advantage."

The "Golden Boy" was the sign of one Sell, a coachmaker in the Lane, who advertises "A Second-hand Machine Coach, lin'd with scarlet Cloth, with a Set of Lanthorn-springs, and with or without a Pair of Harness." [1] The " Golden Lion " in St. Martin's Lane was another coachmaker's sign, at which Richard Payne furnished "Gentlemen and Others with New or Second hand Coaches, Chariots, Landaus, and Chaises. Also Mourning-Coaches, Chariots and Hearses . . . Coach-Glasses to be sold at the most reasonable Rates, etc." [2]

Old Slaughter's Coffee-house, before it was taken down in 1843, when Cranbourn Street was cut through that section of the town to make a thoroughfare between Coventry Street and Piccadilly, stood on the west side of the Lane, three doors from Newport Street. " Old " Slaughter's was as well applied to the landlord as the coffee-house, for Thomas Slaughter, who started it, kept it for no less than forty-seven years. In 1815 it comprised No. 74 as well as 75 St. Martin's Lane, and it is worthy of remark that when the streets of London were all completely paved in the improved style of the beginning of the nineteenth century, " Slaughter's " was called the " coffee-house on the pavement." [3] It was *the* great resort for the artists who congregated in St. Martin's Lane, Gerrard Street, Greek Street, Soho Square, &c., before the establishment of the Royal Academy. They used to arrive in the evenings, and Hogarth was

---

[1] *Daily Advertiser*, July 14, 1742.

[2] *St. James's Evening Post*, October 27, 1737.

[3] *Epicure's Almanack*, 1815. I think Mr. Thornbury is mistaken in calling the landlord *John* Slaughter.

a constant visitor. Previously, in 1753, they used to meet at the "Turk's Head" in Greek Street, and thence their secretary, Mr. F. M. Newton, dated a printed letter to the principal artists, to form a select body for the protection and encouragement of art.

Old Pierre Desmaizeaux, the literary historian, author of "Vie de Bayle" and "Vie de Boileau," a scholar and man of wit and pleasantry, was drinking his coffee at "Slaughter's" when two strangers came in and began a warm dispute about some subject in literature. One was very polite and moderate, for he had reason on his side ; the other was rude and violent, for he was wrong. After some time, the polite man, unable any longer to bear the violence of the other, left the room. The *soi-disant* champion therefore turned about to Desmaizeaux, and said, "Well, sir, don't you think I have mauled my antagonist finely ?" "Yes, sir," replied the old man, "that you have ; and if ever I fight the Philistines, I should like to make use of your jaw-bone."[1] It is a little surprising, when the rough-and-ready wit that prevailed at the coffee-houses is considered—not always either by any means in good taste—that the *badinage* which passed for wit really did not give rise to more duels than it did. Henry Angelo, in his "Reminiscences," says how he once, during his usual visit to "Old Slaughter's" to read the papers, sat near Sir William Chere, who had a very long nose, and was playing at backgammon with old General Brown ; during this time, Sir William, who was a snuff-taker, was continually using his snuff-box, seldom making the application necessary to keep pace with the indulgence. Observing him lean continually over the table, and being at the same time in a very bad humour with the game, the General said, "Sir William, blow your nose." The General's antagonist seems to have been in an equally bad humour, for he said, "Blow it yourself ; 'tis as near you as me !"[2]

John Beard, the celebrated English tenor, a man whose character

---

[1] This is said, with some reason, to have given its origin to the vulgar phrase "to jaw," for Desmaizeaux died in 1745, and the earliest instance noted in the Great English Dictionary of Dr. Murray is from Smollett's *Roderick Random* (1748), ch. xxiv. : "He swore woundily at the lieutenant . . . whereby the lieutenant returned the salute, and they jawed together fore and aft a good spell.'

[2] There is a pencil drawing of "Old Slaughter's" as it was just before being pulled down in May 1843, by Edward Spencer, junr., dated May 31, 1742. This is in the Creed Collection of Tavern Signs in the British Museum Library. There is also an engraving of the coffee-house in Thornbury's *Haunted London*, 1880, p. 260, and a drawing of the same house by T. H. Shepherd on the walls of St. Martin's Library.

was highly esteemed in private life, dwelt at the first house, in St. Martin's Lane, from the corner of Newport Street, next door on the north side, apparently, to Old Slaughter's. Beard first became a great favourite of the town by his splendid style of singing Galliard's famous hunting-song "With early horn," contained in the music to an entertainment of Galliard's, called "The Royal Chase, or Merlin's Cave." Beard sang this song for a hundred nights. At his house in the Lane Mr. J. T. Smith describes his father smoking a pipe with Beard and George Lambert, the latter having been the founder of the Beef-steak Club, and the clever scene-painter of Covent Garden Theatre.[1] On which side of Old Slaughter's is not clear, but next door to that historic coffee-house, well known to Pope, Collins, Roubiliac, Wilkie, Hogarth, I think Dryden, and to many others with famous names, was the house of Monsieur Muilment. Mr. Walter Thornbury in his "Haunted London" erroneously states that the house first became known as "Old Slaughter's" in 1760; it was, however, certainly thus known so early at least as 1742, for on April 10 of that year a "Benefit" is announced, of "Monsr. Muilment, At the Theatre Royal in Drury Lane, on Friday the 23rd instant," when "will be presented a Comedy, call'd 'The MERCHANT of VENICE,' with Entertainments of Dancing by Monsr. Muilment, &c., and Singing by Mr. Beard, as will be particularly express'd on the Bills. Tickets at Monsr. Muilment's House, next to Old Slaughter's Coffee House, St. Martin's Lane";[2] and in 1757 there is another announcement from *Old* Slaughter's.[3]

Two doors from Slaughter's, south, lived Ambrose Philips, whose nickname "Namby Pamby" was applied to him by Carey and Pope on account of his verses addressed to Lord Carteret's children. The nickname is merely a jingling reduplication of "Namby," a baby-name, or one of endearment like "Nunkey" for uncle, and a play upon the poet's Christian name of Ambrose. Pope, in his "Dunciad," has :

> And Namby Pamby be preferred for wit.[4]

Philips lived here from 1720 to 1725, when "gone" is against his name.[5] Between Nos. 84 and 90 St. Martin's Lane is the New Theatre, occupying the site of what were in 1897 the National Penny Bank (87); the (Young Women's) Wantage Club ; the British

---

[1] *Nollekens and his Times*, vol. ii. p. 222.
[2] *Daily Advertiser* of that date.
[3] *Whitehall Evening Post*, May 13, 1756.   [4] Book III. 322.
[5] Cunningham's *London*.

Israel Association (86) ; as far as Miss F. Luker's Ladies' School (85) The front decoration of the theatre, for which Mr. Sprague, the architect, was instructed to prepare plans and designs in 1901, is of the free classic order, and is at once dignified and effective, while the interior satisfies all the modern requirements of theatre construction. The scheme of decoration is of the period of Louis XVI., which has been adhered to down to the minutest details. Mr. Sprague has been responsible for the designs of no fewer than thirty of the modern theatres in the metropolitan district.[1]

The site of New Slaughter's, or Young Slaughter's as it was sometimes called, is now occupied by the Westminster County Court. Mr. Wheatley must be in error when he says that New Slaughter's was established about 1760, for it certainly, like Old Slaughter's, existed so early as 1742, when a solution of the unemployed problem was even then being sought : " Any Workhouse or Parish that wants Employment for a large Number of Poor in London, or within ten Miles thereof, may be treated with on directing a Letter to A.B. at Young Slaughter's Coffee-house in St. Martin's Lane." [2]   And again : " If any Nobleman or Gentleman has Occasion for a Person to teach Latin, French, or Italian, let them be pleas'd to direct to A. F. at New Slaughter's Coffee-house in St. Martin's Lane, and they shall be waited on." [3]   About the year 1765, Smeaton, Solander, Banks, John Hunter, Captain Cook, and other scientific and literary men used New Slaughter's for club meetings.[4]   In 1815 the good dinners of this tavern had gained it great reputation "among gentlemen of the army and navy, as well as among private gentlemen, and functionaries in the public offices. At the back entrance to this house from St. Martin's Court, there is a hot and cold larder, which serves in some sort as a chapel of ease to the main refectory. You may dine here on prime roast and boiled, with plum-pudding and apple-pie, for one shilling and ninepence." [5]   That fine madness ot incongruity, says Mr. Austin Dobson, which tempted Charles Lamb into laughter at a funeral led him, at the top of Skiddaw, to think upon the ham-and-beef shop in St. Martin's Lane. "Where," he asks, "was this historic ham-and-beef shop ? " Surely this was the renowned " Finch's," at the corner of St. Martin's Court at the Lane

[1] *Vide* the *London Argus*, March 14, 1903, and the *Builder*, August 24, 1901.
[2] *Daily Advertiser*, July 6, 1742.
[3] *Ibid.* April 6, 1742.
[4] *A Paladin of Philanthropy*, 1899, p. 312.
[5] The *Epicure's Almanack*, 1815.

end—"one of the oldest and best ham-and-beef repositories in London." This was in 1815. It had belonged to the family of the then Finch for many years, during which two ample fortunes had been made at it. "In addition to rounds and flanks of beef, and to hams, here were also fillets of veal and tongues kept ready dressed," and the essayist might be "sure of a supply of beef marrow"[1] when wanted, or Yorkshire and Westmoreland hams, purchasers of which might have them boiled in Mr. Finch's capacious coppers.[2] Probably the ham-and-beef shop that dwelt thus in Lamb's memory was at the south-eastern corner of the court, for at the north-eastern corner, at either No. 88 or 89, dwelt Hogarth's particular friend John Pine, whom the caricaturist drew, much to his annoyance, as the fat friar eyeing the beef at the "Gates of Calais"—"the *prodigy*, which appeared before the Gates, when the French were *surprised*, being the Roast Beef of Old England." But if the Peace had not, just previously to his visit, been actually signed, he would have been hanged off-hand, and it is sad to relate that Hogarth behaved with such barbarous rudeness generally while on his visit that three gendarmes escorted him three miles off from shore, and then spun him round on deck like a top and left him.[3]

The memory of the unhappy author of "The Orphan" and "Venice Preserved" was kept alive in St. Martin's Court by the sign of the "Otway's Head," appertaining to a bookseller and publisher, F. Noble, who was also the proprietor of a Circulating Library.[4] Here he published, "Price 12s., in Two Volumes, Octavo, with above sixty Copper Plates, 'THE ANTIQUITIES OF ST. PETER's,' or the Abbey Church of Westminster . . . Inscriptions and Epitaphs . . . Lives, Marriages, and Issue of the most eminent Personages therein reposited, and their Coats of Arms truly emblazon'd, adorn'd with Draughts of the Tombs."[5] All "Connoisseurs in Musick" are apprised that catalogues might be had of F. Noble at the "Otway's Head," of "a large Collection of MS. Musick in Italian to be sold at White's Coffee-house in Bedford Court by Covent Garden at two

---

[1] So late as 1847, in one of Macaulay's *Letters*, he says he gave his guests fowl, ham, and *marrowbones* (*Life and Letters*, 1877, vol. ii. p. 213).

[2] The *Epicure's Almanack*, 1815. Charles Mathews's impersonation of Dicky Suett in pawn for the cheesecakes and raspberry tarts, at the pastrycook's in St. Martin's Court, was no less faithful than convulsing (Daniel's *Merry England*, 1881, p. 329).

[3] Nichols and Steevens's *Hogarth*, 1808, vol. i. p. 144.

[4] Mortimer's *Universal Director* (*circa* 1760), p. 171.

[5] *Daily Advertiser*, Nov. 7, 1742.

o'clock in the Afternoon."[1]   Noble also published the second edition
of "Columna Rostrata ; or A History of the English Sea Affairs,"
by Samuel Colliber.[2]   This work, in spite of its unsatisfactory brevity,
is of unwonted value from the fact of the author having been
familiar with Dutch and French, and having examined the works of
writers in those languages.

A relative of Hogarth's master, Ellis Gamble, goldsmith, in
Cranbourn Street, appears to have been a fan-dealer in St. Martin's
Court :

"This Day is publish'd (Price 2s.) The Church of England Fan,
being an Explanation of the Oxford Almanack for the Year 1733,
on which the several Characters are curiously done in various
beautiful Colours from the Original ; with several Motto's and
Pieces now first made known to the Publick.

"Sold by M. Gamble at the Golden Fan in St. Martin's Court,
near Leicester Fields."   Especially is a relationship suggested in the
conclusion of the announcement—" Likewise a new Edition of the
Harlot's Progress in Fans, or singly to frame."[3]

Gamble also advertises the " new EXCISE FAVORS, proper for
all Gentlemen and Ladies to wear upon my Lord Mayor's Day,
with this present Lord Mayor's Picture upon them, and this Motto :

> Barber behold, congratulate his Fate,
> Who trimm'd the City, and who shav'd the State.

(This is evidently an allusion to the present excise system, which
was settled about the year 1733.)   "Also is sold the true Original
ORANGE FAN, and Mrs. Oldfield's Picture for Watches."[4]

At the "Round Table," Nos. 22 and 23 St. Martin's Court, the
American champion John C. Heenan put up when he visited
England to "lift" the English belt, but was beaten by Tom Sayers.
Perhaps the following lines, popular at the time, will be of interest
as evincing British sentiment with regard to what was still a national
sport :

> He bears, for dear old England,
>   The belt of British fight ;
> And proudly will he meet the man,
>   Who dare contest his right.

---

[1] *Daily Advertiser*, Dec. 18, 1741.
[2] *Ibid.* Feb. 18, 1742.
[3] *London Evening Post*, Jan. 20, 1733.
[4] *St. James's Evening Post*, Oct. 20–23, 1733.

He'll meet him with a friendly hand,
    He'll meet him as a brother ;
But that which heart and hand can hold
    He yields not to another.

Give welcome to the manly heart,
    That bravely crossed the sea,
To battle for his country's sake,
    Whatever land it be.
Whichever way the fortune falls (*sic*)
    Twill be our pride to show,
An honest lad, from any land,
    Shall find no Briton foe.

We want no pistol ball or blade,
    But muscle, thew, and bone :
A hand to hand, for friend or foe,
    We trust in that alone.
Then honour fall, where honour's due,
    While honour reigns within :
America and England, ho !
    And may the best man win.

At the south-eastern corner of St. Martin's Court was another
tavern associated with the name of one who was at one time
perhaps the best known man in England, Ben Caunt, the pugilist,
whose portrait once adorned the walls alike of cottage and palace.
There is a portrait of Caunt in Miles's " Pugilistica," taken at the
period of his famous fight with Bendigo in 1842. His head was
certainly a strong one, and in a phrenological way he was better
than many of the men among his contemporaries who did better
things.[1]   The house is now either the " Salisbury " or " Salisbury
Stores," I think, but before it was better known as " Old Ben
Caunt's " it was the " Coach and Horses." At the " Coach and
Horses " in St. Martin's Lane, aged 28, died Robert Baldwin, a
noted prize-fighter, known as " White-headed Bob." [2]   The parlour,
in Caunt's time, was a general resort of aspirants for pugilistic
honours and their patrons, Ben busying himself in bringing forward
and occasionally backing, or finding backers for men, among whom
may be named Bob Caunt, his brother ; Burton of Leicester
(January 20, 1846) ; George Gutteridge (beaten by Nat Langham,
September 23, 1846), and others.[3]

[1] See " A Collection of Death-masks " in *Harper's Magazine*, Sept. 1892,
by Mr. Laurence Hutton.

[2] *Gentleman's Magazine*, 1831 (part 2), p. 282.

[3] H. D. Miles's *Pugilistica*, vol. iii. pp. 92-93.

"To be Sold for the Benefit of Creditors, At the Coach and Horses Inn in St. Martin's Lane, A Crain-Neck Chariot, lin'd with Crimson Cassoy, with one pair of Town Harness.

"A Travelling Coach, lin'd with Scarlet Cloth, and Harnesses for six Horses; both Chariot and Coach very little the worse for wear.

"Also a Machine or Half Berlin; all which was the Property of William Nepuen Esq.; late a Prisoner of the Fleet."[1]

Ben Caunt died universally respected—fistically (I understand that it was only for his fighting prowess that he was respected, not otherwise), and it used to be the fashion for country visitors to look up the old hostelry and drink to the departed champion's memory. There is a fine Staffordshire mug extant, exhibiting his half-length figure, which was modelled from life by Bentley, whose name and date are impressed round the base, with a record of the principal events in Caunt's pugilistic career.

There was another St. Martin's Court, which led from the south side of the church to the Strand.

At the Leicester Fields end of Cecil Court, St. Martin's Lane, was "To be Sold, a great Pennyworth. A large Parcel of Hollands, Cambricks, Muslins, Ell-wide Hollands for Sheeting, Irish Linnen Yard and Ell-wide, Nuns Hollands, Garlix,[2] 3-4ths, 7-8ths, and Yard wide, check'd Cottons, Yard and Ell-wide, Dowlas,[3] strip'd Hollands, Fustian, Dimities, Diaper, Canvas, black Shalloons,[4] &c."

This Cecil Court, nearly opposite New Street, led, before Charing Cross Road was formed, from St. Martin's Lane into Castle Street, and in 1735 was the scene of a conflagration of such magnitude as to burn no fewer than fourteen houses, causing the death from fright of Hogarth's mother.[5] The fire happened on the 9th, and began at the house of Mrs. Calloway, who kept a brandy-shop in the court. This woman was committed to Newgate. She had

---

[1] *London Evening Post*, Oct. 7, 1738.

[2] "Garliz" or "Garlitz" is probably meant—a kind of linen cloth imported from Germany, "whereof there are several sorts: the first is a blew whiting. There is another sort of Ell-wide Garlitz, which is of a browner whiting" (J.F., *Merchant's Ware-house*, 1696, p. 21, quoted in the *New English Dictionary*).

[3] "Dowlas" was a coarse linen, imported from Brittany, and chiefly worn by the lower classes (Halliwell's *Dictionary of Archaic Words*).

[4] A sort of woollen stuff from Châlons in France. With Chaucer, I think, "shalons" were blankets. "Chaperon," a hood, was in the same way called a shapperoone:

"Her shapperoones, her perriwigs and tires."—Taylor's *Works*, 1630.

[5] *Gentleman's Magazine*, June 11, 1735.

threatened "to be even with the landlord for having given her warning, and that she would have a bonfire on June 20 that should warm all her rascally neighbours." One house belonging to John Huggins, late Warden of the Fleet, was greatly damaged.[1] Abraham Raimbach, the line engraver of "Village Politicians," "Blind Man's Buff," and others, after Sir David Wilkie, was born in Cecil Court in 1776. The court has been entirely rebuilt.

No. 94 is now, since 1896, the famous old perfumers' Bayley & Co., with whom "Farmer George" and his frugal Queen Charlotte had fewer dealings than the Prince Regent, who spent £600 a year or more in perfumery.[2]

At No. 96 St. Martin's Lane, where, as already mentioned, wine was produced from a remarkable vine nearly a hundred feet long, was a large staircase, painted with figures viewing a procession, by a French artist named Clermont, who claimed one thousand guineas for his work, and received five hundred. Behind the house was the room which Hogarth has painted in "Marriage à la Mode." The quack is Dr. Misaubin, whose vile portrait the satirist has given. The woman is his Irish wife. Dr. Misaubin, who lived in this house, was the son of a pastor of the Spitalfields French Church. The quack realised a great fortune by a famous pill. His son was murdered ; his grandson squandered his money, and died in St. Martin's Workhouse.[3]

At No. 100 dwelt during 1784–8 Fuseli, the Swiss painter patronised by Reynolds, at the house of John Cartwright, a mediocre portrait-painter. There Fuseli remained until his marriage with Miss Rawlins in 1788, when he removed to Foley Street, a continuation eastward of Foley Place, Marylebone, into Cleveland Street, Fitzroy Square, and here he commenced his acquaintance with Professor Bonnycastle, producing his popular picture of "The Nightmare" (1781) by which the publisher of the print realised £500. In the same period he revised Cowper's version of the "Iliad," and became acquainted with Sir Joshua Reynolds and Dr. Moore, the author of "Zeluco."[4] At No. 100, too, he painted "Œdipus and his Daughters," and planned that Cyclopean enterprise, the "Illustrated Shakespeare" of Boydell.[5] Later, in the years 1817–18,

---

[1] See Nichols and Steevens's *Hogarth*, 1808, 4to., vol. i. p. 67.
[2] See further under "Cockspur Street."
[3] Thornbury's *Haunted London*, 1880, p. 253, and Smith's *Nollekens*, ii. 228.
[4] *Haunted London*, 1880, p. 259.
[5] See further *A Paladin of Philanthropy*, by Austin Dobson, 1899, pp. 302–3.

these premises were occupied by Messrs. Flight and Robson, the organ-builders, and here, in a room at the rear, they exhibited to a wonder-loving public their invention known as the "Apollonicon," which was an elaborate musical instrument constructed on the principle of the organ.[1] Mr. Harrison learnt from elder relatives of his that these "Apollonicon Rooms" were much frequented for the sake of the performances given on that instrument. This is quite correct, for it is described in 1818 as being exhibited to "crowded audiences."[2] The Apollonicon was made for Lord Kirkwall at immense expense.

The room was afterwards opened as a Casino, which Mr. J. W. Harrison believes to have been the first resort of its kind in London. Here the adoption of the "Rational" costume was advocated, known as the "Bloomer," and a "Bloomer Ball" was given, which much shocked the many. The Adelaide Gallery, which I am informed by Mr. Harrison was a forerunner of the Polytechnic, was also run as a Casino,[3] and also had a "Bloomer" Entertainment, which, however, proved distasteful to the public.

From No. 103 to No. 107, the sites of which are now occupied by the Duke of York's (formerly the Trafalgar Square) Theatre, is a portion of the Lane redolent of memories prominent in the early annals of art, and I think it must have been when the Trafalgar Square Theatre was built that I remember the dismantling of Sir James Thornhill's house, No. 104, with its grand allegoric staircase painted by himself. Sir James could obtain but 40s. a yard square for painting the cupola of St. Paul's,[4] which reminds one of the

[1] A full account of this instrument will be found in the *Picture of London* for 1818, p. 281. Timbs also mentions it somewhere.

[2] The *Picture of London*, 1818.

[3] Of the Casino at the Adelaide Gallery the *Mirror*, Oct. 1848 (p. 483), says: "M. Laurent was the first who introduced the Casino into the Metropolis, and, as he commenced, so has he continued. With the proper determination to render it a *réunion* for the lovers of dancing, he was determined to banish from it all that might tend to depreciate such an establishment in the eyes of the most fastidious . . . . the result proves that under proper regulations the Casino is not only beneficial to health, but tends to give an added impetus to the more serious duties of society. The orchestra has become celebrated for the excellence of its instrumentalists, its musician-like arrangements, the ever-varying nature of its selections, the admirable judgment of the conductor. The concert forms an agreeable feature, and the vocalists are excellent. There are few more pleasant ways of passing an hour than in joining in the exhilaration of the polka, the valse, or quadrille."

[4] Horace Walpole's *Anecdotes of Painting*, 1871, p. 328.

sculptor of the Shakespeare statue [1] in Leicester Square, Signor Fontana, who, in answer to the question in a " Confessional Album," " Who was his favourite painter," wrote in his broken English, " Put the paint on thick," humorously pretending that it was he who could earn most money by a lavish use of paint. One of Thornhill's successors at 104 was the Van Nost whose gilt statue of George I. in Leicester Fields preceded that of Shakespeare by Fontana. And here lived Francis Hayman, whose principal productions were historical paintings, with which some of the apartments at Vauxhall were decorated. Originally a scene-painter, he was with Hogarth at Moll King's when Hogarth drew the girl squirting brandy at the other for his picture of the " Rake's Progress." When Hayman buried his wife, a friend asked him why he spent so much money on the funeral. " Oh, sir," he replied, " she would have done as much or more for me with pleasure." How frequently we find either the limbs, the face or the features, or other peculiarities of the painter and sculptor reflected in his work ! This seems to have been the case with Hayman, who filled so many eighteenth-century books with noses à la Cyrano and spindle-shanks ; his own legs probably being the model, we may judge, says Mr. Dobson, from those of Viscount Squanderfield in the " Marriage à la Mode," for whom he was the admitted sitter.[2]

Nos. 108 and 109 are the premises of a very old-established accoutrement-makers, Messrs. Firmin and Sons, who some ten or fifteen years ago carried on business at Nos. 153–4–5 Strand, where I remember an old shop-bill framed and placed in the window showing that their sign was the " Red Lyon." Firmins appear to have been originally sword-cutlers, as indeed they are now. The Strand house stood " over against Norfolk Street," its origin having been traced in the Record Office over two hundred years back. The old bill, of which I made a note, but which now appears to have been lost, describes the proprietor as having " made and sold all Sorts of Gilt and Silver Buttons, in Box Moulds, and Livery Buttons of any kind, White or Yellow, wholesale or retail, at the lowest Prices." They are now Government contractors for the army.

The studio in St. Peter's Court,[3] in which Roubiliac commenced

[1] In the Shakespeare statue in white marble which adorns the centre of Leicester Square, the figure is an exact reproduction by the late Signor Fontana, of the statue (designed by Kent, and executed by Scheemaker) on the Westminster Abbey cenotaph.

[2] " The Grub Street of the Arts " in *A Paladin of Philanthropy.*

[3] There is an interesting engraving of this court as it was then, in *St. Martin's Scrap Book* (St. Martin's Library).

on his own account, from having been, as Allan Cunningham says, "a favourite haunt of artists," became for a long period the abode of the St. Martin's Lane Academy, the Royal Academy in embryo. J. T. Smith, in his "Streets of London," says that the society met under the auspices of Mr. Moser, in this court, from the year 1739 to 1767; but the following paragraph would point to its existence quite sixteen years before 1739: "This Week the Academy for the Improvement of Painters and Sculptors by Drawing after the Naked, open'd in St. Martin's Lane, and will continue during the Season as usual. N.B.—The Company have agreed not to draw on Mondays or Saturdays."[1] Later the Academy in the Lane became the chartered "Society of Artists," because of a charter granted to them in 1765. The present premises of Messrs. Chatto and Windus, numbered 110 and 111 St. Martin's Lane, cover the old St. Peter's Court, through which, from an entrance which stood about the middle of Heming's Row, access might be had to the Friends' Meeting-house. This Meeting-house afterwards occupied the site of the Academy, and was removed later to its present site, No. 52, on the east side of St. Martin's Lane. Although this Heming's Row entrance to St. Peter's Court is not indicated in Stow's Plan of St. Martin's Parish, it is given in R. Horwood's Plan of the Cities of London and Westminster, dated 1799, where the Court forms an L-shaped passage from Heming's Rents into St. Martin's Lane. After continued squabbles which lasted many years, the principal artists forming the St. Peter's Court society, including Benjamin West, Richard Wilson, Edward Penny, Joseph Wilton, Sir William Chambers, G. M. Moser, Paul Sandby, and J. M. Newton, met at the "Turk's Head" in Greek Street, where others joined them in a petition to George III. to become patron of a Royal Academy of Art.[2] The King consented, and selected from the principal artists of the society those he considered the most able. These he embodied as the Royal Academy in 1768. And in Pall Mall, near the Carlton Palace Screen, they opened their first exhibition, where also the venerable President, Mr. West, for several years exhibited his paintings, and, by the liberal patronage of George III., to whom the place of exhibition belonged, he was permitted to do so until his decease.[3]

The remnant of the society built the Lyceum, lately converted

[1] The *London Journal*, Oct. 12, 1722.
[2] J. T. Smith's *Streets of London*, 1849, p. 77.
[3] *Ackermann's Repository*, Nov. 1, 1822.

into a music-hall, for their exhibits, but the honours attendant on the Royal Academy, more immediately under the influence of Royal favour, detached its members. And the Royal Academy's greater attractions to the public effected the decline of the Lyceum.[1] The society remained in Pall Mall until, in 1771, the King gave them apartments in Old Somerset House, where they remained until 1838, when they removed to the National Gallery.[2] The present Royal Academy in Burlington Gardens was erected in 1868, the hundredth anniversary of its foundation.

The house in which the eminent physician to Henry of Navarre, James I., and Charles I., Sir Theodore Turquet de Mayerne, lived, stood here on the west side of what was then the "West Church-lane." Mayerne was himself closely associated with art, for it was he who introduced Petitot to Charles I., and Petitot owed the perfection of his colouring in enamel to some chemical secret communicated to him by Mayerne, who is described by Walpole as a "great chymist."[3] At a toyshop with the sign of the Plough in New Exchange might be had "Sir Theodore Mayerne's Opiate for the Teeth," which "makes them clean and white as Ivory, tho' never so black and rotten, fastens and preserves them from the Tooth-Ach, being an excellent Thing for preventing and Killing the Scurvy" &c., &c.[4] It is narrated of Mayerne that a friend consulting him, and expecting to have the fee refused, ostentatiously placed on the table two gold broad pieces of the value of six-and-thirty shillings each. Looking rather mortified when Mayerne swept them into his pouch, the latter said gravely, "Sir, I made my will this morning, and if it should become known that I refused a fee the same afternoon I might be deemed *non-compos*."[5]

A few doors from Mayerne dwelt Sir John Finet, courtier and favourite of James I. He was assistant-master of the ceremonies, author of "Finetti Philoxenis" ". . . touching the reception and precedence, &c., of forren ambassadors in England," which was published by James Howell in 1656 ; and translated from the French "The Beginning, Continuance, and Decay of Estates," 1606.[6]

---

[1] *Ackermann's Repository*, Nov. 1, 1822.

[2] Interesting information respecting the Academy's constitution and scope in 1831 will be found in Elmes's *Topographical Dictionary* ; see also Thornbury's *Haunted London*, and *A Paladin of Philanthropy*, by Austin Dobson.

[3] Walpole's *Anecdotes of Painting*, 1871, p. 197.

[4] *Tatler*, Dec. 15, 1709.

[5] J. C. Jeaffreson's *Book of Doctors*, p. 109.

[6] Wood's *Athenæ Oxonienses*.

To briefly mention other distinguished residents on the west and fashionable side of the Lane before the plan of numbering the houses was adopted, there were Daniel Mytens, the painter, two doors from Mayerne ; Carew Raleigh, son of Sir Walter Raleigh ; Sir John Suckling ; Sir Kenelm Digby ; Sir William Alexander, afterwards Earl of Stirling, author of " Monarchic Tragedies," whom James I. used to call his " philosophic poet " ; Dr. Thomas Willis, the celebrated physician ; Dr. Tenison, then vicar of St. Martin's ; Sir Benjamin Rudyerd ; the Earl of Shaftesbury ; Ambrose Philips ; Sir James Thornhill ; and Sir Joshua Reynolds.[1]

Charing Cross Road, leading from the east or Tottenham Court Road end of Oxford Street to St. Martin's Church and the National Portrait Gallery, was opened for public traffic by H.R.H. the Duke of Cambridge in January 1887. It was suggested by the " Builder " that it should be called Nelson Avenue, or Alexandra Avenue, just as it was also proposed that the present Shaftesbury Avenue should be known as Piccadilly Road. Charing Cross Road takes its course along Crown Street, which has been widened—crosses Shaftesbury Avenue at Cambridge Circus, takes in the new Sandringham Buildings, crosses Coventry Street, and continues its course to Charing Cross along Castle Street, which was widened.[2] The writer purchased many an interesting relic of the Stuart period during the necessary excavations.

[1] Cunningham's *London.*

[2] Wheatley's *Cunningham*, 1891, vol. i. p. 359 ; and the *Builder*, Feb. 19 and 26, 1887.

CHAPTER XV.

KING STREET.

A S the husband is usually "the head of the wife," so King
Street, Covent Garden, named after King Charles I., was a
street of greater importance for some time after it was built than
Henrietta Street, which with Great Queen Street, Lincoln's Inn
Fields, commemorates the ill-fated monarch's consort, on her
mother's side a Medici. Both King Street and Henrietta Street
were built in 1637, four years after the erection of what subsequently
became the great fruit and vegetable market. In 1865 King
Street had a narrow escape from losing its historic designation,
for the Metropolitan Board of Works agreed to a proposition
that King Street and New King Street should cease to bear
those names. By "New King Street" is probably meant "New
Street," which is to this day a continuation of King Street. The
object was to lessen the confusion arising from the existence of
so many King Streets in London, no fewer, at that time, than
thirty. But a due sense of historic sequence in the maintenance
of our old street nomenclature seems, fortunately, to have prevailed over mere considerations of utility.[1] Between the two
thoroughfares, King Street and Henrietta Street, was "sandwiched"
St. Paul's Church, which, like the "refreshment-room" sandwich,
is of the Tuscan order of architecture. In speaking, however, of
this church, it should be remembered that Inigo Jones, the original
architect, was in no way responsible for its later inharmonious
surroundings. Although the square was formed from his designs,
it was never completed accordingly. One can gather, in fact, from
what remains of the Piazza, that the plan was a supremely grand
one, in which the Tuscan church of St. Paul, after all said and
done by way of apology, would by no means have run severely
counter to the plan's uniformity. Such as Covent Garden is, it

---

[1] A glimpse of the original street is afforded in Hollar's view of the Covent
Garden Piazza.

is the church and remaining arcade that we should be thankful for, painfully ignoring the miserable alloy in the true metal, and deploring the fact of such a noble square having been put to the use of a market-place at all. Grignon, the engraver after Gravelot, Hayman, Wale, &c., who lived at No. 27 James Street on the north side of the market—or perhaps it was his son—informed the author of a scarce pamphlet, published for the instruction of "Gentlemen visiting Evans's Supper-rooms," that he was told by the then Marquis of Tavistock how the south of Covent Garden Piazza was not erected as was intended, because his (the Marquis's) ancestor was fined very heavily in the Star Chamber for commencing to build the other parts without a licence. This vexed him so much that he would not proceed.[1]

The thoroughfare, dirty and circuitous, known as Rose Street— the scene of the "Rose Alley Ambuscade," in which Dryden was so barbarously assaulted by the hirelings of the Earl of Rochester[2]—was not demolished, as Timbs in his "Walks and Talks about London" implies, for it exists to this day,[3] and its winding course may still be followed by taking the first "entry" on the right, from the north-west corner of King Street. The new Garrick Street, in fact, began at the *top* of Rose Street, only a small portion of the latter having been requisitioned for the beginning of the new street.[4] Not a vestige, of course, remains of the old houses in Rose Street, but there is a quaint little old tavern at No. 33 with the sign of the "Lamb and Flag," which Mr. Laurence Hutton erroneously describes as having been built about 1880. This cannot possibly be the case, for the western elevation, up a curious old court, Lazenby Court, leading into Long Acre, is all timber-built in the oldest manner, and this timber wall is part of the "Lamb and Flag" public-house. What connection there could have been between the armorial bearings

[1] In his endeavour to introduce a taste for something approaching the Italian Piazza, Inigo Jones seems to have taken as his model that at Livorno, which has itself been attributed to him.

[2] See advertisement offering the reward of fifty pounds for the apprehension of his assailants in *Domestic Intelligence, or News from City and Country* (No. 50), Dec. 26, 1679, in the Burney Collection.

[3] Compare the plan in Gwynn's *London and Westminster* and Horwood's map with the present map of the London Post Office Directory.

[4] There is a drawing by T. H. Shepherd of the making of Garrick Street— view from St. Martin's Lane—in the St. Martin's Library, Charing Cross, and another of houses in King Street that were demolished on that occasion.

of the Middle Temple (the "Lamb and Flag") and this part is open to speculation, but possibly the sign was set up by some former servant of the Templars. At the time when Rose Street had no flagged pavement, and hackney-coaches could be driven close to the very door of their destination, Saunders Welsh, the magistrate, once captured a rogue in Rose Street in a singular manner. He had good information that a most notorious offender, who had for some time annoyed Londoners in their walks through the green lanes to Mary-le-bone, and who had eluded the chase of several of his men, was in a first floor of a house in Rose Street. After hiring the tallest hackney-coach he could select, he mounted the box with the coachman, and when he was close against the house he ascended the roof of the coach, threw up the sash of a first-floor window, entered the room, and actually dragged the fellow from his bed out at the window by his hair, naked as he was, upon the top of the coach, and so carried him off.

In this street lived Samuel Butler, the author of "Hudibras," [1] and here he dragged, in his last years, a miserable existence to his tomb in St. Paul's Church, Covent Garden, unpatronised, but respected for his integrity and beloved for his social qualities. Probably, however, his existence was not so miserable that consolation was not afforded by the pursuit of letters, for he is described as living here "in a studious retired manner." Aubrey says he "dyed of a consumption September 25 (Anno Domini 1680), and buried 27, according to his own appointment, in the churchyard of Covent Garden ; sc. in the north part next the church at the east end. His feet touch the wall. His grave, 2 yards distant from the pilaster of the dore (by his desire), 6 foot deepe. About 25 of his old acquaintance at his funerall: I myself being one." [2] He was interred, at the charge of his friend Mr. Longueville, at the west end of the churchyard, on the north side, under the wall of the church. With the exception of Westminster Abbey, the burial registers of St. Paul's, Covent Garden, contain probably the names of more men of genius than those of any other church in London. Among these are Sir Peter Lely, the painter ; Dick Estcourt, the actor and wit ; Edward Kynaston, the celebrated actor of female parts at the Restoration ; Wycherley, the dramatist ; Pierce Tempest, who drew "The Cries of London," known as Tempest's Cries; Grinling Gibbons,

---

[1] In a note in the *Biographia Britannica*, p. 1075, this is stated on the authority of the younger Mr. Longueville. (Johnson's *Lives*.)

[2] Aubrey's *Lives*, ii. 263.

the sculptor and carver in wood; Susannah Centlivre, author of
"The Busy Body" and "The Wonder"; Robert Wilkes, the original
Sir Harry Wildair, celebrated by Steele for acting with the easy
frankness of a gentleman; James Worslade, the painter,

> Eager to get, but not to keep the pelf,
> A friend to all mankind except himself;

Dr. John Armstrong, the author of "The Art of Preserving Health,"
a poem; Tom Davies, the bookseller, and his "very pretty wife";
Sir Robert Strange, the engraver; Thomas Girtin, the father of the
school of English water-colours; John Wolcot (Peter Pindar); and
Macklin. Charles Macklin, the actor and dramatist, of some
celebrity for talent, and more for longevity, was buried in the vault
beneath the altar of the church. He died at the great age of 107,
in 1797. The following pathetic description of the veteran treading
the boards at the age of 86 as Macbeth occurs in the Theatrical
Intelligence of the "Middlesex Journal," December 2–3, 1776:
"*Mr. Macklin*, with all the foolhardiness of a daring veteran, who
having been cut and hacked through numberless Campaigns, till he
is desperate enough to regard neither life nor limb—sallied forth
last night again in the character of *Macbeth*; perhaps with the
cynical view of courting the universal contempt of mankind; for as
an actor, no contempt can overpay his presumption in persisting
to appear in this character. We have given him credit from the
first for the judicious getting up of this tragedy, in all its parts, and
thro' all its stages; and only condemn him for counteracting his
own good design, in bringing him into the foreground as the leading
figure of the piece, an object every way repugnant to grace and
nature, as his own prodigious self! In the celebrated dagger scene,
instead of addressing that matchless soliloquy in low and broken
measures to his own mind, he raved and stamped about like a
Smithfield drover after a mad ox! To trace him thro' all his
imperfections would be as disagreeable as tiresome a task. He
may conceive the character right for all we know; but if he does,
he has the most unfortunate manner of bringing his ideas into articu-
lation, or action, that we ever remember. To do him justice, he has
at last corrected those ill-timed roarings on his entering Duncan's
chamber agreeable to our remarks; and the effect of the alteration
was generally felt; the light within the staircase was abundantly
glaring, when the circumstance and situation required, if anything,
the extreme of darkness (*this hint to the scene-shifters*). The other
characters of the play were in general well supported as usual."

In an old newspaper cutting, the source of which is erroneously given as " Domestic Intelligence " for December 26, 1679, is the following : " Mr. Gerrill informs me that the cook-shop the corner of Rose Street was where Butler died ; and that the house next door to him, towards Longacre, was kept by a Lord and a Baronet." [1] Edmund Curll was living in Rose Street when he published Mr. Pope's "Literary Correspondence," and here, at the " Pope's Head," he published (price 5s.)

" THE Merryland Miscellany ; containing the ten following pieces, viz. : 1. New Description of Merryland ; being a topographical, geographical, and natural History of that Country. Address'd to Dr. Cheyne of Bath. 2. Arbor Vitae : or The Tree of Life, &c. 3. The Potent Ally : or Succours from Merryland. Address'd to Alderman Parsons. 4. Merryland Display'd : Being Observations on the new Description of Merryland. Written by an eminent Physician, and address'd to the Author of that Pamphlet. 5. The Poetical History of Pandora's Box. 6. Armour : A Poem. 7. Κυνλυμοζενια (?) : A Tale. 8. Consummation : or, The Rape of Adonis. An original Poem. 9. The Resurrection : A Tale. 10. Ερωτο Πολις : or The Present State of Bettyland. Written by that great Master of Humour, Charles Cotton, Esq., author of Virgil Travestie, &c." [2]

Garrick Street was probably so named because of the Garrick Club having found a new home there in 1864. Until this removal it was situated at No. 35 King Street, where it was established in 1831. The ground is now occupied by the Capital and Counties Bank, but previously to its occupation by the club the house, says Timbs, was a family hotel. Garrick himself resided in King Street. In 1745 he received a letter from A.B. " To Mr. David Garrick, at his lodgings at Mr. West's, Cabinet-maker, in King Street, Covent Garden." [3]

The club-house was a snug old-fashioned tenement that had for many years been " Probatt's Family Hotel." [4]   Before its hotel time

---

[1] See Collection of Cuttings, &c., relating to the neighbourhood of Covent Garden, in the British Museum Library.   Mr. Gerrill was the landlord of the " Salutation " in Tavistock Street.

[2] *Daily Advertiser*, March 1, 1742.

[3] The *Private Correspondence of David Garrick*, 1831, vol. i. p. 33.

[4] In a list of hotels in the *Picture of London* for 1818, mention is made of Probatt's Hotel, King Street, Covent Garden ; and a list of coffee-houses following has Probatt's Coffee-house, King Street, Covent Garden (pp. 413 and 416).

it was the residence of the incomparable comedian, William Lewis, an airy, light performer, of whom there are no less than four portraits in the club.[1] The Garrick was established, mainly by the exertions of Mr. Frank Mills, with the design of constituting "a society in which actors and men of education and refinement might meet on equal and independent terms."[2]

The famous array of theatrical portraits in the Garrick Club were originally collected chiefly by Charles Mathews the elder. Among them are Henderson, by Gainsborough; the elder Coleman, by Sir Joshua Reynolds; Munden, by Opie; a drawing, by Lawrence, of J. P. Kemble; another, by Harlow, of Elliston; and another, by Lawrence, of Mrs. Siddons; Nat Lee; Doggett; Quin; Foote; Moody; Bannister; Tom Sheridan; head of Garrick, by Zoffany; King, by Richard Wilson, the landscape-painter; Emery; the elder Dibdin; Mr. Powel and Family, by R. Wilson; Nell Gwynne; Mrs. Oldfield (half-length), by Kneller; Mrs. Bracegirdle; Mrs. Pritchard Mrs. Cibber; Peg Woffington; Mrs. Abington, by Hickey; Mrs. Siddons, by Harlow; Mrs. Yates; Mrs. Billington; Miss O'Neil, by Joseph; Nancy Dawson; Mrs. Inchbald, by Harlow; Miss Stephens; head of Mrs. Robinson, by Sir Joshua; Joseph Harris, as Cardinal Wolsey; Anthony Leigh, as the Spanish Friar; Colley Cibber, as Lord Foppington, by Grisoni; Griffin and Johnson, in "The Alchemist," by P. Van Bleeck; 'The School for Scandal" (the Screen Scene), as originally cast; Mrs. Pritchard, as Lady Macbeth, by Zoffany; Mr. and Mrs. Barry, in "Hamlet"; Rich, in 1753, as Harlequin; Garrick, as Richard III., by the elder Morland; King, and Touchstone, by Zoffany; Weston, as Billy Button, by Zoffany; King and Mr. and Mrs. Baddely, in "The Clandestine Marriage," by Zoffany; Moody and Parsons, in "The Committee," by Vandergucht; Garrick and Mrs. Cibber, by Zoffany; "Love, Law and Physic" (Mathews, Liston, Blanchard, and Emery), by Clint; Powell, Bensley, and Smith, by J. Mortimer; Dowton, in "The Mayor of Garratt"; busts by Mrs. Siddons, of herself and brother.

This splendid collection, as Mr. Percy Fitzgerald observes, is Charles Mathews's monument. Mathews was extravagant, not in his pleasures, but in gratifying his tastes. He had no idea of the value of money, and was constantly being robbed or taken in. The

---

[1] The *Garrick Club*, by Percy Fitzgerald, 1904, p. 3.
[2] The *Garrick Club: Notices of One Hundred and Thirty-five of its former Members*, by the Rev. R. H. Barham.

beginning of his collection of portraits was thus : he once let his house to an "agreeable" family of the name of Thompson, who paid no rent, until one day his eyes fell on an account of the auction at the cottage, where he found that everything had been sold off and the family had disappeared ! Seven hundred pounds was his loss. Something, however, escaped, and that something was a number of old portraits stored in an outhouse. This was the germ of the dramatic collection which he had just begun to form.[1]

What were "Chinese Brogdanones" and "Lillepushes"? Mrs. Leadbeater, at the "Three Stags' Heads"[2] in King Street, Covent Garden, announces the sale of her "entire Stock in Trade of China Ware, she being oblig'd to clear on or before Lady Day next. Note.—There are some very great Curiosities, particularly Images of extraordinary Stature, representing Chinese Brogdanones, Lillepushes, &c., which must be dispos'd of; also some India Pictures."[3]

When the four "Indian Kings," commemorated in the "Tatler" and "Spectator," visited England in Queen Anne's reign, to obtain assistance against the French in Canada, they lodged in King Street, Covent Garden, at the house of the musician Dr. Arne's father, an upholsterer, who hung out the sign of the "Two Crowns and Cushions." Timbs says Arne's house was next door to the Garrick Club. The king and queen, for whom Arne, as an upholsterer, made the two cushions probably, if not the two crowns, and so begot his sign, were perhaps William and Mary, unless the sign, as might well be the case, existed before his tenancy of the house. This was the Arne who was so full of other people's affairs that he neglected his own. As satirised in the "Tatler" No. 155, he had a wife and several children, but was much more anxious as to what passed in Poland than in his own family, and was "in greater pain and anxiety of mind for King Augustus's welfare than that of his nearest relations."[4] This trait in his character was not an un-

---

[1] The *Garrick Club*, by Percy Fitzgerald, 1904, p. 118.

[2] Three stags' heads are the arms of the D'Oylys, and also, I think, of the Stanleys, Earls of Derby ; but the connection with the sign is not apparent. According to Burke's *Gen. Armoury*, the Doyles or Doyleys bear three stags' heads, the Doylys three bucks' heads (or 2 bends).

[3] *Daily Advertiser*, March 18, 1742. Possibly the Brogdanones and Lillepushes had some connection with the popularity of *Gulliver's Travels* and with Brobdingnag and the Liliputians.

[4] See, further, *Tatler* Nos. 155 and 171, and *Spectator* No. 50.

qualified misfortune, however, for the "nobly non-utilitarian" interests of music were promoted by the quidnunc upholsterer's absence from his home in King Street. The future composer of the air "Rule, Britannia," no doubt profited by this circumstance by day as well as by night. At night he secreted himself with his spinet in his room, just as Handel did with his clavichord, where, muffling the strings with a handkerchief, he used to practise in the night, while the rest of the family were asleep. But if his father had discovered how he spent his time "he would probably have thrown the instrument, if not the player, out of the window."[1] To return to the four "Indian Kings"—their names were of an extraordinary syllabic character—Tee Yee Neen Ho Ga Prow, and Sa Ga Yean Qua Prah Ton, of the Maquas; Elow Oh Kaom, and Oh Nee Yeabh Ton No Prow, of the river Sachem and the Ganajohbore Sachem. On April 18 they were conveyed in two of the Queen's coaches to St. James's, and introduced to their public audience by the Lord Chamberlain, the Duke of Shrewsbury; Major Pidgeon, an officer who had come over with them, acted as interpreter. "They had with one consent," they said, "hung up the kettle and taken in their hands the hatchet, in token of their friendship to the Great Queen and her children, and on the other side of the great waters they had been a strong wall of security to their Great Queen's children, even to the loss of their best children." They rejoiced in the prospect of the English conquest of Canada, after which they should have free hunting, and a great trade with their Great Queen's children, and as a token of the sincerity of the Six Nations they, in the name of all, presented their Great Queen with the belts of wampum. In conclusion they besought their Great Queen to give their case her gracious consideration, and petitioned her to send them more of her children to teach them, as, since their friendship with her children, they had obtained some knowledge of the Saviour of the World.

They remained a fortnight longer in London, being entertained by various persons of distinction, and taken to see the principal "sights." By way of Hampton Court and Windsor they were conveyed to Portsmouth, where they embarked on board the "Dragon" man-of-war, and arrived at Boston, in New England, on July 15, 1710. In 1712, according to an old newspaper excerpt, was published "A full and true account of a most cruel and dreadful fire, which happened betwixt two and three in the morning,

[1] See the *Musical Review*, vol. i. p. 201.

in King Street, Covent Garden, and burnt down the Crown and Cushion, being the house where the 'Indian Kings' lived, and several other houses, having done nearly ten thousand pounds damage." Consequently it must have been the house rebuilt on the site of Arne's, and not the same house as stated, which was for many years afterwards tenanted by Mr. William Cribb, whose father published the magnificent mezzotint by G. Clint, from Harlow's picture of the trial of Queen Katherine. This celebrated painting —known as "The Kemble Family," from its introducing their portraits—was the last work of Harlow, whom his master, Sir Thomas Lawrence, characterised as "the most promising of all our painters." To Mr. Cribb is due the credit of having been the first to appreciate the genius of the late Mr. Sydney Cooper, whose Cuyp-like pictures are so justly admired. The incident is agreeably told by Miss Mitford in her "Belford Regis." Mr. Cribb was struck with a small cattle-piece by Cooper, which he saw in a shop window in Soho ; he sought out the young painter, and gave him his first commission. The painting was seen by artists and amateurs at Mr. Cribb's picture-room in King Street, and it was chiefly from this work that commissions poured in, and urged the artist on the road to fortune.

Three doors from the Capital and Counties Bank, on its west side at No. 33 King Street, lodged one of our most famous actors, George Frederick Cooke, whose reckless manner of living brought him to a comparatively early grave in his fifty-sixth year. It is related how he threw his pocket-book, containing £300, on the fire because a working man who had been a soldier, and with whom he had quarrelled, refused to fight with him, making the excuse that Cooke was a rich man. "Cooke lodged here in 1805," says Wheatley, " at £3 a week."

The Westminster Fire Assurance Company's Office is stated by Cunningham to occupy the site of the house of Lenthall, Speaker of the House of Commons in the time of the Commonwealth.[1] The Company, incorporated in 1717, has already been alluded to as having originally held its meetings at Tom's Coffee-house, in St. Martin's Lane, and we have seen how its engine went nobly to work in sub- duing the fire at Allen's Coffee-house. It was removed from St. Martin's Lane to Bedford Street and from Bedford Street to King Street about the year 1830 or 1831, when it was under the manage- ment of William Crake, Esq., chairman, and twenty-three other

---

[1] *Garrick Correspondence*, i. 33.

directors; George How Brown, Esq., secretary; and James Gray Mayhew, Esq., surveyor of buildings.[1]

The building at the King Street end of Garrick Street was erected when the latter thoroughfare was formed, in 1860, by Messrs. Debenham, Storr and Sons, the auctioneers, from the designs of Mr. Arthur Allom. The style must be called Italian, says the "Builder." It is a good bold front; the blocking course of the frontispiece has an incised ornament, and the heads on the key-stones on the ground floor are very well modelled. The site, an irregular triangle, presented some difficulties, and the building has a frontage of 117 feet.

King Street was honoured by the residence of a poet laureate in the person of the amiable Nicholas Rowe, the editor of Shakespeare, and author of "Jane Shore" and other sentimental tragedies. He lived at a house in this street, however, only during the latter years of his life, but on which side is not stated. Dr. Johnson esteemed his version of Lucan's "Pharsalia" a masterpiece, and he was honoured on the signboard, for his head served as the sign of F. W. Feales, "over against St. Clement's Church in the Strand," in 1737. In the same street lived another poet, Samuel Taylor Coleridge, from 1799 down to 1802. He was then earning his livelihood as an unknown writer on political subjects for the "Morning Post."

[1] Elmes's *Topographical Dictionary*, 1831.

CHAPTER XVI.

SOME CURIOUS ASSOCIATIONS OF KING STREET.

ON the south side of King Street there still exists a most curious sign for a tavern—the "Essex Serpent," at No. 6. There can hardly be any doubt that this is a very old taverner's sign, dating from soon after the formation of the street itself. In the British Museum Library there is a unique pamphlet which evidently relates to this "Essex Serpent."[1]   "One of the most venomous Serpents in former time," says the narrative, "lurked about the Meads near Saffron Walden, in Essex, who by his very sight killed so many as the town became almost depopulated, when a valerous knight, making him a Coat of Christal Glass, boldly went to assail this Cockatrice, but her venomous Nature not able to indure the purity of that fine metal, she suddenly dyed, in memory whereof his Sword was hung up in Walden Church, the effigies of the Cockatrice set up in Brass, and a Table hanged close by, wherein was continued all the story of the adventure; but in these late times of Rebellion, it being taken for a monument of superstition, was by the lawless Souldiers broken in pieces, to show they were also of venomous Nature as well as the Cockatrice."

The terrifying attributes of the Cockatrice, or Basilisk, as this Essex Serpent was also called, were enough to curdle the blood in the veins of the hardiest peasantry.   He is described as the most venomous of all the serpent tribe : "It breaketh stones, blasteth all Plants with his breath, it burneth everything it goeth over ; no Herb can grow near the place of his abode, it is poison to poison, and frighteth away all other Serpents, only with a hissing.   If a man touch it though with a long pole it kills him, and if it see a man a far off it destroys him with its looks.   It is not above a foot in length, of colour between black and yellow, having very red eyes, a sharp head, and a white spot hereon like a Crown.   It goeth not winding like other Serpents, but upright on his breast."

[1] *Strange News out of Essex, or the Winged Serpent*, an eight-page tract.

There was another sign of the " Essex Serpent " in Charles Street, Westminster, but this has disappeared, and the King Street one is the only remaining instance in London. It was, no doubt, adopted by some enterprising tavern-keeper at the time the pamphlet quoted above was in circulation, and when the wonder was fresh in people's minds. It is mentioned by Oldys the antiquary, who died in 1761, but the sign in King Street is probably as old as the publication of the pamphlet in 1669. It was, strictly speaking, not Saffron Walden that the serpent haunted, but Henham-on-the-Mount, four miles from Saffron Walden, and "the truth of the Relation of the Serpent" was attested by: Richard Jackson, churchwarden ; Thomas Presland, constable ; John Knight, overseer of the poor ; Barnaby Thurgood, Samuel Garret, Richard Seely, and William Green, householders.

King Street was the birthplace of mahogany furniture. Dr. Gibbons, an eminent physician of the time, was building a house in King Street, when his brother, a West Indian captain, brought over some mahogany as ballast, and thinking the wood might be of service to his brother the doctor, he sent him a quantity of it ; but the carpenters finding it too hard to work, it was laid aside. Soon after this, Mrs. Gibbons wanting a candle-box, the doctor called on his cabinet-maker in Long Acre, and asked him to make one of some wood which lay in his garden. He complained, however, that it was too hard for his tools, and the doctor said he must get stronger tools. The box was made and approved, so that the doctor had a bureau made of the same wood ; the fine colour and polish were so pleasing that he invited his friends to come and see the bureau ; and among them was the Duchess of Buckingham, through whose patronage of it the wood came into general use. The doors of a few of the better class of old houses in King Street were remarkable for some time afterwards, up, in fact, to the middle of the last century, for being made of solid mahogany. The "Mahogany Door," in fact, really occurs as a sign in 1742 :

"To be SOLD, for the Importer,
At the 'Mahogony Door,' the third above the Church,
in Ludgate Street,
The best Coniac Brandy and Jamaica Rum at the lowest Price. Arrack at 14*s.* per gallon," &c., &c. [1]

The wood seems to have come from Jamaica—at all events in

---

[1] *Daily Advertiser,* June 22, 1742.

1738 : "Yesterday was entered at the Custom-House from ——,
Jamaica, 10,500 lb. of Indigo, and 117 Tons of Mahogony." [1]

Quin, the actor, was born in King Street, in circumstances
associated in later life with his misfortunes. His father, an Irish
barrister, unfortunately married a supposed widow who turned out
to be of the " grass " variety, for her husband, after a long absence,
returned and claimed her, on which account Quin, who was the
offspring of the connection, was deemed illegitimate, and upon his
father's death was left without a fortune. Garrick, once his rival,
lived in the same street, and afterwards became his friend, writing
in due time his epitaph in Bath Cathedral.

The " snuffing gentleman " was an institution of sufficient commercial importance to suggest a snuff-dealer's sign so called,[2] though
not in King Street. In King Street, however, was a snuff-dealer
who hung out the sign of the " Golden Cup," and the " snuffing
gentleman " might purchase there not less than a pound of " superfine Muslin Havanna Snuff at 3s. 6d. a Pound. Also a small, but
neat, Harpsichord to be sold cheap." This snuff-dealer was also a
hosier, one Wilson by name. [3]

The National Sporting Club, No. 43 King Street, was founded
on the ruins of the " Pelican." [4] Situated at the north-west end of
the Piazza, the premises may justly be said to be, in point of the
residence they have afforded to distinguished persons, among the
most historic in London. The site of this famous nursery of the
" noble art " is, in the first place, identical with that occupied by
the house of Sir Kenelm Digby, which is distinctly indicated by
Aubrey in his " Lives," where he says :—" Since the restauration of
Charles II., he lived in the last faire house westward in the north
portioo of Covent Garden, where my lord Denzill Holles lived since.
He had a laboratory there. I think he dyed in this house, sed Qu." [5]
Of this Lord Holles, who was a man of great courage, it is narrated
that being one day engaged in a very hot debate in the House, in
which some rude expressions fell from Ireton, " Colonel Hollis "
persuaded him to walk out with him, and then told him that he
would presently go over the water and fight him. Ireton replied

---

[1] *St. James's Evening Post*, Feb. 9, 1738.

[2] The " Jessamine Tree and Snuffing Gentleman."

[3] *Daily Advertiser*, April 5, 1742.

[4] The *National Sporting Club*, edited by A. F. Bettinson and Wm. O.
Tristram, 1901, pp. 6-7.

[5] *Lives of Eminent Men*, 1813, p. 327.

that "his conscience would not suffer him to fight a duel," where-upon Holles pulled him by the nose, telling him that "if his con-science would keep him from giving men satisfaction, it should keep him from provoking them."[1]   Cunningham says that Denzil Holles, also known as Colonel Holles, the celebrated member of the Long Parliament, "lived in the Piazza in 1644 ; and in 1666 and after in a house on the site of Evans's Hotel."   In or about 1662–3, Holles addressed a letter to the Lord Mayor, Sir John Frederick, requesting a quill of water for the use of his son and daughter, at their residence in St. Martin's Lane.[2]   Sir Harry Vane the younger, also, in the year 1647, dwelt in this house in King Street.[3]   The mansion was subsequently altered, if not rebuilt, for the Earl of Orford, better known as Admiral Russell, and his occupancy is commemorated to this day by a tablet outside, which says :

HERE

LIVED AND DIED

ADMIRAL EDWARD RUSSELL

EARL OF ORFORD.

Born 1651.   Died 1727.

Admiral Russell was gentleman of the bed-chamber to James, Duke of York, but on the execution of his cousin, Lord William Russell, he retired from Court, and was an active promoter of the Revolution.   In the battle of La Hogue, when the French fleet, under Admiral Trouville, was utterly destroyed by the English and the Dutch, Admirals Russell and Rooke gained a most im-portant victory, which not only put an end to the threatened French invasion, and overthrew the hopes of James II. of recovering his throne, but so crippled the navy of France that it ceased to be formidable.   The fine old staircase of what was afterwards Low's Family Hotel was formed of part of the vessel—the "Britannia," 100 guns—that Admiral Russell, Lord Orford, commanded at La Hogue.[4]   Low's was the first "Family" hotel in London.   The house of Admiral Russell, only partly rebuilt, succeeded that in which Sir Kenelm Digby and other distinguished persons lived, and

[1] Guthrie's *History of England*, vol. iii. p. 175 ; see also edition 1751, vol. iv. p. 1173.   This incident, however, detracted little, if anything, from the reputation for courage which Ireton had acquired on the field of battle.

[2] *Remembrancia of the City of London* (1579–1664), 1878, p. 560.

[3] Cunningham's *London*, 1850, p. 595.

[4] Among the items in the Parish Register of St. Paul's, Covent Garden, is one, " Rec^d of Admiral (La Hogue) Russell, for his pew in the gallery, 10*s*."

is said, with extreme probability, to have been the scene of the first Cabinet Council (in which, unlike the Privy Council, the presence of the reigning Sovereign is not considered necessary) ever held in England. The first Lord Archer of the revived barony [1] married into the Russell family, to Lord Orford's sister, I think, [2] but it was the second baron who, in 1761, married Sarah, elder daughter of James West the bibliographer, and member for Alscot, Warwickshire, into whose possession the house had passed. With the second Lord Archer, not only did the barony become extinct, but the owner of the title is said to have been the last nobleman to reside in Covent Garden. It was not the tendency of the everyday speech of the time to call a spade a horticultural implement, and when Lady Archer asked a nobleman why he did not admire her daughter, he said he was "no judge of painting." Her ladyship's wit, however, saved the situation, for, not in the least disconcerted, she asked whether he had "ever seen an angel that was not painted." [3] Here, at No. 43, dwelt the famous bibliophile and connoisseur, James West, and here was sold *in suo proprio loco* his valuable library, which it took the auctioneer six weeks to dispose of. His MSS. passed to the Marquis of Lansdowne. His books, with many important antiquarian notes by Bishop White Kennett, were sold by auction by Mr. Landford, and the catalogue was arranged by Mr. Paterson. Many, of the greatest literary value, sold for a few shillings. The sale of the prints and drawings occupied thirteen days ; the coins and medals, seven.

After the sale the house became Low's Family Hotel. Then it was successively known as the Grand Hotel, Froome's, Hudson's, Richardson's, Joy's, Evans's, and then the Covent Garden Hotel. During all these tenancies the house appears to have remained the dwelling built, or partially rebuilt, by Admiral Russell. Low is said to have had gold, silver, and copper medals struck as advertisements for his hotel. The gold were given to princes, the silver to the nobility, and the copper to the ordinary guests. Before he took

[1] This barony was very ancient. See Burke's *Dormant and Extinct Peerages.*

[2] Thus Burke (*Extinct Peerages*) ; but Mr. Dobson says that Lord Archer married Russell's grand-niece Catherine Tipping (*Eighteenth Century Vignettes,* third series).

[3] See *Court Anecdotes.* There are some curious engravings extant of this Lady Archer, who survived her husband, and there is a view of Bowles's extant, showing the Market, the Church of St. Paul, and Lord Archer's house (1751). A shoeblack who stood at the end of Lord Archer's rails had saved between £70 and £80.

West's historic house, Low was a hairdresser of Southampton Street. His venture, however, ruined him. The next adventurer was Froome, landlord of the " White Hart" in Long Acre, afterwards Stubb's, the coachmaker's. The back gateway and the sides of the White Hart Inn were still to be seen from Hart Street at the beginning of last century. It was a house of ill-fame, but Froome kept Low's very respectably.[1] About 1790 Mrs. Hudson became the proprietor. She was something of a Mrs. Malaprop, for one of her advertisements ended "with stabling for one hundred noblemen and horses." Of Mr. Richardson, who next succeeded, nothing seems to be known.[2] Next came Mr. Joy, when what afterwards became even better known as " Evans's," was called the " Star" dinner and coffee room, because of the number of men of rank who visited it. It was said that it was no uncommon thing for nine dukes to dine here, at this period in the house's history, in one day. Then it became "Evans's." This Mr. W. C. Evans, of Covent Garden Theatre, died in 1854, having in 1844 resigned the rooms and hall into the hands of Mr. Green. Evans was a comedian.

Sir Kenelm Digby, while living here, possessed a piece of ground at the back of the house, afterwards known as " Digby's Garden," where was formerly a small cottage, in which the Kembles lived while in the zenith of their fame at Covent Garden Theatre, and here the highly-gifted Fanny Kemble was born. On the site of this garden was built a very handsome music-hall or singing-room by Mr. Green, the successor of Evans. This music-room was remarkable for the transition in the character of its entertainments, though still known as Evans's, from downright grossness to music of a higher class. This is attested by the publication of a now rare pamphlet which includes a selection of songs, glees and madrigals, and was published about 1855-6 "for the acceptance of gentlemen visiting Evans's Supper Rooms." It was built from the designs of Mr. William Finch Hill. The proportions of the room, which may still be seen at the National Sporting Club, looking at it in section, was nearly square, being about 53 feet high, and as many wide ; it was about 72 feet long from end to end, and with the old room, through which it was approached, the hall was 113 feet in length.[3] As Evans's

---

[1] See a scarce pamphlet printed for " Gentlemen visiting Evans's Supper Rooms, Covent Garden."

[2] Unless he was the well-known waiter of that name at the Shakespear Tavern, Covent Garden.

[3] *Illustrated London News*, January 26, 1856.

Music Hall it was finally closed in 1880, and soon after the building, with the hotel adjoining, was converted into a club-house, the "Falstaff," a club somewhat similar to the "Garrick."

A distinguished actress dwelt in King Street, Covent Garden, in the person of Mrs. Butler, who was said to be an illegitimate daughter of a noble duke whose monument is erected in Westminster Abbey. Her rendering of the character of Celia in Jonson's "Volpone" was "extremely interesting."[1] She was the original actress of Millwood in "Barnwell," and the sometime rival of Mrs. Cibber. While impersonating the Countess of Rousillon in "All's Well that Ends Well" she was "seized with a distemper."[2] In what year this occurred is not stated, but the following advertisement appeared in 1742 :

"For the Benefit of M[rs]. BUTLER.

At the Theatre Royal in Drury Lane, next Tuesday, the 30th instant, will be presented a Comedy

The DOUBLE GALLANT.

The Part of the Double Gallant by Mr. Cibber; Sir Solomon Sadlife, Mr. Johnson ; Careless, Mr. Mills ; Clerimont, Mr. Havard ; Old Wilful, Mr. Shepard ; Old Atall, Mr. Turbutt ; Captain Strut, Mr. Neale ; Dr. Bolus, Mr. Taswell ; Apothecary, Mr. Gray ; Finder, Mr. Berry ; Supple, Mr. Ray ; *Lady Dainty, Mrs. Butler* ; Sylvia, Mrs. Mills ; Clarinda, Mrs. Woffington ; Lady Sadlife, Mrs. Clive ; Wishwell, Mrs. Macklin ; Situp, Miss Bennet ; China-Woman, Mrs. Egerton.

To which will be added a Farce, call'd

The LOTTERY.

Jack Stocks, alias Lord Lace, Mr. Cibber ; Chloe, alias Lady Lace, Mrs. Clive ; Lovemore, Mr. Beard.

And Entertainments of Singing and Dancing as will be express'd in the Bills. Places for the Stage to be taken of Mr. Moor, in the Playhouse Passage.

Tickets to be had at Mrs. Butler's house in King Street, Covent Garden ; and at Mr. Bradshaw's, Box-Book-Keeper, at the King's Arms in Russel-Street, near the Playhouse.

Servants will be admitted to keep Places on the Stage."[3]

---

[1] *Dramatic Miscellanies*, by Thomas Davies, 1785, vol. ii. p. 100.
[2] *Ibid.* p. 9.
[3] The *Daily Advertiser*, March 27, 1742. *Ibid.* March 3.

I have not been able to ascertain whether this Mrs. Butler is identical with one of the same name, but known also as "Mother Butler," who at the beginning of the last century kept the notorious "night-house" called the "Finish," originally known as the "Queen's Head." It was, however, on the south side of the Market, about half-way between Southampton Street and the "Hummums."[1] For some time before Mrs. Butler's tenancy it was called Carpenter's Coffee-house, so named after a singular character who, originally a porter, became lessee of the Market. When fetching fruit from the wharf at the Fox-under-the-Hill, he had a very peculiar knack of piling as many as fifteen half cherry-sieves upon his head, and would throw off at pleasure from one to any number, a knack he had acquired to such a certainty that he never failed. He was a worthy man and much respected.

The "Finish" was, down to a recent date, a gloomy, disreputable coffee-house, kept by one Smith, where, in interdicted hours, beer and spirits could be obtained when all the public-houses were closed. It had in 1866 been recently pulled down.[2] The "School of Reform" was another night resort for "choice spirits" on the south side of Covent Garden, which was contemporary with, and in character similar to, the "Finish."[3]

Four doors from the National Sporting Club at No. 38 King Street is another house of literary, as well as commercial, fame in the annals of Covent Garden. This is Stevens's Auction Rooms, where scientific instruments, &c., are sold, and, at the proper season, bulbs and choice plants. The large photograph immediately within the office premises, entitled "Worn Out," is of special interest. It is that of an old woman in her donkey-cart. "The surest sign of age is loneliness," says the author of "Ophic Sayings," and here we have the quintessence of loneliness. She probably lives, thinks, and has her being alone, yet not alone, for her faithful donkey is with her, and does he not help her to dispose of the poor marketable produce at her command? And who spliced the shafts of the broken-down antediluvian cart for her, of which even the tyres are bound to the wheel, by some kind friend, with cords? This faithful and pathetic picture earned the "Graphic's" £20 award for photography, over the heads of some thousands of competitors.[4] Much as

---

[1] See account in the *Windsor Magazine* for January, 1901.
[2] *History of Signboards*, 1884, p. 511.
[3] The *Epicure's Almanack*, 1815.
[4] This was on March 7, 1905.

we should like to know the history of the two carved ship's figure-heads of Indian kings, appertaining probably to the early annals of the tobacco trade, which stand in splendid preservation in the passage leading to the auction-room, we must pass to the story of the house's earlier fortunes.   The auction-rooms appear to have had for their first despot of the hammer the famous Paterson, who, for some time before it was taken down in July 1777, lived in that portion of the old fabric of Essex House, Strand, in which the Cottonian Library was kept from 1712 to 1730.[1]   Paterson, when he came to King Street, was the earliest auctioneer who sold books singly, in lots, the first bidding for which was sixpence, and the advance threepence each bidding until five shillings were offered, when it rose to sixpence ; and, by this manner of disposing of book property, no book was overlooked.   Paterson was believed—so extensive was his reading—to have read most of the works in the English language that he offered for sale.   This, however, was not conducive to commercial success, and he was at length glad to become the librarian of the first Marquis of Lansdowne.   Paterson's was then taken by the triumvirate, King, Collins, and Chapman, who held it for the sale of books and prints.   It was here that the veteran Collins gave what he called his " Evening Brush,"—lectures consisting principally of anecdotes of persons who had left this world before the birth of three-fourths of his audience.   But what renders the room far more memorable is that it was under this roof that Charles Dibdin commenced his " London Amusement," and here his pathetic and popular song of " Poor Jack " was often encored.[2]   And here Paterson delivered a series of lectures upon Shakespeare's Plays when George Steevens, Edmund Malone, and Barry the painter were among his auditors.[3]   Mr. Thomas King at a later period seems to have taken into partnership Mr. Lochée.   A newspaper paragraph, perhaps from the " Gentleman's Magazine " obituary notices (1793), says : " At his house at Margate, Mr. Thomas King, Covent Garden. He is supposed to have died worth £70,000 sterling.   At the death of the late King he cleared £20,000 by a monopoly of black silks, &c." King and Lochée appear to have been succeeded by Hutchins. T. Rawle, the inseparable companion of Grose the antiquary, was one of His Majesty's accoutrement makers ; and after his death his effects were sold by Hutchins in King Street.   Among the lots were a

[1] Cunningham's *London.*
[2] J. T. Smith's *Nollekens and his Times*, pp. 278-83.
[3] *Ibid.* pp. 278-83.

helmet, a sword, and several letters of Oliver Cromwell ; also the doublet in which Cromwell dissolved the Long Parliament. Another singular lot was a large black wig, with long flowing curls, stated to have been worn by King Charles II. : it was bought by Suett the actor, who was a great collector of wigs.[1]

The name of a famous auctioneer was given to Robins's Auction Rooms in the north-east wing of the Piazza. In this house Zoffany, the clever theatrical portrait-painter, executed that of Foote in the character of Major Sturgeon. George Robins is buried in Kensal Green Cemetery beneath a conspicuous tomb. One of his advertisements, presumably an early one, runs as follows :

"PAWNBROKERS' UNREDEEMED PLEDGES.—Messrs. Robins beg most respectfully to acquaint their numerous Friends and the Publick in general, that their first Sale of unredeemed property (this year) will take Place at their Rooms, under the Great Piazza, Covent Garden, on Tuesday next and three following Days, at half after Twelve o'clock each Day, where will be found Lots worthy the Attention of Country Dealers, &c. The names of the Pawnbrokers will appear in this paper on Monday, on which day the goods may be viewed." [2]

Robins's Sale Rooms seem to have been identical with those of another famous auctioneer named Cock whom Fielding introduced into the "Historical Register" as "Mr. Auctioneer Hen"; and here, says Mr. Austin Dobson, between 1745 and 1750, the "Marriage à la Mode" was exhibited *gratis* to an ungrateful world. In the front apartments of Cock's, and in convenient proximity to a favourite house of call, the "Constitution," in Bedford Street, lodged Richard Wilson. It was afterwards Messrs. Langford's, and later George Robins's.[3]

---

[1] Timbs's *Clubs and Club Life.*

[2] *Daily Advertiser*, March 1, 1742.

[3] *Eighteenth Century Vignettes*, third series, 1896, p. 335 ; but it will be seen from the above advertisement that there was a Robins, auctioneer, under the Great Piazza as early as 1742.

CHAPTER XVII.

HUNGERFORD MARKET.

THE great and honourable family of the Hungerfords became extinct in England with the death, in 1711, of Sir Edward Hungerford, the owner of Hungerford House, Charing Cross. This mansion did not occupy the site exactly of Hungerford Market, but, as will be remarked anon, if we may judge from an entry in Pepys's Diary, stood further eastward, near Durham Yard. It was the gardens attached to the inn or mansion-house that were surrendered for the groundplot, first of the ill-starred market buildings, and afterwards of the hotel and booking-offices of the present South-Eastern and Chatham Railway. The Market, Stairs and Bridge owed their name to the Hungerfords, of Farleigh Castle, Farleigh being a town situated partly in Somersetshire and partly in Wilts. The Castle was a stately stronghold which the family had built with the ransoms obtained from noble prisoners at Cressy and Poictiers.

Time has not erased one or two of those blemishes that are sometimes incidental to the history of old families. On February 20, 1523, Alice, Lady Hungerford, who is questionably said to have been the self-made widow of John Cotell, scrivener, was led from the Tower of London to Holborn, and there placed in a cart and so carried to Tyburn to be hanged.[1] She was buried in the Grey Friars Church, London,[2] in the body of the church.[3]

It is not especially material to our purpose whether Dame Hungerford was hanged or not, but there seems to be some doubt concerning the identity of the Lady Hungerford who adorned the "deadly never-green" at Tyburn. Until the discovery, about forty years ago, of an "Inventory of goods belonging to the King's grace, &c.," it was generally believed to have been Lady *Alice* Hungerford who suffered the extreme penalty for murder. But in this inventory the name of the erring woman is Agnes, as to whose

---

[1] Stow's *Annales*, 1615 (Feb. 15, 1523).   [2] *Ibid.*
[3] Allen's *London*, 1828, vol. iii. p. 554.

identity we are still in the dark. The story, however, is that close by Farleigh Castle, in the early years of Henry VIII.'s reign, dwelt this John Cotell, who acted as steward to the then Sir Edward Hungerford. Cotell's wife was young and beautiful, and so unscrupulous as to employ her charms to fascinate the Lord of Farleigh. She was, moreover, prudent enough to respond to his advances with affected modesty. But the knowledge that it rested only with herself to become Lady Hungerford, and mistress of the Hungerford castles and manors, beguiled her into the path of crime. She bribed a couple of yeomen to make away with her husband. He was therefore waylaid, strangled, and flung on the blazing hearth of the kitchen of Farleigh Castle, where his body was speedily consumed. Some plausible fiction was invented to account for his disappearance, and Sir Edward lost no time in making the fair widow mistress of himself and his fortune.

Not long, however, did she enjoy her unaccustomed rank. Sir Edward died in the second year of her married life, and proved that his affection had undergone no diminution by bequeathing to her all his property, except the lands which his son (by a former marriage) necessarily inherited. After her husband's death, Lady Hungerford proceeded to London, completed the usual legal formalities, and entered into possession of her wealth. But in the meantime the story of the murder of John Cotell seems to have leaked out, and her stepson Walter, afterwards Baron Hungerford [1]—a man of many vices— is said to have taken it up (if indeed he did not wholly concoct it), and turned it to account in revenging himself on the woman who had come between him and the bulk of his father's property, with the result mentioned above. [2]

[1] "Harry, marquis of Exeter, ... Sir William Sandes knight, Lord Sandes, Sir Thomas S. Cheyne knight, Sir Richard Sandes knight, Henry White and Richard Andrewes, and Walter Hungerford, esquire of the body of the lord the King. A messuage called Hungerfordes Inn, and a garden next Charynge Crosse, in the county of Middlesex, and various manors and lands in the counties of Berkshire and Wiltshire. O.C., Mich. Anno 21 Hen. VIII." (*Calendar to the Feet of Fines for London and Middlesex*, by W. J. Hardy, 1893).

[2] Mr. W. H. Davenport Adams does not give his authority for this story, although there cannot be much doubt that the poisoning occurred, judging from allusions to it by other authorities. See his *Streets of London*, 1890, p. 90. Timbs, quoting an "Inventory of the goods belonging to the King's grace by the forfeiture of the Lady Hungerford, attainted of murder in Hilary term, anno xiiij. Regis Henrici VIII.," says that according to this document the Lady Hungerford in question was really a widow and that her name was Agnes, not Alice as stated in the *Grey Friars Chronicle* (Camden Soc.) to which Stow was indebted. See

Possibly, taking all accounts into consideration, she was hanged on the evidence of her stepson Lord Walter, and this *after* her husband's death, for she was then a widow, and the second wife of Sir Edward. Perhaps the public records will at some future time render the identity of the poisoner a matter of greater certainty.

The Hungerford mansion at Charing Cross was, on April 25, 1669, destroyed by fire. Pepys records the event in his Diary. . . . " A great fire happened in Durham Yard last night, burning the house of one Lady Hungerford, who was to come to town to it this night ; and so the house is burned, new furnished, by carelessness of the girl sent to take off a candle from a bunch of candles, which she did by burning it off, and left the rest, as is supposed, on fire. The King and Court were here, it seems, and stopped the fire by blowing up the next house." [1] The Lady Hungerford mentioned by Pepys was the mother, apparently, of the Sir Edward Hungerford to whose extravagance, as Burke says, was wholly and solely attributable the decadence of the family.[2] Known as the "Spendthrift," the story is often quoted of his having given 500 guineas for a wig, incidental to shining at some Court ball.[3] He is said to have disposed of no less than twenty-eight manors in all. He had a son, also named Edward, who, however, died before him without surviving issue, and a daughter Rachel, who was married to Clotworthy, Viscount Massereene. A very flourishing offshoot of the family still remains in Ireland, one branch being seated at the Island, near Clonakilty, co. Cork, and the other at Cahirmore, near Rosscarbery in the same county.[4] But at the hands of Sir Edward Hungerford the glory and good fortune of the English family departed, and the property, immense though it was, was utterly destroyed. The large mansion at Charing Cross was his last card. In 1681 he settled in Spring Gardens.

By way of restoring his fortunes he obtained permission in 1679 to hold a market on Mondays, Wednesdays, and Saturdays, on the

further Timbs's *Ancestral Stories and Traditions of Great Families*, 1869, p. 108 *et seq.*

[1] Pepys's *Diary*, ed. with notes by Lord Braybrooke, 1849, vol. v., p. 188.

[2] *Vicissitudes of Families*, 1st series, 1859, pp. 194–5–6.

[3] *Hungerfordiana*, by Sir R. C. Hoare, 1823, p. 116.

[4] Burke's *Dormant and Extinct Peerages*, 1883, pp. 292–3. That this family was related to the English one now extinct, except for Holdich Hungerford (*County Families*), is evident from the will, dated May 24, 1729, of an English kinsman, who in that document speaks of Colonel Richard Hungerford of the Island as " cousin," and Captain Thomas Hungerford, who died in 1680, is described on his monument in Rosscarbery Cathedral as " descended of Sir Edward Hungerford, of Down Ampney, in the County of Gloucester."

site of the demolished Hungerford House and grounds. In 1682 a market-house was consequently erected there, of which there is an interesting engraving in the "Gentleman's Magazine" of 1832, where there is a full account of the old and the new market-buildings, with engravings and plans of the new also. The first market-building seems to have been erected from the designs of Sir Christopher Wren. A bust of Sir Edward Hungerford, the head enveloped in a flowing wig, to which Pennant alludes, was placed on the north front, with an inscription stating that the market had been built at his expense with the King's sanction.[1] One wonders what has become of this relic of departed greatness.

> Thriftless himselfe but, lyke the goode manure,
> His rotten waste did fertilise the land ;
> And others' thrifty toil hath wrought the cure,
> A goodly Mercatt (Market) joines the busy Strand.[2]

But all the thrift and toil of others failed to redeem the market from a lingering failure. It was at first devoted especially to the sale of fruit and herbs on the "live and let live principle" that Covent Garden should not be allowed to have things all its own way, and it was considered a most propitious circumstance that it possessed stairs convenient for the gardeners to land their produce from the river without the trouble and charge of porters to carry it, as was the case with Covent Garden, by land. But the Bedford mart, having got the start, balked the enterprise of the Hungerford.[3] In 1735 the large room in the market-house was used as the school for the charity children of St. Martin's parish. In 1761 the room had become a French chapel, *i.e.* the room over the market-house.[4] In 1815, the market scarcely supported half-a-dozen butchers, and there remained "a very good shop for fine tripe, calves' feet, and trotters."[5] Then it dwindled to a single row of stalls and shops. The hall was

---

[1] See engraving in the *Gentleman's Magazine*, 1832, vol. ii. p. 113. The inscription was as follows : "Forum utilitati publicæ perquam necessarium, Regis Caroli 2^{di} innuente Majestate, propriis sumptibus erexit perfecitque D. Edvardus Hungerford, Balnei miles, Anno M. DC. lxxxii." Sir Bernard Burke, in his *Vicissitudes of Families*, 1st series, 1859, pp. 194–5–6, speaks of the last baronet as Sir *Henry* Hungerford. It is evident, however, from the above inscription that this is an error.

[2] *Gentleman's Magazine, ibia.*, p. 115.

[3] Strype's *Stow*, 1720, Book vi. p. 76.

[4] Dodsley's *London and Environs*, 1761, vol. iii.

[5] The *Epicure's Almanack*, 1815, p. 292.

let as stables, and the place was principally used as a thoroughfare to and from Hungerford Stairs.[1]

Mr. Charles Fowler, the architect, had only just completed the construction on his own designs of Covent Garden Market for the Duke of Bedford, when he was called upon to erect the new Hungerford Market for the sale, this time, of fish *extensively*, fruit, vegetables, and butchers' meat. The building was of the Italian character, and " cheerful and interesting on the water-side exterior." The upper part consisted of three avenues, with shops on each side ; the whole roofed in.[2] It was refounded on June 18, 1831, and opened July 2, 1833. The opening was signalised by the ascent of a balloon, but one of the aeronauts, being inexperienced, not long after lost his reason. The new market had no sooner been built than an indignant protest came from an inhabitant of the Strand with respect to one of "the boldest, coolest, most unblushing acts of practical impertinence that has ever been perpetrated within the circle of the metropolis." The spacious gallery, it appears, which was carried along that part of the quadrangle that faced the river, was flanked by two public-houses, and the portion which lay between them formed one of the most pleasing features in the whole market-place. The landlords actually had the impudence to run a high iron railing from the corner of one of these taverns to the other. Thus the public were shut out from one of the most pleasant spots in London, for the benefit of the "boozers" who frequented these taverns. "To walk on this terrace," says the writer, " to view the river, with the animated scenes on its banks and on its bosom, and, at the same time, to breathe the current of pure air borne along its surface, was a pleasure of no ordinary description. To the citizen, after his day's confinement—to the professional man—to all the denizens of the brick-and-mortar regions, who could not conveniently go out into the parks, it was an absolute luxury ! The pleasure that it thus afforded was the more felt from the circumstance of its being comparatively free from the hordes of boatmen, market people, sottish Saint-Monday folk, *cauponibus atque malignis*, who congregate round the doors of the two public-houses below, and occupy the entire wharf."

[1] Timbs's *Romance of London* (Warne), p. 299.

[2] Weale's *Handbook of London* (Bohn, 1854). A view of this new Hungerford Market, taken from the Terrace in 1834, may be seen among the admirable collection of drawings and prints relating to the parish in St. Martin's Library, Charing Cross. There is also one of the Old Market, from a sketch made at the request of the Hungerford Market Company, by Charles Fowler, the architect.

A large exhibition-hall and bazaar were built in 1851, when Mr. Bouton produced his dramatic views of Fribourg and Venice ; but again the premises and the pictures were destroyed by fire, March 31, 1854.

The conversion of the Market into a general mart gave an importance to the locality which led to the erection of Hungerford Suspension Bridge, constructed under the direction of Mr. I. K. Brunel, son of Sir Mark Isambard Brunel, the constructor of that marvel of engineering skill—the Thames Tunnel. His son, Isambard Kingdom, was responsible also for the huge iron ship known as the "Great Eastern," the prototype of the modern leviathan. The Hungerford Bridge had a wider span than any similar structure in England, and was thrown across the Thames on the assumption that it would prove a great boon to those who lived on the Surrey side, where there was no fish-market. It only added to the failures, however ; the bridge cost £110,000, and was sold for £226,000 ; but only the first instalment was paid, and the purchase was thus void. In 1863 the bridge was taken down in order to construct a girder bridge for the railway from Charing Cross to London Bridge, when, the chains of Hungerford Suspension Bridge being thus set at liberty, examination of them was made by Mr. Hawkshaw and Mr. Barlow, who found that, with certain modifications in the design, they might be adapted to the piers of Clifton Suspension Bridge at Bristol, and to the preparations for anchorage.[1] The two piers of Hungerford Bridge are retained in the present great red-brick piers of the railway bridge, the only relics of the old Brunel structure which existed for eighteen years. The central span, the widest, as has been noted, of any similar bridge in England, was 676 feet. The width of the river at the point where the bridge crosses is 1,350 feet, and the depth of water at high tide 30 feet. I do not know what the cost of the line between the London Bridge and Waterloo stations proved to be, but including land and compensation, and the cost of the iron-girder bridges over the streets to be crossed, it was set down at the time at £464,000 ; between Waterloo Road and the south bank of the Thames at £126,000 ; and the bridge across the Thames at £160,000. This sum was exceeded, for there were four lines of rail to be reckoned with, instead of two as originally intended. On each side of this eight or nine-spanned girder bridge was a foot-

---

[1] The *Builder*, April 8, 1863. There is a water-colour drawing of the Suspension Bridge, taken from Waterloo Bridge, by G. Pyne, 1850, in the St. Martin's Library.

way twelve feet wide, secured in perpetuity for the free use of the public by the Metropolitan Board of Works, at a cost of £98,540. Like the Cannon Street Bridge, it was built by Mr. Hawkshaw, C.E., the cost being about £200,000. Begun in 1863, it was completed in 1866. For Charing Cross Station, including land, compensation, trade, and other matters, the cost was £320,000, while the outlay altogether was computed at the time to be £1,070,000.[1] This, as might be supposed, proved twenty-six years after to be inadequate to the increasing demands of the railway traffic, and in 1886 the bridge had to be widened as much as forty-eight feet, so as to admit of the laying down of four additional lines of rail, and it was this widening which necessitated the removal of the Charing Cross Swimming Bath, moored immediately to the west of the bridge. The widening at the same time involved the destruction of a large number of houses on the east side of Craven Street.[2]

No fewer than 900,000 persons, steamboat passengers, passed through Hungerford Market to the stairs in 1843.[3] The river-front, in fact, became the great focus of the upper Thames steam navigation, with a million embarkations and landings annually.[4]

The Charing Cross Hotel has an importance in the architectural history of London, since it seems to have been the pioneer effort in a new class of building adapted to the uses of the modern hotel. Facing the West Strand it forms the front of the railway station and booking offices that displaced Hungerford Market and many surrounding houses. It was built by Mr. E. M. Barry, the son of the architect of the new Houses of Parliament. It is a noble edifice, the high Mansard roof[5] being especially admired. The "Builder," under the editorship of George Godwin, and not given to exaggerated praise, thought fit to publicly thank the architect for his work.[6] It is worthy of remark that the front of the building facing the West Strand is not

---

[1] The *Builder*, Sept. 29, 1860.

[2] *Ibid.*, June 19, 1886, p. 904, col. 3.

[3] *Descriptive Particulars of the Hungerford Suspension Bridge*, 1845, p. 6. A detailed description of the bridge by George Godwin, jun., will also be found in Peter Cunningham's *London*, 1850.

[4] Timbs's *Romance of London* (Warne), p. 300.

[5] A Mansard roof is one formed with an upper and under set of rafters, on each side, the under set less and the upper set more inclined to the horizon, so called from François Mansard, its inventor. Also called a curb roof (French *courber*, to bend), owing to the double inclination of its sides. François Mansard's portrait-figure occurs among the sculptures on the north front of the podium of the Albert Memorial in Kensington Gardens.

[6] The *Builder*, Dec. 3, 1864, p. 876.

parallel with the street, a deviation from the rectangularity of the forecourt concealed in a great measure by the misplaced Cross in or near the centre. This obliquity is, however, noted as being rather advantageous to the effect from the Strand and Duncannon Street.

Although, for the time being, pigeon-holed, it is not altogether improbable that at some future time the proposal will again be on the *tapis* by which the London County Council thought of acquiring Charing Cross Station and Hungerford Bridge, and of providing the South-Eastern and Chatham Railway Company with a new site on the south side of the river, so as to make way for a new road-bridge, linking the northern and southern tramway systems. The cost, however, of reinstating Charing Cross Station on a site adjoining the southern end of Hungerford Bridge is, for the present, considered too great. The Company are alive to the advantages to themselves accruing from the present state of things, and indeed contemplate widening still further Hungerford Bridge, as well as enlarging Charing Cross Station. The removal enterprise was mooted about the close of the year 1904.

The shops of Richardson, the celebrated printseller, then No. 31 Strand, at the corner of Villiers Street, a site that is now occupied by the forecourt of Charing Cross Station, are represented in a water-colour drawing in St. Martin's Library, Charing Cross.

It should be borne in mind that Hungerford Stairs, now, like the jolly waterman, "so far gone that no Jew would lend upon them," were relics of Hungerford House, which, like the other Thames palaces, had a water-gate from the Thames. The watermen at these and the adjacent stairs, as the population around Charing Cross increased, must have found in the plying of their oars a corresponding increment in their earnings. They had latterly, no doubt, ceased to sing :

Heave and how, rumbelow,

as in the days of the Plantagenets, neither probably did the river echo any longer with " Row thy boat, Norman, row to thy leaman," [1] but they were still much in request—especially individual watermen who were fortunate enough to be deaf—for lovers, for barristers who wished to air their eloquence, and for young members of Parliament who wanted to recite their speeches undisturbed. In the time of the

---

[1] Sir John Norman, Lord Mayor of London in 1453 (or 1454), was thus honoured in song because he was the first to introduce the custom of proceeding on state occasions, when Lord Mayor, by water from London to Westminster, instead of past Charing Cross on horseback.

Rump, two Rump Parliament-men, having hired a pair of oars, in the course of some customary banter, told the waterman that he and his fellows as a class were hypocrites, for they rowed one way and looked another. Upon which the retort came, "O sir, we have not plyed so long at Westminster as to have learnt nothing of our masters, who pretend to do one thing, and do another."[1]

"HUNGERFORD-MARKET REGATTA TO-MORROW.—The Tenth Annual Prize Wherry, given by Subscription of the Inhabitants of St. Martin's-in-the-Fields, to be Rowed for by Twelve Watermen of Hungerford-stairs, two pair of sculls in each boat, THIS DAY (Wednesday), September 9, in Three Heats. First Heat to start at Two o'clock from Hungerford Stairs, round a boat moored off the Speaker's House down round the Port Mahon, back again, and down to Hungerford. Second and Third Heats, the same as above. The first two boats in the first and second heats to row for the grand heat."[2]

It was in the neighbourhood of Hungerford Stairs[3] that Charles Dickens witnessed much of that low life, the pathetic side of which he represents with so much power in his novels. It was, in fact, at the blacking warehouse at Old Hungerford Stairs—a crazy, break-down old house abutting on the river, and swarming with rats, that his daily avocation consisted in tying up pots of blacking. He relates how, when the factory removed to Chandos Street, he always avoided the street by a detour, so great was the disgust which he felt for his former occupation. From his biographer we learn how he spent his dinner-hour in playing about on the coal-barges, or strolling about the back streets of the Adelphi, and exploring the recesses of its dark arches, in company with his youthful friends, "Poll" Green and Bob Fagin. In "David Copperfield" we are told how he remembered having sat outside the "Fox-under-the-Hill," "eating something on a bench, and looking at some coal-heavers dancing before the house." "No words," he says, alluding to the drudgery that he underwent when a boy of ten at Warren's blacking warehouse, "can express the agony of my soul as I sank into this companionship, and felt my hopes of growing up to be a learned and distinguished man crushed in my breast." But the "Fox-under-the-Hill," the blacking factory, coal-wharves, dancing bargees, and the sea-coal (as coal conveyed by coasting vessels was called) have all disappeared before that

[1] *Coffee-house Jests*, 1760, p. 10.

[2] Newspaper cutting, 1835.

[3] There is a representation of Hungerford Stairs, from a sketch by Charles Fowler, on the walls of St. Martin's Library.

Titanic undertaking, the Thames Embankment. If one is of a sufficiently inquiring turn of mind, while wandering among the mysterious Adelphi arches, to ask *habitués* where the " Fox-under-the Hill" stood, he will find that it is still a tradition, although information thus elicited from one and another is hopelessly at variance as to its exact site, which is now, I think, occupied by that part of the Embankment near the Adelphi Terrace.

An entry, under the date of July 1833, from a printed but unpublished Diary by Mr. Payne Collier, appeared lately in the " Athenæum," having reference to Dickens at the time when he first obtained employment as a reporter, and connecting itself with what Mr. John Forster, his biographer, has related of those childish sufferings. " We walked together through Hungerford Market, where we followed a coal-heaver, who carried his little rosy but grimy child looking over his shoulder ; and C. D. bought a half-pennyworth of cherries, and as we went along he gave them one by one to the little fellow without the knowledge of his father. . . . He informed me as he walked through it that he knew *Hunger*ford Market well. . . . He did not affect to conceal the difficulties he and his family had had to contend against." [1]

It may be thought worthy of note that Jonathan Warren, of the blacking factory alluded to, has a descendant, a grand-nephew, in the person of Mr. E. Warren, saddle and harness maker, of 109A, Westbourne Park Road, Bayswater, who informs me that his grand-uncle died suddenly in the street from shock, through heart disease, upon being told that his factory—presumably the Chandos Street place to which he had removed—was on fire. Mr. Robert Warren, a commissionaire at the Admiralty,[2] is another descendant ; but they have no traditions as to Dickens's early life at this period.

It does not appear when the Hungerford Coffee-house facing the Strand ceased to exist or what was its exact site, but it was a well-known resort of literary characters, since it was one of the few early public places where, as at Peele's in Fleet Street and the " Chapter " in St. Paul's Churchyard, files of London and provincial newspapers were kept for years back, which might be consulted " on the payment

---

[1] *Life of Charles Dickens*, by John Forster, 1903, vol. ii. p. 488, note. See also vol. i. pp. 24–29, where there is a most interesting account by himself of his early hardships ; *The Origin and Progress of the Watermen's Company*, by Henry Humpheris, vol. iii. p. 181 ; and *Charles Dickens : the Story of his Life and Writings*, by B. W. Matz, p. 2.

[2] Mr. E. Warren has served in the Navy, as his brother has in the Army.

Q

of a moderate fee not smaller than sixpence." This Coffee-house
was a meeting-place of the

" BENEVOLENT INSTITUTION
For delivering poor married
Women at their own
Habitations.

The Quarterly General Meeting of the Governors and Friends of
this Institution will be held at the Hungerford Coffee-house, Strand,
on Monday next, at Seven o'clock in the Evening precisely, to
receive the Report of the Committee, and regulate the Affairs of
the Charity.   " THOMAS SAMUEL LEMAGE, *Secretary.*

" No. 12, Queen Street, Soho."[1]

Adorned as the river-strand between Charing Cross and St. Clement
Danes Church was formerly with the splendid inns of the nobility, it
is somewhat surprising that their arms and badges do not survive
more than is the case, in the neighbouring tavern-signs. The " Blue
Lion " of the Percies and the Percy Arms occur, although not in the
immediate neighbourhood. The crest of the Hungerford family was
a wheatsheaf derived from the Peverills, supported by two lions ram-
pant.[2] Sometimes, however, two sickles take the place of the lions.
On the keystone of the gateway of old Hungerford Market was
carved a garb or wheatsheaf between two sickles.[3] But the " Two
Lions and Wheatsheaf" was the sign hung out by Mr. Rogers near
Temple Bar in 1733. Here he advertised Dr. Rogers's " SPECIFIC
OIL for the GOUT, RHEUMATISM and SCIATICA." This medicine,
OLEUM ARTHRITICUM, " was made publick to the World through
Dr. Stukeley's Letter, which he read at the Royal Society on
February 1732-3 about my Oils externally apply'd with Success in
Cure of the Gout, and since printed. . . . My Son, who only sells
them in London, etc." Dr. Rogers the father dwelt at Stamford,
Lincolnshire, so that the reason for adopting the " Two Lions and
Wheatsheaf" is not apparent. Possibly it was already the sign

---

[1] *Daily Advertiser*, Jan. 4, 1794.

[2] *Hungerfordiana*, by Sir R. C. Hoare, 1823, pp. 110 and 116. Three sickles
and as many garbs, elegantly disposed within the garter, form one of the principal
bosses of the cloisters to St. Stephen's Chapel, Westminster. This was the badge
of Walter, Lord Hungerford, K.G., beheaded 32 Henry VIII.—*Collect. Topog. et
Geneal.* vol. iii. p. 71.

[3] *Gentleman's Magazine*, 1832, vol. ii.

of the house when taken over for distributing relief to sufferers from the ailments described.

Charles Court Stairs were on the eastern side of Hungerford Stairs, so named from Charles Court, the fifth turning on the right going from Charing Cross.[1] It led into Hungerford Market, and to the watermen's stairs named after it. The following, perchance, describes the original of the useful modern invention, linoleum :—

" To be SOLD,

At Powell's Painted Floor-Cloth Warehouse and Turner's Shop, against Charles-Court near Hungerford-Market in the Strand, THE best of painted Floor-Cloths of all Sorts and Sizes ready made, with the most beautiful Carpet-Colours, and other very curious Figures, done to the greatest Perfection : They are done well in Oil, thorough dry, and well harden'd, on the best Cloth that may be depended on for Goodness in every Respect ; likewise Listed Carpets, neatly made with lively Colours, and very durable Hair Cloth Matting, with Variety and good Choice of all Sorts of Turnery Wares ; sold Whole-sale or Retail at reasonable Rates." [2]

The site of Hungerford Street, a thoroughfare not mentioned by Cunningham, is now occupied by the railway station. Here were the business premises of the very old-established firm of wine merchants, Messrs. Hedges and Butler, who in their present Regent Street offices preserve a table and two arm-chairs made from an oak post which stood at the corner of their old house in what was afterwards Hungerford Market.

Stow mentions a Heley Alley, by the One Tun Tavern, a passage which " falleth into Hungerford Market." [3]

---

[1] Elmes's *Topog. Dict.*, 1831.
[2] *London Evening Post*, May 11–13, 1738.　　　[3] Ed. 1755.

CHAPTER XVIII.

NORTHUMBERLAND HOUSE.

THE destruction of the fine old Jacobean mansion, Northumberland House, the last of the river-strand inns of the nobility between Whitefriars and Whitehall, was much regretted by many men of taste and judgment, who were of opinion that its removal was a needless act of vandalism. Certainly an entrance equally fine and suitable, and one which would have lent itself well to the arrangement of the new Avenue, could have been made by removing a few of the houses on the west of the mansion, and cutting off the S.W. angle of the garden behind. But the Metropolitan Board of Works, in its eagerness for "improvements," failed sometimes in a due appreciation of what the word "improvement" meant, and this was a glaring instance. Consequently arrangements for the handing over the home of the Howards, the Percies, and the Seymours to the Board of Works' housebreakers were completed in 1873, and the then Duke of Northumberland was more or less compelled to sell his magnificent London home for £500,000, the Board's Charing Cross and Victoria Embankment Approach Act (36–7 Vict. c. 100) empowering them to make a new street to the Embankment which was completed only three years previously.

Of the original Northampton House, built about 1605 by Henry Howard, Earl of Northampton,[1] son of the Earl of Surrey, the poet, there was doubtless, at the time of its demolition, very little left ; but it was built out of the ruins of the Hospital of St. Mary Rouncevall.[2] Bernard Jansen and Gerard Christmas are said to have been the architects. They erected a front of 162 feet in length and a court 81 feet square. The Earl of Northampton's death transferred the property to his kinsman Thomas Howard, Earl of Suffolk, in 1614, in whose time the only change it underwent was in being renamed Suffolk House. Then Algernon, Earl of Northumberland

---

[1] Rate-book of St. Martin's.

[2] Newcourt's *Repert. Eccles.* vol. i. p. 693.

and Lord High Admiral, married Lord Suffolk's daughter and became the proprietor about the year 1642, since when, till its destruction, it was known constantly as Northumberland House. The new owner, the tenth Earl of Northumberland, built the southern front and the stone stairs after a design, 1642, ascribed to Inigo Jones. This addition is erroneously described in the "Builder" (January 7, 1905, p. 9) as a *rebuilding*, instead of which it was merely the completion of the quadrangle, which until then had only three sides. Charing Cross had many years before begun to pass from the suburban to the metropolitan period of its history, so much so that the hurry and noise of passengers and coaches outside the north front greatly disturbed the earl and his household, and in consequence the river-side front was erected which afforded all the advantages of retirement and of a country seat.

The coping above the Strand front was "a border of capital letters," and at the funeral of Anne of Denmark, 1619, a young man among the spectators was killed by the fall of the letter "S," pushed off by the incautious leaning forward of sightseers on the roof.[1] On the portal, in a frieze near the top, were the initials in capitals C. Æ., which Vertue and Walpole construed to signify "Christmas Ædificavit." Vertue's drawing of the portal with the letters C. Æ. upon it was sold at the Strawberry Hill sale, and passed into the hands of the Rev. Henry Wellesley, D.D., Principal of New Inn Hall, Oxford.[2]

It was this, the tenth, Earl of Northumberland who received General Monk here at a meeting when King Charles's restoration was for the first time proposed in direct terms, as a measure absolutely necessary to the peace of the kingdom.

Josceline Percy, the eleventh Earl of Northumberland, who succeeded his father in possession, died in 1670 without male issue, and Northumberland House became the property of his only daughter, Elizabeth Percy, the heiress of the Percy estates, who contributed a page of romance to the annals of her ancient house, which will be referred to again. Suffice it at present to say that she was twice a virgin widow, and three times a wife, before she was seventeen. With her third husband, the "proud" Duke of Somerset, she lived here in great state and magnificence, and died in 1722. The Duke died in 1748 and was succeeded by his eldest son Algernon, Earl of Hertford and seventh Duke of Somerset, created

---

[1] Register of Burials at St. Martin's-in-the-Fields, May 14, 1619.

[2] Wheatley's *London*.

Earl of Northumberland in 1749. It was by this earl that the
north front was rebuilt about 1750, and it is reasonable to infer, says
the author of " London and its Environs " (1761), from some letters
discovered in the front during rebuilding, that one Miles Glover was
the architect of the original mansion that succeeded Rouncevall
Priory.[1]

There is also a very interesting contemporaneous description of
the alterations then made, in a letter from the Countess of Hertford,
afterwards Duchess of Somerset, to Lady Luxborough, which settles
the date of the erection of the façade as it existed immediately before
demolition. This was, with another dated January 21, 1749-50,
taken from a printed transcript, and communicated to the " Builder "
as follows by Mr. Wyatt Papworth :—

" Piercy Lodge [situated near Colnebrook, as appears from a later letter],
June 17, 1749

" Dear Madam,—Your Ladyship bids me give you an account of
what alterations we are making at present, but I feel myself much
less able to describe the fabric and furniture of a palace than a
hermitage ; and while I am attending to all my Lord's designs there,
I fancy I am no better acquainted with the effect it will produce
than a person would be with the beauty of a piece of tapestry who
saw only the wrong side of it. My Lord will do a good deal to the
front of the house in order to make it appear less like a prison ; he
builds a new wing on the right-hand side of the garden, which will
contain a library, bedchamber, dressing-room, and a waiting-room.
I think I told you that all the sashes, doors and ceilings in both
apartments must be entirely new, and the floors in my Lord's ; the
staircase is very noble, but will require as large a lanthorn to light it
as at Houghton, so much celebrated in the newspapers. The
chimney-pieces in both apartments are to be all new, and some
of them very expensive ; the draughts are mighty pretty. My
Lord's bed on the ground-floor is crimson-damask, with tapestry
hangings ; the next room is furnished with green damask on

---

[1] Dodsley's *London and its Environs*, 1761, vol. v. p. 50. There is a most
interesting contemporary drawing, from the Wellesley Collection, presenting a view
of St. Mary Rouncevall Chapel, Whitehall, &c., in the Library of the Corpora-
tion of London ; and in the Hartridge Collection at the City Library is a print of
the garden front of Northumberland House from an original sketch. Canaletto's
view of Northumberland House shows the Golden Cross Inn or Tavern with the
sign suspended outside.

purpose to set off his pictures ; the next with a very fine old set of the Duke of Newcastle's horsemanship, with his own picture on horseback, as big as life ; and, now they are clean, looking neat, as when new. The parlour to be hung with some very good pictures ; above stairs, the great waiting-room, with Saxon green cloth chairs with gilt nails, and green lute-string window curtains, marble table, and large glass between the windows ; first drawing-room, new crimson damask, with lute-string window curtains, two very fine Japan tables and glasses between the windows, with carved and gilt frames ; inner drawing-room, tapestry hangings with small figures, very pretty and as fresh as new. He lays two rooms together in the right wing of the court, on the ground-floor, in order to make a chapel, with a Gothic wainscot, ceiling, and painted windows ; there is to be a Dutch stove in it, which is so contrived as to represent a tomb with an urn upon it. The court is to be paved and the footway altered ; and my Lord is in treaty for nine houses on the other side of the way, in order to pull them down and build stables (for there are none belonging to the house), whose gates are intended to open directly against those of the court ; if he can agree for this purchase he will widen the street in that part about 8 ft. Now, dear madam, I have obeyed you in the best manner I am able ; but upon looking back into my letter, I find I have forgot my bedchamber, dressing-room, and closet, which, one would think, should not appear least interesting to myself ; the first of these is to have a new bed-hanging, and chairs of crimson queen's damask ; the dressing-room, which has two large sashes, will have tapestry hangings and green damask chairs ; the closet, which is small, and has only one sash exactly facing the chimney, furnished with painted paper ; the chimney-piece in the dressing-room is to be of statuary marble and *giallo di Siering* ; and just in front of it the fable of the stork inviting the fox to dinner, very neatly carved. There is another little waiting-room at this end of the apartment, for the groom of the chambers to be in, in the morning, or, when I am not in form, in the evening.

" To return to my *bergerie*. Nothing has been done in it this summer, nor have I the heart to propose anything, for I am actually frightened with the sum my Lord is laying out about Northumberland House ; and I find that by living long in strait circumstances one contracts a narrowness of mind which makes launching out at once into great expense not so desirable as it would be thought by young, gay people.

The architect was Daniel Garrett,[1] of whom nothing appears to be known.

It was in this restored building that poor Oliver Goldsmith met with his ludicrous experience of the patronage of the great. Among the persons of rank who were struck with the merits of "The Traveller" was the son-in-law, apparently, of the writer of the foregoing letter, the Earl (afterwards the Duke) of Northumberland.[2] He procured several other writings of Goldsmith, the perusal of which tended to elevate the author in his good opinion, and to gain for him his good will. The earl held the office of Lord-Lieutenant of Ireland, and, understanding that Goldsmith was an Irishman, was disposed to extend to him the patronage which his high post afforded. He intimated the same to his relative, Dr. Percy, who, he found, was well acquainted with the poet, and expressed a wish that the latter should wait upon him. Here, then, was another opportunity for Goldsmith to better his fortune, had he been knowing and worldly enough to profit by it. Unluckily, the path to fortune lay through the aristocratic mazes of Northumberland House, and the poet blundered at the outset. The following is, according to Washington Irving, the account he used to give of his visit :—" I dressed myself in the best manner I could, and after studying some compliments I thought necessary on such an occasion, proceeded to Northumberland House, and acquainted the servants that I had particular business with the duke. They showed me into an ante-chamber, where, after waiting some time, a gentleman very elegantly dressed made his appearance : taking him for the duke, I delivered all the fine things that I had composed, in order to compliment him on the honour he had done me ; when, to my great astonishment, he told me I had mistaken him for his master, who would see me immediately. At that instant the duke came into the apartment, and I was so confounded on the occasion that I wanted words barely sufficient to express the sense I entertained of the duke's politeness, and went away exceedingly chagrined at the blunder I had committed."[3]

Sir John Hawkins, in his "Life of Dr. Johnson," says that when the earl expressed a desire to do Goldsmith some kindness on the

---

[1] See further Mr. Wyatt Papworth in the *Builder*, April 15, 1871, pp. 282-3.

[2] Formerly Sir Hugh Smithson, who married the heiress of the Percies, Elizabeth Baroness Percy, whose monument may be seen in the Chapel of St. Nicholas, Westminster Abbey.

[3] *Oliver Goldsmith : a Biography*, by Washington Irving, 1850, pp. 89-90.

strength of the latter's Irish nationality, the poet said that he had a brother there, a clergyman, that stood in need of help. . . . . "Thus," says Sir John, "did this idiot in the affairs of the world trifle with his fortunes, and put back the hand that was held out to assist him."

With regard to this forgetfulness of self, however, Irving justly remarks that he cannot join in Sir John's worldly sneer at the conduct of the poet. While we admire that honest independence of spirit which prevented his asking favours for himself, we love that warmth of affection which instantly sought to advance the fortunes of a brother.[1]

Whether his brother benefited we are not told, but his visit was not fruitless so far as himself was concerned, for Dr. Percy—the heir male of the Percies—influenced his kinswoman the countess to such purpose that under her auspices was introduced to the world the beautiful ballad of "The Hermit," originally published under the name of "Edwin and Angelina. Printed for the amusement of the Countess of Northumberland."[2]

A companion-piece to Goldsmith's blundering at Northumberland House was a similarly humorous position in which he found himself, owing to his absent-mindedness, at the Duke of Northumberland's house in Bath. He was staying with Lord Clare, whose house was next door to that of the duke, and returning home one morning from an early walk, he mistook the house and walked up into the duke's dining-room, where he and the duchess were about to sit down to breakfast. Goldsmith, still supposing himself in the house of Lord Clare, and that they were visitors, made them an easy salutation, being acquainted with them, and threw himself on a sofa in the lounging manner of a man perfectly at home. The duke and duchess soon perceived his mistake, and while they smiled internally, endeavoured, with the considerateness of well-bred people, to prevent any awkward embarrassment. They accordingly chatted sociably with him about matters in Bath, until, breakfast being served, they invited him to partake. The truth at once flashed upon the heedless Goldsmith ; he started up from his free-and-easy position, made a confused apology for his blunder, and would have retired perfectly disconcerted, had not the duke and duchess treated the whole as a lucky occurrence to throw him in their way, and exacted a promise from him to dine with them.

[1] Washington Irving's *Life of Goldsmith*, 1850, p. 90.
[2] *Ibid.* pp. 90–91.

It was from Northumberland House, Charing Cross, that the party consisting of the Duke of York, Lady Northumberland, Lady Mary Coke, Lord Hertford and Horace Walpole, all in one hackney coach, set out to see the Cock Lane ghost, while the rain fell in torrents.   One Kent, a broker, having lost his wife, was visited by his sister-in-law Fanny, with whom he fell in love.   They took lodgings with Parsons, parish clerk of St. Sepulchre's, and each made a will leaving all to the survivor.   Fanny died suddenly, and Parsons gave out that Kent had murdered her.   In proof of this, certain knockings and scratchings were heard every night in the chamber lately occupied by Fanny, and these were attributed to her ghost. When questions were asked, "the ghost knocked once to signify *yes*, twice to signify *no*, and scratched to indicate displeasure."   Parsons's daughter, a child of twelve, took a board into her bed, and made these knockings and scratchings, which for many months set all London agog.

When the Northumberland House party arrived in the pouring rain Cock Lane was, says Horace Walpole, "full of mob, and the house so full we could not get in ; at last they discovered it was the Duke of York, and the company squeezed themselves into one another's pockets to make room for us.   The house which is borrowed, and to which the ghost has adjourned, is wretchedly small and miserable ; when we opened the chamber, in which were fifty people, with no light but one tallow-candle at the end, we tumbled over the bed of the child to whom the ghost comes, and whom they are murdering by inches in such insufferable heat and stench.   At the top of the room are ropes to dry clothes.   I asked if we were to have rope-dancing between the acts.   We heard nothing ; they told us (as they would at a puppet-show) that it would not come that night till seven in the morning : that is, when there are only 'prentices and old women. We stayed, however, till half-an-hour after one.   The Methodists have promised them contributions ; provisions are sent in like forage, and all the taverns and alehouses in the neighbourhood make fortunes.[1]   An inquiry, in which Dr. Johnson was concerned, resulted in the gaping world of credulous London being undeceived.   Parsons, one of the contrivers of the fraud, was set three several times in the pillory, and imprisoned for one year in the King's Bench prison. Probably the mob that collected subscriptions for Parsons, instead of pelting him in the pillory, was largely composed of those who had

[1] The *Letters of Horace Walpole*, by Mrs. Paget Toynbee, 1904, vol. v. p. 169 (Feb. 2, 1762).

profited by the swindle, like the taverns in the neighbourhood of this very "thin" ghost's pranks. The noises, it was said, were made for the detection of some human crime, and it was owing to this statement that many eminent men were beguiled into an investigation. But the ghost overreached itself, and publicly promised, by an affirmative knock, that it would attend any one of the gentlemen into the vault under the church of St. John's, Clerkenwell, where the body of Fanny was deposited, and give a token of her presence by a knock upon her coffin. The investigation took place, and Johnson, who was present, printed an account of what they saw and heard. The spirit was solemnly required to perform its promise, but nothing more than silence ensued ; the person supposed to be accused by the spirit then went down with several others, but no effect was perceived. Upon their return they examined the girl, but could draw no confession from her. Between two and three she desired and was permitted to go home with her father. It was, therefore, the opinion of the whole assembly that the child had some art of making or counterfeiting a particular noise, and that there was no agency of any higher cause.

On an unfortunate occasion when Horace Walpole was to have dined at Northumberland House (April 1765), he came perilously near "dining with Duke Humphrey." He writes in one of his delightful letters to the Earl of Hertford :

" You will laugh at it, though it was woeful to me. I was to dine at Northumberland House, and went a little after four. There I found the countess, Lady Betty Mekinsy, Lady Stafford ; my Lady Finlater, who was never out of Scotland before ; a tall lad of fifteen, her son ; Lord Drogheda, and Mr. Worsley. At five arrived Mr. Mitchell, who said the lords had begun to read the Poor Bill, which would take at least two hours, and perhaps would debate it afterward. We concluded dinner would be called for, it not being very precedented for ladies to wait for gentlemen. No such thing. Six o'clock came ; our coaches came——well ! We sent them away, and excuses were we were engaged. Still the countess's heart did not relent, nor uttered a word of apology. We wore out the wind and the weather, the opera and the play, Mrs. Cornely's and Almack's, and every topic that would do in a formal circle. We hinted, represented—— in vain. The clock struck eight. My lady at last said she would go and order dinner, but it was a good half-hour before it appeared. We then sat down to a table for fourteen covers, but instead of substantials there was nothing but a profusion of plates striped red, green, and yellow, gilt plate, blacks, and uniforms! My Lady Finlater, who had never seen those embroidered dinners, nor dined after three, was famished. The first course stayed as long as possible, in hopes of the lords; so did the second. The dessert at last arrived, and the middle dish was actually set on when Lord Finlater and Mr. Mackay arrived. Would you believe it?——the dessert was remanded, and the whole first course brought back again! Stay, I have not done. Just as the second first course had done its duty, Lord Northumberland, Lord Stafford, and Mekinsy came in, and the whole began a third time! Then the second course and the dessert! I thought we should have dropped from our chairs from fatigue and fumes! When the clock struck eleven we were asked to return to the drawing-room and drink tea and coffee; but I said I was engaged to supper, and came home to bed. My dear lord, think of four hours and a half in a circle of mixed company, and three great dinners, one after another, without interruption; no, it exceeded our day at Lord Archer's!"[1]

The first husband of the heiress of the Percy name and estates was Henry Cavendish, Earl of Ogle, who died before he was of age to cohabit with her, and between the first and third husbands of one who was "thus twice a virgin widow and three times a wife before she was seventeen" came Thomas Thynne, of Longleat, in Wilts, who was barbarously murdered in his coach in Pall Mall, on Sunday, February 12, 1681-2, by ruffians hired by Count Königsmarck,[2] a Swedish nobleman, the lady's rejected suitor. Thynne had, a short time before, succeeded in carrying off the youthful widow. He was descended from an ancient family, and on account of his large income was called "Tom of Ten Thousand." He lived in a style of magnificence, and became the Issachar of Dryden's glowing description of the Duke of Monmouth's progresses, in "Absalom and Achitophel":

> From east to west his glories he displays,
> And like the sun, the Promised Land surveys.
> Fame runs before him as the morning star,
> And shouts of joy salute him from afar;
> Each house receives him as a guardian god,
> And consecrates the place of his abode.
> But hospitable treats did most commend
> Wise Issachar, his wealthy western friend!

---

[1] *Walpole's Letters*, ed. Peter Cunningham, 1891, vol. iv. p. 341 (Ap. 7, 1765).

[2] Königsmarck, like Colonel Panton, was nothing but a successful card-sharper. See Lucas's *Lives of the Gamesters*.

It was on the night of Sunday, February 12, 1681-2, that Thynne was shot at the lower end of the Haymarket. The murderers escaped, and their victim survived his wound only a few hours, during which the Duke of Monmouth sat by the bedside of his dying friend. It was not long before the ruffians employed by Count Königsmarck were captured, and Evelyn in his Diary thus refers to their execution: "This day was executed the Colonel Vratz and some of his accomplices for the execrable murder of Mr. Thynne, set on by the principal, Königsmarck; he went to execution like an undaunted hero, as one that had done a friendly office for that base coward, Count Königsmarck, who had hopes to marry his (Mr. Thynne's) widow, the rich Lady Ogle, and was acquitted by a corrupt jury, and so got away. Vratz told a friend of mine, who accompanied him to the gallows, and gave him some advice, that he did not value dying a rush, and hoped and believed God would deal with him like a gentleman." [1] The monument to Thynne in Westminster Abbey, between the south transept and the choir, bears a curious sculpture by Quellin, representing the assassination.

At the west end of the Chapel of St. Nicholas, also in the Abbey, is the monument erected by Sir Hugh Smithson, who, already earl, was raised to the Dukedom of Northumberland in 1766, to his wife, the heiress of the Percies and daughter of the seventh Duke of Somerset. It bears the following inscription:

"Near this place lies interred Elizabeth Percy, Duchess of Northumberland; in her own right Baroness Percy, Lucy, Poynings, Fitz-Payne, Brian, and Latimer, sole heiress of Algernon, Duke of Somerset, and of the ancient Earls of Northumberland. She inherited all their great and noble qualities, with every amiable and benevolent virtue. By her marriage with Hugh, Duke of Northumberland, she had issue, Hugh Earl Percy, Lady F. Eliz. Percy, who died in 1761, and Lord Algernon Percy. Having lived long an ornament of courts, an honour to her country, a pattern to the great, a protectress of the poor, ever distinguished for the most tender affection for her family and friends, she died December 5, 1776, aged sixty, universally beloved, revered, lamented. The Duke of Northumberland, inconsolable for the loss of the best of wives, hath erected this monument to her beloved memory."

A *lapsus linguæ* to which Sir Hugh Smithson committed himself when he had become the Earl of Northumberland was commented

---

[1] March 10, 1682. See also G. L. Craik's *Romance of the Peerage*, 1850, vol. iv. p. 334.

upon at the time. When Lord March visited him at Alnwick Castle he, a true Douglas, was received at the gates by the earl, who thus addressed him : "I believe, my lord, this is the first time that ever a Douglas and a Percy met here in friendship."

At last arrangements for the sale of what was probably the oldest residential house in the metropolis to the Board of Works, in order to open an entrance to the Thames Embankment, were completed in 1873, the purchase-money being £500,000. The sale was concluded definitely in June 1874. In September 1874 the fine old mansion underwent its final phase of degradation, its materials being brought under the hammer of the auctioneer. The lots consisted of 3,000,000 bricks ; the grand marble staircase, built by the elder Cundy, which, until the erection of that at Stafford House, was considered the handsomest in London ; the elaborate ornamentations of the hall, dining and reception rooms ; the state decorations which adorned the hall and corridors ; and a large quantity of lead, stated to be of the weight of 400 tons. In the following month, the Strand front also was sold for building materials. The aggregate sum realised by the sale amounted to but little more than £6,500, and of this the grand staircase alone fetched £360.[1]

The famous Percy Lion, modelled in lead by Carter in 1752, was removed to the suburban residence of the Dukes of Northumberland, Sion House, at Isleworth, and the marble stairs to the late Mr. F. R. Leyland's house, No. 49 Prince's Gate, S.W.

A few of the pictures were removed to Alnwick Castle ; the rest to No. 2 Grosvenor Place, the duke's town residence. It is unnecessary here to enter upon a description of them, but there is a very interesting account of the collection as it was in 1761, soon after it was formed, in Dodsley's "London and its Environs," published in that year.[2]

Northumberland Avenue, which now occupies the site of mansion and gardens, was opened in March 1876, and is the only road laid out by the Board of Works at a profit, due mainly to the absence of trade interests, and to the eager speculation in the sites ; the surplus amounted to £119,819 over a gross outlay of £711,491.

When booksellers were, like John Newbery, vendors of medicines, quack and otherwise, a Mr. Pratt hung out his sign of the Bible and Crown, near Northumberland House, in the Strand, as a nostrum-

---

[1] Dr. Doran's *In and about Drury Lane*, 1881, vol. i. p. 231.
[2] See also Waagen's *Treasures of Art in Great Britain*.

seller,[1] and a Mr. Greg was a "Bookseller by Northumberland House, Charing Cross," who sold "The Sovereign Salve, or Family Plaister . . . For Hysterick Vapours, a most admirable remedy, exceeding Galbanum by far." [2]

The water difficulty cropped up again in the excavations for building the Victoria Hotel. For a solid foundation for the principal walls a depth of 50 feet was reached, and even then it was necessary to use a 10-h.p. engine with pump *night and day for six or seven months*, whilst a 6-feet concrete bed was laid over the entire area of 32,000 feet. The carving of the main entrance-porch to the hotel is by Mr. J. Boekbinder. Messrs. Isaacs and Florence were responsible for the hotel. -

The Constitutional Club is a noble building, conspicuous for the terra-cotta and glazed faïence of its elevations by Mr. J. C. Edwards, under the direction of Colonel Edis, the architect, who has consistently advocated the extended use of terra-cotta for building purposes. Most of the outer detailed ornament was modelled under Colonel Edis's directions by George J. Frampton, R.A., who executed the statue of Queen Victoria for Calcutta. In the Avenue are also the Royal Colonial Institute, and the new quarters of the Society for Promoting Christian Knowledge, removed from Newcastle (or Powis) House, Lincoln's Inn Fields, in 1879. For the Avenue freehold the Society gave £40,500. The interior of the large block at the corner of the Avenue and Charing Cross was re-arranged by Mr. F. W. Waller for temporary uses of the National Liberal Club, founded in 1882. The Grand Hotel is by Mr. A. Waterhouse, the architect of the Natural History Museum at South Kensington, and of St. Paul's School at West Kensington.

[1] *Daily Advertiser*, No. 3,612.
[2] *Country Journal*, Oct. 1, 1730.

CHAPTER XIX.

CHARING HISTORIC AND PRE-HISTORIC.

IT is not easy to think of Charing Cross as the home of the mammoth, of the lion, the bear, and the rhinoceros ; yet the bones of the cave lion, *felis spelæa*, have been found near the statue of Charles I., and the gigantic fleece-clad mammoth once browsed on Charing's river-banks at a period when the Thames was probably a tributary of the Rhine,[1] and the Straits of Dover were in the lap of the gods. The Siberian mammoth with long black hair and an undercoat of reddish wool, elephants of other species, and the two-horned rhinoceros, all clad in fleeces as if to protect them from the rigours of an Arctic climate, had their home in the basin of the Thames, where the forests afforded them suitable food.

When Drummond's Bank, already alluded to, was rebuilt in 1879, on the site of Lockett's and the Bull's Head taverns,[2] the excavations revealed fossil remains of the cave lion, the mammoth, and the Irish elk, and, in the upper deposits, the Celtic ox, the horse, and the sheep. These foundations, the excavations for which were attended by great difficulties, reached to a depth exceeding thirty feet, and it is said, of course exaggeratedly, that it cost more to draw the water off for the foundations than it did to build the bank itself.[3] The writer has himself seen the shells of freshwater species thrown up

[1] Sir Charles Lyell.

[2] It was at the Bull's Head tavern that Pepys looked down the barrel of his " French gun," newly purchased from Truelocke, the famous gunsmith, with as many misgivings as some persons examine the mouth of a gift horse. " A very good piece of work," he says, " and truly wrought ; but for certain not a thing to be used much with safety ; and he " (*i.e.* the gunsmith) " do find that this very gun was never shot off " (*Diary*, March 29, 1667).

[3] So I was informed by Mr. Dixon Gibbs, of the very old-established tea-dealers in Pall Mall West, whose father had it from Mr. Drummond himself. But probably there is some unconscious exaggeration here, for upon inquiry I was told at Drummond's that Cox's Bank opposite had far greater difficulty in respect to the water to be drawn off for the foundations. The relics discovered on the site of Drummond's are preserved in cases in the upper part of the bank.

in the "alluvial gravel" during excavations both on the site of the new Government Offices in Spring Gardens and during the deep diggings for the lavatories near the King Charles statue—the first conveniences, reputedly, of their kind in London. The purchasing from a labourer is also remembered of a fossil nautilus, which, except for the remnants of its silvery shell, was a mass of white clay exuding moisture at every pore. This was discovered at a depth of about thirty or forty feet, while digging foundations in Water Lane, Blackfriars. The nautilus also came from the "alluvial gravel." [1]

But long before the Celtic Briton had emerged from his conflict with the lesser *feræ naturæ* into the smooth waters of a comparative civilisation, the awful-looking animal depicted with such exquisite humour by Mr. E. T. Reed seems to have become extinct in Britain. It is, however, believed to have co-existed at *some* remote time with the ancient Briton, from whatever race that anthropological enigma may have sprung, or by whatever unknown race of people, if any, he may have been preceded. But that man himself existed in this particular locality of Charing Cross contemporaneously with the hairy elephant (*elephas primigenius*) there is, at present, no evidence to show, although, apart from flint implements having been found with remains of the mammoth, there is undoubted testimony to the existence in other parts, and that contemporaneously, of man and mammoth. This testimony consists in the discovery in the caves of Périgord, in France, of the figure of a mammoth engraved on a fragment of its own tusk. [2] Mr. Worthington Smith, in his comparatively recent work, "Man, the Primeval Savage," says: "The fossil bones associated with the stone implements of primeval man show that the mammoth, among many other animals, was the companion of man; .... the hippopotamus reached what is now the Thames, by rivers and the seashore, from Africa." But even if Mr. E. T. Reed had himself dwelt at a pre-historic "Punch" Office in Fleet Street, surrounded by the mammoth, he would have found him by no means the terrifying creature that his humour suggests. For, not being a flesh-eating animal, none but the old bulls would have made things unpleasant. Neither the hairy mammoth nor the straight-tusked elephant would molest humanity further than by an

---

[1] The nautilus has been found near Charing Cross, however. Two found in Jermyn Street, in the London clay, one twenty-six feet below the pavement, may be seen in the Geological Museum in that street, in the upper gallery.

[2] Lartet and Christy's *Reliquiæ Aquitanicæ*, 1875, B, Plate xxviii.

R

occasional charge from a furious old bull. But the rhinoceros was always a dangerous animal.[1]

Then at a later period it is not so difficult to picture the site of stony, staring Trafalgar Square and its immediate neighbourhood as it was when a refuge for the coney, and when unenclosed pasture-land, where no sound broke the stillness but the song of the lark and the tinkling of the sheep-bell. During the Middle Ages it was a common, parts of which were latterly walled in for the use of St. Giles's Hospital. At this period it was known as the "Down" (Le Doune),[2] by which we may suppose, as the word conveys, that it was a tract of land left "in down" for the pasturage of such sheep as were required by the inhabitants of London and Westminster. In Aggas's map (temp. Eliz.) cattle are, in fact, depicted grazing. In a deed 9 Richard II. mention is made of one acre and three roods of land "apud le Doune in St. Martin's Campis" granted to one Stephen Chise.[3] At a period before the erection of the Eleanor Cross, John Mugge, rector of St. Clement's, owned all the site of the present Pall Mall East, as well as a considerable space beyond northward, which he gave to St. Giles's Hospital, and which is described as being then "a garden walled in, situate next les Mwes, and containing twenty-seven acres," together with another garden (the extent not mentioned) "at Cherryng," &c.

The "common" state, as it existed in Richard II.'s time, seems to have continued until the reign of Henry VIII., when it is described as Charyng Cross Field—"Two acres of lande in Charinge-crosse Felde, in the parysshe of Seynt Martyn-in-the-Felde." At this period it partly belonged to St. Giles's Hospital, as already mentioned (which owned the north-western part), the Abbey of Abington, and the Abbey of Westminster; the latter foundation being proprietors of the part abutting on St. Martin's Lane, together with the adjoining Convent Garden, now Covent Garden. At the dissolution of the monasteries Henry VIII. granted the right of "commoning" on this land to the parishioners of St. Margaret's and St. Martin's, who held such right until the beginning of Elizabeth's reign. Aggas's map during this reign shows the country still quite open but for the Mews and a few houses on the east side of what was afterwards St. Martin's Lane. Cattle are grazing, and the clothes-line does not seem to have yet become, in this part, a sequel to the laundry, for women are spreading clothes on the ground to dry in what was not yet

---

[1] *Man, the Primeval Savage,* by Worthington Smith.
[2] Strype's *Stow,* 1720, bk. vi. p. 78.   [3] *Ibid.*

known as Leicester Fields, and in St. James's Fields, west of the Haymarket. Elizabeth, some time after her accession, leased the greater part of this land to a person named Dawson, who, having divided and enclosed it with fences and ditches, thereby deprived the parishioners of their right of common. This, in the year 1592, occasioned a violent commotion, the particulars of which Strype has given in his edition of Stow's " London and Westminster," derived from papers in his possession which had belonged to Lord Burghley.[1] The inhabitants assembled with pickaxes and spades, destroyed the fences, filled up the ditches, and made the whole as level as before, and it was not until some time after, on the matter being represented to the Queen, that an amicable arrangement between the parties was concluded.[2] It was proved at the time that the annual rent of the whole of the Crown land in this neighbourhood, reaching beyond Knightsbridge and Chelsea westward, and comprehending Tothill Fields and the ground unbuilt on southwards as far as the Thames, did not amount to fifty pounds !

Leicester Fields was known in 1627 as Military Street or Military Garden,[3] when no doubt it had ceased to become a laundry-woman's drying-ground, for some twenty or thirty years later two noblemen's houses adorn the landscape, and in Faithorne's map there is evidence of the Lammas-common being first generally built upon. One of these houses belonged to Mountjoy Blount, Earl of Newport, and stood on what is now the site of Newport Street. The other was Leicester House. The White Bear stables, at No. 25½ Lisle Street, are traditionally believed to have appertained to this historic mansion.[4]

---

[1] Strype's *Stow*, bk. vi. pp. 78–9.

[2] Cf. also *Memories of Westminster*, by W. E. Harland-Oxley, in the *Westminster and Pimlico News*, Sept. 30 or Oct. 7, 1904.

[3] Cunningham.

[4] A photograph of these interesting premises may be seen in *Two Centuries of Soho*, by the Clergy of St. Ann's, Soho, 1898, p. 209.

CHAPTER XX.

THE KING'S MEWS.

THE Mews, part of whose site is now occupied by the National Gallery, have given their name generally to any range of stabling, since the stables where the royal falcons were kept were here rebuilt. A mew is a cage for hawks when in the condition of moulting, the word being, says Professor Skeat, from the French *muer*, to change or moult, and allied to the Latin *mutare*.[1] Little or nothing seems to be known with respect to the history of the royal Mews in the hey-day of hawking as a sport, although the office of Grand Falconer of England, as an hereditary service of the Crown, was only abolished in the lifetime of the late Duke of St. Albans. The King's Falconer was an officer of great account, as appears by a record of King Richard II., in the first years of his reign.[2] The office can, how-ever, be traced some eighty or ninety years earlier than this, for in the Wardrobe Accounts of Edward I., in 1299, it is shown that Hankin, the King's Falconer, had 2s. 4d. allowed him for shoes.[3] Then, in the 13th Edward II., John De La Becke had the custody of the King's Mews, called "de mutis apud Charryng juxta West-monasterium," delivered to him. In the reign of Richard II., the King's favourite, Sir Simon Burley, held the office. But the expense and trouble connected with this exacting sport were so great that when an improvement had been effected in firearms, shooting was readily adopted as a more convenient and certain form of sport. The transition in the uses to which the King's Mews were put, from the place where the hawks were kept while they "mewed" or moulted, to stablings for the royal stud, took place in the year 1534,

---

[1] Thus also Minshew.   [2] Strype's *Stow*, 1755, vol. ii. p. 576.

[3] "Hankino custodi mutarum Regis apud Westm' pro calceamentis suis hiemalibus anni presentis, per compotum secum factum apud Westm' mense Januar' anno 29" (*Liber Quotidianus Contrarotulatoris Garderobæ, Anno regni Regis Edwardi Primi vicesimo octavo*, MCCXCIX et MCCC : published by the Society of Antiquaries).

the 26th of Henry VIII.,[1] when the king, having "fair stabling" in Lomesbury, now Bloomsbury, which was " burnt," transferred his horses to the Mewse, by Charing Cross, where so early at least as the time of Richard II. the royal falcons were cared for.[2] These stablings were rebuilt in the reigns of Edward VI. and Queen Mary,[3] and so continued until they were again rebuilt by Kent in the reign of George II. (1732).[4] Thence they continued to be the royal stables until the reign of George IV., when, in 1830, having latterly been used to shelter Cross's menagerie from Exeter Change, the Records of Great Britain, and as a " National Repository," they were finally taken down, never to be rebuilt.

" Feeding the Wild Beast.

Change of Hour ! !

Menagerie, King's Mews, Charing Cross.

At the recommendation and particular desire of many of the Nobility, who complain that the Hour of 8 o'Clock is inconvenient, the Proprietor respectfully announces that on June 1 next, and till further notice,

The Animals will be fed at Four o'clock in the afternoon, at which time he trusts he shall be honoured with their patronage ; the grandeur of appearance, and high state of excitement in which they are seen at that time is interesting beyond description.

Admission to the whole Menagerie, One Shilling."

At the Pavilion near the National Repository was exhibited the Gigantic Whale, 95 feet in length and 18 in breadth, which was found by fishermen floating in the North Sea between Belgium and England on November 3, 1827.

The " National Repository " was a temporary gallery for the exhibition of valuable and curious specimens of British ingenuity which was, in fact, a Science and Art Exhibition, and in which Edward Marmaduke Clarke, the originator of the Panopticon at the Alhambra in Leicester Square, took a prominent part, i.e. before the establishment of that particular Panopticon. Among the board of management of this excellent and truly patriotic undertaking appear the names of

---

[1] *Stow*, p. 167 (Cunningham).

[2] Geoffrey Chaucer, the poet, was Clerk of the Works to the King's Mews (temp. Rich. II.) at Charing Cross.　　　　[3] *Stow*.

[4] From the designs of the celebrated amateur architect, the Earl of Burlington (Elmes's *Topog. Dict.*).

Lords Clare, Ebrington, Gower, Morpeth, and Sandon ; and among
the committee of inspection are enrolled some of the most eminent
scientific and literary characters in the kingdom.[1]   So late as
1821 we read, "Several beautiful Hanoverian horses have arrived
at the King's Mews from the Continent.   They are intended to
be used in some of the State equipages at the Coronation."[2]   It
was from the Mews, near Charing Cross, that the Lincolnshire rebels
under Robin of Redesdale, a political tool of the Lancastrian
Nevilles, took Lord Rivers and his son John, carried them away,
and beheaded them at Northampton.[3]   But the records of the
Master of the Horse are acknowledged by a late holder of the office,
the Earl of Cork and Orrery, to be "rather chronologically confused."   The Earl has, however, rescued from oblivion the picturesque Eastern pedigree of an Arab horse presented to the King
in 1773, whose name was "Dervish" ; his colour like the wood-
pigeon, white and grey ; his dam a bay mare, and, like his sire of
the Holihan (?) race "Sheik Mehemed Bey," known to all Arabs.
"Famous and race-renowned among Arabs is this horse, whose age is
seven years, and whose race has never been mixed nor ever conquered
in war ! "[4]   In 1824 the royal stud, gilt coach, &c., were transferred
to the fine stables of Buckingham Palace.   The respective positions
of the Great Mews, the Green Mews, and the Back Mews are liable
to confusion in the memory.   As shown in a plan in the British
Museum, dated 1690, the whole still consisted then of these three
separate buildings, the Great, the Green, and the Back Mews ; and
they continued so until, in 1732, the façade of the Green Mews was,
with its three stone cupolas, rebuilt by Kent.   Kent's building
stood as nearly as possible on the site of the front of the present
National Gallery, as may be seen in a print in Thornton's "Survey
of London and Westminster."   The Green Mews was also called
the Upper Mews, to distinguish it from the Great or Lower Mews.
The Great Mews did not extend so far back as the present National
Gallery, which occupies the site of the *Green* Mews.   The Green
Mews abutted on Orange Court, while the Back Mews occupied
ground on the west side of the present square, between where the
fountains now play and Whitcomb Street, then Hedge Lane, which
reached so far as the Union Club, and even beyond—within a few

[1] Allen's *London*, 1829, vol. iv. p. 267 note.
[2] *Globe*, June 18, 1821.
[3] Entick's *Hist. and Surv. of Lond. and Westmin.*, vol. i. p. 398.
[4] The Earl of Cork and Orrery, in the *Pall Mall Mag.*, January 1896.

feet, in fact, of the entrance to St. James's Park.[1] On the west side, "between St. Martin's Lane and the Mewse, was situate an Hospital for Lunaticks, which the King caused to be removed to Bethlem Hospital, without Bishopsgate."[2] But the gods must have frowned on the stiff-necked Tudor's treatment of the poor "lunies," for in the twenty-sixth year of his reign, " on the xvi. August was burned the Kynges stable at Charyng crosse otherwise called the Mowse, wherein was brent many great Horses and great store of haye."[3]

Southwards the Great Mews abutted on the space of ground in which the statue of Charles I. is so conspicuous an object and landmark. Its principal entrance was here, south of Landseer's Lions. It was nearly opposite Mermaid Court, which was, however, a little further west, with an entrance into St. James's Park. This Mermaid Court marks the site of the " Mermaid " tavern, " over against the Mews," where George Fox was lodged when Colonel Hacker, in 1654, sent him to be examined by the Protector.[4] The "Mermaid" tavern at Charing Cross was closely connected with the history of lotteries in the seventeenth century.

One of the methods adopted by Charles II., after his restoration, to reward those loyal and necessitous officers who resided within the district defined in the bills of mortality, and had served Charles I. and himself with fidelity in the most discouraging periods of the interregnum, was the granting them one or more Plate lotteries, by which is to be understood a gift of plate from the Crown, and permission to sell tickets : the former to serve as the prizes. In the month of April 1669, Charles II., the Duke of York, and many of the nobility were present, says the "Gazette," "at the grand Plate lottery which, by his Majesty's command, was then opened at the sign of the Mermaid, over against the Mews." This was the origin of the endless schemes under the titles of Royal Oak, Twelve-penny Lotteries, etc. ;[5] but their introduction will be still

---

[1] Strype's *Stow*, 1755, vol. ii. p. 645 (Map of the Parish of St. Martin's).

[2] Maitland's *London*, 1756, vol. ii. bk. vii. p. 1345. See also Bishopsgate Ward.

[3] Hall's *Chronicle*, edited by Sir Henry Ellis, 1809, p. 816. But this is probably an error on the part of Hall, for it was the Bloomsbury stables that were "brent." Cf. *Stow*.

[4] Fox's *Journal*, vol. i. p. 265.

[5] It was not, however, the origin of lotteries in this country, nor even the first lottery opened in London, which was drawn at the west door of St. Paul's Cathedral in 1569. This consisted of 40,000 tickets at 10s. each, the profits of which were to be appropriated to repairing the havens of the kingdom. The

farther illustrated by an intimation published soon after in these words : " This is to give notice, that any persons who are desirous to farm any of the counties within the kingdom of England or dominion of Wales, in order to the setting up of a Plate lottery, or any other lottery whatsoever, may repair to the Lottery-Office, at Mr. Philips's house, in Mermaid-court, over against the Mews, where they may contract with the trustees commissioned by his Majesty's letters patent for the management of the said patent, on the behalf of the truly loyal indigent officers." [1]

Close to the " Mermaid " must have been Forrest's Coffee-house, which is also described as " opposite the Mews Gate, Charing Cross."

" To be Sold,

By WILLIAM HEATH (Brother to GEORGE HEATH, the original Maker, from Kingsgate-Street, Holborn), at the third House above Forrest's Coffee-house, opposite the Mews Gate, Charing Cross,

A Parcel of curious Copper brown Tea-Kettles and Lamps, the Colour of brown China—burnt in after the India Manner, which for curious Work and Colour exceed any that come from Holland, or any other Place. They want no other cleaning than to be wiped with a dry Cloth, and the Colour will be always the same. The great Demand there has been for the above Maker's Work is a sufficient Proof that they exceed any Dutch, and give a general Satisfaction. . . . Three-Pint Tea-Kettles and Lamps, at 10s. Two-Quart ditto, at 11s. Five-Pint ditto, at 12s.; and Three-Quart ditto, at 13s. Likewise several other sorts of curious Work in the above Colour, all warranted to be made by the above Maker, and original Inventor, George Heath, having engag'd him and the best Workmen in London, who by me are only employ'd; and sold at little more than prime Cost." [2]

Again :

drawing began on January 11, and continued day and night until May 6. The prizes were all in plate. Another lottery, consisting of rich armour, was drawn here in 1586. On both these occasions a temporary wooden house was erected next to the walls for the purpose. (Allen's *History of London*, 1828, vol. iii. p. 294.) Mr. John Ashton, in his *History of Lotteries*, says there is believed to be only one authentic record of this " plate lottery," and that is in the muniment room at Loseley House, in Surrey. It was projected in 1566, and drawn in 1569.

[1] Malcolm's *Anecdotes of Manners and Customs*, 17th cent., vol. i. pp. 308-9.
[2] *Daily Advertiser*, March 15, 1742.

"A Number of Silver Tickets to be had any Hour of the Day for RANELAGH GARDENS, at FORREST'S COFFEE-HOUSE, near Charing Cross.

Note, Each Ticket at One Shilling and Three Pence, carries in two Persons at any Hour of the Day." [1]

Another Mews Gate stood "next Hedge Lane." This Hedge Lane entrance was in the Back Mews, almost exactly opposite to the present Spring Gardens entrance to St. James's Park, which was a passage-way with the Red Lion inn at the corner.[2] In some year closely subsequent to 1785 strict rules were issued for the porter at the Mews Gate next Charing Cross "to suffer no loose, idle, or suspicious persons, or women of the town, to lurk or harbour near the mews ; to shut the gate next Hedge Lane as soon as it is dusk, and the gate next Charing Cross at ten at night, and *to prevent mobs or riots of loose, idle, and disorderly people.*"[3] In the latter half of the eighteenth century Aldridge's appear to have rescued the Royal Mews from a situation which was anything but creditable to the office of Master of the Horse, for the Mews had become quite a horse-fair and rendezvous for those in quest of all the usual paraphernalia of the stable and the coach-house. So much so, indeed, that in 1785 stringent orders were issued to reform "abuses that have been practised in the mews," viz. the " buying and selling horses and chaises, harness and carriages, by which means the mews has been made a kind of trading-place, to the great dishonour of the King; any servant found guilty of such practises shall be discharged."

Probably there were abuses also among the higher officers of his Majesty's stables. With the corruption in other quarters, it would be an exceptional circumstance in the management of the nation's affairs if there were not. In the ninth year of George I. the list of officers and servants was as follows :

Gentleman of the Horse

Avenar [4] and Clark Martial

[1] *Daily Advertiser*, July 12, 1742.

[2] " At the next door to the Red Lyon Inn-Gate, Charing Cross, London, any Persons that have Estates to Buy or Sell may be there accommodated : And money will be Lent at 5*l.* per Cent. upon Mortgages, from 100*l.* to 10,000*l.*, and 6*l.* per Cent. upon Personal Property from 100*l.* to 500*l.*" (advert. of eighteenth century).

[3] "Concerning the Office of the Master of the Horse " (*Pall Mall Mag.*, January 1896).

[4] The "avenar" was he who had the care of the provender for the horses

Seven "Equeries," Four Pages of Honour, Two "Equeries" of
the Crown Stable

One Sergeant of the Carriages

,, Yeoman of the Carriages

,, Supervisor of the Highways

,,   ,,   ,,   Stables

,, Riding Surveyor

Two Yeoman Riders

Clerk of the Avery

,,   ,,   Stables

Storekeeper

Esquire Sadler

Yeoman Sadler

Sergeant Farrier

Marshal Farrier

Yeoman Farrier

Two Coachmakers

Four Purveyors

Riding Purveyor

Mews-keeper

Four Stable-keepers

Thirteen Footmen

Five Coachmen

Five Postilions

Five Helpers

Four Chairmen

Two Chaise Helpers

Thirteen Grooms

Bottle Groom, Gentleman-Armourer

Page of the Back Stairs, Porter of the Mews

Messenger of the Avery [1]

and

Tregonnel Frampton, Esq., who was paid £1,000 per annum " for
keeping ten Race Horses at Newmarket." [2]

(*avena* = oats). " The master of the horse preferres to the avenarie, and other
clarkesbips, offices and places about the stable " (*Tom of all Trades*, 1631).

[1] The place where the provender was kept (Skinner). Boucher in v. "Aver"
considers it to be the stable. It seems certainly to be derived from *aver*, and not
from *haver*, oats, as Minsheu supposes (Halliwell's *Archaisms*).

[2] *Magnæ Britanniæ Notitia*, by John Chamberlayne, 1723, pp. 556–8, where
the salary of each official is given.

A propos of the office of Master of the Horse, an eighteenth-century story is told of two Irishmen from the banks of the Shannon. Casually meeting outside the "Golden Cross," after mutual congratulations, they inquired after each other's situations, one of them saying that he had been so lucky as to be appointed Master of the Horse. "And pray, Patrick," he said, "what are you?" "Why, I have been still more fortunate, for I am made Under-Secretary of State." "The devil you are! but how so, Pat, when you can neither read nor write?"—"O faith, let me alone for that; my master is a coal merchant, and I keep the tally, and chalk up the numbers of the sacks as they pass under the gateway. Pray, Terence, how are you Master of the Horse?" "Why, I help the ostler's assistant at the 'Golden Cross,' my dear." It was at the King's Mews, in Charles II.'s time, that Rowley, the famous stallion, was stabled, whose name was transferred, by the wits about the Court, to his royal master at Whitehall. Here Cromwell's horses were also probably stabled. At all events, Cromwell made use of the Dutch prison in the Mews to incarcerate Lieutenant-Colonel (sometime Cornet) Joyce. Joyce had a hankering after the possession of Fawley Park, in Hampshire; so had Cromwell's son, "Tumble-down Dick." Carlyle says that "Joyce, then a noisy Anabaptist, was partly minded, and fully entitled to purchase, and that Richard Cromwell was minded and not fully entitled: how Richard's father thereupon dealt treacherously with the said Joyce; spake softly to him, then quarrelled with him, menaced him (owing to Fawley Park); nay, ended by flinging him into prison, and almost reducing him to his thimble and needle again, greatly to the enragement and distraction of the said Joyce."[1] This was about the year 1654; but about nine years before Cromwell made a more important use of the Mews. After the battle of Naseby (1645), 4,500 prisoners and fifty-five captured standards were carried through Islington, and down St. Martin's Lane, guarded by the green and yellow regiments of the city, "and finally lodged in the Mews at Charing Cross till further orders."[2]

There was another entrance to the Mews at the southern end of Castle Street. Castle Street formed the west side of a square, of which the south side was Duke's Court; the north, Heming's Row; and the west, St. Martin's Lane. It enclosed the workhouse,

---

[1] *Cromwell's Letters and Speeches*, by Thomas Carlyle, 1850, vol. iii. p. 328; and *Harleian Miscellany*, v. 557, &c.

[2] Markham's *Fairfax*, p. 227, quoted in Wheatley's *London*, s.v. "Mews."

behind which, in Castle Street, was Archbishop Tenison's School and Library. The origin of the library is related by Evelyn, who was told by Dr. Tenison that there were thirty or forty young men in orders in his parish, either governors to young gentlemen or chaplains to noblemen. These gentlemen, being reproved on one occasion for frequenting taverns and coffee-houses, told him they would study or employ their time better if they had books. "This," says the diarist, "put the pious Doctor on this design of erecting a Library in St. Martin's parish for the public use."[1] Castle Street partook of the art traditions of St. Martin's Lane, for here dwelt Benjamin West, who made it his first London residence, and Sir Robert Strange, the eminent engraver, who, like many others who had fought for the Stuart cause, found a home in London between 1765 and 1774. In 1769 he published "A Descriptive Catalogue of a Collection of Pictures selected from the Roman, Florentine, Lombard, Venetian, Neapolitan, Flemish, French, and Spanish Schools, with remarks on the principal painters and their works, with a list of thirty-two designs from the best compositions of the great masters, collected and drawn during a tour of several years in Italy."[2]

I conceive that it was not the Charing Cross entrance to the Mews, but the Upper Mews Gate at the lower end of Castle Street, that became a bookseller's corner, whence doubtless many a valued work passed into the Tenison Library. "A small number of Francis Drake's History and Antiquities of the City of York, illustrated with 109 Copper Plates," were advertised to be sold by "T. Taylor, the Corner of the Mews Gate, at £1 11s. 6d. bound, *this Day, and no longer* ; after which they will be kept at the original Price, viz. £2 12s. 6d. in Sheets."[3] At the Mews Gate also dwelt "honest Tom Payne," the bookseller,[4] whose little shop in the shape of an L was named the Literary Coffee-house, from its knot of literary frequenters. He was for some time assisted by Edward Noble, and from 1789 to 1797 another of his assistants was John Hatchard, the founder of Hatchard's in Piccadilly. While with Payne, Hatchard lived close by in Monmouth Court, Whitcomb Street.[5] At the Literary Coffee-house by the Upper Mews Gate, says Mr. Austin Dobson, measuring margins, or discussing the merits of wire-wove

---

[1] Evelyn's *Diary*, February 15, 1684.
[2] Aikin's *Gen. Biog. Dict.*
[3] *Daily Advertiser*, June 1, 1742.
[4] Not the author of the *Age of Reason*, whose name was spelt with an " i."
[5] *Piccadilly Bookmen*, by Arthur L. Humphreys, 1893, pp. 14–18.

and black-letter, were daily to be found the "Doctor Dewlaps" of the day, the Greens, the Gilpins, the Gossets, the Grangers, and the like. Payne bought the books of Ralph Thoresby, the Leeds antiquary, at whose sale Horace Walpole acquired for 20s. the vellum volume of York Miracle Plays, of which the price in 1844 had risen to £305. His chief claims to remembrance are his inflexible integrity, his unrivalled knowledge of his business, and his genuine love of letters.[1]

"This is to acquaint Gentlemen

That there will be an Ordinary at the Mews Coffee-house, at Three Shillings a Head, exclusive of Wine, &c., to begin on Monday next, the 14th inst. ; and proper Attendance shall be given, and that in a neat and careful Manner, by

Your most humble Servant,
KATHERINE PERRONET.

Note, Dinner will be ready between Three and Four o'clock."[2]

Its exact site I have failed to identify, but the "Swan at Charing Cross" over against the Mews flourished in 1665, when Marke Rider was the landlord. The token of the house bore the figure of a swan holding a sprig in its mouth. Its memory is embalmed in a curious extempore grace once said by Ben Jonson before King James. These are the verses :

Our king and queen the Lord God bless,
The Palsgrave and the Lady Besse;
And God bless every living thing
That lives and breathes, and loves the King ;
God bless the Council of Estate,
And Buckingham the fortunate ;
God bless them all, and keep them safe,
And God bless me, and God bless Ralph.

The Schoolmaster King being mighty desirous to know who this Ralph was, Ben told him it was the drawer at the Swan tavern, who drew him good canary. For this drollery the king gave Ben a hundred pounds.[3] Possibly this Swan tavern gave its name to the Swan Close, upon the site of which Leicester House was built,[4] for

---

[1] See further "The Two Paynes," in *Eighteenth-Century Vignettes*, 2nd series, by Austin Dobson, pp. 192–203.

[2] *Daily Advertiser*, December 12, 1741.   [3] Aubrey, iii. 415.

[4] See Austin Dobson's *Eighteenth-Century Vignettes*, 1st series, p. 258, note.

the Lammas-lands appertaining to the mansion abutted on the Mews, and would certainly answer to the description of its situation as being "over against the Mews," if by "over against" we may understand the expression as applicable to the back of the Mews.   The situation of the Mews horse-pond cannot, I think, be identified by consulting any map or plan of St. Martin's parish, but Mr. J. T. Smith seems to have located it in this part of the royal stables.   Smith was fond of learning from very old people their reminiscences of London in their youth, and he thus learnt from a conversation with a gentleman named Packer, then in his eighty-seventh year, that in the King's Mews, adjoining Leicester Fields, there was a cistern where the horses were watered, behind which was a horse-pond, where pick-pockets caught in the neighbourhood were taken and ducked.[1]   This was in 1825 ; but nearly a hundred years before an instance is recorded of the pond at that earlier period having been put to the same use.   "Sunday several Gentlemen and others, standing to observe the Ruins " (*i.e.* of a disastrous fire which burnt down several houses), "a Woman attempted to pick a Gentleman's Pocket, who apprehended her in the Fact, and laid her on with his Cane pretty heartily, which drew the Resentment of the Mobb upon him, as not being acquainted with the Reason ; but being acquainted therewith the Offender was hurried away to the Pond in the Meuse, and underwent the Discipline usual in such cases."[2]   The authors of "Old and New London" say that this pond was "between the bottom of the Haymarket and the King's Mews," which would certainly help to locate its site if they had given their authority for the statement.[3]

So that, whether the Mews horse-pond was literally "in the Mews " or not, is at present a matter of uncertainty.   In a kind communication which I have received from Dr. Japp, it is suggested that there must have been something in the nature of a small pond, or bathing or watering place, where due attention was given to the bath for birds kept in the royal mews.   "One element," says Dr. Japp, " in the process of moulting or mewing was the attention to the bath, which, at the least, should have been every other day, if not every day ; so that, in a place where were gathered large numbers of hawks, there would be a necessity for something in the nature of a small pond or bathing place. . . . Great labour would

---

[1] J. T. Smith's *Ramble in the Streets of London*, ed. by Charles Mackay, LL. D., 1849, p. 70.

[2] *St. James's Evening Post*, August 31, 1734.   [3] Vol. iv. p. 227.

have been inevitable, taking baths to each separate bird, which, after all, would not have been so effective . . . and though the pond would be found convenient for watering the horses after the mews were transformed to stables, the pond was a part, and a necessary part, of the establishment when used for its original purpose."

Among the Records in the Archives of the City known as "Remembrancia" there is a letter from the Duke of Albemarle to the Lord Mayor requesting that the Court of Aldermen would take measures for supplying the Mews with water as heretofore, which was so essentially necessary to the king's service (October 13, 1663). There seems to have been a horse-pond in Moor's Yard, for in February 1738 "a gin-informer, since dead," was "Horse-ponded in Moor's Yard." Moor's Yard was on the north side of the church, apparently between what is now St. Martin's Place and the St. Martin's Lane end of Chandos Street. See newspaper cutting without date in the "St. Martin's Scrap Book."

CHAPTER XXI.

TRAFALGAR SQUARE.

ON March 21, 1826, Mr. Arbuthnot, following in the footsteps of Mr. Agar-Ellis two years before, obtained leave to bring in a Bill for the improvement of Charing Cross and its vicinity, little thinking to what strife and heart-burnings the project would lead, from its incipiency to the completion of the Nelson statue. It was then intended to purchase all the "stacks" of buildings situated between the Mews and St. Martin's Lane ; also the further stack of buildings, beyond these, bounded on the north by Chandos Street, extending southward to the Strand, and having its eastern termination near Bedford Street. The practical part of this project has certainly to some extent been accomplished, for it was to make a better communication between east and west. The west side of the proposed quadrangle was already formed by the Union Club House and the College of Physicians, and the intention has been realised, as we see it to-day, of forming the east side on a line with the portico of St. Martin's Church. It was the wish of Mr. Arbuthnot that the paintings, statues, and works of art possessed by the nation should be placed in a "range of buildings" extending on the north side from Pall Mall to St. Martin's Church.[1] It was certainly, according to all accounts, to King William IV. that we owe the opening to the public of the space now known as Trafalgar Square. It is also generally agreed that his Majesty suggested the name of the square, and the placing in its centre some monument to the immortal name of Nelson. The dilatoriness which attended the execution of the scheme can only be accounted for in the slow but sure impulses of the British character. Four years after Mr. Arbuthnot's motion this delay in the proceedings provoked a meeting of the tradesmen and others residing in the vicinity of the improvements. At this meeting, on Friday, June 11, 1830, the propriety was considered of petitioning Parliament for remuneration for severe losses which

---

[1] *Gentleman's Magazine*, March 1826, pp. 198-9-200.

they were sustaining through the removal of the houses and the long-continued dilapidations. Lord Lowther said in reply that the funds in the hands of the Commissioners were small, and that they could not proceed with greater rapidity, nor could they grant the remuneration applied for. One tradesman said he had lost £1,000 in two years.[1] The operations began in 1829, and the square, it will hardly be believed, was not completed even in 1849. The Nelson Column was begun in the year in which Queen Victoria ascended the throne,[2] and the statue, 17 feet in height, was set up in November 1843. The column was designed by Mr. William Railton, who, if he had difficulties in selecting an appropriate form of monument, was in the same predicament as the architect of the National Gallery, and had to cut the coat according to the cloth. The Nelson monument is a copy of one of the huge Corinthian pillars of the temple of Mars Ultor erected in the Forum at Rome by Augustus after taking vengeance upon the murderers of his great-uncle, Julius Cæsar. Thus it was doubtless intended to be in allusion to the great victory of Trafalgar by which the invasion of England was frustrated. There seems to be a general misconception as to the height of the column, which, with *base* and *pedestal*, is said to be 193 feet. Thus Thornbury, in "Haunted London." In Bohn's "Pictorial Handbook of London," edited by Weale, the architect, the column and capital are said to be "176 feet 6 inches in the *whole height*, surmounted with a colossal statue of 18 feet in height."[3] There are still other varying estimates of its height; but "Moderator," writing to the "Builder" of December 15, 1849, does so with a view to correct "a widely circulated error respecting the proportion of the column itself." The opponents of a columnar monument, he says, urged, before its erection, the insecurity of Corinthian proportions; and in a subsequent report by Sir Richard Smirke and Mr. Walker, the engineers, it was recommended that a considerable diminution in the proposed height of the work should be made. This recommendation was followed; but the impression that the clumsy expedient was adopted of chopping the required length off the shaft, and thereby violating the just proportion of the order, is entirely without foundation, although this, at the time, "went the round of the papers." "Moderator" claims that he went to the best source for his information, and found the height of the column

---

[1] *Times*, June 15, 1830, p. 4.
[2] Thornbury's *Haunted London*.
[3] Ed. 1854, p. 826.

as built, from the top of the pedestal to the top of the abacus, to
be 101 feet 6 inches, the lower diameter 10½ feet, and the upper
diameter 9 feet.[1] Now the estimate that has gained currency, in
spite of this statement, would make the Nelson Column no less than
three times the height of the two or three remaining columns of the
temple of Mars Ultor in the Forum at Rome. These are 58 feet
only in height, and themselves exceed those now existing of any
temple in Rome.[2] "Moderator" points out that the upper diameter
of the ancient example is a fraction less than 5 feet 2 inches, and
that as these dimensions are in the exact ratio of 101 feet to 9 feet,
it is evident the classic proportion has been strictly maintained.
But a few months later the state of uncertainty in which we are
thrown by these varying opinions and statements is still further
aggravated by an article in the "Builder," which gives the height
of the column to the top of the capital as 145·6 feet, and its diameter
10·6 feet. The dimensions of the principal columns which have
been erected as monuments are stated to be as follows :

A.D.		Order.	Feet.		Diameter.
118	Trajan	Doric	115	Height of capital to top	12
162	Antonine	Doric	123		13
1671	Monument	Doric	172		15
1806	Napoleon	Doric	115		12
1832	Duke of York	Doric	109		11
1839	Nelson	Corinthian	145·6		10·6

The statue of Nelson, of heroic size, is by Edward Hodges
Baily, R.A., one of whose best performances is considered "The
Graces Seated." This statue is formed of two blocks of stone from
the Granton quarry. The great pedestal of the column is adorned
with four reliefs, each 18 feet square, representing—

On the north side, "The Battle of the Nile," by Mr. Woodington.
On the south side, "The Death of Nelson," by Mr. Carew.
On the east side, "The Bombardment of Copenhagen," by Mr.
Ternouth.
On the west side, "The Battle of St. Vincent," by Mr. Watson.

[1] *Builder*, December 15, 1849, p. 596.
[2] Cf. the *Architectural Antiquities of Rome*, by G. L. Taylor and Edward
Cresy, 1874, pp. 48–50, and plates lxxii., lxxviii. Also *Rome in the Nineteenth
Century*, by Charlotte A. Eaton, 1860, vol. i., letter xix., and illust. of the
Temple, p. 196. As to the height of column and scaffolding see also the *Builder*
Nov. 25, 1843; and *Notes and Queries*, 10th Series, vol. iii. p. 457 (June 10
1905).

The Trafalgar relief on the south side is the largest of the four. It is, in fact, said to be the largest bronze casting of its kind in Europe, containing as it does more surface in superficial inches than the Wellington statue, now removed to Aldershot, but once at Hyde Park Corner. The original signal for the battle of Trafalgar may be seen in the popularly neglected United Service Museum in Whitehall.

The western panel represents the Admiral on board the "San Josef" at St. Vincent, receiving the swords of the Spanish officers. It was on the occasion of the boarding of this vessel that Nelson exclaimed, "Westminster Abbey or victory!"—"and they buried him," gasps Sir Henry Cole, "in St. Paul's!"[1]

The pedestal is raised on a flight of fifteen steps, at the angles of which are the Landseer lions—"the outlines," says the acutely observant naturalist, Richard Jefferies, "the bold curves and firm touches of the master hand, the deep indents, as it were,[2] of his thumb on the plastic metal, all the technique and grasp written there, are legible at a glance. Then come the pose and expression of the whole, the calm strength in repose, the indifference to little things, the resolute view of great ones. Lastly, the soul of the maker, the spirit which was taken from nature, abides in the massive bronze. The only noble open-air work of native art in the four-million city, they rest there and are the centre."

The Trafalgar Square fountains would have been supplied with water by the public water companies *but for the expense* which so vast a quantity would have entailed. So the Commissioners of Woods and Forests were compelled to look to other sources, and in 1843-4 they applied to Messrs. Easton & Amos, who, after a careful survey, recommended artesian wells, of the possibilities of which, however, they seem to have formed exaggerated notions, for they suggested the practicability of supplying not only the fountains, but all the public offices in the vicinity, together with the new Houses of Parliament, and for watering the roads when necessary.[3] This boastful undertaking has, however, literally ended in a fizzle, for, as Mr. Walter Thornbury, in his "Haunted London," has pointed out, the supply had in 1880 dwindled down to a sort of overflow of a ginger-beer bottle once a day. The artist would find a fit subject for genre-painting in the blushes of a British cicerone reflected in the spasmodic eruptions of green water, as he points out to foreigners

---

[1] Sir Henry Cole's *Guide to Westminster Abbey*.

[2] Not "as it were"; he actually modelled them with his own hands.

[3] The *Globe* newspaper, 1844.

the beauties of Peterhead granite in fountain architecture—beauties especially appreciated by the Frenchman and the Italian, whose countrymen have ever been the most celebrated for the architectural taste and symmetry of their fountains. But then, as Fairholt says, we have not yet arrived at anything beyond the simply ridiculous in this respect.[1] The "Builder" voiced the feelings of the discerning public when it expressed annoyance at finding that the much-vaunted fountains were "nothing more nor less in design than might have been purchased, dolphins and all, ready-made, at any of the artificial stone shops in the Paddington Road."[2]

Oases are formed in this desert of stone called Trafalgar Square by the statues which adorn its centre and angles. However carelessly recognised its architectural opportunities may have been, the site of the square is unimpeachably fine. Not only did Sir Robert Peel pronounce it to be one of the finest sites in Europe, but Chantrey, better qualified to express an opinion, said that the square stands on a site the most favourable imaginable for any national work of art. With the exception of the noble church of St. Martin's-in-the-Fields, there is, in fact, no building whose design and dimensions are adequate to the grandeur of the place. When Chantrey's statue of George IV. was cast, it was with a view to placing it upon the Marble Arch, before that arch was removed from its original position at the entrance to Buckingham Palace. But considerations of good taste prevailed against the impropriety of placing an equestrian statue, and a modern one at that, upon an arch in the style of that of Constantine in Rome. For this statue Sir Francis Chantrey was paid £9,000. It is a fine work of art, "graceful, unaffected, not without dignity, but a little tame," and stands at the north-east angle of the square. At the south-east corner is a statue of General Havelock, the hero of the relief of Lucknow, who died in the service of his country in India in 1857. At the opposite (southwest) corner stands the statue of the conqueror of Scinde, Sir Charles Napier, who died in 1853.[3] Never encountering the foe without being victorious, he defeated 35,000 with 2,000 men only under his command at the battle of Meeanee, and 26,000 with 5,000 at

---

[1] Among the most notable fountains in London are those in Hyde Park, presented by the Maharajah of Vizianagram in 1868 ; in Regent's Park, by a wealthy Parsee gentleman in 1869 ; in Victoria Park, by Miss Coutts in 1862 ; and that which stands in front of the Royal Exchange.

[2] The *Builder*, March 8, 1845, p. 119.

[3] There is also a marble statue of Napier, by G. C. Adams, on the north side of the entrance to the north transept of St. Paul's Cathedral.

Hyderabad. Speaking of Napier's victories, the Duke of Wellington said that "he had never heard anything like them." He was the first general in the British army to insert in his despatches the names of privates who had distinguished themselves. Beloved of the rank and file, it will be seen on the inscription that the most numerous subscribers to the statue were private soldiers. The south-western site was for a time occupied by a statue of Dr. Jenner, who, as the discoverer and propagator of vaccination, ranks among the great benefactors of the human race. It was at first thought desirable that he should stand near the College of Physicians, on the west side of the square, but the monument was soon removed to Kensington Gardens—the northern extremity—as a more appropriate spot. The statue is by William Calder Marshall, R.A., who executed the fine sculptures of Hyde, Lord Clarendon the historian, and Lord Somers, in the new Palace of Westminster.

The statue of General Gordon, in the centre of the square, was suitably decorated on January 26, 1905, in commemoration of the twentieth anniversary of his heroic death at Khartoum on January 26, 1885. A large wreath of evergreens and flowers was sent from the Gordon Boys' Home, with a card bearing the words : "Workers and friends of the Ragged School Union and Shaftesbury Society again render a grateful tribute to the memory of one who loved and helped the ragged boys." The "toothache" attitude given to the statue by Mr. Thornycroft, the sculptor, is said to have been the General's favourite one. His sobriquet of "Chinese Gordon" arose from the energy and despatch with which he quelled the formidable Tae-ping rebellion for the Chinese Government in 1863-4. His epitaph by Lord Tennyson may appropriately be reproduced here :

> Warrior of God, man's friend, not here below
> But somewhere dead, far in the waste Soudan,
> Thou livest in all hearts, for all men know
> The earth hath borne no simpler, nobler man. [1]

The College of Physicians, opposite to the north-west angle of the square on the south side of Pall Mall East, was erected from the designs of Sir Robert Smirke at an expense of £30,000, and opened by Sir Henry Halford, June 25, 1825. It was founded in 1523 by Linacre, who, as early as 1518, obtained through Cardinal Wolsey

---

[1] There is a recumbent effigy of Gordon by Boehm in St. Paul's Cathedral ; and his statue, mounted on a camel, by Mr. Onslow Ford, A.R.A., in the barrack square of the corps of Royal Engineers at Chatham.

letters patent for the college, of which he became the first president. The first meetings were held at No. 5 Knightrider Street, at Linacre's house, still standing, and bequeathed by Linacre to the college, which still possesses it. On the accession of Charles I. the college was removed to a house at Amen Corner, which, with nearly the whole of the library, was consumed in the Great Fire. Then a new college was built in Warwick Lane, where the Fellows held their meetings until 1825, when the present handsome edifice in Trafalgar Square was opened.

The Union Club, once the Cannon coffee-house, is also from the designs of Smirke, and contains, or used to contain, paintings by Stanfield and Roberts. The transition from coffee-house to club occurred about 1821–3. In a newspaper of November 1821 is the following : " The Chronicle of yesterday has a letter about the Greeks, signed S. T., which is the production of some wag (perhaps their Dunbar correspondent)—which begs to have a line addressed to the writer at the 'bar of the Cannon Coffee-house, Charing Cross.' Any body who could look strait, would have known that there was no such coffee-house now open."

The Union Club as now constituted is social and non-political, its present members being of all professions. There are a thousand members, and its expenditure is about £10,000 a year. When the late Mr. Clement Scott first joined the club he describes it in " How they Dined in 1860 " as being " one of the oldest and even then the most old-fashioned in London, where a member could get a bottle of the finest old champagne for about 5s. a bottle, and a bottle of magnificent old Madeira that had been in the cellar for years for 4s. 6d."

CHAPTER XXII.

THE NATIONAL GALLERY.

WE have it on very high authority that the English National Gallery of Art is, on the whole, the completest collection of pictures in the world, and that with the highest average of merit.[1] The gallery occupies the whole of the north side of the square, and was erected between 1832 and 1833, from the designs of William Wilkins, the author of " Remarks on the Buildings and Antiquities of Athens," 1807. It was the ape-like fashion to speak of this building as "the Wilkins Greek job " and the "National Cruet-stand," and to allude to its " mustard-pot " cupola and " pepper-caster " campaniles. These, no doubt, interfere with the aspect of the portico, which is composed of the beautiful Corinthian columns from Carlton House. For these columns Henry Holland, the architect, was, I believe, responsible ; and when Carlton House was taken down in 1826, they were ear-marked for the National Gallery. But the chief fault of the National Gallery is that it literally does not *rise* to the occasion of its situation and surroundings. It is, in fact, dwarfed not only by St. Martin's Church, but by buildings of less importance than either the church or gallery, which environ it. But as to the design itself, George Godwin, in one of his leading articles in the early " Builder," confesses that he cannot join in the fashionable chorus of condemnation, although adverse opinions embittered the architect's latter years, and caused his premature death.

Let us take a peep at the fountain-head of the stream that now flows in such splendour through the galleries of this national treasure-house of art. It was, according to Fairholt, at No. 90 Pall Mall that the Angerstein collection was first exhibited, in the house in which the collector of them, Mr. Angerstein, lived. That is, they were so exhibited after they had been purchased by the Govern-

---

[1] The *National Gallery*, by Sir Walter Armstrong, 1904. Mr. Ruskin said that it is " without question now the most important collection of paintings in Europe for the purposes of the general student."

ment ; and there is a view of the interior, by Frederick Mackenzie, in the Victoria and Albert Museum. Perhaps the numbering of the street has been altered since ; but Sir William Armstrong says that Angerstein's house stood on the site now covered by the north-east angle of the Reform Club, and by the private entrance to the club chambers. The Reform Club house and chambers occupy the present Nos. 104 and 105. However this may be, in 1818 the Angerstein collection is described as far from numerous, but perhaps the most select in London, and certainly formed at the greatest expense in proportion to its numbers. The pictures were thirty-eight, among these being four of the finest landscapes by Claude ; the "Venus and Adonis" and the "Ganymede" of Titian, from the Colonna Palace at Rome ; a very fine landscape by Poussin ; and other works by Velasquez, Rubens, Murillo, and Vandyck. Also the invaluable series of Hogarth's "Marriage à la Mode."[1] Owing to the good offices of Mr. G. Agar-Ellis, whose name public gratitude has perpetuated in Agar Street, Strand, and who first proposed, before he became Lord Dover, a National Art Repository,[2] Lord Liverpool announced to his colleagues in 1824 that he had agreed to buy the collection formed by John Julien Angerstein, then lately deceased, to form the nucleus of a gallery for the nation. The thirty-eight pictures cost £57,000, with £3,000 for incidental expenses. But even at this stage there was opposition from a few eminent painters, among whom was Constable, on the ground that the presence of a fine collection of accepted masterpieces might have a deteriorating influence upon the contemporary school of art ! Nevertheless, the approval of the scheme was general, and upon it ensued purchases and bequests, of which the first was from Mr. Hamlet, whose "Bacchus and Ariadne" of Titian cost £5,000; from Mr. Nieuwenhuy, a dealer, of whom was obtained "La Vierge au Panier" of Correggio for £3,800, formerly one of the gems of the Madrid Gallery, but hurt in cleaning ; Sir George Beaumont's bequest of sixteen pictures, valued at 7,500 guineas, which included "The Château," one of Rubens's finest landscapes, and Wilkie's

[1] The *Picture of London* for 1818, pp. 267-8.

[2] Mr. "Welbore Ellis Agar," as he was also known, himself had a very well-chosen and valuable collection of pictures, which might have been seen by application at his house in Norfolk Street, Park Lane. Titian seems to have been his favourite painter, and among the very fine pictures by that master in his possession was "a landscape, with a naked figure sleeping, in which the boughs of the trees are painted with an effect that is magically forcible ; likewise some very fine Claudes" (The *Picture of London* for 1803).

chef-d'œuvre, " The Blind Fiddler." This was in 1825-6. In 1834 followed thirty-four pictures bequeathed by the Rev. Holwell Carr, including fine specimens of the Caracci, Titian, Luini, Garofalo, Claude, Poussin, and Rubens. In 1836 King William IV. presented six pictures. In 1837 Lieut.-Colonel Olney bequeathed eighteen ; in 1838 Lord Farnborough sixteen ; then came the great " Peace and War " (£3,000) by the Marquis of Stafford ; three valuable pictures by Reynolds, Gainsborough, and West ; and a fine Parmigiano—all four presented by the British Institution. The greatest addition, however, was made in 1834, when Parliament purchased from the Marquis of Londonderry the two great Correggios, " Mercury teaching Cupid to read in the presence of Venus," known as the " Education of Cupid," and " Ecce Homo," to which Pungileoni assigns the date 1520. It once belonged to Murat ; and the " Education of Cupid " was in the possession of Charles I.

In 1857 the greatest of landscape painters, J. M. W. Turner, delighted the art world by his munificent gift of 362 oil-paintings, some of which, placed near the rich collection of Claudes, maintain after death the rivalry of the two great masters. In his will Turner particularly desired that a Dutch coast scene and " Dido Building Carthage " should be hung between Claude's " Sea-Port " and " Mill." The Vernon collection is now removed to the museum and galleries at South Kensington. In 1859 twenty pictures were bequeathed by Mr. Jacob Bell, and a few years later twenty-two others were added as a gift by the late Queen Victoria. The Peel collection was bought in 1871. In 1876 accrued the great collection of ninety-four pictures presented by Mr. Wynn Ellis. In this year a new wing was added, after a design by Mr. E. M. Barry, R.A., and the whole collection is now under one roof. In the earlier history of the gallery, owing to the unsatisfactory accommodation which the building afforded, partly occupied as it was, until 1869, by the Royal Academy, it was seriously proposed to remove the galleries to, first, Marlborough House, then to Buckingham Palace, and, later, to the site of the Life Guards Barracks or stables at Hyde Park.[1]

The addition of the new rooms opened in 1887 has enabled the authorities to arrange the pictures in schools, adhering as closely as possible to a chronological order. Handbooks and works of reference relating to the collection are the catalogues of Mr. Wornum, the late keeper of the gallery, who died in 1877—these have been reissued with corrections and additions by Sir F. W. Burton in 1889 ; the

[1] See the *Builders* before that year.

" Handbook of the National Gallery," by Mr. Edward T. Cook, 1901 (this includes an interesting collection of notes on the pictures by Mr. Ruskin and others) ; Mr. Gustave Geoffrey's work, " The National Gallery," a careful guide to the English, Italian, Flemish, Dutch, German, Spanish, and French pictures, with reproductions of the most celebrated originals, and an historical sketch by Sir Walter Armstrong, Keeper of the Dublin Gallery ; Dr. J. P. Richter's " Italian Art in the National Gallery," 1883 ; and Mrs. Jameson's " Handbook of the Galleries."

CHAPTER XXIII.

ST. MARTIN'S CHURCH.

ST. MARTIN'S was apparently elevated to the dignity of parish-hood between the years 1222 and 1275. In documents which were produced at a trial in the Court of King's Bench in the Hilary Term of 1828, " Fenn against Golding and other Churchwardens of St. Martin's-in-the-Fields," [1] lands are described, so early as the year 1225, as being in the parish of St. Martin of Charing, and, after-wards, others appear described as being within the parish of St. Martin's-in-the-Fields. It does not, however, seem to have been a confirmed, and even then not an independent parish, until some time after 1306, which is the first date of the Registry of the Diocese of London. Newcourt, who was principal registrar of that diocese for nearly twenty-seven years, represents the registry not to be defective from its commencement in 1306 to the year 1337, but that no registry existed from the latter date until the year 1361, when it again appeared without being defective for the space of fourteen years. [2] In 1367, about the fortieth year of the reign of Edward III., in a deed of confirmation of certain property, this property is described as being "near to the Cross of Charyng in the parish of St. Martin-in-the-Fields." [3] Not that St. Martin's had yet become a separate parish. It was first made independent of St. Margaret's, Westminster, [4] so

---

[1] *Barnewell and Cresswell's Reports*, vol. vii. p. 766.

[2] Newcourt's *Repertorium*, Preface, p. iv.

[3] *Our Parish*, by H. Simpson, 1836 ; and *Gentleman's Magazine*, July 1826, p. 30. But see further Appendix.

[4] The boundaries of Westminster in 1222 were confined to the single parish of St. Margaret, which at that time comprised not only the present parish of St. Margaret, but those also of the present St. Paul's in Covent Garden, St. Martin's-in-the-Fields, St. Anne's, St. James's, St. George's, Hanover Square, and St. John the Evangelist (*Archæologia*, vol. xxvi. p. 228). An old grant made to the parish by James I. recites that "in Henry VIII.'s reign the inhabitants did resort to the parish church of St. Margaret, and were thereby forced to bring their bodies by the Court-gate of Whitehall ; which the said Henry, then disliking, caused the church in the said parish of St. Martin to be then erected and made a parish there " (*Ibid.*).

late as 1535, and for a curious reason. When Henry VIII. occupied the palace at Whitehall he objected to the many funerals which took their, to him, dismal course beneath his windows on their way to St. Margaret's Church, Westminster. To obviate this the King built the first parochially independent Church of St. Martin,[1] and went on surviving wives as cheerfully as usual. But he also laid out the churchyard—not the present stone-paved area, one-third of an acre in extent, which has been supplied with trees and seats by the Metropolitan Public Gardens Association, and which is maintained by the Vestry, but the piece of ground which lay between Duke's Court and Heming's Row, with the workhouse and Tenison's Library on the west side. This burying-ground was destroyed in 1829, a new one of $1\frac{3}{4}$ acre having already been consecrated in 1805, in Pratt Street, Camden Town. This also is now a well-kept public garden, under the control of the St. Pancras Vestry. A part appears to have been appropriated as a private garden for the almshouses, and as a site for a chapel and other buildings.[2]

This, the most conspicuous parochial church in London, has in its Grecian portico one of the finest pieces of architecture in the metropolis. Everyone speaks well of the portico, which is saying a great deal.[3] The church is a remarkably handsome edifice of the florid Roman or Italian style, open to criticism in respect of the tower and spire, but otherwise of fine proportions, and, with its noble Corinthian columns, an enduring source of pleasure among the scant architectural beauties of London. Possibly the bust of James Gibbs, the architect, is placed inside the church against the western wall

---

[1] There was, however, a church of some sort on this spot at a very early period. In 1225 there was a dispute between the Abbot of Westminster and the Bishop of London, concerning the exemption of the church from the jurisdiction of the latter. It is not improbable that there was a chapel here for the use of the monks when they visited their convent garden, which reached to the church. See Allen's *London*, 1828, vol. iv. p. 240.

[2] *London Burial Grounds*, by Mrs. Basil Holmes, 1896, p. 289.

	Feet	Inches
[3] Extent of portico from end of one plinth to that of the other .	64	10
Intercolumniation from plinth to plinth	7	$4\frac{1}{2}$
Diameter of columns	3	4
Square of the plinth	4	8
Projection of portico from line of wall to front of plinth . .	24	11
Height of columns	33	4
Height of base with the plinth	1	$9\frac{1}{4}$

Builder, Nov. 25, 1843, p. 522.

with a taste that is unquestionable, since he did not so dispose it himself; but, as Pope says,

> Who builds a church to God, and not to fame,
> Will never mark the marble with his name.

The bust is, however, a beautiful work of art by Rysbrack, the sculptor of so many monuments in Westminster Abbey. As another instance of how many inhabitants have their most cherished family and commercial interests interwoven in the history of the parish of St. Martin, Mr. Dickson Gibbs, of the old-established tea firm in Pall Mall, south-west, where you may without difficulty obtain the fragrant brew at sixteen shillings a pound, is a great-nephew of the famous architect of St. Martin's Church—that is, of course, to say that the architect was the brother of the present Mr. Dickson Gibbs's grandfather. Two designs for a Round church were approved by the committee, but were laid aside because of the expense in executing them, "though," says the architect, "they were more capacious and convenient than what they pitch'd upon."

The crown surmounting the steeple of the church still signifies that this is a royal parish.[1] Buckingham Palace is within its confines, and the baptismal register contains the names of the royal children born in the parish. George I. was in fact a churchwarden, the only instance, I believe, of such a position having been filled by a King of England. There is a curious woodcut of the old church, the original building with its subsequent enlargements, in Allen's "History of London."[2] It was taken down in 1721. The new church was consecrated on October 20, 1726. On the laying of the first stone, the King gave a hundred guineas to be distributed among the workmen, and some time after £1,500 to purchase an organ. The whole expense of building and decorating the church amounted to £36,891 10s. 4d. In the tympanum of the pediment over the portico is a bas-relief of the royal arms, beneath which is a Latin inscription relating to the foundation of the church: "D. sacram Ædem S. Martini Parochiani extrui fec. A.D. MDCCXXVI." The capital of St. Martin's has its abacus ornamented, and the centre volutes, or horns, are entwined similar to those of the temple of Jupiter Stator, at Rome. The base, as to the contour of the

---

[1] The fact of the old Palace of Whitehall and St. James's Palace having stood within its confines at the time that St. Martin's was ordained a separate parish will readily account for its position in this respect.

[2] Ed. 1828, vol. iv. p. 241.

mouldings, is the same with that in Palladio's book of archi-tecture.[1]

A few years after the completion of the present edifice, the interior was the scene of a singular exhibition of violence. On September 10, 1729, during evening prayers, a gentleman abruptly entered, and fired two pistols at the clergyman who was reading the service : one of the bullets grazed the surplice, but the other entered the body of Mr. Williams, farrier, of Bedfordbury, who was sitting in a pew near the officiating clergyman. At this, the congregation fled from the church in the utmost alarm, all but a sturdy carman, who proceeded to secure the offender. This he effected after a severe encounter and many bruises on the head. It was subsequently found that the aggressor was one Roger Campaznol by name, son of the governor of Brest in France, and that having been cheated by his landlord, a Huguenot, resident near Seven Dials, of £138, his mind became deranged, so that he had not sufficient discrimination to distinguish the victim of his revenge. After his commitment to Newgate he endeavoured to .hang himself with his garters in the chapel ; but, being prevented, he fastened himself into his cell, and when the door was forced open he was found eating part of a bottle pounded into fragments, with bread.[2] The steeple also lent itself to a daring exhibition soon after the completion of the church. An Italian named Volante (the " flyer," presumably) descended head foremost by a rope from the top, over the houses in St. Martin's Lane, to the farthest side of the Mews (a distance of about 300 yards) in half a minute. The crowd of gazers, we are told, was immense ; and the young princesses, with several of the nobility, were in the Mews.[3] The bells of St. Martin's are the first to announce a naval victory. The bell-ringers still enjoy an annual sum of money which was left by Nell Gwynn, whose remains lie in a nameless grave in one of what are known as the " Vicar's vaults " from the circumstance of their being situated beneath the chancel. Archbishop Tenison, who attended Nell Gwynn's deathbed, preached a sermon extolling her virtues—so, at least, an enemy of his told Mary II. Queen Mary replied with dignity—" Yes, so I

---

[1] Mr. Woodward, in the month of January 1894, suggested the removal of the steps surrounding the portico of St. Martin's Church and the substitution of a *podium*. This proposal, however, was flouted, as tending to undo the original design of the architect. Whether the architect had any preference for steps rather than for a podium is perhaps questionable.

[2] Allen's *London*, 1828, vol. iv. p. 246.   [3] Malcolm's *Anecdotes*.

have heard. It is a sign that the unfortunate woman died penitent; for, if I can read a man's heart, the doctor would never have been induced to speak well of her had she not made a pious and Christian end." While wandering among "the memorials and the things of time that do renown this city," it is pleasant to observe the care which the noble French family of Mayerne have bestowed upon the restoration of the monument to their famous ancestor, Sir Theodore Mayerne, which adorns the crypt. The eminent physician's proper title was Theodore de Mayerne-Turquet, Baron d'Aubonne. The use of the whipping-post preserved here succeeded the custom of whipping at the cart-tail as a form of punishment. So late as 1730, one Mary Williams was "whipped at a cart's tail thrice round Covent Garden Market, pursuant to her sentence at Hicks's Hall, for stealing oranges out of Mrs. Vernon's greenhouse at Twickenham."[1] As to the punishment of the whipping-post, the culprit was tied round the waist by means of a rope which passed through a large hole in the centre, while his hands were fastened to the clasps above. In the case of a stout man his arms only were secured to these clasps. A curious relief of the sentence being carried out is carved in the wood above where the rings were. The post is about 190 years old, and fell into disuse about the year 1786, one year after the invention of the French guillotine.

The writer once secured, at considerable trouble, two fine elm water-pipes, excavated from the bed of the Wall Brook in Copthall Avenue, City. When in quest of them some months afterwards, it was found that they had served admirably as firewood! A similar fate befell the parish stocks formerly preserved in St. Martin's crypt, which were *chopped up for firewood* by a former sexton, about, so I was told by the present sexton, ten or twelve years ago.

There is also a tablet in the crypt to another great name in the annals of medicine, that of Dr. John Hunter, the founder of the College of Surgeons, in Lincoln's Inn Fields.

There are in England about 160 churches dedicated in the name of St. Martin, one of the most illustrious saints of the Middle Ages. The incident in his life depicted in the stone relief over the new St. Martin's Vestry, and also on the quaint door-knobs of the church's interior,[2] happened outside the walls of Amiens, where the legion

---

[1] The *Daily Advertiser*, March 3, 1730.

[2] There is also, or used to be, in a south window, a portrait of St. Martin in the act of dividing his mantle.

was quartered in the year 332. The winter was one of such exceeding severity that men died in the streets from excessive cold, and it happened one day that St. Martin, on going out of the gate of the city, was met by a poor naked beggar, shivering with cold. The saint's compassion being aroused, and having nothing but his cloak and his arms, he with his sword divided his cloak in twain, and gave one half of it to the beggar, covering himself as well as he might with the other half. In the famous picture by Vandyck at Windsor of this incident, the historical treatment has been adopted as regards style and conception. It is said that Vandyck has here represented himself mounted on the white charger which Rubens had presented to him.

For the view of St. Martin's Church looking from Pall Mall East, past the National Gallery, we are indebted especially to two eminent architects. The want of this opening, to be effected by the pulling down of the western side of St. Martin's Lane from Heming's Row to Northumberland House, and by the laying out as a street of Pall Mall East, was complained of in 1735 by the eminent architectural critic, James Ralph, to whom is due the credit of first suggesting the improvement which, to those who knew what the old state of things was, must have formed an architectural view of great beauty. The portico Ralph describes as being "at once elegant and august," and what was lost to the public view before these improvements were achieved may be seen by referring to some old engravings of the time, which exhibit the church entirely obscured to the view from the west by miserable-looking lath-and-plaster hovels immediately opposite, for the removal of which James Elmes also exercised his influence, although, as has been pointed out, it was to Ralph that the credit of the suggestion is due.[1]

Among the eminent artists buried in St. Martin's are Dobson, "the English Vandyck," whom Charles I. called the English Tintoret; Louis Laguerre, the assistant and imitator of Verrio, who painted the Labours of Hercules in chiaroscuro at Hampton Court, but much of whose work was damned by Pope's unpropitious line, " Where sprawl the saints of Verrio and Laguerre "; Paul Vansomer, who in Walpole's estimation trod, as regards merit, on the heels of Vandyck; Nicholas Laniere, patronised by Charles I., who was also a musician, drew for the King a picture of Mary, Christ, and Joseph, and his own portrait done by himself with a palette and

---

[1] *Critical Review of Publick Buildings in London, etc.*, 1734, p. 31.

pencils in hand, and musical notes on a scrap of paper, afterwards placed in the Music School at Oxford ; Nicholas Hilliard, the portrait painter ; and Nicholas Stone, the statuary.

The walls of the spacious vestry-room are adorned with half-length portraits of former vicars, from the year 1670. Almost all of these attained high distinction in the Church.[1]

---

[1] A list of the vicars of St. Martin's will be found in Malcolm's *Londinium Redivivum*.

T

CHAPTER XXIV.

SUFFOLK STREET.

SUFFOLK STREET is recorded in the rate-books of St. Martin's as dating from about 1664. Both Suffolk Street and Suffolk Place were so named from Suffolk House having stood on their site, a mansion which was the residence, in the days of James I., of Thomas, first Earl of Suffolk, and his beautiful and unprincipled Countess, whose names so frequently occur in the profligate annals of that reign. In old Suffolk Street lived the charming actress, Mary Davis, who is said to have captivated the heart of Charles II. by singing, in the character of Celania in "The Mad Shepherdess," the song, "My lodging is on the cold ground." [1] Pepys alludes to her thus : "The King, it seems, hath given her a ring of £700, which she shows to every body, and owns that the King did give it her ; and he hath furnished a house in Suffolke Street most richly for her, which is a most infinite shame." [2] Again : "In Suffolk Street lives Moll Davies ; and we did see her coach come for her to her door, a mighty pretty fine coach." [3] A rift in the lute of the King's pleasures occurred, however, in 1670, when the opponents of the Government proposed in Parliament to levy a tax on playhouses. In the course of the debate Sir John Coventry, commenting on the King's licentiousness, asked "Whether did the King's pleasure lie among the men or the women that acted?" The allusion was obviously intended to apply to Nell Gwynn and Moll Davis. The King's friends expressed great indignation, and prepared to avenge the insult. On December 21, while on his way home to his house in Suffolk Street, Coventry was taken out of his carriage by a band of ruffians, headed by Sir T. Sandys, and his nose slit to the bone. This deed caused the greatest excitement in the House of Commons, and in consequence "Coventry's Act" was passed in 1671 (22 and 23 Car. II. c. 1), declaring nose-slitting or

---

[1] Jesse's *Memorials of London* (Nimmo, 1901), 2nd series, p. 25.
[2] *Diary*, January 14, 1667-8.　　　[3] *Ibid*. February 15, 1668-9.

other mutilation of the person to be felony without benefit of clergy. Coventry's assailants were never captured.

In 1678 Stanley, the author of the " Lives of the Philosophers," died in old Suffolk Street, and was buried in St. Martin's Church. The street became notorious on account of a riot which took place here, generally, but erroneously, supposed to have been in connection with a meeting of the "Calves Head Club" at the Golden Eagle. The Calves Head Club, however, had nothing whatever to do with it. Sundry noblemen and gentlemen, finding time hang heavily on their hands during a relaxing of their parliamentary duties, dined here rather in the direction of "too well" than of "wisely." Malcolm's account is evidently derived from the hunger-spurred narratives of "the garretteers in Grub Street," and is quite an erroneous one.[1] Perhaps it will be as well to give the exact words of one, Lord Middlesex, who was present, as they occur in Spence's "Anecdotes." ". . . The mixture of the company," he says, "has convinced most reasonable people by this time that it was not a designed or premeditated affair. We met then, as I told you before, by chance upon this day (Jan. 30, 1734, anniversary of King Charles's execution), and after dinner, having drunk very plentifully, especially some of the company, some of us going to the window unluckily saw a little nasty fire made by some boys in the street, of straw I think it was, and immediately cried out ' D——n it, why shouldn't we have a fire as well as anybody else ? ' Up comes the drawer. 'D——n you, you rascal, get us a bonfire !' Upon which the imprudent puppy runs down, and without making any difficulty (which he might have done by a thousand excuses, and which, if he had, in all probability some of us would have come more to our senses) sends for the faggots, and in an instant, behold ! a large bonfire blazing before the door. Upon which some of us, wiser, or rather soberer than the rest, bethink themselves then for the first time what day it was, and fearing the consequences a bon-fire on that day might have, proposed drinking loyal and popular healths to the mob (out of the window), which by this time was very great, in order to convince them that we did not intend it as a ridicule upon that day. The healths that were drunk out of the window were these, and only these : ' The King, Queen, and Royal

---

[1] Malcolm's *Manners and Customs of London in the Eighteenth Century*, 1810, vol. ii. pp. 47–8. At the house where this is said to have taken place was hung out the sign of the " Golden Eagle." Creed, in his *Collection of Tavern-Signs* (vol. vi.), says there are two prints extant of this club.

Family,' 'The Protestant Succession,' 'Liberty and Property,' 'The present Administration.' Upon which the first stone was flung, and then began our siege, which, for the time it lasted, was at least as furious as that of Phillipsburgh.[1] It was more than an hour before we got any assistance; the more sober part of us, during this time, had a fine time of it: fighting to prevent fighting, in danger of being knocked on the head by the stones that came in at the windows, in danger of being run through by our mad friends, who, sword in hand, swore they would go out, though they first made their way through our bodies. At length the justice, attended by a strong body of guards, came and dispersed the populace. The person who first stirred up the mob is known: he first gave them money, and then harangued them in a most violent manner. I don't know if he did not fling the first stone himself. He is an Irishman, and a priest belonging to the Venetian Envoy. This is the whole story from which so many calves' heads, bloody napkins, and the Lord knows what, have been made. It has been the talk of the town and the country, and small beer and bread and cheese to my friends the garretteers in Grub Street for these few days past. . . ."[2] Whatever feelings the proceedings aroused, the particular company there assembled on this occasion appear from all accounts to have had no connection with the nebulous Calves' Head Club further than that the political opinions of individuals present might accidentally have been of a strong Whig tendency. But it seems to have been quite distant from their unpremeditated design to drink:

> " To the pious memory of Oliver Cromwell."
> " Damnation to the race of the Stuarts."
> " To the glorious year 1648."
> " To the Man in the Mask," &c., &c.

Or if it *was* their intention thus to arouse the Stuart sympathies of the mob, the latter seem to have been actuated in return by the

---

[1] Philipsburg on the Rhine, taken by the French in 1734, when the Duke of Berwick was killed at the siege.

[2] Spence's *Anecdotes*, 1858, 2nd ed. pp. 300-305, where in another Letter (No. VI.), from Mr. A. Smyth to Mr. Spence, the writer states that there was no calf's head exposed at the window, and afterwards thrown into the fire, no napkin dipped in claret to represent blood, nor anything that could give colour to such reports. Among the healths drunk, that to the "present Administration," which did not happen to be very popular, "was the only cause of the riot."

sentiment expressed in a Calves' Head Club burlesque drawing by Heemskirk :

> New Regicides, bad as the old, dare call
> The Martyr's blood on their own heads to fall ;
> And black as those who Frocks or Vizors wore,
> These Sons of Hell thus trample on his Gore.

The authors of "Old and New London" are probably in error when they suggest the "Cock" tavern in Suffolk Street as the scene of this escapade. Malcolm says it was the "Golden Eagle." At the "Cock," in Suffolk Street, the Councillors of the Board of Trade dined together ;[1] and Pepys relates how he "did walk to the Cock at the end of Suffolke Street, where I never was, a great ordinary mightily cried up, and there bespoke a pullet, and while dressing he and I walked into St. James's Park, and thence back and dined very handsome, with a good soup and pullet, for 4s. 6d. the whole."[2]

"At the MILITARY PROMOTION OFFICE, in Suffolk Street, Charing Cross," were to be sold "a Company in a young Regiment on distant service ; and one with five months' rank and half-pay. A Lieutenancy in a young Regiment on service; Cornetcy of Horse, and one in old Cavalry, both with uncommon advantages ; several Ensigncies in old Regiments ; a 2d Lieutenancy of Fuzileers in a young Regiment returning from service (this commission takes rank of all Cornets and Ensigns) ; an Adjutancy of Dragoons on the British and one on the Irish Establishment ; one of Infantry, and one in a Regiment of Militia. Wanted to purchase, a Lieutenant-colonelcy, a Majority, and an old Chaplaincy. Exchanges wanted from half to full pay, for all ranks. A Captain in a young Regiment, not likely to be soon disbanded, wishes to exchange into the Guards.

"Several Commissions to be sold and exchanged, with great advantages. Letters post paid will be punctually attended to.

"J. BURNE."[3]

Adam Smith lodged in Suffolk Street during one of his sojourns in London. No. 23 was the residence of Richard Cobden, and here he died. A memorial tablet to this effect was erected outside on August 15, 1905. James Barry, R.A., dwelt at No. 29 between the years 1773 and 1776. Lord Winchilsea was living at No. 7 when challenged in 1829 by the Duke of Wellington. Neither the exact spot nor the number of the house is known in which Swift's

---

[1] Evelyn's *Diary*, December 23 1671.　　　　[2] *Ibid.*
[3] *Morning Herald and Daily Advertiser*, December 15, 1783.

Vanessa sat at the receipt of praises from wits and of visits from people of quality. Vanessa was the daughter of a Dutch merchant, and inherited a fortune. The following passage from the Dean's poem of "Cadenus and Vanessa" presents some traits of manners in those times :

> A party next of glittering dames,
> From round the purlieus of St. James,
> Come early out of pure good will
> To see the girl in deshabille.
> Their clamour 'lighting from their chairs
> Grew louder all the way upstairs ;
> At entrance loudest, where they found
> The room with volumes littered round.
> Vanessa held Montaigne and read,
> Whilst Mrs. Susan combed her head.
> They called for tea and chocolate,
> And fell into their usual chat,
> Discoursing with important face
> On ribbons, furs, and gloves and lace ;
>
> .   .   .   .   .   .
>
> Dear Madam, let me see your head ;
> Don't you intend to put on red ?
> A petticoat without a hoop !
> Sure you are not ashamed to stoop.[1]

On the east side of Suffolk Street is the Gallery of the Society of British Artists, designed by the eminent architect James Elmes, and built under the superintendence of John Nash. It consisted of an entrance under a tetrastyle portico of the Roman Doric order, designed by John Nash, which led to a wide staircase. This opened to a square vestibule that led to a suite of five spacious exhibition rooms or galleries, all of which were on the same floor, communicating with each other, and lighted by large lanterns in the ceiling, which, being inclined from the perpendicular, diffused an even light over the whole surface of the walls. The angles of all the galleries were taken off octagonally, to prevent dark corners.[2]

It was in the year 1823 that a number of artists formed themselves into a Society of British Artists, principally for the purpose of exhibiting their works more advantageously than by the means afforded at the Royal Academy. About the year 1852 Queen Victoria conferred a charter on the society. The Gallery is open to all artists from April to July, and from October to February.

A Mr. Chenevix was a famous toy-dealer of the middle of

---

[1] Leigh Hunt's *Saunter through the West End*, 1861, pp. 217, 218.
[2] Elmes's *Topographical Dictionary*.

the eighteenth century, whose widow's name constantly occurs as carrying on the business in other parts of London at a later date. Chenevix's shop was "against Suffolk Street, near Charing Cross," whence he advertises the loss of a "Coat of Arms Seal, engraved on a Chrystal, and set transparent in Gold, the Arms, Argent, a Lyon rampant, and a Border engrail'd, Sable, with a Crescent." A guinea and a half reward, and "no questions ask'd."[1] At this celebrated toy-shop tickets for most of the West-End "shows" and exhibitions were sold.

Three years after the death of the great Sir Isaac Newton, his "Head" served as the sign at "the Corner of Suffolk Street" of J. Pote, who published "THE FOREIGNER'S GUIDE; or, A Necessary and Instructive Companion, both for the Foreigner and Native, in their Tower thro' the Cities of London and Westminster," at Sir Isaac Newton's Head.[2]

Among the eminent inhabitants of Suffolk Street were Sir Philip Howard from 1665 to 1672, and the Earl of Suffolk from 1666; Mr. Secretary Coventry (Charles II.), after whom (and not because of Lord Keeper Coventry's residence being situated there) Coventry Street, Haymarket, was so named; Sir Edward Spragg, one of the admirals of the Dutch war under Charles II.; Dean Swift, five doors from Mrs. Vanhomrigh, the mother of Vanessa. The last and most unfortunate King of Poland, Stanislaus Augustus, lodged in 1754 in Suffolk Street, at the house of a Mr. Cropenhole.[3]

The United University Club House, at No. 1 Suffolk Street, for members of the Universities of Oxford and Cambridge, was built by the architect of the National Gallery, William Wilkins, R.A., and J. P. Gandy, and opened February 13, 1826. The entrance fee was then twenty-five guineas; the annual subscription, six guineas. It is now forty-two guineas, with an annual subscription of eight guineas.

The small-pox scourge must have been terribly rife in the seventeenth and eighteenth centuries. Evidence of this is repeatedly occurring in the newspaper advertisements of the time, when allusions to its ravages, as in the following, are painfully common:

"On the 12th of this instant April, one Abraham Councel took away a Sum of Money from his Master the Marquis de Rochegude: The said Abraham Councel is middle-sized, aged about 25, marked

---

[1] *Daily Advertiser*, April 13, 1742.

[2] The *Craftsman*, February 20, 1729, which contains a further description of the *Guide*.

[3] Malcolm.

with the Small-Pox, and has all black Stumps of Teeth ; he wears a light Wig, and speaks both English and French very well. Whoever secures him, and gives notice to Mrs. Benoit, in Suffolk-street near Charing-cross, London, shall have 3 Pounds Reward, and Charges." [1]

One case of small-pox like the above might be multiplied by the score. The disease was incredibly frequent. Time after time and time again one encounters mention of such facial disfigurement.

Little Suffolk Street, which in 1831 was seven houses on the right going up the Haymarket from Cockspur Street, is perhaps identical with what is now Suffolk Place. In Little Suffolk Street was the "Goat," mentioned as a well-known tavern in the newspapers of the Civil War period,[2] and between James Street (which is still the third turning on the left in the Haymarket from Coventry Street) and Little Suffolk Street was the King's Head inn.

[1] *London Gazette*, April 17–20, 1699.
[2] *Illustrations of the Life and Neighbourhood of the New Post Office*, pp. 65-6.

CHAPTER XXV.

COCKSPUR STREET.

THE earlier history of this interesting byway of western London has already been alluded to, and an origin has been imputed to it, closely associated with the sale of cock-spurs in connection with the cockpits royal of Whitehall and St. James's.[1] The latter pit was taken down in 1816, but had been deserted long before in favour of that behind Gray's Inn.[2] The St. James's cockpit, however, which stood at some steps leading from Birdcage Walk into Dartmouth Street, near the top of Queen Street, Westminster, was still in vogue so late as 1780, for in that year was published, price 1s. 6d. :

" Directions for Breeding Game Cocks. With the method of treating them from the time they are hatched, until fit to fight. . . . Articles for a Cock Match. Key to a Match Bill. Rules and Orders in Cocking, *as abided by at the Cock-pit Royal, Westminster, &c.*"[3] And even fourteen years later, in 1794, a match is advertised as follows :

" At the Cockpit-Royal, the South Side of St. James's Park, on Monday next, and all the Week, will be fought the Gentlemen's annual Trial Subscription Cock-Match. To begin fighting at Six o'Clock. Walter and Fisher, Feeders. By Order of the Gentlemen, Dinner on Table at Four o'Clock on Monday, Wednesday and Saturday."[4] The silver spurs used on these occasions[5] were, no doubt, at that time purchased in Cockspur Street or its immediate neighbourhood, where they are still to be had, as anyone who may take the trouble to inquire will find.

The Courts of Requests, also known as the Courts of Conscience, for the recovery of small debts, were superseded in 1846–7, so far as

[1] See pp. 21–2.
[2] See *A New Guide to London*, 1726, 2nd ed., p. 8, quoted by Cunningham. In this case, however, it must have reverted later to its former use, as will be seen by the announcements which follow.
[3] The *Morning Chronicle and London Advertiser*, March 3, 1780.
[4] The *Daily Advertiser*, January 4, 1794.   [5] *Ibid.*, May 20–25, 1742.

the extra-mural jurisdiction of the city was concerned, by the County Courts, of which there are now over 500. One of these courts was in Cockspur Street : others were in Osborn Street, Whitechapel; in Castle Street, Leicester Square; in Vine Street, Piccadilly ; in Kingsgate Street, Holborn ; near the Guildhall; and on St. Margaret's Hill, Southwark.

" To be sold by AUCTION,

By Mr. PINCHBECK, senior,

This Day and To-morrow, at the British Coffee-House, adjoining to his Shop in the Court of Requests,

The entire Collection of original Pictures of the late Capt. John Mitchell, Commander of the Yacht belonging to his Grace the Duke of Bedford, a Gentleman well known and esteem'd by the Connoisseurs in Painting ; among which are several very capital Pictures by the best Masters, particularly of Backhuzen [*sic*], Snyders, &c.

.　　　.　　　.　　　.　　　.　　　.

N.B. At the particular Desire of several Noblemen and Gentlemen, the curious Chamber-Organ and Cabinet in Mr. Pinchbeck's Shop, made by Old Smith, and which likewise plays ten pieces of Musick of itself, will be put up To-morrow, exactly at Two o'Clock.

Catalogues are deliver'd gratis at the Place of Sale, and at Mr. Pinchbeck's Shops in Fleet-Street and the Court of Requests.

Note, Thursday next being Ascension-Day, when the Courts will not sit, and it is apprehended the Houses may not, is the Reason for beginning this Sale a Day sooner than was before advertised." [1]

The Panopticon was an instrument exhibited by Pinchbeck at the " Repository " over his shop in Cockspur Street. A handbill describes it as "That celebrated and well-known Triangular Musical Machine, the PANOPTICON ; with six moving Pictures, which is universally allowed, from its beautiful Structure, the vast Variety of its Motions, and the Harmony of its Music, to be the first Piece of Mechanism of its Magnitude in Europe. Its first Picture represents a Concert of Music in a Country Fair, with the Musicians, and all the other Figures, in their proper Motions." There were many other models, pieces of machinery, and ingenious contrivances, to the number of considerably over twenty exhibited at the same time, which certainly seem to have suggested the Panopticon of the Alhambra. The date of the handbill from which the above descrip-

----

[1] The *Daily Advertiser*, May 20–25, 1742.

tion is taken is not given. There is a letter from John Pinchbeck concerning this Panopticon in the "London Gazette," June 12, 1751.

The fact of there having been two Christopher Pinchbecks and two Pinchbecks, senior, besides John and Edward Pinchbeck, has given rise to some confusion. The truth seems to be that while old Christopher Pinchbeck, the *reputed* inventor of the metal to which he gave his name, was alive, his son was known as Christopher Pinchbeck, junior ; and that, when the old man died, his eldest son Christopher, while in Cockspur Street, described himself as Mr. Pinchbeck, senior. The authors of "Old and New London" are evidently incorrect in stating that the *elder* Pinchbeck died in 1783. He died in 1732, as advertisements of that period testify ; in one of which his son Edward describes himself as his father's sole executor.[1] Christopher the second, who died in 1783, and not Edward, was the eldest son. Even the lives of the Pinchbecks in the "Dictionary of National Biography" have made Christopher the *second* son. But that this was not the case appears from the following in the "London Evening Post" for October 6, 1733 :

"N.B. It having been insinuated in an Advertisement in the publick Papers, that Christopher Pinchbeck, *eldest Son of the late Mr. Christopher Pinchbeck*, was the only Son brought up to his Father's Business, and that his Father's Workmen were ready to attest that *he only* assisted him in making the curious Metal above-mentioned ; this is to satisfy the Publick, that those Insinuations are entirely false, as will plainly appear by the following Particulars :

"First, Mr. Edward Pinchbeck has been brought up to his Father's Business ever since he was ten Years of Age, *by whose Means the Discovery of the aforesaid Metal was first made, tho' afterwards improv'd and brought to Perfection by his Father ;* and to the said Edward Pinchbeck alone his Father on his Death-Bed communicated the Secret, with his Improvements of it.

"Secondly, Mr. Edward Pinchbeck appeals to ocular demonstration for the Truth of this Assertion, and doubts not but all those Noblemen and Gentlemen who have done him the Honour to deal with him, will testify that the Composition of his curious Metal is the same with his late Father's, and answers the Purpose in every Particular.

"Thirdly, To shew that Mr. Edward Pinchbeck's is the only true and valuable Metal, he promises, that whoever shall hencefor-

---

[1] See the *London Evening Post*, December 12, 1732.

wards purchase any of it, he will allow them 2s. 6d. per Ounce for it, after they have used it as long as they think proper." [1]

From the foregoing one gathers two remarkable facts, inserted as the advertisement obviously is by Edward Pinchbeck himself. These are that Christopher and not Edward was the eldest son; but that it was Edward by whom the discovery of the beautiful alloy was first made; and, further, that the first Christopher Pinchbeck's apparent favouritism of his second son in confiding to him the whole secret process was entirely owing, probably, to Edward having discovered the first principles applicable to the manufacture of the alloy.

Christopher *fils* died somewhere between 1783 and 1788, at his residence in Cockspur Street.

" By Mr. CHRISTIE,

On the Premises THIS DAY,

ALL the remaining STOCK in TRADE, models, pieces of machinery, particularly Winstanley's Perpetual Motion, improved; pictures, china, books, glass-cases, nests of drawers, tools, &c., &c., of the late

Mr. CHRISTOPHER PINCHBECK, deceased,

At his late Dwelling house, Cockspur Street, Charing Cross.

The whole to be sold without reserve, the present Possessor removing to Bond-Street, and the Premises must be cleared immediately.

To be viewed till the sale, which will begin at twelve o'clock. Catalogues may be had on the premises; the Rainbow Coffee-house, Cornhill; and in Pall Mall." [2]

Three doors from Pinchbeck's in Cockspur Street dwelt the celebrated conjurer, Breslaw, whose commodious house faced the lower end of the Haymarket. The old Cockspur Street rooms certainly were "commodious," for Breslaw describes the particular room in which he performed as "prepared with pit and boxes in the most elegant manner," and illuminated with wax candles. The charge for admission was five shillings and half-a-crown, and the programme comprised " new amazing performances with pocket-pieces, rings, sleeve-buttons, purses, snuff-boxes, swords, cards, hours,

---

[1] See the *London Evening Post*, October 6, 1733.
[2] The *Gazetteer and New Daily Advertiser*, February 26, 1788.

dice, letters, thoughts, numbers, watches, particularly with a leg of mutton."

Being at Canterbury on one occasion with his troupe, Breslaw met with such ill-success that they were almost starved. He repaired to the churchwardens, and promised to give the profits of a night's conjuration to the poor if the parish would pay for hiring a room, &c. The charitable bait took, the benefit proved a bumper, and next morning the churchwardens waited upon the wizard to touch the receipts. " I have already disposed of dem," said Breslaw. " De profits were for de poor. I have kept my promise and given de money to my own people, who are de poorest in dis parish ! " "Sir ! " exclaimed the churchwardens, "this is a trick ! " " I know it," replied Hocus Pocus ; " I live by my tricks." [1]

He met with defeat once, however, from an unexpected quarter. He was exhibiting a mimic swan, which floated on real water and followed his motions, when the bird suddenly became motionless. He approached it more closely, but the swan did not move.

" There is a person in the company," he said, " who understands the principle upon which this trick is performed, and who is counteracting me. I appeal to the company whether this is fair ; and I beg the gentleman will desist." [2]

The trick was performed by magnetism, and the counteracting agency was a magnet in the pocket of Sir Francis Blake Delaval. Cockspur Street was the scene of Breslaw's triumphs for nine successive seasons.

A famous firm of ecclesiastical artists at 25 Cockspur Street is that of Messrs. Hardman & Co. The massive brass gates under the south door of the Peers' Lobby, the chief approach to the House of Lords, are splendid specimens of intricate and masterly workmanship by Hardman, in weight 1½ ton, and are only equalled in beauty of design and workmanship by those to the tomb of Henry VII. in Westminster Abbey, of the fifteenth century. Surrounding the centre of the floor of the lobby is a very fine enamel, inlaid with brass by Hardman. The stained glass windows, representing the arms of the early families of the aristocracy of England, are also manufactured by Hardman, who is again responsible for the beautiful little medallions of Tennysonian subjects in the windows of the Queen's Robing Room.

---

[1] George Daniel's *Merrie England in the Olden Time*, 1881, p. 321.

[2] Thomas Frost's *Lives of the Conjurers*, 1881, pp. 129 *et seq.*, and *Notes and Queries*, 9th Series, viii. 228-9.

A wonderful piece of mechanism is exhibited over the Charing Cross wayfarer's head, if he would only look upwards exactly at 1 P.M. as he passes the famous clock and watch makers, Messrs. M. F. Dent & Co., at No. 34 Cockspur Street. This is their outside timeball; and viewing the automaton at the specified time, the passer-by should handle his watch and compare his time with that of the timeball, for that timeball represents the opinion on the matter of the Royal Greenwich Observatory, and is discharged downwards exactly at 1 P.M. every day by an electric current from the Observatory, where, at the same time, captains of vessels about to leave the river at Greenwich are afforded an opportunity to rate their chronometers by means of a similar contrivance. Messrs. Dent's timeball is 5 feet 4 inches in diameter, and 16 feet 9 inches in circumference. There is a smaller timeball in their shop which is discharged from Greenwich hourly, so that Greenwich mean time may be obtained at any hour.[1]

The timeball signal upon the roof of the Electric Telegraph Office, No. 448 Strand, at the corner of Adelaide Street, was considered an even more noteworthy sight for visitors to London than the Fleet Street clock-figures before they were removed by the Marquis of Hertford to his villa in the Regent's Park.

The signal consisted of a zinc ball six feet in diameter, supported by a rod, which passed down the centre of a column, and carried at the base a piston, which in its descent plunged into a cast-iron air-cylinder; the escape of the air being regulated so as at pleasure to check the momentum of the ball, and prevent concussion. The raising of the ball half-mast high took place daily at ten minutes to one o'clock; at five minutes to one it was raised to the full height; and at one precisely, and simultaneously with the fall of the timeball at Greenwich Observatory (by which, as it has been remarked, navigators correct their chronometers), it was liberated by the galvanic current sent from the Observatory, through a wire laid for that purpose. The same galvanic current which liberated the ball in the Strand moved a needle upon the transit-clock of the Observatory, the time occupied by the transition being about $\frac{1}{300}$th part of a second; and by the unloosing of the machinery which supported the ball, less than one-fifth part of a second. The

---

[1] The Greenwich timeball is raised half-mast high at five minutes before 1 P.M., at 2 minutes before 1 it is raised to the top, and it falls at 1 precisely. By this, time is also, at stated hours, sent by electricity to public offices, postal, telegraph, railway, and various other stations.

true moment of one o'clock was therefore indicated by the first appearance of the line of light between the dark cross over the ball and the body of the ball itself. There was a similar timeball on the roof of a clock-maker's in Cornhill.

In the Museum of the College of Surgeons, in Lincoln's Inn Fields, is preserved the skeleton of the Irish giant O'Byrne, who, in the flesh, was 8 feet 4 inches in height, but as an osteological curiosity measures only 8 feet. Four inches certainly seems a "tall" margin for the measurement in addition to his skeleton, from scalp to cushioned heel; but possibly he had a luxuriant head of hair. The following obituary notice of him occurs in the "Annual Register":

"In Cockspur Street, Charing Cross, aged only twenty-two, Mr. Charles Byrne, the famous Irish giant, whose death is said to have been precipitated by excessive drinking, to which he was always addicted, but more particularly since his loss of almost all his property, which he had simply invested in a single bank-note of £700.

.   .   .   .

"Neither his father, mother, brother, nor any other person of his family was of an extraordinary size."[1]

In what was formerly No. 58 Cockspur Street lived Mr. William Holland, the eminent publisher of caricatures, and a patron of Woodward, Rowlandson, Newton, Buck, and other artists. He was himself a man of genius, and wrote many popular songs, as well as a volume of poetry, besides being the author of the pointed and epigrammatic words which accompanied most of his caricatures. In 1793 he was imprisoned six months for selling a copy of Paine's "Letter to the Addressers." He died in 1815, a few minutes after coming out of the warm bath at the Hummums in Covent Garden.[2]

Smollett was in the habit of frequenting "a small tavern in the corner of Cockspur Street, called the Golden Ball," where he had a frugal supper and a little punch, as the finances of none of the company were in very good order. Dr. Carlyle was there with him when the news of the Battle of Culloden arrived, and relates the stratagems that they resorted to on leaving, lest they should be detected by the mob as Scotchmen, and roughly handled.[3]

[1] Vol. xxvi. (June 1783), p. 209.
[2] A newspaper excerpt without date.
[3] *Autobiography of Dr. Alexander Carlyle*, and the *Collector*, by Dr. Doran, p. 43.

The first station of the Phœnix Fire Office was in Cockspur Street. There are perspective views of it extant. The Company was established by the sugar-bakers of the metropolis in 1782 for insuring property at home and abroad from fire. It was probably so named because *phœnix* is the Greek name of the date from the juice of which sugar was prepared. There is a water-colour drawing of the original fire office in Cockspur Street in the Crace Collection of Prints and Drawings relating to London (portfolio xi. 129), and in an illustration in " Old and New London " flames and smoke appear in the distance, a cry of " Fire ! " is being raised, and passers-by are making a lane and stopping the traffic for the better passage of the engine as it issues from the portals of the fire station :

> The engines thundered through the street,
> Fire-hook, pipe, bucket, all complete ;
> And torches glared, and clattering feet
> 　　　　Along the pavement flew.
> The Hand-in-Hand the race begun,
> Then came the Phœnix and the Sun,
> The Exchange, where old insurers run,
> 　　　　The Eagle, where the new.

A curious, and I think a unique, trade-sign occurs in Cockspur Street—that of the " King of Clubs," in 1742, apparently the sign of a cardmaker.

" To be Sold by HAND.

This Day and To-morrow only,

THE entire Household Goods of Mr. John Bennett, Card-Maker, at the King of Clubs in Cockspur-Street, facing Suffolk-Street, near Charing Cross ; consisting of useful Furniture, China, Linnen, Leaden Cisterns, two Coppers, a Malt-Mill and Brewing Vessels, &c., likewise his Stock in Trade, as Presses, Copper-Plates, Stamps, and divers Utensils ; also a large Quantity of Pasteboard and Cartridge-Paper, some hundred Pieces of divers sorts of printed Paper Hangings for Rooms, at Three Halfpence a Yard, and the other Goods for Dispatch, at Great Loss. The House to be lett." [1]

Having omitted, in remarks about St. Martin's Lane, to mention the old firm of Bayley & Co., one did so under the impression that they were still at No. 17 Cockspur Street. But they removed to No. 94 St. Martin's Lane in 1896, where, no doubt, there is more scope for their wholesale trade. The antiquity of the business

---

[1] *Daily Advertiser*, February 4, 1742.

may be gauged by their having been established in Long Acre for some time before they went, in 1739, to Cockspur Street. The portrait of William Bayley, founder of the firm, was painted by Harlow, while the sign of the " Old Civet Cat," in oils, originally suspended over the door of the Long Acre shop, is attributed to Hogarth, an old crony of the founder, and a constant frequenter at No. 17 Cockspur Street. The curious may also see, in an old ledger, an account with the Prince Regent, afterwards George IV., who spent—though not necessarily all at Bayley's—£600 a year on perfumery alone. Towards the end of the eighteenth century the firm was known by the style of Bayley & Lowe. Mr. J. W. Harrison, of St. Martin's Lane, informs me that Dr. Golding, the founder of Charing Cross Hospital, married Miss Blew (? Lowe) of Bayley & Blew (? Bayley & Lowe). Messrs. Golding & Son were also perfumers in Cornhill, and at both places might be had the "True Essential Salt of Lemons, for removing Ink Spots, Iron Moulds, Stains, &c. . . . without injury even to the very finest laces."[1] Bayley & Lowe, or rather William Bayley, also produced " By the King's Patent . . . a most excellent shining liquid blacking, much superior to anything known; it gives the finest black, and most beautiful gloss to the leather, yet never renders it stiff or hard, but, on the contrary, prevents it cracking and preserves it soft and pliable to the very last, whereby it is rendered more agreeable to the wearer, as well as much more durable ; and the shoes that are blacked with it will neither soil the fingers in putting on, nor the stockings in wearing," etc., etc.[2]

Between the Haymarket Theatre and Cockspur Street, and opposite to the Opera House, Broughton, the champion of England, as he called himself, in the reign of George II. kept a public-house, with the sign of his own head, minus wig, as in the character of a bruiser. Underneath the sign was the line from Virgil (Æn. v. 484) :

Hic victor cæstus artemque repono.

Broughton's first patron was the Duke of Cumberland, who took him on the Continent, and showed him the Grenadier Guards at Berlin, all of whom Broughton expressed himself ready to fight.[3] The present outlet from Spring Gardens into Cockspur Street was

---

[1] *Morning Herald and Daily Advertiser*, December 15, 1783.
[2] *Ibid.* March 29, 1783.
[3] Wheatley's *Round About Piccadilly*, 1870, p. 112.

made familiar in the drawings of Morland and Stothard ; and when the latter had finished his painting of the Death of Lord Robert Manners, son of the Marquis of Granby, who was killed on his ship the " Resolution," in an engagement with the French in 1782, it was exhibited in Cockspur Street.

" Mr. Macklin begs leave to acquaint his Subscribers, and the Public in general, that the Picture of the Death of Lord Robert Manners, who so nobly fell, on board the ' Resolution,' on the 12th of April, 1782, in defence of his country, and painted by Mr. Stothard, being now finished, is exhibiting at Mr. Haynes's, the corner of Cockspur Street, facing the end of Pall Mall. The Proprietor thinks it unnecessary to say anything in praise of the performance, as he flatters himself the Picture, when seen, will sufficiently recommend itself. Every subscriber will have a Ticket for one admittance gratis, by applying to the Proprietor at his Print Shop, No. 39, Fleet Street. Admittance to non-subscribers one shilling each.

" The above Picture is an engraving by Mr. J. K. Sherwin, the size of General Wolfe ; and as the Proprietor is to pay the greatest price for the engraving ever given in this country to any artist for such a sized Plate, he flatters himself he shall be able to produce to the public a most excellent Print." [1]

[1] *Morning Herald and Daily Advertiser*, March 29, 1783.

CHAPTER XXVI.

THE "ALENTOURS" OF COCKSPUR STREET.

IN the open space between Cockspur Street and Pall Mall East is the equestrian statue of George III., by Matthew Cotes Wyatt. It is in bronze, and was erected in the year of the late Queen Victoria's accession to the throne. It is admired chiefly as affording a perfect likeness of the King. When it was cast in 1835 or 1836, permission was obtained for its erection on this triangular spot of waste ground. But some of the tenants of the adjacent houses, finding that in their leases it was covenanted that the open space should not be occupied, raised objections which were held valid by the then Vice-Chancellor, but were set aside on appeal to the Lord Chancellor.

Of this statue it is justly remarked that it may very reasonably be asked why a plain English gentleman should be represented in the dress of a Roman tribune? Let the man appear, even in a statue, in his habit as he lived, and, whatever we may say, posterity will be grateful to us. We should like to know exactly the ordinary walking dress of Cæsar or Brutus, and how they wore their hair; and we should not complain if they had cocked hats or periwigs, if we knew them to be exact copies of nature.[1]

Immediately behind the south-east corner of Cockspur Street, down the passage leading past Lord Fitzharris's house on the left into the Park, was Cox's Museum, afterwards Wigley's Auction Rooms. Its site, with that of the French chapel, was later occupied by the offices of the old Metropolitan Board of Works, and now by those of the London County Council.[2]

The famous Katterfelto, who was the son of a Prussian colonel of Hussars, made his bow to a London audience in the spring of 1781, at Cox's Museum, Spring Gardens. Katterfelto was the first of his

[1] J. T. Smith's *Streets of London*, 1849, p. 62.
[2] There is an exhaustive account of Cox's and similar museums in Mr. G. L. Apperson's *Bygone London Life*.

U 2

profession of conjuring, since the time of Faust and Agrippa, to give a philosophical character to his entertainments, and to avail himself of the resources afforded by science for the purpose of illusion. But in 1782 he removed to 22 Piccadilly, alleging that there was not enough light in Spring Gardens for the exhibition of his great solar microscope.[1]

It was in the "Great Room" appertaining evidently to Wigley's house that the Society of Artists of Great Britain held their famous exhibition, for which Hogarth illustrated a catalogue, with a compliment to the young King and a caricature of rich connoisseurs. In 1766 was issued a "Catalogue of Pictures, Sculptures, Designs in Architecture, Models, Drawings, Prints, &c., exhibited by the Society of Artists of Great Britain at the Great Room, Spring Gardens." The Society had its origin in the meetings of certain artists, in 1753, at the Turk's Head, Gerrard Street, Soho.

The two "milkmaids," Mrs. Kitchen and Miss Burry, who so picturesquely maintained, until February 1905, the time-honoured traditions of Milk Fair in St. James's Park, immediately behind Cockspur Street, received, I believe, a hint from the matter-of-fact Office of Works that they must not look upon the spot occupied by their anything but pretty kiosk just within the Park railings, and immediately opposite the Horse Guards, in the light of freehold. They received due compensation for their inevitable loss, and the processional road has already overtaken the two gigantic elms, the railings that surrounded their "pitch," and the cows that pretended they were enjoying rural surroundings. However, we, the public, also have our compensation in George Morland's picture, linking the days of the Stuarts with our own, and showing the milk-stall as it was probably soon after the owners' squatting rights were ratified by Charles II.—some say by James I. For two and a half centuries, at all events, milk warm from the cow has been dispensed by the two old ladies' ancestors on the same spot. Latterly the number of cows had been reduced in 1901 from six to two. The spot, however, from which they have just been evicted was not the original one, and the late Queen Victoria in 1885 (as well as his present Majesty King Edward later) intervened on a similar occasion when there were more than two stall-keepers, and when the cows were more numerous. This pasturage for the cows extended further Whitehall way, although they were tethered to posts, and towards evening

---

[1] See further Thos. Frost's *Lives of the Conjurors*, 1881, p. 135 *et seq.*

the lowing herd wound slowly towards "the gate which leads from the Park to the corner of Whitehall." [1]

Sir Richard Phillips, in his "Morning's Walk from London to Kew," 1820, p. 5, says that "the privilege of keeping these cows and of selling their milk on this spot belongs to the gate-keepers of the Park; and it must be acknowledged to be a great convenience to invalids and children."

Warwick Street, lying *perdu* behind Cockspur Street, would, if all were known, vouchsafe a long series of historic incidents. The rate-books of its parish of St. Martin show that it was built about the year 1681, having been named to commemorate Warwick House,[2] the suburban retreat of Sir Philip Warwick, member for Westminster, after the Restoration, and author of the interesting "Memoirs of King Charles the First." [3] Here dwelt the Dowager Duchess of Shrewsbury,[4] widow of the twelfth Earl, whose father was killed in the atrocious duel with the second Villiers, Duke of Buckingham, while the dreadful Countess of Shrewsbury held her paramour's horse. Warwick House was at the west end of the street, and was inhabited for a time by the Princess Charlotte with a small household, the lamented Princess being thus near the residence of her father, the Prince of Wales, at Carlton House. From Warwick House, "wearied out by a series of acts all proceeding from the spirit of petty tyranny, and each more vexatious than another, though none of them very important in itself," she made her escape in a hackney-coach, on July 16, 1814, to the house of her mother in Connaught Place.[5] On a fine evening in July, about the hour of seven, when the streets were deserted by all persons "of condition," she rushed out of her residence in Warwick House un-

---

[1] *A Tour to London*, 1772. They were probably, therefore, driven through New Street to the exit which was at the corner where Drummond's Bank stands. See "Old London Refreshment Places," in the *Leisure Hour*, November 1885.

[2] Demolished when the offices of the Metropolitan Board of Works were built.

[3] Concerning Sir Philip Warwick see also Marvell's *Letters* xiii. and xiv.

[4] The *Stranger's Guide to London*, 1721.

[5] "All the London world was startled by hearing that the Princess Charlotte had left Warwick House unobserved, and gone off in a hackney-coach to the Princess of Wales in Connaught Place. The cause of this sudden and unaccountable proceeding has never transpired to the world at large. That it was perfectly unexpected and unwished for by the Princess of Wales there seems to be lit le doubt. The Duke of York, the Duke of Sussex, Lord Eldon, and Mr. Brougham all repaired to Connaught Place, and after several hours of discussion the Princess Charlotte returned to Warwick House" (The Countess Brownlow's *Slight Reminiscences of a Septuagenarian*, 1868, pp. 112-3).

attended, hastily crossed Cockspur Street, flung herself into the first hackney-coach she could find, and drove to her mother's house. The Princess of Wales having gone to pass the day at her Blackheath villa, a messenger was despatched for her, another for her law adviser, Mr. Brougham, and a third for Miss Mercer Elphinstone, the young Princess's bosom friend. He arrived before the Princess of Wales had returned, and Miss Mercer Elphinstone had alone obeyed the summons. Soon after the royal mother came, accompanied by Lady Charlotte Lindsay, her lady-in-waiting. It was found that the Princess Charlotte's fixed resolution was to leave her father's house, and that which he had appointed for her residence, and to live thenceforth with her mother. But Mr. Brougham is understood to have felt himself under the painful necessity of explaining to her that by the law, as all the twelve judges but one had laid it down in George I.'s reign, and as it was now admitted to be settled, the King or the Regent had the absolute power to dispose of the persons of all the Royal Family while under age. . . . As soon as the flight of the young lady was ascertained, and the place of her retreat discovered, the Regent's officers of state and other functionaries were despatched after her. The Lord Chancellor Eldon first arrived, but not in any particularly imposing state, "regard being had" to his eminent station ; for, indeed, he came in a hackney-coach. Whether it was that the example of the Princess Charlotte herself had for the day brought this simple and economical mode of conveyance into fashion, or that concealment was much studied, or that dispatch was deemed more essential than pomp and ceremony—certain it is that all who came, including the Duke of York, arrived in similar vehicles, and that some remained enclosed in them, without entering the royal mansion. At length, after much pains and many entreaties used by the Duke of Sussex and the Princess of Wales herself, as well as Miss Mercer Elphinstone and Lady Charlotte Lindsay (whom she always honoured with a just regard), to enforce the advice given by Mr. Brougham that she should return without delay to her own residence and submit to the Regent, the young Princess, accompanied by the Duke of York and her governess, who had now been sent for, and arrived in a royal carriage, returned to Warwick House, between four and five o'clock in the morning.[1]

It is to be hoped that the extremely interesting painted signboard, about four feet by three, of the "Two Chairmen," preserved

---

[1] Lord Brougham, quoted by Cunningham.

on the premises of the tavern with that sign at No. 1 Warwick Street, will find a home, eventually, in the City Museum, for it is evidently a painting almost contemporary with the introduction of the sedan-chair. At all events, it appears to date from the time of Charles II., to judge from the costume of the chairmen and the royal monogram ƆC, two C's interlocked, surmounted by a royal crown, which adorns the panel of the door of the chair.

There was a court leading immediately from the east end of Warwick Street into St. James's Park, called White Horse Court, in 1755. The Red Lion inn stood at the entrance to another court, also leading into St. James's Park, but further east ; and next came "Mearmaid" Court, opposite to the Mews. Then came, in the order given, Pump Court, doubtless named after the pump which stood by the statue (in Pump Court was "one of the Six Offices whence Country Letters and Parcels were, in 1721, conveyed daily to the environs of London" ; it was called the Westminster Office "in Pump Court, near Charing Cross " : "The Stranger's Guide," by W. Stow, 1721, p. 134); Stanhope Court; then Buckingham Court.[1] At the western end of Warwick Street was Stonecutter's Alley, "overagainst St. Alban's Street . . . which leads to the back gate of the King's garden, for the conveniency of Mr. George London, her late Majesty's principal gardener, there inhabiting in a neat and pleasant house." [2]

[1] Strype's *Stow* (Map), 1755.
[2] *Ibid.* book vi. p. 81.

CHAPTER XXVII.

WHITCOMB STREET.

THE hedgerows which gave their earlier name of Hedge Lane to Whitcomb Street, a narrow thoroughfare leading from Pall Mall East to Coventry Street, are shown in Aggas's "Elizabethan Map of London." It was at the bottom of this lane (where, in December 1821, some interesting ruins were discovered, appertaining, it was thought, to the Royal Mews burnt in 1534),[1] that Sir Richard Steele, Eustace Budgell (a relative of Addison), and Ambrose Phillips the poet (Namby-Pamby), all contributors to the "Spectator," on coming out of a tavern, were about to take their course up the lane when somebody told them that some very suspicious-looking fellows were standing at the bottom as if in wait. "Thankye," exclaimed the wits ; and, without waiting for further parley, each cast an alarmed glance behind him, parted company with his fellows, and hurried away as fast as his legs would carry him. Before he removed to Monmouth House, Soho, the Duke of Monmouth had a house in Hedge Lane, in the later years of Charles II.'s reign.

Mauritius Lowe, the painter, reputed to have been a son of the Earl of Sunderland, from whom he had a small annuity, lived for some time in Hedge Lane. Madame d'Arblay, in her "Diary," describes Dr. Johnson's efforts to obtain work as a portrait painter for Lowe, and the state of filth and misery to which Lowe and his family were reduced.[2] Lowe was a pupil of Cipriani, who also lived in the lane. He was born in 1746, and died in 1793. Here too dwelt Joseph Wilton, R.A., the sculptor who executed the monument of General Wolfe in Westminster Abbey. He was born in 1722, and died November 25, 1803. Joshua Marshall, who executed, but did not design, the pedestal of the King Charles statue at Charing Cross, had his workshops in Hedge Lane.

---

[1] There is a plan of the neighbourhood where these ruins were discovered, in the Crace Collection, portfolio xi. 135.

[2] *Diary*, ii. 41.

At No. 48 Whitcomb Street is a tavern with the interesting old sign of the "Hand and Racket," *i.e.* the racket used in court tennis as distinguished from the modern lawn tennis. The sign is unique in London, and, without doubt, had its origin in being contiguous to the Royal Tennis Court, on the south side of James Street, which was one of the favourite haunts of Charles II., when perchance he tired of Paille Maille. It was not closed until 1863, when the building was converted into a storehouse for military clothing. The site is now occupied by Messrs. Simpkin, Marshall, the publishers, outside whose premises is the legend :

"This Building, formerly known as the Royal Tennis Court, Rebuilt A.D. 1887." At the corner of the street is another and older stone tablet : "James St. 1673." Says Stow, "James Street comes out of the Haymarket and falleth into Hedge Lane, of chief note for its Tennis Court, which takes up the south side of the street ; the north side being but ordinarily inhabited." [1]

Fawkes, the famous conjurer, whose show and paraphernalia passed at his death into the hands of his son and his late partner Pinchbeck, exhibited "at his Theatre in James-street, near the Haymarket," in 1729, "his surprizing and incomparable Dexterity of Hand." And here he exhibited the ingenious flower-trick of the Indian conjurers, reproduced nearly a century and a half later by Stodare, and more recently by Dr. Lynn at the Egyptian Hall. Fawkes died in 1732. [2]

The following amusing handbill, probably of the middle of the eighteenth century, is a curiosity preserved in Mr. Mason's valuable "St. Martin's Scrap Book " :

"The delight of the humorous ; come then, my friend, my genius, come along,

AT THE

OLD THEATRICAL SHEW-SHOP, JAMES-STREET, HAY-MARKET.

A little after Owl-light the Game will begin. First a dish of capers on the Tight Rope, by the Master Lawrences, and some celebrated in that art.

By MR. PUNCH and his Queer Company, will be performed

The Wife Well
Managed, or a cure for CUCKELDOM

---

[1] Book vi. p. 68.   [2] Thos. Frost's *Lives of the Conjurors*, 1881, p. 118.

Secondly, Singing by several clear and good pipes, after the manner of the Moderns, as the antient Method is quite exploded.

Thirdly, Several new balances on the Slack Wire by Mr. Lawrence, who will toss the straw from head to foot to heel; and so to all parts of his body, till it falls on the terrestial globe.

Fourthly, By a Company of FANCY TICKLERS—some with heads right—and some with heels light. The first of this class will perform a new piece, called

TRUE BLUE, or THE PRESSGANG.

If any one should be moved to tears, they are desired to withdraw.

By the second, will be some Tumbling, a-la-mode a flip-flap, with such agility that their right ends cannot be distinguished from the wrong. The Master Lawrences exhibit the most amazing Somerset Pieces, in quite a different manner to what has been seen on any Stage in England; they likewise perform the Italian Table Tricks, without spring-boards or tramplings, &c.

A HORNPIPE in taste, by Master LAWRENCE, seven years of age, who will accompany himself on the Violin.

Here will be given a Pantomine called

HARLEQUIN Every Where,

Harlequin by Don PARSLOE,
Furiosa, by DIAGOBABINETTO,
Don Crackemaralio, Signor PRESTO JEAN,
Don Arboebco, by CRACOMAROPO,
Vamponini, by Don VAMPO,
Columbine, by Donna LARIONE,
Clodpate the Clown, by Don JEFFERIES.
Attendents, by Donna Collingham, Miss Twine, Miss Twist, and
Madam Lightfoot from Italy.

First and highest seats, 3d. Second or Middle Gallery, 4d. Third or Pit, 6d. Fourth or Boes (?), 1s. Laugh where we must, be candid where we can. We shall begin at seven, or exactly as the curtain is drawn up, and no money returned that is fit to keep. The what we call a Theatre to be illuminated with lights, and the whole to conclude with being ended.

The candles to be snuffed in the French taste, by a Gentleman for his own diversion. The clothes and scenes are entirely old and worn out, so that nobody can be admitted behind them for fear of making them worse."

In 1742 the Tennis Court buildings appear from an advertisement of that year to have been used for exhibition purposes :

" To all Lovers of Art in Mechanism and Engineering.

At the Theatre in James Street, near the Hay-Market, are to be seen several curious Pieces of Engine-Work, &c., as two Models for draining Mines, Fen-Lands, or Water-Works of any other kind ; the one by a Windmill for that Purpose particular made, with many curious Improvements thereto ; the other by a Wheel, either to be work'd by Men or Horses, in such a Manner as is not at this time in any other, and will perform one-third more Work than any other Wheel now used ; and is capable of draining any Mine, let its Situation be where it will, tho' left off as unworkable by other Machines. There is also a curious Model of a Machine for weighing Waggons of any Burthen whatsoever, without taking off even the Thill-Horse, or retarding the said Waggon more than one Minute. With several other Things very curious, as several Plans, setting forth the Nature, Soil, and Ore of Mines, Fen-Lands, and other places ; all which will be explain'd in a Lecture, wherein the Theory and Practical Parts of Mechanicks will be set forth, and I doubt not will give a general Satisfaction to all Spectators, as well artists as others.

The whole to be shewn at the said Theatre this day, at Eleven o'clock in the Morning, and Seven in the Evening, and so continue during the whole Week ; by

HUGH ROBERTS.
Engineer

Boxes 1s. 6d.   Pit 6d."

The Old White Horse, at No. 51 Whitcomb Street, was a "recruiting house" so early at least as 1794, in which year " Edward Barrat, a mariner, had been ill-treated, and was saved this evening from destruction by the intervention of the military." [1] The tavern rebuilt is still standing.

It was at the Cannon Coffee-house, upon the site of which now stands the Union Club house, that Hackman saw Miss Ray drive past on her way to Covent Garden Theatre, where it is said that she went to sing in " Love in a Village," when he followed and shot her as she was entering her coach after the performance. The Cannon Coffee-house was the last house in Whitcomb Street.

---

[1] *Gentleman's Magazine*, Tuesday, August 19, 1794.

It is not clear when St. Martin's Street, leading from the centre of the south side of Leicester Square into Whitcomb Street, was built. But its existence is certainly remarkable if only for the fact of No. 35, next door to the entrance to Orange Street Chapel, having been the last town residence of the greatest master of the exact sciences that ever existed, Sir Isaac Newton. The last two years of his life were spent at Bullingham House, Pitt Street, Kensington, but this was of course a suburban rather than a town residence. As a memorial tablet outside the St. Martin's Street house indicates, the philosopher dwelt there from 1710 to 1725, two years before his death in the Old Court Suburb. In 1889, possibly it is so still, the house was occupied as the Warrant Officers' Club, but the old red brick had, since 1849, been covered with stucco. In 1709, the year before Newton became its occupier, it was inhabited by the Envoy of Denmark. The observatory built by Sir Isaac at the top of the house, after being used for some years as a Sunday-school, was taken away about the year 1869, and sold to supply some pews for the adjoining chapel. Newton used to say that the happiest years of his life went spent in this observatory. Until 1824 it was kept up for the inspection of the curious, and was visited by thousands.[1] It is narrated of Sir Isaac Newton—with what truth, or whether, if true, it occurred at 35 St. Martin's Street, one cannot say—that his intimate friend Dr. Stukeley, having called and been shown into the dining-room where Sir Isaac's dinner awaited him, got tired of waiting, and, being hungry, consumed a chicken alone, replacing the bones on the dish. Sir Isaac presently entered and sat down, but on taking off the cover, and seeing nothing but the bones, said : " How absent we philosophers are! I really thought that I had not dined." Newton's kinswoman, the "famous witty Miss Barton" of the " Gentleman's Magazine," according to Mr. Austin Dobson,[2] dwelt here, but whether this was while she was " super-intendant of his domestic affairs " to Charles, Earl of Halifax, is not quite apparent. In August 1717 Catherine Barton married John Conduitt, M.P., Newton's successor as Master of the Mint, and when in town continued to reside with her husband under Newton's roof. The house was subsequently tenanted by Dr. Burney when writing his " History of Music," and here Fanny Burney wrote " Evelina,"

---

[1] *Memorable London Houses*, by Wilmot Harrison, p. 4 ; and Sir David Brewster's *Life of Newton*.

[2] See further *Eighteenth Century Vignettes*, 1st Series, 1897, pp. 277–279.

described as "the first realistic novel by a woman in which characters are sketched with vigour and fidelity."

William Bewly, "the philosopher of Massingham," died here during a visit to his friend Dr. Burney. Mr. Thrale, writing to Miss Burney, styles the inmates of the house in St. Martin's Street "dear Newtonians." [1]

[1] Timbs's *Curiosities of London*, 1868, p. 514.

APPENDIX

A SINGULAR record of the ordinary conversation in a reputable tavern, nine years after the accession of the House of Hanover to the English throne, when ominous talk of Jacobite conspiracy filled the air, when the "club," sometimes synonymous for "secret society," was still in its incipiency, occurs in the "Weekly Journal" of October 19, 1723. The conversation by no means has the look of fiction, and, apart from the sketches which we have of the coffee-house life of Pope and his contemporaries, it enables us to form a probably unique conception of the manners and conversation prevailing among the better-class tavern and coffee-house visitors. Addison's observant, if not his literary, style is suggested by the writer, who thus unburthens himself :

" Not long since, I accidentally fell into Company where I was so well diverted, that I could not forbear committing the Conversation to Writing, in hopes it may give the same Amusement to my Readers.

" It is an old Remark, that the Discourse amongst *Englishmen* generally begins upon the Weather, so it happen'd in the Company of which I am speaking, but even in this, Men differ in their Opinions, for while some were praising the Beauties of the Season, a Country Gentleman, with a florid Countenance, whose frank and hospitable Humour appear'd in his Looks, objected, that thro' the extream Dryness of the Season, the Scent would not lye, so that there was no Sporting worth a Farthing : A Yeoman of *Kent*, who was also of the Company, shook his Head, and said, *It was a very bad Season, for they wanted Rain in the Country for their ploughing.*

" Thus, without being able to settle the Weather to our common liking, we pass'd to other Subjects, and what seem'd naturally to occur, was, concerning the new Distempers, which have so universally visited both Town and Country of late ; viz. the Vomiting, Looseness, and Gripes ; one thought they might be occasioned by eating of Oysters, according to the Opinion which some time since prevail'd ;

others attributed the Cause to the excessive devouring of Fruit, which has abounded in greater Plenty this Season than many Years past ; the Yeoman was against this last Opinion, for he had sold fifty Maunds [1] of Kentish Pippins that Morning, and had as many more to sell ; therefore he maintain'd that good Fruit never did any Harm, especially if People did but observe to have a Dram after it ; and it could not proceed from eating of oysters, for he had seen the contrary in Print. [2]

" A young Physician, who was leaning with both Hands upon an Ivory-headed Cane, and teaching his Shoulders to stoop to the Weight of a heavy Head, in affectation of Wisdom and old Age, said, ' Upon my Word, Gentlemen, the late Distemper, which the Learned call a *Diarrhœa*, was neither owing to the eating of Oysters or of Apples, but proceeded from the circumambient Air which was impregnated with saline Particles of a pestiferous Nature, exhaled by the Sun from sweaty Heads, and putrified Mushrooms, which by the continued Dryness of the Season, being condens'd into a kind of *Sal Volatile*, penetrated the *Tunicles* of the *Oesophagus*, and *Intestines*, and caused those unnatural Stimulations.'

" The Country Gentleman said, ' He did not understand *Hebrew*, but in plain *English*, that he differ'd from them all, and declared, it was his Opinion, that all this Vomiting, Looseness, &c., was occasioned by taking the Oaths.'

" This excited a Laugh, and the Physician desired to know what grounds he had for his Opinion ; his Answer was, ' He observ'd it began exactly at the Meeting of the Quarter Sessions,[3] and you all know,' added he, ' what a Pickle we've been in ever since.'

---

[1] Baskets :—

> " Behold for us the naked graces stay
> With maunds of roses for to strew the way."
>
> (*Herrick's Poems*, p. 308).

[2] In 1723, the year to which the above conversation relates, the following enormous mortalities occurred in three successive weeks in London alone :

Week ending	Griping in the guts	Convulsions	All deaths	Births
Sept. 3	23	308	761	396
,, 10	32	251	705	339
,, 17	33	262	768	390

(*History of Epidemics in Britain*, by Charles Creighton, M.A., M.D., 1904, vol. ii., p. 755).

[3] Probably, then as now, one of the four times of sitting was in the first week after October 11, although it was not till 1830 that quarter sessions of the peace were definitely appointed to be held in the first week after October 11, December 28, March 31, and June 24.

" A grave-looking Gentleman in a stiff Band and broad Hat, who sat over against him, look'd stedfastly in his Face, and, shaking his Head, cried out, 'Poor Soul! poor Soul! how thy weak Pastors misguide thee! Wouldst thou hearken to the Truth and Holiness of our Teachers, thou wouldst know that this Opinion was all Vanity, yea, that it was the Vanity of Vanities, and that it was the Foolishness of Folly to believe it.'

" 'Why, old *Testimony* (replies the Country Gentleman), what in thy most sanctified Opinion might be the Cause of it?' The Gentleman with the grave Looks answer'd, 'That all true Protestants were satisfied that it proceeded from the late horrid Conspiracy.' This raised a second Laugh, and the Yeoman of *Kent* ask'd him, 'If he was sure of it?' He answered ' He would not say it for the World if it was not true, for he never told a Lye in his Life.' 'Well,' says the Country Gentleman, 'I never knew a Presbyterian without a Plot, they are as inseparable as the Flesh and the Spirit. I suppose you found this out by the Light of some Revelation; I believe thou art one of those Fellows that dream of strange Things when you are drunk, and when you are sober, run about to snuffle them out for Prophecies; we shall never be at Rest whilst such canting Knaves are suffer'd to go unpunish'd; heark 'e, Sirrah, I tell you one Secret, *If there were no Presbyterians, there wou'd be no Plots.*'

" 'Friend, I value not thy Slanders,' reply'd the other; 'thou dost revile me because I am a Protestant.' 'You a Protestant!' answered the 'Squire, ' a canting Fanatick, pretend to be a Protestant! If you call your self a Protestant before me I'll break your Head!'

" 'Friend, I perceive thou art a Jacobite; nay, I suspect, thou art a Papist; hast thou taken the Oaths to the Government?' The other answer'd with Passion, that by G —— he never took an Oath in his Life and never wou'd.

" Finding the Country Gentleman grew hot, we thought it best to divert the Subject, least he should be provok'd to strike the other, who would be glad of an Opportunity of plaguing him with a vexatious Law Suit; therefore I ask'd him, what he thought of a Project of a certain Gentleman, who had form'd a Scheme for raising Money by laying a Tax upon Oaths, that this would be a great Ease to the Subject; for if his Notion concerning the Occasion of our late Distemper was true, it would prevent *Vomiting* and *Profaneness*; and not only so, but take off from the People the Charge of maintaining the Army; for if this Project should take Effect, the Army wou'd, in a great Measure, be oblig'd to maintain itself ; for a Captain,[1] in a quarter of an Hour, would swear off a Month's Pay, and the Sub-alterns and common Soldiers a great deal more. He rapt out an Oath, and said it was an excellent Design, for he observ'd, the Country swarm'd with Officers and Soldiers,[2] and he did not know what they were good for, except for destroying the Game.

"The old Fellow lifted up his Eyes at hearing the Gentleman swear, cried out ' *Profane! Profane!* ' and muttered many short Sentences concerning Anti-Christ, and the Whore of *Babylon*. While he was in the Midst of his *Soliloqui*, the Country Gentleman spoke softly, and ask'd me, if this was not L—— the Evidence, to which I answered in the Negative, and told him, he need not be afraid. ' Nay, as to that Matter,' answer'd he, ' I never in my Life was afraid of any Thing a Whig could do, except his swearing me into a Plot.'

" He had no sooner said that Word, but we heard the Flourish of a Fiddle at the Door of the Room in which we sat ; having open'd it, a poor Girl led in an old blind Man, who ask'd us if we would be entertain'd with Musick ; the old Gentleman, without giving us Time to answer, immediately began to examine what Parish the poor Man belong'd to, and whether he did not receive Alms from the said Parish, to which Question he gave him satisfactory Answers, and assured him, he never receiv'd Alms from any Parish in his Life, but that he gain'd his Bread by his Fiddle.[3] The other call'd him

---

[1] The allusion is probably to the ' Cock & Bottle captain ' of the time, a vicious production of the army with the character generally of a bully, who, at the beginning and middle of the 18th century, infested the taverns and ale-houses, and whose avocation consisted in thrashing bailiffs, bullying timorous persons, and doing other such exploits for hire. See *A Trip through the Town* (Lond., 1735).

[2] About this time a great increase was effected in the standing army, and soldiers were clad in a regular national uniform.

[3] Harpers, fiddlers, and other tavern musicians moved westward with the fashions of those whom they entertained. Harpers were common at the best taverns. In one of Tom Brown's *Letters from the Dead to the Living* (Works, vol. ii. p. 191), the writer alludes to " Honest John Nichols, the harper," who appears from Ned Ward's "Satyrical Reflections on Clubs," quoted in Kitson's *Ancient Songs*, ed. 1829, p. lviii, to have fixed his quarters at the " Still " in the Strand. This was between 1700 and 1731. Later the harp is seen in Hogarth's third print of the Rake's Progress, behind the door at the Rose tavern in Brydges Street :

" This is to give Notice to all Gentlemen and others, THAT Mr. JONES, the Harper, who play'd for seventeen Years and upwards at the Old Hercules Pillars

.

Vagabond and idle Fellow, and was for sending for a Constable to send him before a certain Justice of Peace, whom he call'd an upright Magistrate, the same that was the Terror of Butchers and Poulterers, who presum'd to sell such Things of a *Sunday* Morning as would not keep till *Monday*; and he was for having the poor Fellow sent to Bridewell, for being blind, for that was all that he could lay to his Charge; but having diverted his Zeal against this Piece of Severity, we represented the poor Man to him as an Object of Charity; then indeed he preached a Sermon to him against *Musick* and *Popery*, but would not give him a Farthing.

"The poor Fellow finding nothing coming, turn'd towards us, and ask'd if we would have a Tune, the Squire answered He lik'd no Musick but the Cry of a good Pack of Hounds on a frosty Morning; however, as he was a poor Man, he gave him a Shilling towards his Daughter's Portion, as he call'd it, and bid him go mind his Business.

"Then looking at his Watch, he call'd to pay, for it was near the Hour, at which a Club he belong'd to, usually met; he ask'd me to go with him, assuring me they were all honest Gentlemen, and that no Presbyterian was ever admitted amongst them, except once, when a Merchant of the City, a member of the Club, brought in two *Jews*, for which he would have been expell'd if he had not begg'd Pardon of the whole Company."[1]

P. 2.

Perhaps George Peele in his "King Edward the First" is responsible for the *chère reine* illusion, when in 1593 he writes:

Let Spanish steeds, as swift as fleeting wind,
Convey these princes to their funeral:

---

in Fleet Street, is now remov'd to the Trumpet in Sheer-Lane, Temple Bar, where all due attendance will be given by
Your most obedient humble Servant to command,
THOMAS EACH."
(*Daily Advert.*, March 5, 1742).

Judging from the company's opinion and treatment of the poor fiddler, the harper was a cut above the fiddler, as to tavern reputation at all events, in the middle of the 18th century. "Fiddlers' news," "Fiddlers' money," and "Fiddlers' fare" (or pay), were all contemptuous phrases which we do not find applied to the harper.

Miss.— "Did your ladyship play?"
Lady Sm.— "Yes, and won; so I came off with fiddlers' fare; meat, drink and money."
(Swift: *Polite Conv.*, iii.)

[1] The *Weekly Journal*, October 19, 1723.

Before them let a hundred mourners ride.
In every time of their enforc'd abode,
Rear up a cross in token of their worth,
    Whereon fair Elinor's picture shall be plac'd.
Arrived at London, near our palace-grounds,
Inter my lovely Elinor, late deceas'd ;
And in remembrance of her royalty,
Erect a rich and stately carvèd cross,
    Whereon her stature shall with glory shine,
And henceforth see you call it Charing Cross ;
For why the chariest and the choicest queen
That ever did delight my royal eyes,
    There dwells in darkness.

P. 4.

St. James's leper-house was of ancient date and provided for fourteen female patients, who came somehow to be called the *leprosæ puellæ* (Rotuli Chartarum, 1199–1216—Charter of Confirmation, 1204—5 Joh. p. 117[b]), although youth is by no means specially associated with leprosy. This house grew rich, and supported eight brethren for the religious services of the sixteen patients. In the *Valor Ecclesiasticus* of Henry VIII. its revenue is put at £100.— *A Hist. of Epidemics in Britain, from* A.D. 664 *to the Extinction of the Plague*, by Charles Creighton, M.A., M.D., 1891, vol. i., p. 88–9.

P. 7.

A "skinker" was a "wine-bibber" as well as a wine-drawer at a tavern :

"Awake, thou noblest drunkard Bacchus,—teach me, thou sovereign skinker."—Decker's *Gull's Hornbook*, p. 26.

To "skink," literally, is to serve out wine from a pipe, probably in contradistinction to the duties of a tapster. It is from the Anglo-Saxon *scencan*, to pour out ; originally to draw off through a pipe. Anglo-Saxon *scanc*, a shank, shank-bone, hollow-bone (hence, a pipe). So also Dutch, *schenken* ; Icelandic, *skenkja* ; Danish, *skienke*; German, *schenken*, to skink.—Skeat : *Etymol. Dict.*

A "tappestere" was a female tapster. In olden times the retailers of beer, and for the most part the brewers also, appear to have been females. The *-stere* or *-ster* as a feminine affix (though in the fourteenth century it is not always or regularly used as such) occurs in Middle English *brewstere*, *webbestere* ; English, spinster. See Skeat's "Principles of Etymology," part 1, §238. *Cf. beggestere*, a female beggar. The friar in the Prologue to the Canterbury Tales :

    Knew . . . everich hostiler and tappestere
    Bet than a lazar or a beggestere.

P. 10.

It appears, from the first rate-books, made in the reign of Elizabeth, that the chief parishioners at that time resided either in the Strand, by the waterside, or close to the church. "Close to the church" is, however, somewhat vague.

P. 19.

In 1876 there was skating on the Thames on "real ice." But the ice, though real, was artificially made, and the skating was "by special permission of the Metropolitan Board of Works," at the Floating Swimming Bath at Charing Cross, which had been turned into a "Glaciarium" on Mr. John Gamgee's system. Spectators One Shilling, Skaters Two Shillings; Tuesday, Thursday, and Saturday afternoons from 2 to 4, Five Shillings, Spectators Two-and-Sixpence, Skates Sixpence.—Handbill in *St. Martin's Scrap Book.*

Pp. 23 and 168.

The name of the Living Colossus from Sweden was, according to a handbill of 1742, in the "St. Martin's Scrap Book," Daniel Cajanus —"near a Foot taller than the late famous Saxon, or any Person ever yet seen in Europe."

P. 32.

At the "Royal Great Rooms," Spring Gardens, Charing Cross, was a "Fashionable Promenade" where there was an Exhibition of Music, by Mechanical Power, called the "Panharmonicon," invented by Mr. Gurk of Vienna. This Panharmonicon consisted of two hundred instruments : viz. French Horns, Trumpets, Kettle-drums, Oboes, Clarinets, Bassoons, Cymbals, Triangles, Great Drum, Bells, and German Flutes, "performing the most select Pieces of Military Music, composed by Mozart, Haydn, Krommer, &c."

During the week to which a handbill in the "St. Martin's Scrap Book" appertains, there were performed :

1. Overture of Clemenza di Tito . . . *Mozart.*
2. Allegretto of the Military Symphony by . *Haydn.*
3. Hunting Piece, with an Imitation of a Thunderstorm, composed for the Pan-harmonicon . . . . . *Fr. Starke.*
4. Ronda, composed for the Instrument by . *Andr. Romberg.*
5. Three Marches, viz. 1st, March of the

Vienna Volunteers; 2nd, March of the
Vienna Grenadiers with Drum solo ;
3rd, Cavalry March with a Trio ; the
whole as performed on the Vienna
Parade . . . . . . *Fr. Starke.*
6. National Waltzes of Vienna . . . *Pechatschek.*
{ Rule Britannia.
{ Prince Regent's Favourite March, by . . *Logier.*
7. { Duke of Gloucester's Volunteer quick Step,
{ composed and arranged for the Pan-
{ harmonicon by . . . . . *Purkis.*
8. God Save the King, with Variations . . *Logier.*
N.B.—The Music is just published for the Piano Forte.

Topping, Printer, Blackfriars, London.

" On Saturday sen'night, at his house, in New-street, Spring
Gardens, (died) John Waxsdale, M.D., aged 76, formerly of Carlisle.
At the coronation of our present sovereign he went from Carlisle to
London, in 28 hours, upon horseback, was present at the ceremony,
and returned there again in 30 hours, after an absence of five nights,
three of which he slept in London. . . . He held the honorary
office of Private Secretary to his Grace the Duke of Norfolk, which
he discharged with the greatest punctuality and honour."—The
Globe, June 20, 1807.

Pp. 40–41.

" There is another Set of Gamblers, commonly called Duffers,
who attend at Charing Cross . . . and invite you to go down some
Alley, and buy some cheap *India* Handkerchiefs and Waistcoats ;
but this Cheat growing stale, they use another Method. . . . They
apply themselves to some young Publican to borrow 20 or 30*l.* to
make up a Sum ; and to shew they do not want Money in general,
they produce a large Purse well crammed with Counters and Brass
Medals, which they give the Publican a distant View of, that he
may take it for Money ; they then produce some Silk Waistcoats
embroidered with Tinsel, which, if not strictly examined, may pass
for Silver ; these they propose, with other India goods made in
Spital-Fields, to leave in the Hands of the Publican or his Wife, as
a Security for the Money they want, who . . . generally fall into the
Trap."—Sir John Fielding's " Cautions to Merchants " &c., in his
Description of London and Westminster, 1776, p. 85.

"Yesterday a large Gang of Pick-pockets in the true Interest of their Country, met according to Desire, at the Cross Keys and Rummer ; whence after drinking the proper Health, they proceeded immediately to the Place of Poll ; where, we are assured they made a considerable Booty, some Part of which they have since *generously subscribed towards the further Continuance of the Election.*"—The *Covent Garden Journal*, December 5, 1749.

P. 49.

"The Luminous Fountain at the Panopticon, Leicester Square.

"Thousands of sight-seers have already seen the magnificent Fountain at the Royal Panopticon, with its central jet leaping from an enamelled base to the height of ninety-nine feet. The sight of this extraordinary column of water subjected to a powerful light so as to exhibit a variety of the most beautiful hues, will surprise the spectator. . . . A strongly concentrated and reflected light at each end of the jet illuminates the whole length, effectually colouring, as well as making brilliant the up-springing shaft with the detached particles which descend like a shower of many tinted gems into the inlaid basin. . . . The times for exhibiting the fountain, under the luminous aspect, are a quarter before five o'clock, at the morning entertainment ; and a quarter to eight in the evening."—*Illust. Lond. News*, March 18, 1854.

P. 55.

Dwarfs . . . See also "St. Martin's Scrap Book" (*General* volume).

Private quarrels were sometimes publicly ventilated after a fashion that reminds us forcibly of the homely proverbial stricture about "dirty linen " :

"Whereas an advertisement was lately put in Heathcote's 'Halfpenny Post,' by way of challenge for me to meet a person (whose name to me is unknown) at Old Man's Coffee-house near Charing Cross, the 28th instant, in order to hear that said person make out his assertions in that Dialogue we had in Palace Yard, the 11th of November, 1718, This will let that person know that as he would not then tell me his name, nor put it to his advertisement, I conclude he is ashamed to have it in print. When he sends me his name in print, that I may know who to ask for, I shall be willing to meet him at any convenient time and place, either by ourselves or with two friends on each side, till then I shall have neither list nor leisure to obey his nameless summons.

"ROBERT CURTIS."

Southwark, Jan. 13th, 1719–20.

—Daily Post, Jan. 16, 1720.

P. 61.

At 26 Charing Cross was exhibited "The Wonderful American Hen with Three Wings and Four Legs, The Greatest Living Curiosity in the World." The poor humanities in the form of giants and dwarfs must all have departed this life. There is no date to this handbill, but it was probably early 19th century. "Last Wednesday, one Williams, a young man boasting the hardness of his teeth, at a baker's shop under the Piazza in Covent Garden, undertook to carry a tailor's goose in his mouth to Charing Cross and back for a wager of half-a-crown, which he won with ease."—Newspaper cutting, 1700.

P. 64.

"This is to give Notice to all Gentlemen, Ladies, and Others, That there is lately arriv'd, and is now to be seen at the Mitre Tavern at Charing Cross,

A French Woman 20 Years Old

One Foot 3 Inches and a Quarter High ;

Who has had the Honour to be shewn before the King and Queen of France, and all the Royal Family ; As likewise before Sir Hans Sloan and the rest of the Royal Society with great Satisfaction. She sings a Song to please the Company, and discourses with the Company, as if she was Forty Years Old ; She likewise takes a Glass of Wine off her Toe, and drinks it off before the Company.

Note : Any Gentlemen or Ladies may have her brought to their own Houses, by giving an Hour's Notice.

To be seen from Ten in the Morning, till Nine in the Evening."
—Handbill in *St. Martin's Scrap Book.*

P. 66.

Houdin, the conjurer, discovered the secret of this piece of ingenuity. A vase, containing seed steeped in water, was placed before the bird. The motion of the bill in dabbling crushed the food, and facilitated its introduction into a pipe placed beneath the lower bill. The water and seed thus swallowed fell into a box placed under the bird's stomach, which was emptied every three or four days. The other part of the operation was thus effected : Bread crumb, coloured green, was expelled by a forcing pump, and carefully caught on a silver salver, as the result of artificial digestion. This was handed round to be admired, while the ingenious trickster laughed in his sleve at the credulity of the public.—*Memoirs of Robert Houdin*, 1859.

P. 71.

The approximate date of the demolition of Charing Cross—*i.e.* of the old Cross itself—is indicated by " an Accompt concerning the digging of the stones, being the foundation of Charing Cross, and for levelling and Paveing in of ye ground in the yeare 1657."—Thos. Mason's *Catalogue of Books and Documents belonging to St. Martin's-in-the-Fields*, 1895, p. 5.

P. 79.

"M. H.," writing in the " Home Counties Magazine " with regard to the statue of Charles I. (and referring to "Middlesex and Herts Notes and Queries," vol. iv., p. 1), says : " I notice reference, under date 6th May, 1692, to a ' Yorkshire ' tavern (*i.e.* a tavern which visitors from Yorkshire frequented), with the sign of ' The King on Horseback ' at Charing Cross. This sign, no doubt, had reference to Le Sueur's famous statue so ably described by Lord Dillon, and figured in the pages of the ' Home Counties Magazine' for January, 1898. The tavern in question was in 1692 suspected as a sojourning place for Jacobites (Home Office Warrant Book 6, p. 321)."— *Home Counties Magazine*, 1900, vol. ii., p. 165.

P. 92.

A curious custom or superstition was in evidence at the hanging of Dr. Dodd at Charing Cross. After he had hung about ten minutes, a very decently dressed young woman went up to the gallows in order to have a wen in her face stroked by the doctor's hand, for it was a received opinion among the vulgar that it is a certain cure for such a disorder. The executioner, having untied the doctor's hand, stroked with it the part affected several times. (Brand's " Antiquities," Bohn, 1855, vol. iii., p. 276.) Grose says that "a dead man's hand is supposed to have the quality of dispelling humours, such as *wens*, or swelled glands, by stroking with it, nine times, the place affected. It seems as if the hand of a person dying a violent death was deemed particularly efficacious; as it very frequently happens that nurses bring children to be stroked with the hands of executed criminals, even whilst they are hanging on the gallows. Again, at the execution of a Jew named Abraham Abrahams, after the body had hung some time, several persons applied for permission to rub the hand of the deceased over their wens; but the Jews in attendance told them they could not suffer the body to be touched by any but their own people, it being contrary to their customs."

P. 99.

Hugh Hewson (the reputed Hugh Strap of " Roderick Random ") is stated to have dwelt at No. 17 May's Buildings, where he died in 1809 at the advanced age of 95. In his latter years he was employed as keeper of a promenade in Villiers-walk, York Buildings, and was much noticed and respected by the inhabitants who frequented the place."—See further newspaper cutting (without date) in the *St. Martin's Scrap Book*, St. Martin's Library.

At the sale of garden ornaments and other objects forming a collection which was dispersed on September 30, 1905, by Messrs. Robinson & Fisher, a leaden tank was sold which was once in the possession of the family of the Duke of Buckingham, and was a short time ago removed from that portion of old Buckingham House situated still at the bottom of Buckingham Street. It was of the Early Georgian period, and dated 1722.

P. 101.

" For the Benefit of Mrs. Hemings,

On the 14th Instant, at Mr. Clayton's House in York Buildings, will be performed, The Passion of Sappho and Feast of Alexander. Tickets at a Crown each, are to be had at St. James's Coffee-house in Swithen's Ally, by the Royal Exchange, at Squire's Coffee-house in Fulwood's Rents, and at Nando's Coffee-house at Temple-Bar."—Newspaper cutting (in *St. Martin's Scrap Book*) Dec. 12, 1711.

P. 119.

" MAGIC CAVE.

The only SUBTERRANEOUS EXHIBITION in London, in which may be seen 16 beautifully painted Cosmoramic Views, by eminent artists, so well arranged as to give the spectator a better idea of the scenes before him than any thing short of reality possibly can. Admission 6*d.* Open from Ten o'clock in the Morning until Ten at Night at the

LOWTHER BAZAAR,

No. 35, Strand."—(Cutting with no date.)

P. 121.

At the Polygraphic Hall, April 29, 1859, W. S. Woodin being the lessee was given a farewell entertainment of the Wizard Jacobs before retiring from the profession. The programme consisted of:

PART I.	PART II.
The Invisible Miller	The Enchanted Seat
The Wizard's Target	The Old Oak Chest
The Lilliputian Hornpipe	The Mysterious Gold Fish
The Miraculous Handkerchief	The Incantation Kettle
The Extraordinary Cash-box	
The Magic Banquet	
The Magician's Dejeuner	
The Grand Transformation	
The Escamotage de Sprightly	

At this Hall in King William Street there also "held forth" Emma Hardinge, the "Celebrated Extemporaneous Speaker." The "Celebrated and Original Christy Minstrels from 472, Broadway, New York, and late of the St. James's Theatre." Mr. Costello with his "Budget of Eccentricities. Hussey, Sweny and Felton as the New American Minstrels, from the Academy of Minstrels, New York. The only legitimate delineators of Negro Life and Plantation Melodies, each Performer a Star in his Line." They sang "Meet me in the Lane," "Walk Along, John," "I'm Lonely since my Mother Died," "The German Band," "Good Old Friends," etc., etc.

Woodin's Carpet Bag entertainments. See "An Artistic Olio," the "Builder," May 26, 1855.

P. 125.

"A REAL SALE OF SILKS

AT the Coventry Cross, Chandos Street, Covent Garden. Consisting of a very great assortment of Rich brocades, Tissues, flowered and plain Sattins, Tabbies, Ducapes, black Armozeens,

Rasdumores, Mantuas, &c.   Being purchased of the executors of an eminent weaver and factor, deceased, and of another left-off trade.

Merchants, &c., may be supplied with rich Silks fit for exportation, fresh and fine patterns, greatly under prime cost, for ready money only, the price marked on each piece.

It is hoped Ladies will not be offended that they cannot possibly be waited on at their own Houses."—*British Chronicle*, Feb. 10–12, 1763.

P. 128.

"Mr. Benjamin Ferrers, Face-painter, the gentleman that can't neither speak nor hear, is removed from the Crown and Dagger at Charing Cross into Chandois Street, next door to the sign of the Three Tuns in Covent Garden."—*Postman*, July 19–22, 1707.

P. 135.

Pon's Coffee House was at the corner of New Street, Covent Garden, where a collection of pictures, prints, and drawings of Thomas Munley, painter, "lately deceased," were to be viewed preparatory to their sale by auction.—*St. Martin's Scrap Book* (Covent Garden), p. 178.

At the "Civet Cat" in New Street, Covent Garden, Mrs. Hugg, in 1782, opened a shop and advertised a much-lauded pomade as a hair-restorer.   Also a "fine Camphire Paste that takes tan and freckles off the skin," &c.—*Ibid.*

"At the 'Swan' in New Street, Covent Garden, is sold (as imported) Arrack, Brandy, Rum, and Wines of all Sorts, Wholesale and Retale, very old, strong, and of an excellent Flavour.   Samples of Arrack at 3*s.* 6*d.* per Quart ;   red and white Ports, Mountain and Lisbon, at 1*s.* 6*d.* per Quart ; other Wines in Proportion.

"☞   An Ordinary every Day at Three o'Clock, consisting of four Covers, at 1*s.* 6*d.* each, including Table Beer, Wine or Punch, &c., &c."—*Ibid.*, p. 178.

In the "London Gazette" for January 18, 1651, the library of Mr. Paul Colomier, Library-Keeper to the late Archbishop of Canterbury, is advertised to be sold on Wednesday, the 20th inst., at 3 after Noon at Mr. Arnaudin's, Chirurgeon, in New Street, Covent Garden.

P. 138.

In the "London Evening Post" for 1735 an advertisement of P. Desca, snuff-dealer, bears an interesting illustration of the use of the "rappoir," which is held in the left hand while the right holds a roll of tobacco which is being grated. Desca dwelt at the sign of the "Spaniard" in New Street, Covent Garden, and there he made and sold French Rappee, Rappee Clarac (? or Clarao), Rappee Brazil, St. Domingue Rappee, Havannah Rappee, fine Rappee Rolls, &c.

There was a sign of the "Corner Pin," probably indicating facilities for the game of Ninepins, at the corner of New Street, St. Martin's Lane.—*St. Martin's Scrap Book.*

P. 143.

Clay's Papier-mâché tray shop was at 17 and 18 King Street, Covent Garden. Here they sold "every variety of fancy JAPANNED PAPER GOODS, popularly, but erroneously, called 'Papier Mâché,' including Chairs, Tables, Work-tables and Work-boxes, Chess-tables and Boards, Cabinets, Desks, Tea-trays, Tea-chests, Tea-caddies, Inkstands, Blotting-books, Envelope Cases, Secretaires, Card-boxes, Card-baskets, Card-racks and Card-cases, Glove and Netting-boxes, &c."

Clay seems to have been famous, like Pinchbeck, for his "Musical Clock," for Cock, the Robins of his time, advertises the sale by auction, among other articles,

" PARTICULARLY

"That most celebrated Musical Clock, made by the late famous Mr. Clay, which was won some time since by Mr. Foubert's Mathematical Wheels. Which may be view'd at his late Dwelling House, the further End of Southampton Row, Bloomsbury, next the Fields, till the Hour of Sale, &c."—*Daily Advertiser, circa* 1742.

P. 147.

When Mr. Innes, one or two of whose accounts I have in my own possession with the sign of the tradesman with whom he dealt on the billhead, dealt with James Baughan, shoemaker at the sign of the Angel in Henrietta Street, Covent Garden, he purchased :

	£	s.	d.
" 2 pr. of Blue Call°. (? Callico) Pumps	0	13	0
2 pr. „ Pink „	0	13	0
2 pr. „ Green „	0	13	0
6 pr. „ Black „	1	19	0
	3	18	0 "

From the "London Gazette" of August 26, 1689, it appears that a Mr. John Green was a goldsmith in Henrietta Street.

The Burton Ale House, kept by J. Field in Henrietta Street, seems to have been one of the earliest of its kind, if not the actual first instance in London.—See Newspaper cutting in *St. Martin's Parish Scrap Book* (Covent Garden), p. 141.

Henrietta Street was a great quarter of London for Petticoat Warehouses or Shops. At No. 15 might be had " coats " of " Sattin, Sarsnet, Persian, Russel, Callimanco, and Stuff Quilted Coats." This was in March 1780. Customers are warned that " there are other Petticoat Shops in the same Street."

Mr. John Salt, " a very great man's mercer . . . by his great Assiduity and close Attendance in the Service of his Country, as one of the Middlesex Jury last Sessions at the Old Bailey, caught a violent Cold, which flung him into a Fever and was the Cause of his Death. He died at his house in Henrietta Street."—Newspaper cutting, January 7, 1736.

George Pressey, Nos. 3 and 4 Henrietta Street, advertises " the very best wax candles and flambeaux," about the year 1780.—*St. Martin's Scrap Book*.

To the " Parrot," in Henrietta Street, Daniel Mallory, Laceman (Late Partner with Mr. John Mallory at the Indian Queen in the Strand), announces that he has removed.—June 28, 1729.

P. 153.

This ancient shop-front, with its richly carved private door-case at the side, is evidently that of which there is a water-colour illustration in the *St. Martin's Scrap Book* (Library of St. Martin's-in-the-Fields).

P. 158.

"PRUDENCE REED,"

picturesquely named, dwelt at the equally picturesque sign of the Green Shutters in Duke's Court, St. Martin's Lane, whence she announces her removal to a shop at the end of the same court, opposite to St. Martin's Church.—Newspaper cutting without date in *St. Martin's Scrap Book*.

P. 162.

" Many will remember, as the writer does, a stout-built, clean-shaven old man, who used to take up his stand in the queer passage on the north side of the church in St. Martin's Place. He was a disabled South Wales miner who had been blind for eight and twenty years. He used to arrive at his stand by 'bus every morning and turn to his knitting, which he sold to passers-by. His dog Nell always met him as he alighted from the 'bus, having run across the park (St. James's) for that purpose. But one morning poor Nell, a small rough-haired dog, waited in vain for his master. The second and third 'buses brought not the expected arrival, and Nell's whining brought to the spot sympathisers in the form of the recruiting-sergeant, matchseller, and shoeblack. 'Why, what's the matter with Nell?' asked the shoeblack. 'She's looking for old blind Welsh, and he hasn't been here for a week or more. The cold weather has taken him off. His daughter's over there in the passage where he used to sit by the vestry-hall door, knitting, but the dog's fretting and won't touch a copper now.'

" ' Nell ! Nell ! '

" At the call a pepper and salt Dandie Dinmont came scampering down the rickety staircase into a back lane in the poorest part of Westminster.

" ' There she is, sir ! '

" Nell put up her intelligent face, came to be patted, and ran to the penny lying on the ground. But she let it lie there after taking it in her mouth as she used when taking toll of the passers-by at St. Martin's, and went sniffing up and down the pavement. 'That's it—she's never been the same dog since my father died. I buried him last week. . . . Yes, I've been offered a good sum for the dog, but I don't want to part with her—if I can help it.' "—See the *Daily Graphic*, Jan. 27, 1894.

St. Martin's Workhouse, in Castle Street, Leicester Square, occupying a large spot of ground, was erected in 1772, when £11,775 was raised on annuities for the building of it. According to the " London Guide," 1806, one of the inmates was 104 years of age. But this is not the only instance of longevity in the parish. James Colman, born on St. Valentine's Day, 1750, reached his hundredth year on the same sentimental occasion in 1850. On February 3, 1850, he received the Sacrament of the Eucharist at the hands of the Rev. Sir Henry Dukenfield, Bart., having attended the church as usual without assistance. He was educated at Tenison's School, and remembered witnessing the funeral procession of King George II. in November 1760. On the fifth of the month in which he died, he, without difficulty, mounted four flights of stairs to sit

for his Daguerréotype portrait.—See *St. Martin's Scrap Book*
("Leicester Square," vol. ii.).

Pp. 169-70.

"The Round House must have witnessed some remarkable disturbances. About eleven o'clock one morning in May, 1744, twenty
thieves and gamblers appeared with 'cutlashes,' bludgeons, and
pistols before its portals. Their object was to rescue some notorious
offenders confined there. To these they passed arms through the
windows, with which the keeper and beadles were wounded while
the party outside attempted to break open the door. But a detach-
ment of Horse Grenadiers and Foot Guards coming up, four of the
rioters were taken and brought before Sir Tho. de Veil, who, after
five hours' examination, committed them to Newgate."—*Gentleman's
Magazine*, vol. xiv., May 1744.

"On Saturday, three Men who had given Information against
People for retailing Spirituous Liquors, appeared publicly in St.
Martin's Lane; and tho' it was intimated to them that they were
known, and that the mob was going to rise upon them, they not-
withstanding walked several Times up and down the Lane in an
insulting and daring Manner; till at length the Gentry in Moor's
Yard, who, it seems, are a very considerable Body, almost every
Family keeping their Wheel-barrow, rose one and all, and disciplin'd
two of the Fellows (the third making his Escape) in such a Manner
that they were carried half dead to the Round House, all other
Houses, both Publick and Private, refusing to give them Sanctuary."
—News-cutting in the *St. Martin's Scrap Book*.

P. 174.

On the site of No. 35 St. Martin's Lane, now occupied by the
mammoth house of entertainment, were two cells which were used
by the watchmen as a lock-up when the Round House outside the
church was full, and here I am informed by Mr. J. W. Harrison
were confined many of those involved in the O. P. riots at Covent
Garden Theatre.

P. 176.

Among a small collection of antiquities which were unearthed on
the premises of Messrs. J. W. Harrison and Sons in 1889 is an

earthenware bleeding-cup, examples of which, in pewter and in Delft and Lambeth ware, may be seen in the City Museum. The occasion of the discovery of these seventeenth century remains was the subsidence of the pit of one of Messrs. Harrison's printing machines, when the soil was removed down to the gravel for the purpose of ascertaining the cause, and for underpinning. The building in which the machine stood was on the site of the houses in Chymister (Kynaston's) Alley. And since Sir Francis Kynaston dwelt in "Berrie" (*i.e.* Bedfordbury) it seems probable that the Alley was so named from having occupied the site of some buildings appertaining to the poet, who, Cunningham says, quoting a somewhat vague entry in the rate-books of St. Martin's, lived "on the east side of the street towards Berrie." So that possibly the utensils, much fractured for the most part, which were found, once belonged to Sir Francis Kynaston. Scarifying was one form of bleeding : this consisted in letting blood by incisions of the skin, commonly after the application of cupping-glasses. It also meant to cut the skin with, or as with a lancet. A cupping glass was a sort of glass vial, applied to the fleshy parts of the body, to draw away "corrupt blood or windy matter"—See Bailey's *Dictionary*, 1740.

"Last Week Mr. Knight, a Gentleman at Plaistow, was suddenly seized with an Apoplectick Fit as he was making merry with his Friends ; and Mr. Hunter, a neighbouring Surgeon, being sent for, used the proper Means of Bleeding, Cupping, *Scarrifying*, &c. but to no Purpose, for he died soon after."— *Weekly Journal*, Sept. 23, 1721.

P. 181.

There was one Robb, a Colourman at No. 64 St. Martin's Lane, of whose shop (probably seventeenth century) there is a water-colour in the "St. Martin's Scrap Book." Hogarth is said to have resided in the house above the shop. The sketch was apparently made in October 1884.

P. 182.

At No. 70 Gt. St. Martin's Lane (five doors from the bottom of Long Acre) "The Original New Grand Peristrephic or Moving Panorama of the Defeat of the Turks by the Greeks, at Sea and upon Land, Together with the Storming of Seringapatam," was exhibited in "The Great Room, entrance 70 Gt. St. Martin's Lane."—See further a handbill in the *St. Martin's Scrap Book*.

Opposite Slaughter's Coffee-house in 1821, Fentum's Grand Masquerade (A Grand Mask'd Fête) took place at the New Museodeum Rooms in St. Martin's Lane.—See further a handbill in the *St. Martin's Scrap Book.*

P. 184.

The National Penny Bank (Limited), now on the east side of the Lane, was established for the purpose of receiving sums ranging from one penny to any superior amount, upon which it gives three per cent. interest. It is under distinguished patronage.

P. 186.

Among the earliest and most successful rivals of Wright, the originator in London of circulating libraries, were the Nobles in Holborn and St. Martin's Court ; and Lowndes in Fleet Street.

There was a Penny Post Office in St. Martin's Court in 1774, as a newspaper cutting in "St. Martin's Scrap Book" shows.

·The Rev. G. C. Wilton, Vicar of St. Mary's, Soho, writing to the "Daily Mail," May 31, 1905, from the Vicarage, 109 Charing Cross Road, calls the attention of lovers of Dickens to the gold-beater's shop in Manette-street, Soho, the sign of which is mentioned in the "Tale of Two Cities."

"After forty-five years of work in the quaint panelled shop, the gold-beater, Mr. Dickson, whose trade has been ruined by foreign competition, is compelled to give up his work," and aid is solicited for him in his distress.

P. 187.

There was a Sturgis's Coffee-house in St. Martin's Court, St. Martin's Lane.— *Weekly Journal,* December 2, 1721.

P. 191.

Handbills relating to the Apollonicon will be found in the "St. Martin's Scrap Book," a valuable collection of printed matter relating to this historic parish which has been formed by Mr. Mason, the late librarian.

P. 192.

Signor Fontana was the successful competitor for the execution of the monumental effigy of the late Mr. Graves, M.P. for Liverpool, a work destined to occupy a prominent place in St. George's Hall. The Leicester Square statue, of Sicilian marble, similar to that used for the Albert Memorial in Hyde Park, is a modified repetition of the Shakespeare in Westminster Abbey, and was selected as having become the traditional figure of the great poet, recognisable by everybody at a glance, without any label. The quotation on the scroll—

There is no darkness but ignorance,

is from "Twelfth Night," Act iv. scene 2. The statue was by Signor Fontana, of Chelsea, and the pedestal by Mr. Thorn, also of Chelsea. The rest of the fountain, with its surrounding vases, consoles, &c., by Messrs. Walker, Emley, and Beall, of Newcastle. The dolphins were carved by Mr. Daymond, of Westminster: the gilded cresting on the lower marble rim was cast by the Coalbrookdale Company, and the works were carried out by Messrs. Easton and Anderson.

The north face of the pedestal bears the inscription :

" This Enclosure
was Purchased, Laid out, and Decorated
as a Garden
By ALBERT GRANT, ESQ., M.P.,
and
Conveyed by him on July 2, 1874,
to the
Metropolitan Board of Works
To be preserved for ever
For the Use and Enjoyment
of the Public."

P. 195.

Mr. E. H. Bousfield, the arbitrator, awarded Lord Salisbury £11,070 in October 1905 for the compulsory sale of three houses in Charing Cross Road for the Cranbourn Street station of the Charing Cross, Euston, and Hampstead Railway. The houses occupied an area of 2,780 superficial feet.

P. 202.

An extraordinary representation was made to Sir Richard Ford, the magistrate, on the part of a linen-draper in King Street, Covent

Garden, on November 4, 1805. He stated that a gentleman, between forty and fifty years of age, and to all appearance a youth about fourteen years old, lodged in his house, but whom his (the linen-draper's) family suspected to be a female. Suspicion first became aroused through the "youth" endeavouring to conceal his face when the servant went into the room, by putting a book close to it. This suspicion became confirmed, and it was thought that the suspect was the young lady who lately eloped from a boarding-school, at Beverley in Yorkshire, with an officer of the Lincolnshire Militia. Sir Richard, in consequence, despatched Taunton and S. Lavender, who went to the lodging of the parties, and, having knocked at the door, it was opened by the supposed youth, who hesitated at first to acknowledge whether his father was within : but, having done so, the gentleman made his appearance, when the officers made him acquainted with the information that had been laid before Sir Richard Ford, who required them to appear before him. The parties appeared much confused, but acknowledged that the information was correct, and the supposed youth proved to be Miss ——. She wore loose nankeen trousers, a yellow Marseilles waistcoat, and a brown coat or jacket. Miss —— requested permission to change her dress, to which the officers consented. She was about nineteen years of age, very small in stature, and appeared, when dressed in male attire, not more than fourteen. At Bow Street they gave such a satisfactory account of themselves as to convince the magistrate that they were not the pair who had lately taken their flight from Yorkshire. The "boy" had been for the last four months with her companion, who is a native of Ireland, in Germany, and was to have thrown off her disguise a short time after the officers went to apprehend them. Let us hope it ended happily "through the church door."

P. 203.

"On Wednesday the Indian Chiefs were carried from their Lodgings in King Street, Covent Garden, to the Plantation Office at Whitehall, guarded by two Files of Musqueteers. When they were brought up to the Lords Commissioners, they sang four or five Songs in their Country Language ; after which the Interpreter was order'd to let them know that they were sent for there to join in Peace with King George and his People ; and were desired to say, if they had anything further to offer relating to the Contract they had before enter'd into. Upon which the King stood up, and gave a large Feather that he had in his Hand to the Prince, who thereupon spoke to the Lords Commissioners to this effect."—September 12, 1730.

At the "Spinning Wheel" in King Street, Covent Garden, is advertised "a choice Parcel of Irish Linnens from 7d. to 9s. 6d. per yard." This was in 1756.—Newspaper cutting without further date.

P. 206.

On the site apparently of the "Essex Serpent" Tavern, at No. 6 King Street, Covent Garden, "at the Great Room," Jaquez Droz, inventor, exhibited his "SPECTACLE MECHANIQUE" at 5s. a head, about the years 1775–1777.

There was a Rainbow Coffee-house in King Street, Covent Garden.—Newspaper cutting, September 2, 1775.

P. 207.

"MAHOGANY, &c.

To be Sold by Auction by JOSEPH COLE.

On the Premises, the Honduras Wharf, No. 74, Bankside, Southwark, in a few Days. Forty Thousand Feet of fine sizeable Honduras Mahogany Logs and Planks, 20,000 Feet of Hispaniola ditto, a Parcel of 14 Feet Clapboard Logs and dry sawed ditto, Half Inch Dutch Wainscot, Norway Deals, Baulks, &c. Catalogues of which will be timely delivered by J. Cole, Broker, No. 5, Albion Street, Black-Friars Road."—*Daily Advertiser*, January 4, 1794.

P. 208.

What is believed to have been the first "Divan" in London was in King Street. It was "A Rustic Smoking Promenade," which was illuminated in the evening. 1s. Admission included "a matchless Cigar, and Mocha coffee, or Lemonade, Orgeat, Sherbet, Soda Water, &c., &c. Eight Morning and Evening Newspapers and all the Magazines and Reviews of the Day—Chess, Draughts, etc. Open daily from 11 o'clock ; on Sundays from Five." This was in 1831. The Divan was between sixty and seventy feet in length, and by artistic skill was converted into "a beautiful Grecian Temple." Fluted columns of Sienna marble supported the cornice—rich crimson draperies with a classic bordering hung in luxuriant folds, through which were seen the following subjects : Isola Bella, Lago di Como, the Forum at Rome, Bingen on the Rhine, Coblenz, Tower of Andernach, Val D'Aosta and the Dogano at Venice. The views, the last mentioned of which was twenty-five feet long, were selected from the works of Stanfield, Prout, Harding, and Turner, and were executed by a young artist named Hillyard. "The hotel next door" is described as being the same as in Hogarth's "Frosty Morning."

P. 210.

General Guise was in his last years so feeble that he used to be supported up the long flight of steps to Langford's auction room by his own servant and one of Langford's men, to whom he used to exclaim, as they were ascending, " Damme, sirs, if you let me fall, I'll knock you down."—*Memoirs of Charles Macklin*, 1804, p. 22.

P. 211.

At Evans's Hotel (Supper Rooms) the Institute of British Architects held their meetings when first established, and here the first medal awarded by them was presented by the president, Earl de Grey, to the successful candidate in 1836. The capacious 'singing-room" or "music-hall" was completed in 1855. A description of the new room will be found in the " Builder," December 22, 1855, p. 622. The staircase may still be seen, which was formed of part of the vessel commanded by Russell, and exhibits in the carvings, anchors, and ropes the initial letters of Lord Orford.

P. 212.

No. 42, King Street, Covent Garden, was in 1825 known by its Bowling Alleys, of which an illustration may be seen in " St. Martin's Scrap Book " in St. Martin's Library, Charing Cross. They appear to have been kept by Thomas Kilpack, Tobacconist. Hence, one may suppose, it was an easy transition from Bowling Alley to Smoking Divan, for the house became such until 1877, when it was taken down. When the change took place, however, is not clear, but Gliddon's Cigar Divan was the first place of its kind in this country. It was next door on the west side to Evans's, and attached to the Divan was a garden.

P. 214.

Collins's Evening Brush.

"At the Auction Room, King Street, Covent Garden, To-Morrow, the 3rd of February, for the Seventh time this Season, will be presented that favourite and fashionable Pasticcio,

COLLINS'S EVENING BRUSH.

By the Author.

As exhibited at the Lyceum last Season, and at the Royalty Theatre the Season before, to crowded audiences, and unbounded applause.

In which the various Abuses of the Drama, by the itinerant Quacksalvers of the Sock and the Buskin, are held up to ridicule in a multiplicity of ludicrous and laughable (*sic*) examples.

Interspersed with Comic Strictures on Readers and Readings, Orators and Oratory, and embellished with the Author's Last new selection of

ORIGINAL SONGS,
Comic, Satyric, and Sentimental.

Doors opened at Seven.—Begin precisely at Eight.

Admittance Three Shillings.

Good Fires in the Room every Day, and all Day long. No more than one step from a Carriage to the Door; and no accommodation spared to render it an inviting receptacle for persons of fashion and respectability.

London, February 2, 1790."

P. 223.

Richardson's extensive collection of prints was noted for portraits, topographical and antiquarian prints, and for public sales of that class of property. In February and March, 1800, he sold an amazing collection of British portraits, which continued for thirty-one days, and which appears to have been accumulating for forty years. Dr. Thomas Rees used to attend the sales held in the evening, and met there "several gentlemen with whom I became intimate, from congeniality of attachments, amongst whom were Mr. Alexander of the British Museum, Mr. Baker of St. Paul's Churchyard, Mr. R. Holford, Mr. Bentham, Mr. Bindley, Dr. Gossett, Mr. Molteno, and several others, whose hoards have since been again brought to the hammer, and distributed to amuse other illustrators. Richardson published several portraits, *fac similes* of scarce prints, and also three different-sized prints of the "Felton Shakespeare," as it is usually named. At his rooms were sold by auction the famed collections of Musgrave and Tighe.—*Reminiscences of Literary London*, by Dr. Thomas Rees, 1896, p. 155.

P. 224.

"Have You Seen the

WHALE

Recently Captured and fresh as when caught, measuring 50 feet in length, and now Exhibiting at the

Fox Under the Hill,
Opposite the Adelphi Theatre, Strand,

THE HALFPENNY STEAM BOAT PIER

Only a Few Days

Admission Threepence."
(Handbill without date, *St. Martin's Scrap Book*.)

P. 225.

Messrs. Day and Martin were not the inventors or the first makers of blacking, neither, I think, do they claim to be. Mr. Benjamin Martin, the founder of the house, was a barber at Doncaster, and one day in 1780 a soldier, who had been shaved in his shop, stated that he had to go on foot to join his regiment at York, as he had no money to pay his coach fare. Mr. Martin lent the soldier money to pay his fare, and received in return a recipe for the manufacture of a mixture which the soldier said he had long used with effect upon the boots of his officers. This was the origin of the world-famed blacking of Day and Martin's.—See history of the firm in the weekly journal *Commerce* of some years ago.

The use of blacking for boots is, I think, traceable to an even earlier date than the following, which, however, has not, so far as one knows, been noted. In the "London Evening Post," May 11–13, 1738, the sale is announced "Wholesale, with an Allowance to sell again, by John Kirby, next Door to the Black Bull in Devonshire-street, near Bishopsgate, London ; Retail at Forrest's Coffee-House at Charing Cross, etc. . . .

"KIRBY's New German Blacking-Balls for shoes approv'd of by some thousands of Gentlemen and Servants that do daily buy of them, to be the best in England, for leaving a fine Jet-black Gloss, without so much as soiling the Stockings, Hands, or Ruffles, in putting on, and are exceeding proper for Sea and foreign Parts, at 1s. each Ball, Retail, and the Brush proper to be used with them Price 6d."

P. 240.

Mr. W. Davies, of the Palæontological Department of the British Museum, identified the bones of the cave lion (*Felis leo spelæa*); portions of antlers of a variety of the fallow deer (*Cervus dama*, var. *Brownii*), a molar of the "straight-tusked" elephant (*Elephas antiquus*), and remains of the rhinoceros. Also tusks, teeth, and bones of the woolly elephant (*Elephas primigenius*); the great extinct Irish deer (*Cervus megaceros*), the red deer (*Cervus elaphus*), and a number of bones belonging to extinct bovidæ (*Bos primigenius*). All the above were from deposits of the Quaternary or Pleistocene period, whilst from the comparatively recent or superficial deposits were obtained bones of the Celtic short horn (*Bos longifrons*), the probable ancestor of the small breed of Scotch or Welsh oxen; the sheep and the horse.

This is the first instance of the remains of *Felis spelæa* having been found in London proper.—See further the *Illustrated London News*, January 13, 1883, p. 54.

In September 1905, at Agen in France, the sinking of the soil under the weight of a ploughing-team of oxen, which were almost buried, led to the discovery of a cavern, very extensive, but not differing greatly from others known in various parts of Europe. On the flooring, however, were found some exceedingly rare animal foot-prints, and among others those of the *Felis spelæa*, or prehistoric cave lion. From plaster casts this petrified footprint has been measured to be 9¼ inches long by 8¾ inches broad, and the claws are 2¾ inches long. These footprints were then being closely studied by experts.— The *Globe*, September 19, 1905.

P. 247.

Before Porridge Island and the Bermudas were swept away, there is said to have been on the east side of the Square, where Morley's Hotel now stands, a mean-looking building which had been used as a state coach-house in the reign of George II.

P. 247.

At No. 9 Charing Cross was the lottery office of T. Bish, one of the principal office-keepers of the period, who showered millions of bills and miles of doggerel verse on London just before the final draw took place. Although the last lottery was expected to take place on July 18, it was not until October 18 that the closing scene in an eventful history took place. For this Bish, among many other handbills, produced the following :

"THE AMBULATOR'S GUIDE
To the Land of Plenty
By purchasing a TICKET
in the present Lottery

You may *reap* a golden *harvest* in *Cornhill*, and pick up the *bullion* in *Silver*-street, have an interest in *Bank-buildings*, possess a *Mansion House* in *Golden Square*, and an estate like a *Little Britain* ; never be in *Hunger*ford Market, but all your life continue a *Mayfair*.

By purchasing a HALF,

You need never be confined within *London Wall*, but become the proprietor of many a *Long Acre*, represent a *Borough* or an *Aldermanbury*, and have a share in Threadneedle-street.

By purchasing a QUARTER,

Your affairs need never be in *Crooked-lane*, nor your legs in *Fetter Lane* ; you may avoid *Paper-buildings*, steer clear of the *King's Bench* ; and defy the *Marshalsea* ; if your heart is in Love-lane you may soon get into Sweeting's Alley, obtain your lover's consent for *Matrimony-place*, and always live in a *High*-street.

By purchasing an EIGHTH,

You may secure plenty of provision for *Swallow-street*, finger the *Cole* in *Coleman-street*, and may never be troubled with Chancery-lane. You may cast *anchor* in *Cable-street*, set up business in *Fore-street*, and need never be confined within a *Narrow-wall*.

By purchasing a SIXTEENTH,

You may live *frugal* in *Cheapside*, get merry in *Liquorpond-street*, soak your *hide* in *Leather-lane*, be a wet sole in *Shoe-lane*, turn *maltster* in *Beer-lane*, or *hammer* away in Smithfield.

In short, life must indeed be a *Long-lane* if it's without a turning. Therefore, if you are wise, without *Mincing* the matter, go Pall Mall to *Cornhill* or *Charing Cross*, and enroll your name in the Temple of Fortune."—Sampson's *History of Advertising*, 1874, pp. 466-67.

P. 255.

Queen Elizabeth's Bath formerly stood among a cluster of old buildings adjoining the King's Mews at Charing Cross, and was removed in 1831. Of this Bath a plan and view were presented to the Society of Antiquaries, February 9, 1832, and are engraved in the "Archæologia," xxv. 588-90. The building on the plan was nearly square, and was constructed of fine red brick. Its chief merit consisted in its groined roof, which was of very neat workmanship, and formed by angular ribs springing from corbels. The form of the arch denoted the date of this building to be the fifteenth century.— See Timbs's *Curiosities of London*, 1868, p. 39.

P. 256.

The following alterations in the Square were proposed by the Navy League in October 1905, the month and year of Nelson's glorious centenary :

" That the Square be made a fitting termination to the processional road to the Palace.

" That fine groups of statuary should be placed at each end of the terrace, on the two large pedestals, one of which is now occupied by the George IV. statue.

" That new majestic fountains should take the place of the bald Euston Road productions.

" That pillars should be placed at the south end of the enclosing walls of the Square, surrounded by figures of Victory and inscribed with the names of our great admirals.

" That the Tube station be balanced by a drinking-fountain of a similar design on the west side of the Nelson Column, both being used to commemorate admirals or victories.

" That the revetment walls be decorated with bronze reliefs.

" That there be new decorative lamp-posts. And that the monuments and other decorations represent the general history of the growth of British supremacy at sea."

With regard to the improvements at Charing Cross and Trafalgar Square proposed some few years ago, see the "Westminster Budget,"

January 19, 1894, and the "St. James's Budget" of the same date.
Also the "Sketch," January 24, 1894; and the "British Architect,"
January 26, 1894.

P. 260.

Other fountains of remarkable design in the metropolis are the
famous St. George's Fountain in majolica ware, exhibited by Messrs.
Copeland, of Stoke-upon-Trent, at the International Exhibition of
1862, which stood, and possibly still stands, outside the Bethnal
Green Museum; and the beautiful production commemorative of the
good deeds of the Earl of Shaftesbury, in Piccadilly Circus.

INDEX

PRINTED BY
SPOTTISWOODE AND CO. LTD., NEW-STREET SQUARE
LONDON

ImTheStory.com

Personalized Classic Books in many genre's

Unique gift for kids, partners, friends, colleagues

Customize:

- Character Names
- Upload your own front/back cover images (optional)
- Inscribe a personal message/dedication on the
  inside page (optional)

Customize many titles Including
- Alice in Wonderland
- Romeo and Juliet
- The Wizard of Oz
- A Christmas Carol
- Dracula
- Dr. Jekyll & Mr. Hyde
- And more...

CPSIA information can be obtained at www.ICGtesting.com
Printed in the USA
BVOW08s1134290713

327229BV00017B/635/P